The Diversity of Life

interactive
SCIENCE

Boston, Massachusetts
Chandler, Arizona
Glenview, Illinois
Upper Saddle River, New Jersey

AUTHORS

You're an author!

As you write in this science book, your answers and personal discoveries will be recorded for you to keep, making this book unique to you. That is why you are one of the primary authors of this book.

✏️ **In the space below, print your name, school, town, and state. Then write a short autobiography that includes your interests and accomplishments.**

YOUR NAME
_____

SCHOOL
_____

TOWN, STATE
_____

AUTOBIOGRAPHY

_____

_____

_____

_____

_____

_____

_____

_____

Your Photo

Acknowledgments appear on pages 307–310, which constitute an extension of this copyright page.

ISBN-13: 978-0-13-368490-2
ISBN-10: 0-13-368490-3
17 16

ON THE COVER
A Hidden Defense
The nudibranchs pictured on the cover are sea slugs—snails without shells. Most sea slugs are tiny, only about 1.27 cm long. Sea slugs can't move very fast. So why don't faster animals target them as an easy meal? The sea slugs store poison from animals they eat. If other animals eat the sea slugs, they get a mouthful of poison.

Program Authors

DON BUCKLEY, M.Sc.
Information and Communications Technology Director,
The School at Columbia University, New York, New York
Mr. Buckley has been at the forefront of K–12 educational technology for nearly two decades. A founder of New York City Independent School Technologists (NYCIST) and long-time chair of New York Association of Independent Schools' annual IT conference, he has taught students on two continents and created multimedia and Internet-based instructional systems for schools worldwide.

ZIPPORAH MILLER, M.A.Ed.
Associate Executive Director for Professional Programs
and Conferences, National Science Teachers Association,
Arlington, Virginia
Associate executive director for professional programs and conferences at NSTA, Ms. Zipporah Miller is a former K–12 science supervisor and STEM coordinator for the Prince George's County Public School District in Maryland. She is a science education consultant who has overseen curriculum development and staff training for more than 150 district science coordinators.

MICHAEL J. PADILLA, Ph.D.
Associate Dean and Director, Eugene P. Moore School of
Education, Clemson University, Clemson, South Carolina
A former middle school teacher and a leader in middle school science education, Dr. Michael Padilla has served as president of the National Science Teachers Association and as a writer of the National Science Education Standards. He is professor of science education at Clemson University. As lead author of the *Science Explorer* series, Dr. Padilla has inspired the team in developing a program that promotes student inquiry and meets the needs of today's students.

KATHRYN THORNTON, Ph.D.
Professor and Associate Dean, School of Engineering
and Applied Science, University of Virginia,
Charlottesville, Virginia
Selected by NASA in May 1984, Dr. Kathryn Thornton is a veteran of four space flights. She has logged over 975 hours in space, including more than 21 hours of extravehicular activity. As an author on the *Scott Foresman Science* series, Dr. Thornton's enthusiasm for science has inspired teachers around the globe.

MICHAEL E. WYSESSION, Ph.D.
Associate Professor of Earth and Planetary Science,
Washington University, St. Louis, Missouri
An author on more than 50 scientific publications, Dr. Wysession was awarded the prestigious Packard Foundation Fellowship and Presidential Faculty Fellowship for his research in geophysics. Dr. Wysession is an expert on Earth's inner structure and has mapped various regions of Earth using seismic tomography. He is known internationally for his work in geoscience education and outreach.

Instructional Design Author

GRANT WIGGINS, Ed.D.
President, Authentic Education,
Hopewell, New Jersey
Dr. Wiggins is a co-author with Jay McTighe of *Understanding by Design, 2nd Edition* (ASCD 2005). His approach to instructional design provides teachers with a disciplined way of thinking about curriculum design, assessment, and instruction that moves teaching from covering content to ensuring understanding.

UNDERSTANDING BY DESIGN® and UbD™ are trademarks of ASCD, and are used under license.

Planet Diary Author

JACK HANKIN
Science/Mathematics Teacher,
The Hilldale School, Daly City, California
Founder, Planet Diary Web site
Mr. Hankin is the creator and writer of Planet Diary, a science current events Web site. He is passionate about bringing science news and environmental awareness into classrooms and offers numerous Planet Diary workshops at NSTA and other events to train middle and high school teachers.

ELL Consultant

JIM CUMMINS, Ph.D.
Professor and Canada Research Chair,
Curriculum, Teaching and Learning
department at the University of Toronto
Dr. Cummins focuses on literacy development in multilingual schools and the role of technology in promoting student learning across the curriculum. *Interactive Science* incorporates essential research-based principles for integrating language with the teaching of academic content based on his instructional framework.

Reading Consultant

HARVEY DANIELS, Ph.D.
Professor of Secondary Education,
University of New Mexico,
Albuquerque, New Mexico
Dr. Daniels is an international consultant to schools, districts, and educational agencies. He has authored or coauthored 13 books on language, literacy, and education. His most recent works are *Comprehension and Collaboration: Inquiry Circles in Action* and *Subjects Matter: Every Teacher's Guide to Content-Area Reading.*

REVIEWERS

Contributing Writers

Edward Aguado, Ph.D.
Professor, Department of Geography
San Diego State University
San Diego, California

Elizabeth Coolidge-Stolz, M.D.
Medical Writer
North Reading, Massachusetts

Donald L. Cronkite, Ph.D.
Professor of Biology
Hope College
Holland, Michigan

Jan Jenner, Ph.D.
Science Writer
Talladega, Alabama

Linda Cronin Jones, Ph.D.
Associate Professor of Science and Environmental Education
University of Florida
Gainesville, Florida

T. Griffith Jones, Ph.D.
Clinical Associate Professor of Science Education
College of Education
University of Florida
Gainesville, Florida

Andrew C. Kemp, Ph.D.
Teacher
Jefferson County Public Schools
Louisville, Kentucky

Matthew Stoneking, Ph.D.
Associate Professor of Physics
Lawrence University
Appleton, Wisconsin

R. Bruce Ward, Ed.D.
Senior Research Associate
Science Education Department
Harvard-Smithsonian Center for Astrophysics
Cambridge, Massachusetts

Content Reviewers

Paul D. Beale, Ph.D.
Department of Physics
University of Colorado at Boulder
Boulder, Colorado

Jeff R. Bodart, Ph.D.
Professor of Physical Sciences
Chipola College
Marianna, Florida

Joy Branlund, Ph.D.
Department of Earth Science
Southwestern Illinois College
Granite City, Illinois

Marguerite Brickman, Ph.D.
Division of Biological Sciences
University of Georgia
Athens, Georgia

Bonnie J. Brunkhorst, Ph.D.
Science Education and Geological Sciences
California State University
San Bernardino, California

Michael Castellani, Ph.D.
Department of Chemistry
Marshall University
Huntington, West Virginia

Charles C. Curtis, Ph.D.
Research Associate Professor of Physics
University of Arizona
Tucson, Arizona

Diane I. Doser, Ph.D.
Department of Geological Sciences
University of Texas
El Paso, Texas

Rick Duhrkopf, Ph.D.
Department of Biology
Baylor University
Waco, Texas

Alice K. Hankla, Ph.D.
The Galloway School
Atlanta, Georgia

Mark Henriksen, Ph.D.
Physics Department
University of Maryland
Baltimore, Maryland

Chad Hershock, Ph.D.
Center for Research on Learning and Teaching
University of Michigan
Ann Arbor, Michigan

Jeremiah N. Jarrett, Ph.D.
Department of Biology
Central Connecticut State University
New Britain, Connecticut

Scott L. Kight, Ph.D.
Department of Biology
Montclair State University
Montclair, New Jersey

Jennifer O. Liang, Ph.D.
Department of Biology
University of Minnesota–Duluth
Duluth, Minnesota

Candace Lutzow-Felling, Ph.D.
Director of Education
The State Arboretum of Virginia
University of Virginia
Boyce, Virginia

Cortney V. Martin, Ph.D.
Virginia Polytechnic Institute
Blacksburg, Virginia

Joseph F. McCullough, Ph.D.
Physics Program Chair
Cabrillo College
Aptos, California

Heather Mernitz, Ph.D.
Department of Physical Science
Alverno College
Milwaukee, Wisconsin

Sadredin C. Moosavi, Ph.D.
Department of Earth and Environmental Sciences
Tulane University
New Orleans, Louisiana

David L. Reid, Ph.D.
Department of Biology
Blackburn College
Carlinville, Illinois

Scott M. Rochette, Ph.D.
Department of the Earth Sciences
SUNY College at Brockport
Brockport, New York

Karyn L. Rogers, Ph.D.
Department of Geological Sciences
University of Missouri
Columbia, Missouri

Laurence Rosenhein, Ph.D.
Department of Chemistry
Indiana State University
Terre Haute, Indiana

Sara Seager, Ph.D.
Department of Planetary Sciences and Physics
Massachusetts Institute of Technology
Cambridge, Massachusetts

Tom Shoberg, Ph.D.
Missouri University of Science and Technology
Rolla, Missouri

Patricia Simmons, Ph.D.
North Carolina State University
Raleigh, North Carolina

William H. Steinecker, Ph.D.
Research Scholar
Miami University
Oxford, Ohio

Paul R. Stoddard, Ph.D.
Department of Geology and Environmental Geosciences
Northern Illinois University
DeKalb, Illinois

John R. Villarreal, Ph.D.
Department of Chemistry
The University of Texas–Pan American
Edinburg, Texas

John R. Wagner, Ph.D.
Department of Geology
Clemson University
Clemson, South Carolina

Jerry Waldvogel, Ph.D.
Department of Biological Sciences
Clemson University
Clemson, South Carolina

Donna L. Witter, Ph.D.
Department of Geology
Kent State University
Kent, Ohio

Edward J. Zalisko, Ph.D.
Department of Biology
Blackburn College
Carlinville, Illinois

Museum of Science.

Special thanks to the Museum of Science, Boston, Massachusetts, and Ioannis Miaoulis, the Museum's president and director, for serving as content advisors for the technology and design strand in this program.

CONTENTS

Lab zone® Enter the Lab zone for hands-on inquiry.

Chapter Lab Investigation:
• Directed Inquiry: Please Pass the Bread
• Open Inquiry: Please Pass the Bread

Inquiry Warm-Ups: • Is It Living or Nonliving? • Can You Organize a Junk Drawer? • What Organism Goes Where? • Observing Similarities

Quick Labs: • React! • Compare Broth Samples • Classifying Seeds • Make a Classification Chart • Living Mysteries • Staining Leaves • Common Ancestors

my SCIENCE ONLINE.com

Go to MyScienceOnline.com to interact with this chapter's content.
Keyword: Introduction to Living Things

> UNTAMED SCIENCE
• What Can You Explore in a Swamp?

> PLANET DIARY
• Introduction to Living Things

> INTERACTIVE ART
• Redi's and Pasteur's Experiments
• Taxonomic Key

> ART IN MOTION
• Finding a Common Ancestor

> VIRTUAL LAB
• Classifying Life

Lab zone®
Enter the Lab zone for hands-on inquiry.

Chapter Lab Investigation:
• Directed Inquiry: Comparing Disinfectants
• Open Inquiry: Comparing Disinfectants

Inquiry Warm-Ups: • Which Lock Does the Key Fit? • How Quickly Can Bacteria Multiply? • What Lives in a Drop of Pond Water? • There's a Fungus Among Us

Quick Labs: • How Many Viruses Fit on a Pin? • How Viruses Spread • Classifying Bacteria • Drawing Conclusions • Observing Pseudopod Movement • Predicting • Observing Slime Mold • Do All Molds Look Alike? • Considering Fungi as Decomposers

my science online.com

Go to MyScienceOnline.com to interact with this chapter's content. **Keyword:** Viruses, Bacteria, Protists, and Fungi

> UNTAMED SCIENCE
• What Good Are Mushrooms?

> PLANET DIARY
• Viruses, Bacteria, Protists, and Fungi

> INTERACTIVE ART
• Virus Reproduction • Exploring Protozoans

> ART IN MOTION
• The Benefits of Bacteria

> REAL-WORLD INQUIRY
• Using Organisms in the Enviro

CONTENTS

Lab zone® Enter the Lab zone for hands-on inquiry.

Chapter Lab Investigation:
• Directed Inquiry: Investigating Stomata
• Open Inquiry: Investigating Stomata

Inquiry Warm-Ups: • What Do Leaves Reveal About Plants? • Will Mosses Absorb Water? • Which Plant Part Is It? • Make the Pollen Stick • Can a Plant Respond To Touch? • Feeding the World

Quick Labs: • Algae and Other Plants • Local Plant Diversity • Masses of Mosses • Examining a Fern • Common Characteristics • The In-Seed Story • Modeling Flowers • Plant Life Cycles • Where Are the Seeds? • Watching Roots Grow • Seasonal Changes • Everyday Plants

my science online.com

Go to MyScienceOnline.com to interact with this chapter's content. Keyword: **Plants**

> PLANET DIARY
• Plants

> INTERACTIVE ART
• Plant Cell Structures • The Structure of a Flower • Seed Dispersal

> ART IN MOTION
• Plant Tropisms

> VIRTUAL LAB
• Classifying Plants

Introduction to Animals

CHAPTER 4

Lab zone® Enter the Lab zone for hands-on inquiry.

Chapter Lab Investigation:
• Directed Inquiry: Earthworm Responses
• Open Inquiry: Earthworm Responses

Inquiry Warm-Ups: • Is It an Animal? • How Many Ways Can You Fold It? • How Do Natural and Synthetic Sponges Compare? • How Is an Umbrella Like a Skeleton? • Exploring Vertebrates

Quick Labs: • Get Moving • Classifying Animals • Organizing Animal Bodies • Front-End Advantages • Characteristics of Vertebrates • Keeping Warm • It's Plane to See

my science ONLINE.com

Go to MyScienceOnline.com to interact with this chapter's content. Keyword: Introduction to Animals

> UNTAMED SCIENCE
• Eating Like an Animal

> PLANET DIARY
• Introduction to Animals

> INTERACTIVE ART
• Structure of a Sponge • Where Could They Live?

> ART IN MOTION
• Invertebrate Diversity

> VIRTUAL LAB
• Classifying Animals

CONTENTS

Lab zone® Enter the Lab zone for hands-on inquiry.

Chapter Lab Investigation:
• Directed Inquiry: A Snail's Pace
• Open Inquiry: A Snail's Pace

Inquiry Warm-Ups: • Will It Bend and Move? • Sending Signals • Hydra Doing?

Quick Labs: • Comparing Bone and Cartilage • What Do Muscles Do? • Design a Nervous System • Compare Nervous Systems • Webbing Along

my science online.com

Go to MyScienceOnline.com to interact with this chapter's content. Keyword: **Getting Around**

> **UNTAMED SCIENCE**
• Science in a Bat Cave

> **PLANET DIARY**
• Getting Around

> **INTERACTIVE ART**
• Water Vascular System • Adaptations for Movement • Types of Skeletons

> **ART IN MOTION**
• Nervous Systems at Work

> **REAL-WORLD INQUIRY**
• Responding to the Environment

Lab zone® Enter the Lab zone for hands-on inquiry.

Chapter Lab Investigation:
• Directed Inquiry: Looking at an Owl's Leftovers
• Open Inquiry: Looking at an Owl's Leftovers

Inquiry Warm-Ups: • How Do Snakes Feed? • How Does Water Flow Over a Fish's Gills? • Getting Oxygen

Quick Labs: • Planarian Feeding Behavior • How Do Animals Get Oxygen? • Comparing Respiratory Systems • Comparing Circulatory Systems • Double-Loop Circulation • Modeling a Kidney

my science online.com

Go to MyScienceOnline.com to interact with this chapter's content.
Keyword: Obtaining Energy

> **UNTAMED SCIENCE**
• Cephalic Feeding Is Soo Much Fun

> **PLANET DIARY**
• Obtaining Energy

> **INTERACTIVE ART**
• Vertebrate Circulatory Systems • Alien Mouth Match-Up

> **ART IN MOTION**
• Respiratory Structures at Work

> **REAL-WORLD INQUIRY**
• Frog Fill-Up

CONTENTS

Lab zone® Enter the Lab zone for hands-on inquiry.

Chapter Lab Investigation:
• Directed Inquiry: One for All
• Open Inquiry: One for All

Inquiry Warm-Ups: • Making More • "Eggs-amination" • What Behaviors Can You Observe? • Communicating Without Words

Quick Labs: Types of Reproduction • Types of Fertilization • "Eggs-tra "Protection • Cycles of Life • To Care or Not to Care • Animal Behavior • Become a Learning Detective • Modeling Animal Communication • Behavior Cycles

my science online.com

Go to MyScienceOnline.com to interact with this chapter's content. Keyword: Animal Reproduction and Behavior

> **UNTAMED SCIENCE**
• Is That Dance Just for Me?

> **PLANET DIARY**
• Animal Reproduction and Behavior

> **INTERACTIVE ART**
• Build a Life Cycle

> **ART IN MOTION**
• Animal Learning

> **REAL-WORLD INQUIRY**
• Predicting Animal Behavior

Video Series: Chapter Adventures

Untamed Science created this captivating video series for interactive SCIENCE featuring a unique segment for every chapter of the program.

Featuring videos such as

Chapter 1
What Can You Explore in a Swamp? Follow the crew as they sort out living and nonliving things in a cypress swamp and in a forest.

Chapter 2
What Good Are Mushrooms? See the surprising roles mushrooms play in the environment.

Chapter 3
Amazing Plant Defenses Take a closer look at how plants fend off hungry insects and other animals looking for a meal.

Chapter 4
Eating Like an Animal Follow the Untamed Science crew as they investigate how people explain what they think an animal is.

Chapter 5
Science in a Bat Cave The crew sees how animal movements relate to where and how animals live.

Chapter 6
Cephalic Feeding is Soo Much Fun Explore some of the unusual ways that animals get their food.

Chapter 7
Is That Dance Just for Me? See how a talent for dancing helps some birds find a mate.

interactive SCIENCE

This is your book. You can write in it!

THE BIG

?

Get Engaged!

At the start of each chapter, you will see two questions: an Engaging Question and the Big Question. Each chapter's Big Question will help you start thinking about the Big Ideas of Science. Look for the Big Q symbol throughout the chapter!

HOW CAN WIND KEEP YOUR LIGHTS ON?

THE BIG **?**

What are some of Earth's energy sources?

This man is repairing a wind turbine at a wind farm in Texas. Most wind turbines are at least 30 meters off the ground where the winds are fast. Wind speed and blade length help determine the best way to capture the wind and turn it into power. Develop Hypotheses Why do you think people are working to increase the amount of power we get from wind?

> UNTAMED SCIENCE Watch the Untamed Science video to learn more about energy resources.

Wind energy collected by the
turbine does not cause air pollution.

174 Energy Resources

Untamed Science™

Follow the Untamed Science video crew as they travel the globe exploring the Big Ideas of Science.

Interact with your textbook. **Interact with inquiry.** **Interact online.**

Energy Resources

CHAPTER **5**

Build Reading, Inquiry, and Vocabulary Skills

In every lesson you will learn new ↺ Reading and ◢ Inquiry skills. These skills will help you read and think like a scientist. Vocabulary skills will help you communicate effectively and uncover the meaning of words.

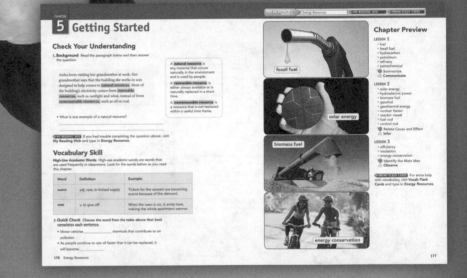

Go Online!

Look for the MyScienceOnline.com technology options. At MyScienceOnline.com you can immerse yourself in amazing virtual environments, get extra practice, and even blog about current events in science.

UNLOCK THE BIG ?

Explore the Key Concepts.

Each lesson begins with a series of Key Concept questions. The interactivities in each lesson will help you understand these concepts and Unlock the Big Question.

MY PLANET DiARY

At the start of each lesson, My Planet Diary will introduce you to amazing events, significant people, and important discoveries in science or help you to overcome common misconceptions about science concepts.

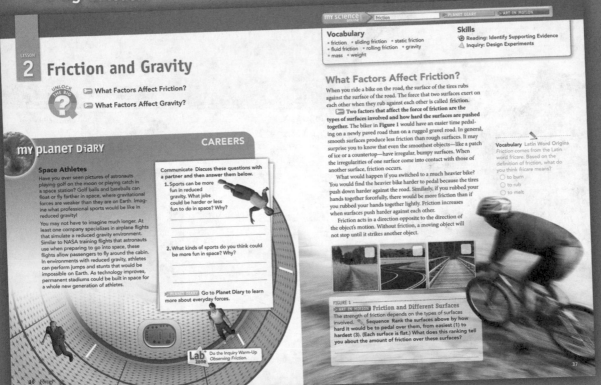

LESSON 2 — Friction and Gravity

UNLOCK THE BIG ?
- What Factors Affect Friction?
- What Factors Affect Gravity?

MY PLANET DiARY — CAREERS

Space Athletes

Have you ever seen pictures of astronauts playing golf on the moon or playing catch in a space station? Golf balls and baseballs can float or fly farther in space, where gravitational forces are weaker than they are on Earth. Imagine what professional sports would be like in reduced gravity!

You may not have to imagine much longer. At least one company specializes in airplane flights that simulate a reduced gravity environment. Similar to NASA training flights that astronauts use when preparing to go into space, these flights allow passengers to fly around the cabin. In environments with reduced gravity, athletes can perform jumps and stunts that would be impossible on Earth. As technology improves, permanent stadiums could be built in space for a whole new generation of athletes.

Communicate Discuss these questions with a partner and then answer them below.

1. Sports can be more fun in reduced gravity. What jobs could be harder or less fun to do in space? Why?

2. What kinds of sports do you think could be more fun in space? Why?

PLANET DIARY Go to Planet Diary to learn more about everyday forces.

Lab zone Do the Inquiry Warm-Up Observing Friction.

MY SCIENCE > Friction | PLANET DIARY | ART IN MOTION

Vocabulary
- friction · sliding friction · static friction
- fluid friction · rolling friction · gravity
- mass · weight

Skills
- Reading: Identify Supporting Evidence
- Inquiry: Design Experiments

What Factors Affect Friction?

When you ride a bike on the road, the surface of the tires rubs against the surface of the road. The force that two surfaces exert on each other when they rub against each other is called friction.

Two factors that affect the force of friction are the types of surfaces involved and how hard the surfaces are pushed together. The biker in Figure 1 would have an easier time pedaling on a newly paved road than on a rugged gravel road. In general, smooth surfaces produce less friction than rough surfaces. It may surprise you to know that even the smoothest objects—like a patch of ice or a countertop—have irregular, bumpy surfaces. When the irregularities of one surface come into contact with those of another surface, friction occurs.

What would happen if you switched to a much heavier bike? You would find the heavier bike harder to pedal because the tires push down harder against the road. Similarly, if you rubbed your hands together forcefully, there would be more friction than if you rubbed your hands together lightly. Friction increases when surfaces push harder against each other.

Friction acts in a direction opposite to the direction of the object's motion. Without friction, a moving object will not stop until it strikes another object.

Vocabulary Latin Word Origins Friction comes from the Latin word fricare. Based on the definition of friction, what do you think fricare means?
- ○ to burn
- ○ to rub
- ○ to melt

FIGURE 1
ART IN MOTION **Friction and Different Surfaces**
The strength of friction depends on the types of surfaces involved. Sequence Rank the surfaces above by how hard it would be to pedal over them, from easiest (1) to hardest (3). (Each surface is flat.) What does this ranking tell you about the amount of friction over these surfaces?

37

Desertification If the soil in ____ of moisture and nutrients, the ____ advance of desertlike condition ____ fertile is called desertification ____

One cause of desertification ____ is a period when less rain than ____ droughts, crops fail. Without pl____ blows away. Overgrazing of gra____ cutting down trees for firewood____

Desertification is a serious p____ and graze livestock where deser____ people may face famine and sta____ central Africa. Millions of rural ____ cities because they can no longe____

apply it!

Desertification affects many areas around the world.

❶ **Name** Which continent has the most existing desert?

❷ **Interpret Maps** Where in the United States is the greatest risk of desertification?

❸ **Infer** Is desertification a thr____ is existing desert? Explain. Circle ____ your answer.

❹ **CHALLENGE** If an area is facin____ things people could do to possi____

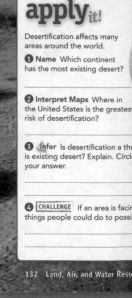

Explain what you know.

Look for the pencil. When you see it, it's time to interact with your book and demonstrate what you have learned.

apply it!

Elaborate further with the Apply It activities. This is your opportunity to take what you've learned and apply those skills to new situations.

Lab Zone

Look for the Lab zone triangle. This means it's time to do a hands-on inquiry lab. In every lesson, you'll have the opportunity to do a hands-on inquiry activity that will help reinforce your understanding of the lesson topic.

...ertile area becomes depleted
...become a desert. The
...eas that previously were
...t uh fih KAY shun).
...te. For example, a **drought**
...falls in an area. During
...r, the exposed soil easily
...by cattle and sheep and
...se desertification, too.
...People cannot grow crops
...n has occurred. As a result,
...Desertification is severe in
...there are moving to the
...rt themselves on the land.

Land Reclamation Fortunately, it is possible to replace land damaged by erosion or mining. The process of restoring an area of land to a more productive state is called **land reclamation**. In addition to restoring land for agriculture, land reclamation can restore habitats for wildlife. Many different types of land reclamation projects are currently underway all over the world. But it is generally more difficult and expensive to restore damaged land and soil than it is to protect those resources in the first place. In some cases, the land may not return to its original state.

FIGURE 4 ·······························
Land Reclamation
These pictures show land before and after it was mined.

✎ **Communicate** Below the pictures, write a story about what happened to the land.

...in areas where there
...a on the map to support

Key
■ Existing desert
■ High-risk area
■ Moderate-risk area

North America, Europe, Asia, Atlantic Ocean, South America, Africa, Indian Ocean, Australia, Antarctica

...tification, what are some
...its effects?

Lab Do the Quick Lab
zone Modeling Soil...

🔑 **Assess Your Understanding**

1a. Review Subsoil has (less/more) plant and animal matter than topsoil.

c. Apply Concepts ...
that could prev...
land reclama...

b. Explain What can happen to soil if plants are removed?

got it?

○ I get it! Now I know that soil management is important becau...

○ I need extra help with _____
Go to **MY SCIENCE COACH** online for help with this subject.

got it?

Evaluate Your Progress.

After answering the Got It question, think about how you're doing. Did you get it or do you need a little help? Remember, **MY SCIENCE** ⑤ **COACH** is there for you if you need extra help.

Explore the Big Question.

At one point in the chapter, you'll have the opportunity to take all that you've learned to further explore the Big Question.

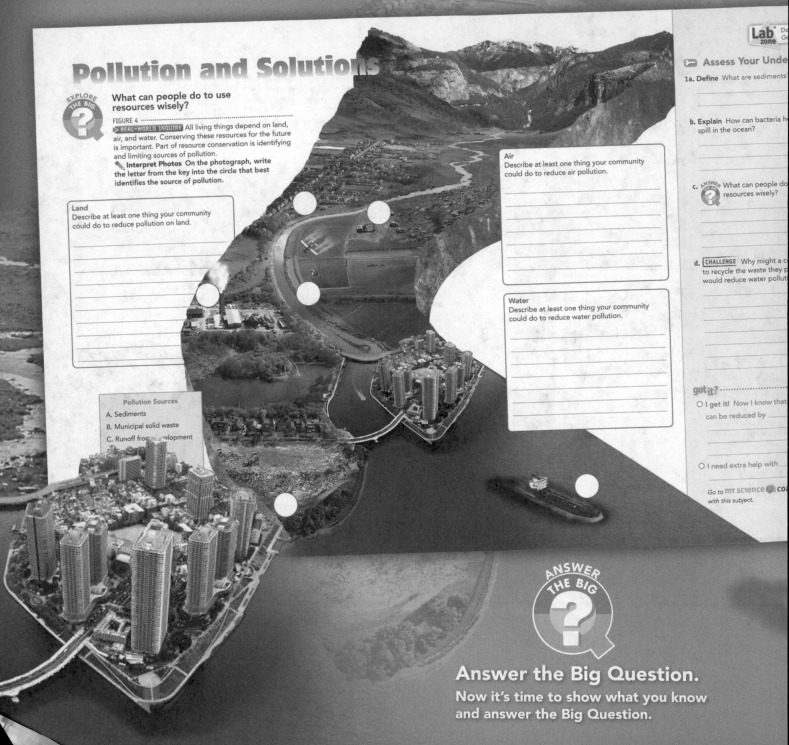

Pollution and Solutions

EXPLORE THE BIG ?

What can people do to use resources wisely?

FIGURE 4 ....
> **REAL-WORLD INQUIRY** All living things depend on land, air, and water. Conserving these resources for the future is important. Part of resource conservation is identifying and limiting sources of pollution.

✎ **Interpret Photos** On the photograph, write the letter from the key into the circle that best identifies the source of pollution.

Land
Describe at least one thing your community could do to reduce pollution on land.

_____
_____
_____
_____

Pollution Sources
A. Sediments
B. Municipal solid waste
C. Runoff from ___elopment

Air
Describe at least one thing your community could do to reduce air pollution.

_____
_____
_____
_____

Water
Describe at least one thing your community could do to reduce water pollution.

_____
_____
_____
_____
_____
_____
_____

Lab zone

Assess Your Unde___

1a. Define What are sediments

_____

b. Explain How can bacteria h___ spill in the ocean?

_____
_____

c. ANSWER What can people do ___ resources wisely?

_____
_____
_____

d. CHALLENGE Why might a c___ to recycle the waste they p___ would reduce water pollut___

_____
_____
_____
_____

got it? ....

O **I get it!** Now I know that ___ can be reduced by ___
_____

O **I need extra help with** ___
_____

Go to MY SCIENCE ___ co___ with this subject.

ANSWER THE BIG ?

Answer the Big Question.

Now it's time to show what you know and answer the Big Question.

interactiveSCIENCE
Interact with your world.

Review What You've Learned.

Use the Chapter Study Guide to review the Big Question and prepare for the test.

my science | Land, Water, and Air Resources | MY SCIENCE COACH | PRACTICE TEST

CHAPTER
4 Study Guide

To use resources wisely, people can reuse or _____ materials and they can properly dispose of hazardous wastes and other _____.

LESSON 1 Conserving Land and Soil

Three uses that change the land are agriculture, mining, and development.

Without soil, most life on land could not exist. Poor soil management results in three problems: erosion, nutrient depletion, and desertification.

Vocabulary
• litter • topsoil • subsoil • bedrock
• erosion • nutrient depletion • fertilizer
• desertification • drought • land reclamation

LESSON 2 Waste Disposal and Recycling

Solid waste is burned, buried, or recycled.

Recycling categories include metal, glass, paper, and plastic.

Hazardous wastes are stored depending on the type and potential danger.

Vocabulary
• municipal solid waste • incineration
• pollutant • leachate • sanitary landfill
• recycling • biodegradable • hazardous waste

LESSON 3 Air Pollution and Solutions

A major source of outdoor air pollution is vehicle emissions. Indoor air pollution has a variety of causes.

The major cause of the ozone hole is CFCs.

Reducing air pollution requires reducing emissions.

Vocabulary
• emissions • photochemical smog • ozone
• temperature inversion • acid rain
• radon • ozone layer • chlorofluorocarbon

LESSON 4 Water Pollution and Solutions

Water on Earth is about 97 percent saltwater.

Most water pollution is caused by human activities.

The keys to keeping water clean include cleaning oil spills, proper sewage treatment, and the reduction of pollutants.

Vocabulary
• groundwater • pesticide • sewage • sediment

LESSON 5 Ocean Resources

Resources in the ocean include organisms such as fish and nonliving things such as oil.

Most ocean pollution is related to human activities.

Vocabulary
• nodule
• upwelling

168 Land, Air, and Water Resources

Review and Assessment

LESSON 1 Conserving Land and Soil

1. What is an agricultural use of land?
   a. growing crops on land
   b. collecting water from land
   c. building structures on land
   d. removing minerals from land

2. Plant roots absorb nutrients and water from the layer of soil called _____.

3. **Relate Cause and Effect** What type of land use can result in nutrient depletion? Explain.

LESSON 3 Air Pollution and Solutions

7. Which of the following describes a pollutant that has been released into the air?
   a. sewage   b. leachate
   c. sediment   d. emissions

8. The _____ in the upper atmosphere prevents some of the sun's ultraviolet radiation from reaching Earth.

9. **Predict** Do you think the hole in the ozone layer will increase or decrease in size? Why?

CHAPTER
4 Review and Assessment

LESSON 4 Water Pollution and Solutions

11. Why is fresh water a limited resource?
    a. because most water on Earth is in lakes
    b. because most water on Earth is in clouds
    c. because most water on Earth is in the ground
    d. because most water on Earth is salt water

12. A _____ is a chemical that kills crop-destroying organisms.

13. **Draw Conclusions** Rain may wash fertilizers into bodies of water, such as ponds. How might fertilizer affect a pond?

LESSON 5 Ocean Resources

14. The ocean contains living resources such as _____ and nonliving resources such as _____.
    a. fuel; water   b. fish; minerals
    c. seaweed; shrimp d. organisms; pollution

15. _____ is the movement of cold water from the deep ocean to the surface.

16. **Relate Cause and Effect** How might oil used as fuel result in ocean pollution?

What can people do to use resources wisely?

17. Every individual, including young people, can make decisions to use resources wisely. Use the terms *reduce, reuse,* and *recycle* to explain how the students in the picture below can help minimize solid waste.

170 Land, Air, and Water Resources

159

Practice Taking Tests.

Apply the Big Question and take a practice test in standardized test format.

INTERACT ... WITH YOUR TEXTBOOK ...

Go to **MyScienceOnline.com** and immerse yourself in amazing virtual environments.

> THE BIG QUESTION

Each online chapter starts with a Big Question. Your mission is to unlock the meaning of this Big Question as each science lesson unfolds.

Unit 4 > Chapter 1 > Lesson 1

<< | The Big Question | Unlock the Big Question | Explore the Big Question | >>

The Big Question   Check Your Understanding   Vocabulary Skill

Populations and Communities

Tools

The Big Question

Unit 2 > Chapter 4 > Lesson 1

Engage & Explore   Explain

Planet Diary

my planet diary

> VOCAB FLASH CARDS

Practice chapter vocabulary with interactive flash cards. Each card has an image, definitions in English and Spanish, and space for your own notes.

Unit 4 > Chapter 1 > Lesson 1

<< | The Big Question | Unlock the Big Question | Explore the Big Question | >>

The Big Question   Untamed Science   Check Your Understanding   Vocabulary Skill   Vocabulary Flashcards

Vocabulary Flashcards

Tools

Card List | Create-a-Card   10 Cards Left | Test Me

Lesson Cards   My Cards

- Birth Rate
- Carrying Capacity
- Commensalism
- Community
- Competition
- Death Rate
- Ecology
- Ecosystem
- Emigration
- Habitat
- Host
- Immigration
- Limiting Factor

Science Vocabulary

▸ Term: **Community**

▸ Definition: All the different populations that live together in a particular area.

View Spanish

Add Notes

<<

Card 5 of

Unit 6 > Chapter 1 > Lesson 3

Engage & Explore   Ex

Apply It   Directed Virtual Lab

Color in Light

Exit

Reset Lab

Unit 6 > Chapter 1 > Lesson 1

Engage & Explore | Explain | Elaborate | Evaluate

Apply It   Do the Math   Art in Motion   Interactive Art   Real World Inquiry

The Nebraska Plains

▸ **Bald Eagle**

Information   Media

Haliaeetus leucocephalus
Bald Eagles are 80-95 cm tall with a wingspan of 180-230 cm. These birds are born with all brown feathers but grow white feathers on their head, neck, and tail.

Layers List   ▲ Show

Next

22 of 22

Back

> INTERACTIVE ART

At MyScienceOnline.com, many of the beautiful visuals in your book become interactive so you can extend your learning.

WITH INQUIRY...

interactive SCIENCE
GO ONLINE

my science online.com | Populations and Communities > PLANET DIARY > LAB ZONE > VIRTUAL LAB

http://www.myscienceonline.com/

PLANET DIARY

My Planet Diary online is the place to find more information and activities related to the topic in the lesson.

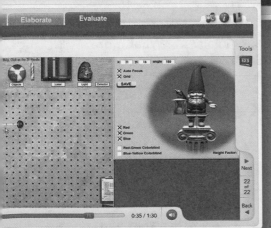

Elaborate | Evaluate

Everest   Tools

Still Growing! Mount Everest in the Himalayas is the highest mountain on Earth. Climbers who reach the peak stand 8,850 meters above sea level. You might think that mountains never change. But forces inside Earth push Mount Everest at least several millimeters higher each year. Over time, Earth's forces slowly but constantly lift, stretch, bend, and break Earth's crust in dramatic ways!

Planet Diary Go to Planet Diary to learn more about forces in the Earth's crust.

Next
22 of 22
Back

VIRTUAL LAB

Get more practice with realistic virtual labs. Manipulate the variables on-screen and test your hypothesis.

Find Your Chapter

1 Go to www.myscienceonline.com.

2 Log in with username and password.

3 Click on your program and select your chapter.

Keyword Search

1 Go to www.myscienceonline.com.

2 Log in with username and password.

3 Click on your program and select Search.

4 Enter the keyword (from your book) in the search box.

Other Content Available Online

> UNTAMED SCIENCE Follow these young scientists through their amazing online video blogs as they travel the globe in search of answers to the Big Questions of Science.

> MY SCIENCE COACH Need extra help? My Science Coach is your personal online study partner. My Science Coach is a chance for you to get more practice on key science concepts. There you can choose from a variety of tools that will help guide you through each science lesson.

> MY READING WEB Need extra reading help on a particular science topic? At My Reading Web you will find a choice of reading selections targeted to your specific reading level.

? BIG IDEAS OF SCIENCE

Have you ever worked on a jigsaw puzzle? Usually a puzzle has a theme that leads you to group the pieces by what they have in common. But until you put all the pieces together you can't solve the puzzle. Studying science is similar to solving a puzzle. The big ideas of science are like puzzle themes. To understand big ideas, scientists ask questions. The answers to those questions are like pieces of a puzzle. Each chapter in this book asks a big question to help you think about a big idea of science. By answering the big questions, you will get closer to understanding the big idea.

✏ **Before you read each chapter, write about what you know and what more you'd like to know.**

BIGIDEA

Living things are alike yet different.

Grasses and wildflowers look different, but they all grow in soil and need sunlight and water.

What do you already know about how all living things are alike yet different? ✏ **What more would you like to know?**

_____

_____

_____

Big Questions:

? How are living things alike yet different? Chapter 1

? How are living things other than plants and animals important to Earth? Chapter 2

? How do you know a plant when you see it? Chapter 3

? How do you know an animal when you see it? Chapter 4

✏ **After reading the chapters, write what you have learned about the Big Idea.**

_____

_____

BIGIDEA

Structures in living things are related to their functions.

Using its wings, a hawk flies through the air and coasts to a landing.

What do you already know about how animals move in water, on land, or in air? ✏ **What more would you like to know?**

_____

_____

_____

Big Question:

? How do animals move? Chapter 5

✏ **After reading the chapter, write what you have learned about the Big Idea.**

_____

_____

Living things get and use energy.

A salmon lunch provides energy for this hungry bear.

What do you already know about how animals get and eat food? ✎ **What more would you like to know?**

_____

_____

_____

_____

Big Question:

❓ How do animals get and use energy? Chapter 6

✎ **After reading the chapter, write what you have learned about the Big Idea.**

_____

_____

_____

_____

Living things grow, change, and reproduce during their lifetimes.

Tadpoles hatch from frog eggs and grow into adults.

What do you already know about how animals survive and produce offspring? ✎ **What more would you like to know?**

_____

_____

_____

_____

Big Question:

❓ How does an animal's behavior help it survive and reproduce? Chapter 7

✎ **After reading the chapter, write what you have learned about the Big Idea.**

_____

_____

_____

_____

HOW ARE THIS MANATEE AND HYRAX ALIKE?

How are living things alike yet different?

Living in Florida waters, a manatee can grow to be longer than 3 meters and weigh over 350 kilograms. A rock hyrax is a small, tailless, rodentlike animal that lives in rocky areas of Africa. While these animals appear to be very different, they are actually related.

Develop Hypotheses **What could these two animals have in common?**

_____

_____

_____

_____

_____

_____

> UNTAMED SCIENCE Watch the **Untamed Science** video to learn more about living things.

Introduction to Living Things

1 Getting Started

Check Your Understanding

1. **Background** Read the paragraph below and then answer the question.

You eat microscopic organisms all the time without realizing it! Some microscopic organisms are necessary to prepare common foods. Yeast, for example, is a tiny organism that is used to make bread. Bacteria are used to make yogurt, sauerkraut, and many other foods.

> Something microscopic is so small that it cannot be seen without a magnifying lens or a microscope.
>
> Yeast is a single-celled organism that has a nucleus.
>
> Bacteria are single-celled organisms that do not have nuclei.

• What is one kind of food that bacteria are used to make?

_____

> MY READING WEB   If you had trouble completing the question above, visit **My Reading Web** and type in *Introduction to Living Things.*

Vocabulary Skill

Greek Word Origins Many science words come from ancient Greek words. Learning the word parts that have Greek origins can help you understand some of the vocabulary in this chapter.

Greek Word Part	Meaning	Example
autos	self	autotroph, *n.* an organism that makes its own food
taxis	order, arrangement	taxonomy, *n.* the scientific study of how living things are classified
homos	similar, same	homeostasis, *n.* the maintenance of stable internal conditions

2. **Quick Check** Circle the part of the word *taxonomy* that lets you know that the word's meaning has something to do with ordering or classifying things.

organism

species

eukaryote

branching tree diagram

Chapter Preview

LESSON 1
- organism
- cell
- unicellular
- multicellular
- metabolism
- stimulus
- response
- development
- asexual reproduction
- sexual reproduction
- spontaneous generation
- controlled experiment
- autotroph
- heterotroph
- homeostasis

↻ Compare and Contrast
△ Control Variables

LESSON 2
- classification
- taxonomy
- binomial nomenclature
- genus
- species

↻ Ask Questions
△ Observe

LESSON 3
- prokaryote
- nucleus
- eukaryote

↻ Identify the Main Idea
△ Classify

LESSON 4
- evolution
- branching tree diagram
- shared derived characteristic
- convergent evolution

↻ Summarize
△ Infer

▷ VOCAB FLASH CARDS For extra help with vocabulary, visit **Vocab Flash Cards** and type in *Introduction to Living Things.*

What Is Life?

🔑 **What Are the Characteristics of All Living Things?**

🔑 **Where Do Living Things Come From?**

🔑 **What Do Living Things Need to Survive?**

my planet Diary

TECHNOLOGY

It's Kismet!

If you hear a loud noise, do you turn toward the sound to see what caused it? When someone smiles at you, do you smile back? If somebody shook something in front of your face, would you back away? Most people react in these ways, and so does Kismet, a humanlike robot! Scientists developed Kismet to interact with, cooperate with, and learn from humans. Kismet can understand information that it sees and hears as if it were a young child. When responding to information, Kismet's face changes so that it seems interested, happy, or frightened. Kismet's expressions are so convincing that it is sometimes hard to remember that Kismet isn't really alive!

Answer the questions below.

1. What does Kismet do that makes it seem human?

_____

_____

_____

2. What are some things you think Kismet might not be able to do that humans can?

_____

_____

_____

▸ **PLANET DIARY** Go to **Planet Diary** to learn more about living things.

 Lab zone® Do the Inquiry Warm-Up *Is It Living or Nonliving?*

Vocabulary

- organism • cell • unicellular • multicellular • metabolism
- stimulus • response • development • asexual reproduction
- sexual reproduction • spontaneous generation
- controlled experiment • autotroph • heterotroph • homeostasis

Skills

↻ **Reading: Compare and Contrast**

△ **Inquiry: Control Variables**

What Are the Characteristics of All Living Things?

If you were asked to name some living things, or **organisms,**
you might name yourself, a pet, and some insects or plants. You
would probably not mention a moss growing in a shady spot, the
mildew on bathroom tiles, or the slime molds that ooze across
lawns. But all of these things are organisms that share several
important characteristics with all other living things. 🔑 **All living
things have a cellular organization, contain similar chemicals,
use energy, respond to their surroundings, grow and develop,
and reproduce.**

FIGURE 1 ·······························

It's Alive . . . or Is It?

✎ **Look at the photos. Then
answer the questions.**

1. **Identify** List the letter of the

   photo(s) that you think show

   living thing(s). _____

2. **Describe** What
   characteristics helped
   you decide whether or
   not the things shown
   were living or nonliving?

   _____

   _____

   _____

Cellular Organization

All organisms are made of small building blocks called cells. A **cell,** like the one shown here, is the basic unit of structure and function in an organism. Organisms may be composed of only one cell or of many cells.

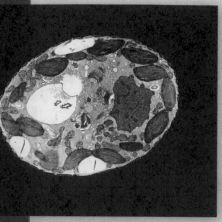

Single-celled organisms, like bacteria (bak TIHR ee uh), are **unicellular** organisms. The single cell is responsible for carrying out all of the functions necessary to stay alive. Organisms that are composed of many cells are **multicellular.** For example, you are made of trillions of cells. In many multicellular organisms, the cells are specialized to do certain tasks. Specialized cells in your body, such as muscle and nerve cells, work together to keep you alive. Nerve cells carry messages to your muscle cells, making your body move.

Characteristics of Living Things

The Chemicals of Life

The cells of living things are made of chemicals. The most abundant chemical in cells is water. Other chemicals, called carbohydrates (kahr boh HY drayts) are a cell's main energy source. Two other chemicals, proteins and lipids, are the building materials of cells, much as wood and bricks are the building materials of houses. Finally, nucleic (noo KLEE ik) acids are the genetic material of cells—the chemical instructions that cells need to carry out the functions of life.

Energy Use

Organisms get energy from taking in and breaking down materials. The combination of chemical reactions through which an organism builds up or breaks down materials is called **metabolism.** The cells of organisms use energy to do what living things must do, such as grow and repair injured parts. An organism's cells are always hard at work. For example, as you read these words, not only are your eye and brain cells busy, but most of your other cells are working, too. Young sooty terns, like the one shown above, need lots of energy to fly. These birds can fly four to five years without ever setting foot on land!

FIGURE 2 ....

Living Things

All living things share the same characteristics.

✎ **Make Judgments** Which characteristic on these two pages do you think best identifies an object as a living thing? Explain your choice.

_____

_____

_____

_____

_____

Response to Surroundings

If you've ever seen a plant in a sunny window, you may have observed that the plant's stems have bent so that the leaves face the sun. Like a plant bending toward the light, all organisms react to changes in their environment. A change in an organism's surroundings that causes the organism to react is called a **stimulus** (plural *stimuli*). Stimuli include changes in light, sound, and other factors.

An organism reacts to a stimulus with a **response**—an action or a change in behavior. For example, has someone ever knocked over a glass of water by accident during dinner, causing you to jump? The sudden spilling of water was the stimulus that caused your startled response.

Lab ® Do the Quick Lab
zone *React!*

Growth and Development

All living things grow and develop. Growth is the process of becoming larger. **Development** is the process of change that occurs during an organism's life, producing a more complex organism. As they develop and grow, organisms use energy and make new cells.

Reproduction

Another characteristic of organisms is the ability to reproduce, or produce offspring that are similar to the parents. Organisms reproduce in different ways. **Asexual reproduction** involves only one parent and produces offspring that are identical to the parent. **Sexual reproduction** involves two parents and combines their genetic material to produce a new organism that differs from both parents. Mammals, birds, and most plants sexually reproduce. Penguins lay eggs that develop into young penguins that closely resemble their parents.

Assess Your Understanding

1a. Review A change in an organism's surroundings is a (stimulus/response).

b. Infer A bird sitting in a tree flies away as you walk by. Which of the life characteristics explains the bird's behavior?

_____

c. CHALLENGE Trees do not move like birds do, but they are living things. Why?

_____
_____
_____
_____
_____

got it? ....

○ **I get it!** Now I know that all living things
_____
_____
_____
_____
_____

○ **I need extra help with** _____
_____

Go to **MY SCIENCE** Ⓢ **COACH** online for help with this subject.

7

Where Do Living Things Come From?

Today, when people see weeds poking out of cracks in sidewalks or find mice in their cabinet, as shown in **Figure 3,** they know that these organisms are the result of reproduction. 🔑 **Living things arise from other living things through reproduction.**

Four hundred years ago, however, people believed that life could appear from nonliving material. For example, when people saw flies swarming around decaying meat, they concluded that flies were produced by rotting meat. The mistaken idea that living things can arise from nonliving sources is called **spontaneous generation.** It took hundreds of years of experiments to convince people that spontaneous generation does not occur.

FIGURE 3 ···

Spontaneous Generation

Sometimes unexpected visitors, like this mouse, can be found in kitchen cabinets.

✎ **Answer the questions.**

1. **Develop Hypotheses** If you lived 400 years ago, where might you think the mouse in the cabinet came from?

_____

_____

_____

2. [CHALLENGE] Describe a way in which you could test your hypothesis.

_____

_____

_____

_____

_____

_____

_____

_____

_____

_____

_____

Redi's Experiment In the 1600s, an Italian doctor named Francesco Redi helped to disprove spontaneous generation. Redi designed a controlled experiment to show that maggots, which develop into new flies, do not arise from decaying meat. In a **controlled experiment,** a scientist carries out a series of tests that are identical in every respect except for one factor. The one factor that a scientist changes in an experiment is called the manipulated variable. The factor that changes as a result of changes to the manipulated variable is called the responding variable. Redi's experiment is shown in **Figure 4.**

FIGURE 4 ··
Redi's Experiment
Francesco Redi designed one of the first controlled experiments. Redi showed that flies do not spontaneously arise from decaying meat. Here's how he did it:

Uncovered jar   **Covered jar**

STEP ① Redi placed meat in two identical jars. He left one jar uncovered. He covered the other jar with a cloth that let in air.

STEP ② After a few days, Redi saw maggots (young flies) on the decaying meat in the open jar. There were no maggots on the meat in the covered jar.

STEP ③ Redi reasoned that flies had laid eggs on the meat in the open jar. The eggs hatched into maggots. Because flies could not lay eggs on the meat in the covered jar, there were no maggots there. Redi concluded that decaying meat did not produce maggots.

apply it!

Use **Figure 4** to answer the following questions about Redi's experiment.

❶ Control Variables What is the manipulated variable in this experiment?

_____
_____
_____

❷ Control Variables What is the responding variable?

_____
_____

❸ Analyze Sources of Error Name two factors that would need to be kept constant in this experiment to avoid causing error. Why?

_____
_____
_____
_____
_____
_____
_____

Pasteur's Experiment Even after Redi's experiment, many people continued to believe in spontaneous generation. In the mid-1800s, Louis Pasteur, a French chemist, designed another experiment to test spontaneous generation. That experiment, shown in **Figure 5,** along with Redi's work, finally disproved spontaneous generation.

FIGURE 5 ···

> INTERACTIVE ART Pasteur's Experiment
Louis Pasteur's carefully controlled experiment demonstrated that bacteria arise only from existing bacteria. ✎ **Design Experiments** Read each step of the experiment below. Why do you think flasks with curved necks were important?

_____

_____

_____

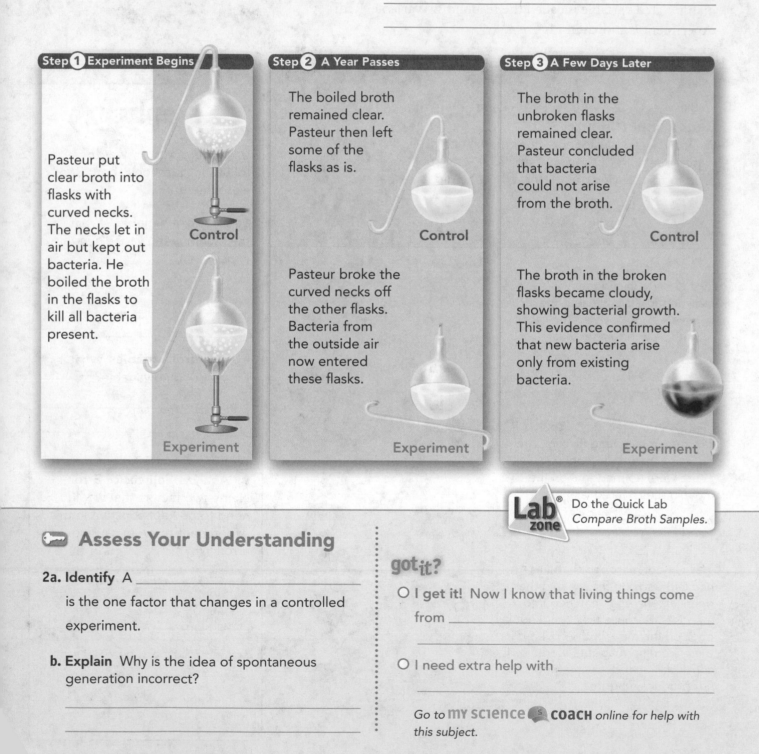

Step ① Experiment Begins

Pasteur put clear broth into flasks with curved necks. The necks let in air but kept out bacteria. He boiled the broth in the flasks to kill all bacteria present.

Control

Experiment

Step ② A Year Passes

The boiled broth remained clear. Pasteur then left some of the flasks as is.

Control

Pasteur broke the curved necks off the other flasks. Bacteria from the outside air now entered these flasks.

Experiment

Step ③ A Few Days Later

The broth in the unbroken flasks remained clear. Pasteur concluded that bacteria could not arise from the broth.

Control

The broth in the broken flasks became cloudy, showing bacterial growth. This evidence confirmed that new bacteria arise only from existing bacteria.

Experiment

Lab zone® Do the Quick Lab
Compare Broth Samples.

🔑 Assess Your Understanding

2a. Identify A _____ is the one factor that changes in a controlled experiment.

b. Explain Why is the idea of spontaneous generation incorrect?

_____

_____

got it?

○ **I get it!** Now I know that living things come

from _____

_____

○ **I need extra help with** _____

_____

Go to **MY SCIENCE** ⓢ **COACH** *online for help with this subject.*

What Do Living Things Need to Survive?

Though it may seem surprising, flies, bacteria, and all other organisms have the same basic needs as you. 🔑 **All living things must satisfy their basic needs for food, water, living space, and stable internal conditions.**

Food Recall that organisms need a source of energy to live. They use food as their energy source. Organisms differ in the ways they obtain energy. Some organisms, such as plants, capture the sun's energy and use it to make food. Organisms that make their own food are called **autotrophs** (AW toh trohfs). *Auto-* means "self" and *-troph* means "feeder." Autotrophs use the food they make to carry out their own life functions.

Organisms that cannot make their own food are called **heterotrophs** (HET uh roh trohfs). Heterotrophs obtain energy by feeding on other organisms. Some heterotrophs eat autotrophs for food. Other heterotrophs consume heterotrophs that eat autotrophs. They use the energy in the autotrophs' bodies. Therefore, a heterotroph's energy source is also the sun—but in an indirect way. Animals, mushrooms, and slime molds are examples of heterotrophs.

⟳ Compare and Contrast As you read, circle how autotrophs and heterotrophs are similar and underline how they are different.

Vocabulary Greek Word Origins The Greek word part *hetero-* means "other." How does this word help you to understand how heterotrophs get their food?

_____

_____

_____

FIGURE 6 ·····················
Food
This giraffe, a heterotroph, obtains its energy by feeding on trees and shrubs.

✏ **Identify** From your own habitat, name two examples of autotrophs and two examples of heterotrophs.

_____

_____

_____

_____

_____

During the summer, when desert temperatures can exceed 47°C, a camel only needs to drink water every five days. At that time, a camel can drink up to 189 liters of water in just a few hours!

Water All living things need water to survive. In fact, most organisms can live for only a few days without water. Organisms need water to obtain chemicals from their surroundings, break down food, grow, move substances within their bodies, and reproduce.

One property of water that is vital to living things is its ability to dissolve more chemicals than any other substance on Earth. In fact, water makes up about 90 percent of the liquid part of your blood. The food that your cells need dissolves in blood and is transported to all parts of your body. Waste from cells dissolves in blood and is carried away. Your body's cells also provide a watery environment for chemicals to dissolve.

Living Space All organisms need a place to live—a place to get food and water and find shelter. Whether an organism lives in the freezing Arctic or the scorching desert, its surroundings must provide what it needs to survive.

Because there is a limited amount of space on Earth, some organisms must compete for space. Trees in a forest, for example, compete with other trees for sunlight above ground. Below ground, their roots compete for water and minerals.

FIGURE 7

Desert Oasis

You might be surprised to see so much green in the middle of a desert. In a desert oasis, there is water beneath the surface. The groundwater can bubble to the surface and create springs.

✎ **Draw Conclusions** How can a small area in the middle of a desert provide an organism what it needs to survive?

_____

_____

_____

_____

_____

FIGURE 8 ·····················

Homeostasis
During the winter months, birds rely on their feathers to maintain homeostasis. By fluffing its feathers, this bluebird is able to trap body heat to keep warm. ✏ **Make Generalizations** How do people maintain homeostasis when exposed to cold temperatures?

_____

_____

_____

 Do the Lab Investigation *Please Pass the Bread.*

Stable Internal Conditions

Organisms must be able to keep the conditions inside their bodies stable, even when conditions in their surroundings change significantly. For example, your body temperature stays steady despite changes in the air temperature. The maintenance of stable internal conditions is called **homeostasis** (hoh mee oh STAY sis).

Homeostasis keeps internal conditions just right for cells to function. Think about your need for water after a hard workout. When water levels in your body decrease, chemicals in your body send signals to your brain, which cause you to feel thirsty.

Other organisms have different mechanisms for maintaining homeostasis. Consider barnacles, which as adults are attached to rocks at the edge of the ocean. At high tide, they are covered by water. But at low tide, the watery surroundings disappear, and barnacles are exposed to hours of sun and wind. Without a way to keep water in their cells, they would die. Fortunately, a barnacle can close up its hard outer plates, trapping some water inside. In this way, a barnacle can keep its body moist until the next high tide. Refer to **Figure 8** to see another example of how an organism maintains homeostasis.

🗝 **Assess Your Understanding**

3a. Describe Which basic need is a fox meeting by feeding on berries?

_____

_____

b. Apply Concepts The arctic fox has thick, dense fur in the winter and much shorter fur in the summer. How does this help the fox maintain homeostasis?

_____

_____

_____

_____

_____

got it? ·····················

○ **I get it!** Now I know that to survive, living

things need _____

_____

_____

○ **I need extra help with** _____

_____

_____

Go to MY SCIENCE ⬤ COACH *online for help with this subject.*

Classifying Life

UNLOCK THE BIG ?

🔑 **Why Do Biologists Classify Organisms?**

🔑 **What Are the Levels of Classification?**

🔑 **How Are Taxonomic Keys Useful?**

MY PLANET DiARY

CAREER

Birds of a Feather

When people first began to travel in airplanes, birds often caused crashes. In 1960, 62 people were killed when birds flew into an airplane's engine. Something had to be done, but no one knew what kinds of birds were causing the crashes. Usually only a tiny, burnt piece of feather remained. Engineers didn't know how big or heavy the birds were, so they couldn't design planes to keep birds out of the engines. Then a scientist named Roxie Laybourne invented a way to classify birds using a tiny piece of feather. She identified the birds from many crashes. Her work helped engineers design engines to reduce bird collisions. She also helped develop bird management programs for major airports. Roxie's work has saved passengers' lives!

Answer the questions below.

1. What did Roxie Laybourne invent?

_____

_____

_____

2. Why was her invention so important?

_____

_____

_____

_____

_____

_____

▷ PLANET DIARY Go to **Planet Diary** to learn more about classification.

Lab zone® Do the Inquiry Warm-Up *Can You Organize a Junk Drawer?*

Vocabulary
- classification • taxonomy • binomial nomenclature
- genus • species

Skills
- Reading: Ask Questions
- Inquiry: Observe

Why Do Biologists Classify Organisms?

So far, scientists have identified more than one million kinds of organisms on Earth. That's a large number, and it keeps growing as scientists discover new organisms. Imagine how difficult it would be to find information about one particular organism if you had no idea even where to begin. It would be a lot easier if similar organisms were placed into groups.

Organizing living things into groups is exactly what biologists have done. Biologists group organisms based on similarities, just as grocers group milk with dairy products and tomatoes with other produce. **Classification** is the process of grouping things based on their similarities, as shown in **Figure 1.**

🔑 **Biologists use classification to organize living things into groups so that the organisms are easier to study.** The scientific study of how organisms are classified is called **taxonomy** (tak SAHN uh mee). Taxonomy is useful because once an organism is classified, a scientist knows a lot of information about that organism. For example, if you know that a crow is classified as a bird, then you know that a crow has wings, feathers, and a beak.

🔄 **Ask Questions** Before you read, preview the headings. Ask a *what*, *why*, or *how* question that you would like answered. As you read, write the answer to your question.

_____

_____

_____

_____

FIGURE 1 ....

Classifying Insects

These bees and wasps belong to a large insect collection in a natural history museum. They have been classified according to the characteristics they share.

✏️ **Observe** What characteristics do you think may have been used to group these insects?

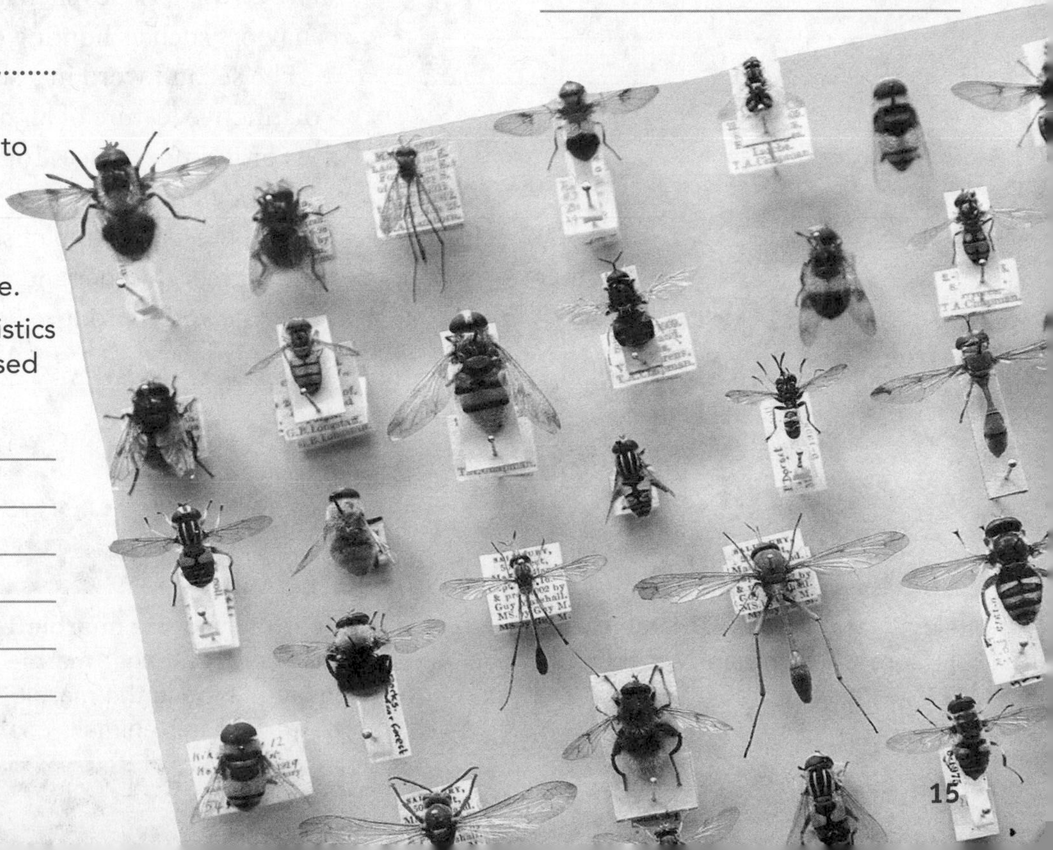

_____

_____

_____

_____

_____

Puma concolor (puma)
Concolor means "the same color" in Latin. Notice that this animal's coat is mostly the same color.

FIGURE 2 ·······················

Binomial Nomenclature

These three different species of cats were once classified in the same genus based on their structures and behavior. But other types of evidence led scientists to classify the puma in the genus *Puma*.

✏️ **Infer** Suppose someone told you that a jungle cat is classified in the same genus as house cats. What characteristics and behaviors do you think a jungle cat might have?

_____

_____

_____

_____

_____

The Naming System of Linnaeus

Taxonomy also involves naming organisms. In the 1730s, the Swedish botanist Carolus Linnaeus devised a system of naming organisms that is still used today. Linnaeus placed organisms in groups based on their observable features. Each organism was given a unique, two-part scientific name. This system is called **binomial nomenclature** (by NOH mee ul NOH men klay chur). *Binomial* means "two names."

Genus and Species The first word in an organism's scientific name is its genus. A **genus** (JEE nus; plural *genera*) is a classification grouping that contains similar, closely related organisms. As shown in **Figure 2,** below, house cats and marbled cats are classified in the genus *Felis*. Organisms that are classified in the genus *Felis* share characteristics such as sharp, retractable claws and behaviors such as hunting other animals.

The second word in a scientific name often describes a distinctive feature of an organism, such as where it lives or its appearance. Together, the two words form the scientific name of a unique kind of organism. A **species** (SPEE sheez) is a group of similar organisms that can mate with each other and produce offspring that can also mate and reproduce.

Felis domesticus (house cat)
Domesticus means "of the house" in Latin.

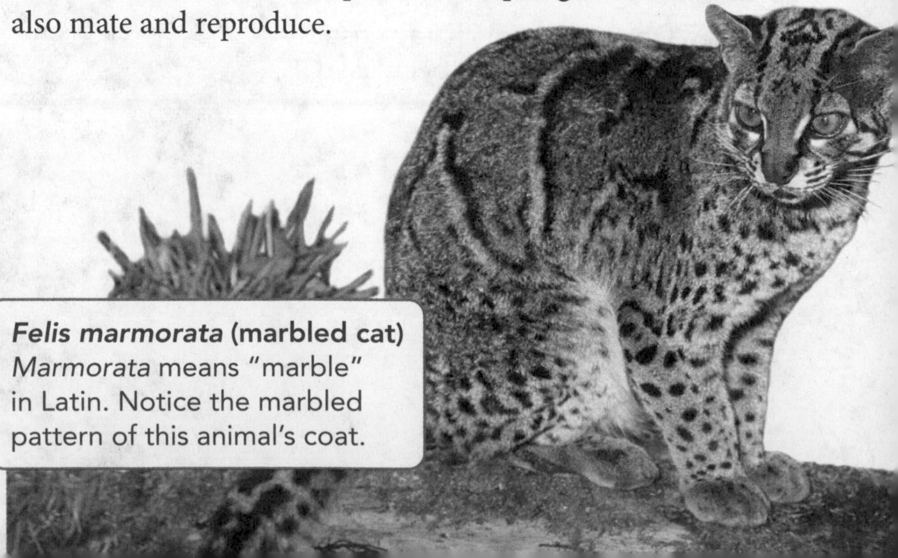

Felis marmorata (marbled cat)
Marmorata means "marble" in Latin. Notice the marbled pattern of this animal's coat.

Using Binomial Nomenclature A complete scientific name is written in italics. Only the first letter of the first word in a scientific name is capitalized. Notice that scientific names contain Latin words. Linnaeus used Latin words in his naming system because Latin was the language that scientists used during that time.

Binomial nomenclature makes it easy for scientists to communicate about an organism because everyone uses the same scientific name for the same organism. Using different names or common names for the same organism can get very confusing, as **Figure 3** describes.

FIGURE 3 ....
What Are You Talking About?
Is this animal a groundhog, a woodchuck, a marmot, or a whistlepig? Depending on where you live, all of these names are correct. Luckily, this animal has only one scientific name, *Marmota monax*.

✎ **Describe** How is a scientific name written?

_____

_____

_____

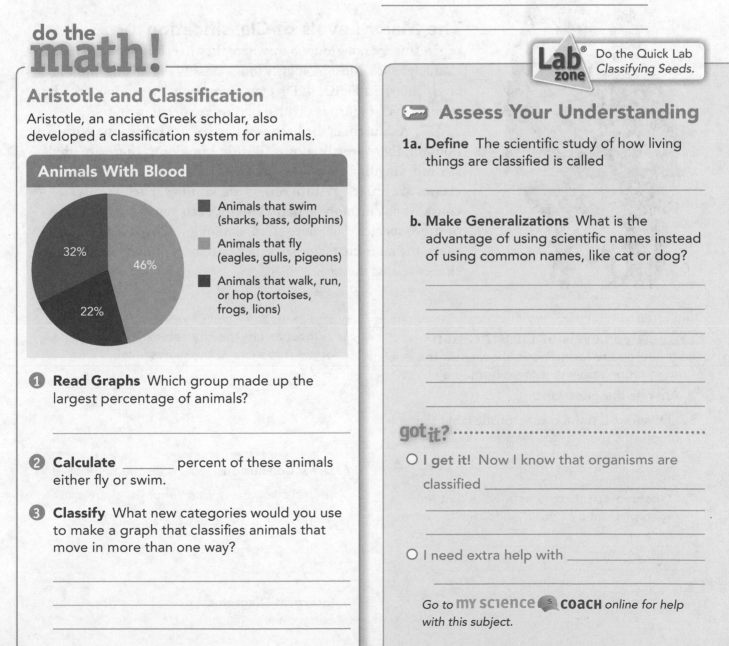

do the math!

Aristotle and Classification
Aristotle, an ancient Greek scholar, also developed a classification system for animals.

Animals With Blood

- 32%
- 46%
- 22%

- Animals that swim (sharks, bass, dolphins)
- Animals that fly (eagles, gulls, pigeons)
- Animals that walk, run, or hop (tortoises, frogs, lions)

❶ **Read Graphs** Which group made up the largest percentage of animals?

_____

❷ **Calculate** _____ percent of these animals either fly or swim.

❸ **Classify** What new categories would you use to make a graph that classifies animals that move in more than one way?

_____

_____

_____

Lab zone® Do the Quick Lab *Classifying Seeds.*

🔑 Assess Your Understanding

1a. Define The scientific study of how living things are classified is called

_____

b. Make Generalizations What is the advantage of using scientific names instead of using common names, like cat or dog?

_____

_____

_____

_____

_____

got it? ....

○ **I get it!** Now I know that organisms are

classified _____

_____

_____

○ **I need extra help with** _____

Go to **MY SCIENCE ⓢ COACH** *online for help with this subject.*

What Are the Levels of Classification?

The classification system that scientists use today is based on the contributions of Linnaeus. But today's classification system uses a series of many levels to classify organisms.

To help you understand the levels of classification, imagine a room filled with everybody who lives in your state. First, all of the people who live in your town raise their hands. Then those who live in your neighborhood raise their hands. Then those who live on your street raise their hands. Finally, those who live in your house raise their hands. Each time, fewer people raise their hands. The more levels you share with others, the more you have in common with them.

The Major Levels of Classification Of course, organisms are not grouped by where they live, but by their shared characteristics. Most biologists today classify organisms into the levels shown in **Figure 4.** First, an organism is placed in a broad group, which in turn is divided into more specific groups.

🔑 **A domain is the broadest level of organization. Within a domain, there are kingdoms. Within kingdoms, there are phyla (FY luh; singular *phylum*). Within phyla are classes. Within classes are orders. Within orders are families. Each family contains one or more genera. Finally, each genus contains one or more species.** The more classification levels two organisms share, the more characteristics they have in common and the more closely related they are.

FIGURE 4 ⋯⋯⋯⋯⋯⋯⋯⋯⋯⋯⋯⋯⋯⋯⋯⋯⋯⋯⋯⋯⋯⋯⋯⋯⋯⋯⋯⋯⋯⋯⋯⋯⋯⋯

▶ VIRTUAL LAB Levels of Classification
The figure on the facing page shows how the levels of organization apply to a great horned owl.

✎ **Answer the questions.**

1. **Observe** List the characteristics that the organisms share at the kingdom level.

   _____

2. **Observe** List the characteristics that the organisms share at the class level.

   _____

   _____

3. **Observe** List the characteristics that the organisms share at the genus level.

   _____

   _____

   _____

4. **Draw Conclusions** How does the number of shared characteristics on your list change at each level? _____

   _____

   _____

5. **Interpret Diagrams** Robins have more in common with (lions/owls).

Levels of Classification

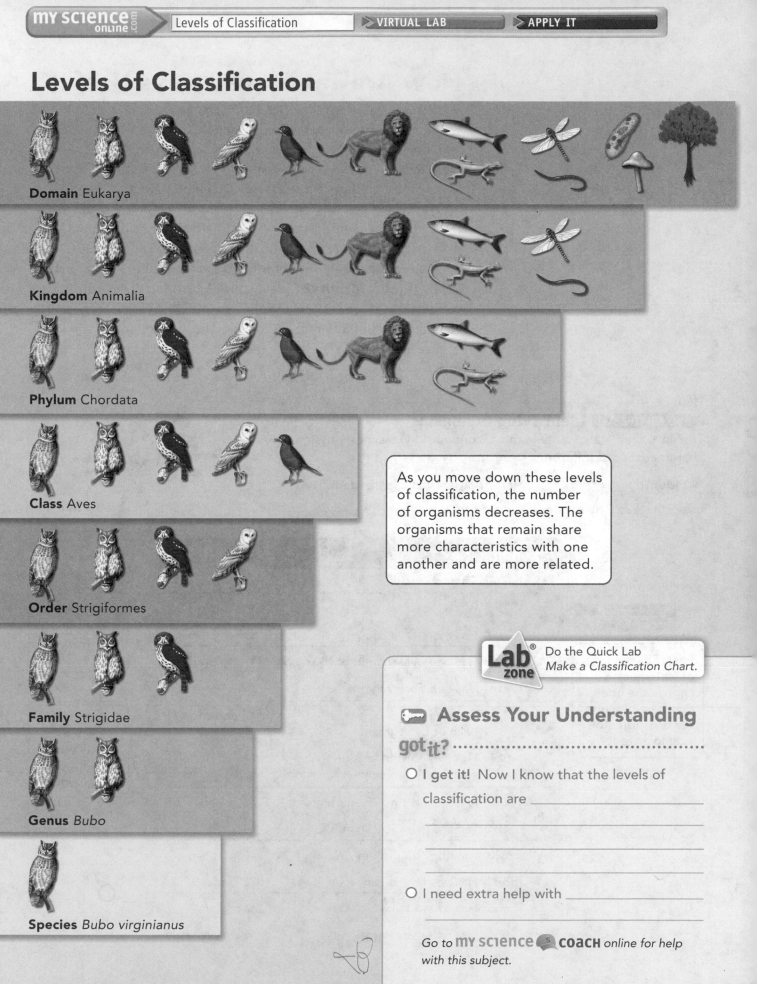

Domain Eukarya

Kingdom Animalia

Phylum Chordata

Class Aves

Order Strigiformes

Family Strigidae

Genus *Bubo*

Species *Bubo virginianus*

As you move down these levels of classification, the number of organisms decreases. The organisms that remain share more characteristics with one another and are more related.

Lab zone® Do the Quick Lab *Make a Classification Chart.*

🔑 Assess Your Understanding

got it? ⋯⋯⋯⋯⋯⋯⋯⋯⋯⋯⋯⋯⋯⋯⋯⋯⋯

○ **I get it!** Now I know that the levels of classification are _____

_____

_____

_____

○ **I need extra help with** _____

_____

Go to MY SCIENCE ⓢ COACH *online for help with this subject.*

How Are Taxonomic Keys Useful?

Why should you care about taxonomy? Suppose that you are watching television and feel something tickling your foot. Startled, you look down and see a tiny creature crawling across your toes. Although it's only the size of a small melon seed, you don't like the looks of its two claws waving at you. Then, in a flash, it's gone.

How could you find out what the creature was? You could use a field guide. Field guides are books with illustrations that highlight differences between similar-looking organisms. You could also use a taxonomic key. 🔑 **Taxonomic keys are useful tools that help determine the identity of organisms.** A taxonomic key consists of a series of paired statements that describe the various physical characteristics of different organisms. The taxonomic key shown in **Figure 5** can help you identify the mysterious organism.

FIGURE 5 ··

> INTERACTIVE ART **Identifying Organisms**
The six paired statements in this taxonomic key describe physical characteristics of different organisms.

✎ **Identify** _____ different organisms can be identified using this key. The mysterious organism is a _____

0.4 mm

Taxonomic Key			
Step		Characteristics	Organism
1	1a.	Has 8 legs	Go to Step 2.
	1b.	Has more than 8 legs	Go to Step 3.
2	2a.	Has one oval-shaped body region	Go to Step 4.
	2b.	Has two body regions	Go to Step 5.
3	3a.	Has one pair of legs on each body segment	Centipede
	3b.	Has two pairs of legs on each body segment	Millipede
4	4a.	Is less than 1 millimeter long	Mite
	4b.	Is more than 1 millimeter long	Tick
5	5a.	Has clawlike pincers	Go to Step 6.
	5b.	Has no clawlike pincers	Spider
6	6a.	Has a long tail with a stinger	Scorpion
	6b.	Has no tail or stinger	Pseudoscorpion

Start Here

First: For each set of statements, choose the one that best describes the organism; for example, 1a.

Second: Follow the direction to the next step.

Third: Continue process until organism is identified.

apply it!

Use the taxonomic key in **Figure 5** to answer the following questions.

1 Interpret Tables Identify each pictured organism.

5 mm

1a, 2b, 4b, 5b, 6b

64 mm

1a, 2b, 4b, 5a, 6a

40 mm

1a, 2b, 4b, 5b, 6b

50 mm

1b, 2a, 3b, 4b, 5b, 6b

7 mm

1a, 2b, 4b, 5a, 6b

25 mm

1b, 2a, 3a, 4b, 5b 6b

2 Draw Conclusions What other information could have been helpful in identifying these organisms?

_____

_____

_____

3 CHALLENGE Is this information necessary for the key in **Figure 5**? Explain your answer.

_____

_____

_____

Lab zone® Do the Quick Lab *Living Mysteries.*

Assess Your Understanding

got it? ....

O **I get it!** Now I know that taxonomic keys are used to _____

_____

O **I need extra help with** _____

Go to MY SCIENCE ⓢ COACH online for help with this subject.

Domains and Kingdoms

🔑 **How Are Organisms Classified Into Domains and Kingdoms?**

MY PLANET DIARY

Unbeelievable!

If you were classifying organisms, would you expect there to be more bees, more birds, or more mammals in the world? The table below shows the number of species of bees, mammals, and birds that scientists have found so far!

Number of Species		
Bees	**Mammals**	**Birds**
19,200	5,400	10,000

SCIENCE STATS

Answer the question below.

Why do you think that bee species outnumber mammal and bird species combined?

_____

_____

_____

_____

▷ PLANET DIARY Go to **Planet Diary** to learn more about domains and kingdoms.

Lab zone Do the Inquiry Warm-Up *Which Organism Goes Where?*

How Are Organisms Classified Into Domains and Kingdoms?

Suppose you helped Linnaeus classify organisms. You probably would have identified organisms as either plants or animals. That's because in Linnaeus' time there were no microscopes to see the tiny organisms that are known to exist today. Microscopes helped to discover new organisms and identify differences among cells.

Today, a three-domain system of classification is commonly used. As shown in the table on the top of the next page, the three domains are Bacteria, Archaea, and Eukarya. Within the domains are kingdoms. 🔑 **Organisms are placed into domains and kingdoms based on their cell type, their ability to make food, and the number of cells in their bodies.**

Vocabulary
- prokaryote
- nucleus
- eukaryote

Skills
- Reading: Identify the Main Idea
- Inquiry: Classify

Three Domains of Life

Bacteria	Archaea	Eukarya			
		Protists	Fungi	Plants	Animals

Domain Bacteria Although you may not know it, members of the domain Bacteria are all around you. You can find them on the surfaces you touch and inside your body. Some bacteria are autotrophs, while others are heterotrophs.

Members of the domain Bacteria are called prokaryotes (proh KA ree ohtz). **Prokaryotes** are unicellular organisms whose cells lack a nucleus. A **nucleus** (NOO klee us; plural *nuclei*) is a dense area in a cell that contains nucleic acids—the chemical instructions that direct the cell's activities. In prokaryotes, nucleic acids are not contained within a nucleus.

Domain Archaea Deep in the Pacific Ocean, hot gases and molten rock spew out from a vent in the ocean floor. It is hard to imagine that any living thing could exist in such harsh conditions. Surprisingly, a group of tiny organisms thrives in such a place. They are members of the domain Archaea (ahr KEE uh), whose name comes from the Greek word for "ancient."

Like bacteria, archaea are unicellular prokaryotes. And like bacteria, some archaea are autotrophs and others are heterotrophs. Archaea are classified in their own domain because their chemical makeup differs from that of bacteria. Bacteria and archaea also differ in the structure of their cells. The bacteria in **Figure 1** and the archaea in **Figure 2** have been stained and magnified to make them easier to see.

FIGURE 1
Bacteria
Most bacteria, such as *Lactobacillus acidophilus,* are helpful. These bacteria help to produce yogurt and milk for people who are lactose intolerant.

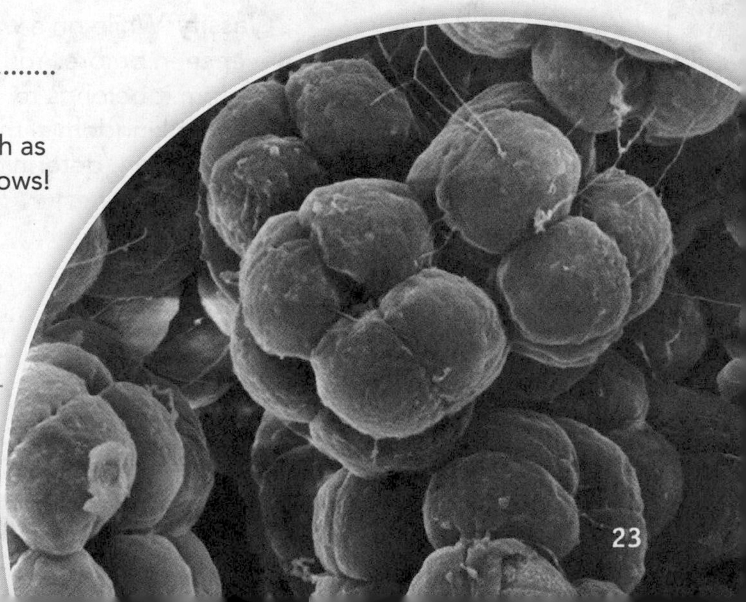

FIGURE 2
Archaea
Archaea can be found in extreme environments such as hot springs, very salty water, and the intestines of cows! Scientists think that the harsh conditions in which archaea live are similar to those of ancient Earth.

Compare and Contrast How are archaea and bacteria similar? How are they different?

_____
_____

23

FIGURE 3 ·······················
Eukarya
You can encounter organisms from all four kingdoms of Eukarya on a trip to a salt marsh.

Three Domains of Life

Bacteria	Archaea	Eukarya			
		Protists	Fungi	Plants	Animals

Domain Eukarya What do seaweeds, mushrooms, tomatoes, and dogs have in common? They are all members of the domain Eukarya. Organisms in this domain are **eukaryotes** (yoo KA ree ohtz)—organisms with cells that contain nuclei. Scientists classify organisms in the domain Eukarya into one of four kingdoms: protists, fungi, plants, or animals.

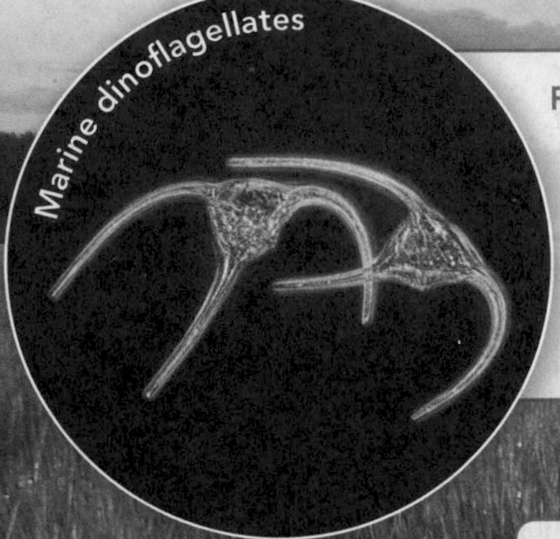

Protists

A protist (PROH tist) is any eukaryotic organism that cannot be classified as a fungus, plant, or animal. Because its members are so different from one another, the protist kingdom is sometimes called the "odds and ends" kingdom. For example, some protists are autotrophs, while others are heterotrophs. Most protists are unicellular, but some, such as seaweeds, are multicellular.

Marine dinoflagellates

Fungi

If you have eaten mushrooms, then you have eaten fungi (FUN jy). Mushrooms, molds, and mildew are all fungi. The majority of fungi are multicellular eukaryotes. A few, such as the yeast used in baking, are unicellular eukaryotes. Fungi are found almost everywhere on land, but only a few live in fresh water. All fungi are heterotrophs. Most fungi feed by absorbing nutrients from dead or decaying organisms.

Aspergillus fumigatus

apply it!

⚠️ **Classify** While on a walk, you find an organism that you've never seen before. You are determined to figure out what kingdom it belongs to. Starting with the first observation below, circle the kingdom(s) the organism could fit into. Using the process of elimination, determine what kingdom the organism belongs to.

❶ There are nuclei present. (Protists/Fungi/Plants/Animals)

❷ You can count more than one cell. (Protists/Fungi/Plants/Animals)

❸ The organism cannot make its own food. (Protists/Fungi/Plants/Animals)

❹ The organism gets nutrients from dead organisms. (Protists/Fungi/Plants/Animals)

❺ Other members of this kingdom can be unicellular. (Protists/Fungi/Plants/Animals)

Plants

Dandelions on a lawn, peas in a garden, and the marsh grass shown here are familiar members of the plant kingdom. Plants are all multicellular eukaryotes, and most live on land. Also, plants are autotrophs that make their own food. Plants provide food for most of the heterotrophs on land.

The plant kingdom includes a great variety of organisms. Some plants produce flowers, while others do not. Some plants, such as giant redwood trees, can grow very tall. Others, like mosses, never grow taller than a few centimeters.

⊙ **Identify the Main Idea** In the text under Domain Eukarya, underline the main idea.

Snowy egret

Animals

A dog, a flea on the dog's ear, and a cat that the dog chases have much in common because all are animals. All animals are multicellular eukaryotes. In addition, all animals are heterotrophs. Animals have different adaptations that allow them to locate food, capture it, eat it, and digest it. Members of the animal kingdom live in diverse environments throughout Earth. Animals can be found from ocean depths to mountaintops, from hot, scalding deserts to cold, icy landscapes.

 Do the Quick Lab *Staining Leaves.*

🔑 Assess Your Understanding

1a. Define A cell that lacks a nucleus is called a (eukaryote/~~prokaryote~~).

b. List Two ways that the members of the two domains of prokaryotes differ are in the

• structure cells

• chemical makeup

c. CHALLENGE You learn that a dandelion is in the same kingdom as pine trees. Name three characteristics that these organisms share.

• multicellular   • autotroph

• eukaryotes

got it?

○ **I get it!** Now I know that organisms are classified into domains and kingdoms based on their _____

_____

_____

○ **I need extra help with** _____

_____

Go to **MY SCIENCE** 💬 **COACH** *online for help with this subject.*

Evolution and Classification

🔑 **How Are Evolution and Classification Related?**

my planet Diary

DISCOVERY

If It Looks Like a Duck...

The first scientist to see the pelt of the platypus thought it was a joke. Could a four-legged, duck-billed, egg-laying mammal exist? How had it evolved? Native people from Australia believed that the first platypus was born when a water rat mated with a duck. But scientists put the platypus into a new group of egg-laying mammals. Then many years later, scientists began to argue. Had the platypus really evolved later with younger marsupials such as kangaroos? Would the platypus have to be reclassified? Scientists studied its DNA and discovered that the platypus was in the right place!

Answer the question below.

How did DNA help classify the platypus?

_____

_____

_____

_____

_____

_____

> **PLANET DIARY** Go to **Planet Diary** to learn more about evolution and classification.

Lab zone Do the Inquiry Warm-Up *Observing Similarities.*

How Are Evolution and Classification Related?

When Linnaeus developed his classification system, people thought that species never changed. In 1859, a British naturalist named Charles Darwin published an explanation for how species could change over time. Recall that the process of change over time is called **evolution.** Darwin thought that evolution occurs by means of natural selection. Natural selection is the process by which individuals that are better adapted to their environment are more likely to survive and reproduce than other members of the same species.

Vocabulary

- evolution
- branching tree diagram
- shared derived characteristic
- convergent evolution

Skills

⟳ Reading: Summarize

△ Inquiry: Infer

As understanding of evolution increased, biologists changed how they classify species. Scientists now understand that certain organisms may be similar because they share a common ancestor and an evolutionary history. The more similar the two groups are, the more recent the common ancestor probably is. Today's system of classification considers the history of a species. 🔑 **Species with similar evolutionary histories are classified more closely together.**

⟳ **Summarize** Name two things that similar organisms share.

_____

_____

_____

Branching Tree Diagrams

Two groups of organisms with similar characteristics may be descended from a common ancestor. A **branching tree diagram,** like the one in **Figure 1,** shows probable evolutionary relationships among organisms and the order in which specific characteristics may have evolved. Branching tree diagrams begin at the base with the common ancestor of all the organisms in the diagram. Organisms are grouped according to their shared derived characteristics.

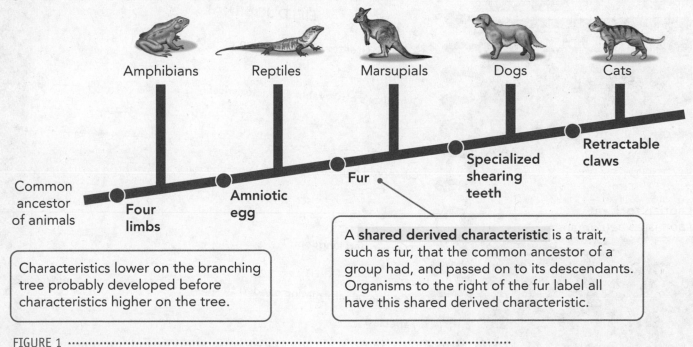

Amphibians   Reptiles   Marsupials   Dogs   Cats

Retractable claws

Specialized shearing teeth

Fur

Common ancestor of animals

Four limbs

Amniotic egg

Characteristics lower on the branching tree probably developed before characteristics higher on the tree.

A **shared derived characteristic** is a trait, such as fur, that the common ancestor of a group had, and passed on to its descendants. Organisms to the right of the fur label all have this shared derived characteristic.

FIGURE 1 ....

▶ ART IN MOTION **A Branching Tree**

This branching tree diagram shows how cats have evolved.

✎ **Complete the tasks.**

1. **Interpret Diagrams** Put squares around the shared derived characteristics.

2. **Interpret Diagrams** Circle the animal(s) that belong to the smallest group.

3. **Apply Concepts** Cats are more closely related to (reptiles/marsupials).

Note the characteristics of Figures A, B, C, and D.

1 ⚠️ **Infer** Which figure is the most similar to Figure B?

_____

2 **CHALLENGE** Suppose these shapes are fossils of extinct organisms. Which organism do you think might be the ancestor of all the others? Why?

_____

_____

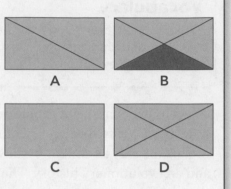

A   B

C   D

Finding a New Species

THE BIG ?

How are living things alike yet different?

FIGURE 2 ···

While on an expedition, you photograph what you think is a new species.

✏️ **Draw Conclusions** Use the camera image of the new species and the photos of organisms previously identified from the same area to record your observations in your field journal.

Laotian rock rat
Laonastes aenigmanus

Golden-crowned flying fox
Acerodon jubatus

FIELD JOURNAL

Location: Greater Mekong region of Asia _____

Date: _____

Organism's observable characteristics: _____

_____

_____

Observed habitat(s): _____

_____

_____

Domain and kingdom: _____

_____

Additional information needed to determine if organism is a new

species: _____

_____

_____

Name (assuming it's a new species): _____

_____

Significance/meaning of name: _____

_____

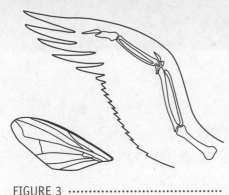

FIGURE 3 ....

Convergent Evolution
Birds and insects both use wings to help them fly. However, these two organisms are not closely related.

Determining Evolutionary Relationships

How do scientists determine the evolutionary history of a species? One way is to compare the structure of organisms. Scientists can also use information about the chemical makeup of the organisms' cells.

Sometimes unrelated organisms evolve similar characteristics because they evolved in similar environments, like organisms that move through the water or eat similar foods. Because the organisms perform similar functions, their body structures may look similar. Look at **Figure 3.** The process by which unrelated organisms evolve characteristics that are similar is called **convergent evolution.**

When studying the chemical makeup of organisms, sometimes new information is discovered that results in reclassification. For example, skunks and weasels were classified in the same family for 150 years. When scientists compared nucleic acids from the cells of skunks and weasels, they found many differences. These differences suggest that the two groups are not that closely related. As a result, scientists reclassified skunks into a separate family.

Lab zone® Do the Quick Lab
Common Ancestors.

🔑 Assess Your Understanding

1a. Identify Look back at **Figure 1.** What characteristics do all reptiles share?

_____

b. ANSWER THE BIG ? How are living things alike yet different? _____

_____

_____

got it? ....

O **I get it!** Now I know that evolution and classification are related because _____

_____

_____

O **I need extra help with** _____

_____

Go to **MY SCIENCE ⑤ COACH** *online for help with this subject.*

CHAPTER
1 Study Guide

Living things can vary. For example, organisms may be prokaryotes or _____.
Yet all living things are made of _____, which grow, develop, and reproduce.

LESSON 1 What Is Life?

🔑 All living things have a cellular organization, contain similar chemicals, use energy, respond to their surroundings, grow and develop, and reproduce.

🔑 Living things arise from other living things through reproduction.

🔑 All living things must satisfy their basic needs for food, water, living space, and stable internal conditions.

Vocabulary
- organism • cell • unicellular • multicellular • metabolism • stimulus • response • development
- asexual reproduction • sexual reproduction • spontaneous generation • controlled experiment
- autotroph • heterotroph • homeostasis

LESSON 2 Classifying Life

🔑 Biologists use classification to organize living things into groups so that the organisms are easier to study.

🔑 The levels of classification are domain, kingdom, phylum, class, order, family, genus, and species.

🔑 Taxonomic keys are useful tools that help determine the identity of organisms.

Vocabulary
- classification • taxonomy • binomial nomenclature
- genus • species

LESSON 3 Domains and Kingdoms

🔑 Organisms are placed into domains and kingdoms based on their cell type, ability to make food, and the number of cells in their bodies.

Vocabulary
- prokaryote
- nucleus • eukaryote

LESSON 4 Evolution and Classification

🔑 Species with similar evolutionary histories are classified more closely together.

Vocabulary
- evolution
- branching tree diagram
- shared derived characteristic
- convergent evolution

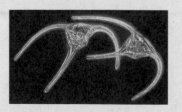

Review and Assessment

LESSON 1 What Is Life?

1. The maintenance of stable internal conditions is called

   a. stimulus.   **b.** autotrophy.

   c. homeostasis.   **d.** response.

2. _asexual reproduction_ involves only one parent and produces offspring that are identical to the parent.

3. **Apply Concepts** Pick an organism in your home and describe how this organism meets the four basic conditions for survival.

A hamster needs food, water, space to live, and stable internal conditions. It must eat and drink to grow, it needs a space to live in, and must have the apropriate temperature.

4. **Control Variables** A student is designing a controlled experiment to test whether the amount of water that a plant receives affects its growth. Which variables should the student hold constant and which variable should the student manipulate?

He should manipulate how much water he gives each plant, and keep them in the same spot.

5. **Write About It** Suppose you are searching for new life forms as part of an expedition in a remote region of Alaska. At one site you find 24 greenish-brown objects, each measuring around 1 cm³. The objects do not appear to have heads, tails, or legs, but you suspect they may be alive. Describe what you would do to determine if the objects are alive.

LESSON 2 Classifying Life

6. Which of the following is the broadest level of classification?

   a. genus   **b.** species

   c. domain   **d.** kingdom

7. The two-part naming system called _binomial nomenclature_ was devised by Linnaeus in the 1700s.

8. **Predict** The scientific name for the red maple tree is *Acer rubrum*. Another organism is called *Acer negundo*. Based on its name, what can you predict about this organism? Explain.

They both have the same genus.

9. **Make Models** Develop a taxonomic key that a person could use to identify each of the plants shown below.

White ash   Red oak   White oak   Pasture rose

LESSON 3 Domains and Kingdoms

10. Which four kingdoms belong to the domain Eukarya?

   a. prokarya, archaea, eukarya, bacteria

   (b.) protists, fungi, plants, animals

   c. mite, tick, scorpion, spider

   d. class, order, family, genus

11. All eukaryotes belong to domain Eukarya, while _prokaryotes_ belong to domain Bacteria or domain Archaea.

12. Compare and Contrast Both plants and fungi belong to the domain Eukarya. What is one main difference between these organisms?

Fungi are heterotrophs and plants are autotrophs.

LESSON 4 Evolution and Classification

13. Which of the following factors is most important when classifying an organism?

   a. size   **b.** shape

   c. habitat   **(d.)** evolutionary history

14. A diagram that shows probable evolutionary relationships among organisms is called a _branching tree diagram_

15. Apply Concepts If you discovered two unrelated organisms that looked very similar, how could you explain it?

They are unrelated but they evolve same characteristics. This process is called convergent evolution.

How are living things alike yet different?

16. With the advances in commercial space travel, some day you may have the opportunity to visit another planet and see things you've never seen before! How would you go about identifying things on the other planet as being living or nonliving? If an object turns out to be living, what characteristics would you look for in order to classify it? Use four vocabulary terms from the chapter in your answer.

I would know that the object is nonliving if it doesn't have any cells. I would also know that it's not living if it doesn't grow and develop. I would know that the object is living if it has unicellular or multi-cellular cells. Another way I would know if it's living is if it reproduces.
— is it prokaryote or eukaryote

Standardized Test Prep

Multiple Choice

Circle the letter of the best answer.

1. How many kingdoms are represented by the organisms shown below?

   — animals & plants

   A 1   B ②
   C 3   D 4

2. According to the system of binomial nomenclature, which of the following is a properly written scientific name?

   A Acer rubrum   B Acer Rubrum
   ⓒ *Acer rubrum*   D *acer rubrum*

3. Which of the following is an example of an autotroph?

   A a lion   Ⓑ a tree
   C an eagle   D a mushroom

4. Which domain does NOT contain prokaryotes?

   A Archaea
   B Bacteria
   ⓒ Eukarya
   D None of the above. All three domains contain prokaryotes.

5. A branching tree diagram shows evolutionary relationships by _____

   A grouping organisms according to their differences.
   B determining the identity of organisms.
   ⓒ grouping organisms according to their shared derived characteristics.
   D giving an organism a unique, two-part scientific name.

Constructed Response

Use the chart below and your knowledge of science to help you answer Question 6. Write your answer on a separate piece of paper.

Some Types of Trees

Common Name of Tree	Kingdom	Family	Species
Bird cherry	Plants	Rosaceae	*Prunus avium*
Flowering cherry	Plants	Rosaceae	*Prunus serrula*
Smooth-leaved elm	Plants	Ulmaceae	*Ultimus minor*
Whitebeam	Plants	Rosaceae	*Sorbus aria*

6. Which one of the four trees is most different from the other three? Explain your answer.

   Smooth-leaved elm because it's family is totally different.

A RECIPE for Success

Before the 1800s, people thought that living things could appear from nonliving material. But Louis Pasteur did not think that this accepted theory was correct. He suspected that bacteria traveled on particles in the air and reproduced when they landed on biological material—like broth. Pasteur experimented to test his theory. His experiments were successful because they followed a good experimental design. Pasteur tested only one variable, included a control, and repeated his experiments.

Pasteur put broth into two flasks with curved necks. The necks would let in oxygen but keep out bacteria in air. Pasteur boiled the broth in one flask to kill any bacteria in the broth. He did not boil the broth in the other flask.

In a few days, the unboiled broth turned cloudy, showing that new bacteria were growing. The boiled broth remained clear. Pasteur then took the flask with clear broth and broke its curved neck. Bacteria from the air could enter the flask. In a few days, the broth became cloudy. Pasteur's results showed that bacteria were introduced into the broth through the air, and did not grow from the broth itself. He repeated the experiment, and showed that the results were not an accident.

Recipe for a Successful Experiment

1. Make a hypothesis.
2. Write a procedure.
3. Identify the control.
4. Identify the variable.
5. Observe and record data.
6. Repeat.
7. Make a conclusion.

Design It The Dutch scientist Jean-Baptiste van Helmont proposed a recipe for generating mice. He set up an experiment using dirty rags and a few grains of wheat in an open barrel. After about 21 days, mice appeared. The results, he concluded, supported his hypothesis that living things come from nonliving sources. What is wrong with van Helmont's experimental design? Using his hypothesis, design your own experimental procedure. What is your control? What is your variable?

Are you going to Eat That?

Bacteria are everywhere. Most bacteria have no effect on you. Some even help you. But bacteria in your food can be dangerous and can make you sick.

Milk and many juices are treated by a process called pasteurization. The process is named after Louis Pasteur, who invented it. Before the milk or juice reaches the grocery store, it is heated to a temperature that is high enough to kill the most harmful bacteria. Fewer bacteria means slower bacterial growth, giving you enough time to finish your milk before it spoils.

Tips for Keeping Food Safe in Homes and Restaurants

- Keep foods refrigerated until cooking them to prevent any bacteria in the foods from reproducing.

- Cook meat thoroughly, so that the meat reaches a temperature high enough to kill any bacteria that has been growing on it.

- Wash fresh foods, such as fruits and vegetables, to remove bacteria on the surface.

- Do not use the same utensils or cutting board for cutting raw meat and fresh foods, so that any bacteria in raw meat are not transferred to other foods.

Write About It Some champions of raw-food diets suggest that traditional methods of pasteurization reduce the nutritional value of milk and cause milk to spoil rather than to sour. Research the debate about raw dairy products and write a persuasive article that explains whether you support pasteurization of dairy products.

WHERE DO MUSHROOMS GROW?

THE BIG
?

How are living things other than plants and animals important to Earth?

> UNTAMED SCIENCE Watch the **Untamed Science** video to learn more about mushrooms.

The mushrooms in this photo have a lacy, delicate covering and bright colors. But don't get too close—these mushrooms smell like rotting meat! Their beauty and powerful smell gives them the name netted stinkhorns. The rotting smell attracts flies. When a fly lands on the mushroom, tiny reproductive structures may stick to the fly's legs. These reproductive structures can then drop off when the fly lands on another rotting surface. If conditions are right, a new netted stinkhorn will begin to grow there.

△Develop Hypotheses **Where might mushrooms grow?**

_____

_____

_____

Viruses, Bacteria, Protists, and Fungi

Check Your Understanding

1. **Background** Read the paragraph below and then answer the question.

"Yes, it is a prokaryote!" said Lena, pulling her head away from the microscope. "No, it's not!" said Kiera. "Stop fighting!" said their friend Isa. "Let me see." Isa looked. "It's not a prokaryote; that's for sure. First of all, it is too large. More importantly, you can clearly see its nucleus. It is obviously a eukaryote."

A **prokaryote** is an organism whose single cell lacks a nucleus.

A **nucleus** is a large oval organelle that contains the cell's genetic material in the form of DNA and controls many of the cell's activities.

A **eukaryote** is an organism with cells that contain nuclei.

• Which organisms have nuclei—prokaryotes or eukaryotes?

_____

▷ **MY READING WEB** If you had trouble completing the question above, visit **My Reading Web** and type in *Viruses, Bacteria, Protists, and Fungi.*

Vocabulary Skill

Prefixes Some words can be divided into parts. A root is the part of the word that carries the basic meaning. A prefix is a word part that is placed in front of the root to change the word's meaning. The prefixes below will help you understand some of the vocabulary in this chapter.

Prefix	Meaning	Example
endo-	inside, within	endospore, *n.* a small, rounded, thick-walled cell that forms inside of a bacterial cell
pseudo-	false	pseudopod, *n.* a "false foot"; a structure used by certain protozoans for movement

2. **Quick Check** Which part of the word *endospore* tells you it is something that forms inside a bacterial cell?

_____

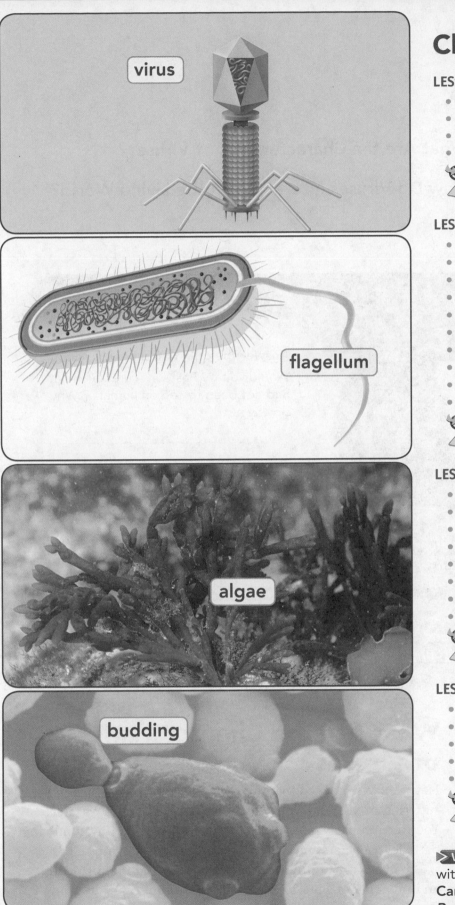

virus

flagellum

algae

budding

Chapter Preview

LESSON 1
- virus
- host
- parasite
- vaccine
- ◑ Identify the Main Idea
- △ Infer

LESSON 2
- bacteria
- cytoplasm
- ribosome
- flagellum
- cellular respiration
- binary fission
- conjugation
- endospore
- pasteurization
- decomposer
- ◑ Compare and Contrast
- △ Predict

LESSON 3
- protist
- protozoan
- pseudopod
- contractile vacuole
- cilia
- algae
- pigment
- spore
- ◑ Summarize
- △ Graph

LESSON 4
- fungus
- hyphae
- fruiting body
- budding
- lichen
- ◑ Identify Supporting Evidence
- △ Observe

> VOCAB FLASH CARDS For extra help with vocabulary, visit **Vocab Flash Cards** and type in *Viruses, Bacteria, Protists, and Fungi.*

Viruses

UNLOCK THE BIG ?

🔑 What Are the Characteristics of Viruses?

🔑 How Do Viruses Interact With the Living World?

my planet diary

VOICES FROM HISTORY

A Mad Choice

Have you ever seen a snarling dog on TV? Chances are this "mad dog" was supposed to have rabies. Rabies is a virus that affects the brain, causing "mad" behaviors and spasms of the throat. Infected animals avoid water, giving the disease the nickname *hydrophobia*, meaning "fear of water."

In the 1800s, if people were bitten by a mad dog, they would likely die. Then, in 1884, the scientist Louis Pasteur said he had a cure. He claimed, "Whoever gets bitten by a mad dog has only to submit to my three little inoculations, and he need not have the slightest fear of hydrophobia."

Answer the question below.
Would you try Pasteur's cure, even if it had not been tested on humans? Why or why not?

_____

_____

_____

_____

_____

_____

▶ PLANET DIARY Go to **Planet Diary** to learn more about viruses.

Lab zone® Do the Inquiry Warm-Up *Which Lock Does the Key Fit?*

What Are the Characteristics of Viruses?

Have you ever noticed that when you spent time with a friend suffering from a cold, you sometimes felt sick a few days later? You were probably infected by a virus. A **virus** is a tiny, nonliving particle that enters and then reproduces inside a living cell. 🔑 **Viruses are nonliving, have a protein coat that protects an inner core of genetic material, and cannot reproduce on their own.**

Vocabulary
- virus • host
- parasite • vaccine

Skills
↻ **Reading:** Identify the Main Idea
△ **Inquiry:** Infer

Virus Needs Why are viruses considered nonliving? They lack most of the characteristics of living things. Viruses are not cells and do not use their own energy to grow or to respond to their surroundings. Viruses also cannot make food, take in food, or produce wastes. Although viruses can multiply like organisms, they can only do so when they are inside a living cell.

The organism that a virus enters and multiplies inside of is called a host. A **host** is an organism that provides a source of energy for a virus or another organism. A virus acts like a **parasite** (PA ruh syt), an organism that lives on or in a host and causes it harm. Almost all viruses destroy the cells in which they multiply.

Influenza virus

Tobacco mosaic virus

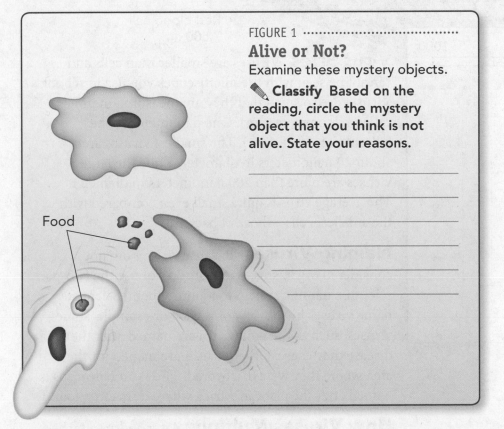

FIGURE 1 ·····························

Alive or Not?
Examine these mystery objects.

✎ **Classify** Based on the reading, circle the mystery object that you think is not alive. State your reasons.

_____
_____
_____
_____
_____
_____

Food

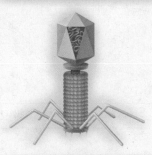

T4 bacteriophage

Virus Shapes As you can see in **Figure 2,** viruses vary widely in shape. Some viruses are round, and some are rod-shaped. Other viruses are shaped like bricks, threads, or bullets. There are even viruses that have complex, robotlike shapes, such as the bacteriophage. A bacteriophage (bak TEER ee oh fayj) is a virus that infects bacteria. In fact, its name means "bacteria eater."

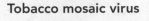

FIGURE 2 ·····························
Virus Shapes
The leglike structures on the bottom of the T4 bacteriophage keep the virus firmly in place as it infects a cell.

41

All measurements represent approximate diameters.

Smallpox virus 250 nm

Cold sore virus 130 nm

Influenza virus 90 nm

Cold virus 75 nm

Yellow fever virus 22 nm

2. Measure Use your calculation from Step 1 to mark and label on the scale the size of the *Streptococcus* bacterium.

3. Make Models Draw the bacterium to scale in the box provided.

Red blood cell
7,500 nm

0 nm   250   1000

100   500

Streptococcus bacterium

Virus Sizes
Viruses are smaller than cells and cannot be seen with the microscopes you use in school. Viruses are so small that they are measured in units called nanometers (nm). One nanometer is one billionth of a meter (m). The smallest viruses are about 20 nanometers in diameter, while the largest viruses are more than 200 nanometers in diameter. The average virus is quite small even compared with the smallest cells—those of bacteria.

Naming Viruses
Because viruses are not considered organisms, scientists do not use the two-part scientific naming system to identify them. Scientists name viruses in a variety of ways. For example, some viruses, such as the poliovirus, are named after the disease they cause. Other viruses are named for the area where they were discovered. The West Nile virus is named after the place in Africa where it was first found.

How Viruses Multiply
After a virus attaches to a host cell, it enters the cell. Once inside a cell, the virus's genetic material takes over many of the cell's functions. It instructs the cell to produce the virus's proteins and genetic material. These proteins and genetic material then assemble into new viruses. Some viruses take over cell functions immediately. Other viruses wait for a while.

The Structure of Viruses
Although viruses have many different shapes and sizes, they all have a similar structure. All viruses have two basic parts: an inner core containing genetic material and a protein coat that protects the virus. A virus's genetic material contains the instructions for making new viruses.

Each virus contains unique surface proteins. These surface proteins play an important role during the invasion of a host cell. The shape of the surface proteins allows a virus to attach only to certain cells in the host. Like keys, a virus's proteins fit only into specific "locks," or proteins, on the surface of a host's cells. So a particular virus can attach only to one or a few types of host cells. For example, most cold viruses infect cells only in the nose and throat of humans. Those cells have proteins on their surfaces that complement or fit the proteins on cold viruses. **Figure 4** shows how the lock-and-key system works.

FIGURE 4 ....

> INTERACTIVE ART **Virus Structure and Invasion**
Some viruses are surrounded by an outer membrane envelope.

✎ **Interpret Diagrams** For the virus on the right, draw a line from the virus surface proteins to the matching cell surface proteins. Circle any of the cell proteins that do not match.

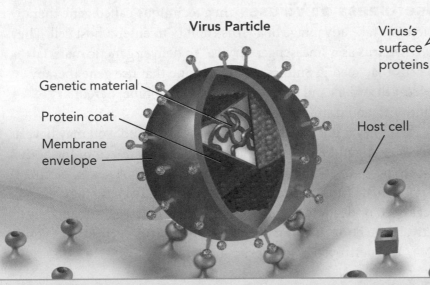

Virus Particle

Genetic material

Protein coat

Membrane envelope

Virus's surface proteins

Host cell

Cell's surface proteins

Lab zone Do the Quick Lab *How Many Viruses Fit on a Pin?*

🔑 Assess Your Understanding

1a. Define A virus is a (living/nonliving) particle that enters a cell and uses it to reproduce.

b. Relate Cause and Effect How do the surface proteins on a virus help it to invade a host cell?

_____

_____

c. CHALLENGE Scientists hypothesize that viruses could not have existed on Earth before organisms appeared. Do you agree? Explain.

_____

_____

_____

_____

got it? ....

○ I get it! Now I know that the characteristics of viruses are _____

_____

○ I need extra help with _____

Go to MY SCIENCE COACH online for help with this subject.

How Do Viruses Interact With the Living World?

You may have only heard of viruses causing colds and diseases. But sometimes viruses help rather than harm. 🔑 **Though viruses can cause disease, they can also be used to treat and prevent illnesses.**

Viruses and Disease
Some viral diseases, such as colds, are mild and pass through the body quickly. Other viral diseases, such as human immunodeficiency virus, or HIV, have much more serious and lasting effects on the body.

Viruses also cause diseases in organisms other than humans. For example, apple trees infected by the apple mosaic virus may produce less fruit. Dogs and cats can get deadly viral diseases such as rabies and distemper.

Usefulness of Viruses
In a technique called gene therapy, scientists take advantage of a virus's ability to enter a host cell. They use the virus as a "messenger service" to deliver genetic material to cells that need it. Studies are being done that use gene therapy to treat disorders and diseases such as hemophilia, hereditary blindness, and immune deficiencies.

If you never got the chickenpox virus as a child, you may have a vaccine to thank! A **vaccine** is a substance introduced in the body to help produce chemicals that destroy specific viruses. A vaccine may be made from weakened or dead viruses. Because they are weakened or dead, the viruses do not cause disease. Instead, they activate the body's natural defenses. If that virus ever invades your body, it is destroyed before it can make you sick.

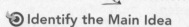

Identify the Main Idea
Read the text about viruses and disease. Then underline the main ideas in each paragraph.

FIGURE 5 ·············
Vaccine Protection
Influenza (flu) and other diseases can be prevented by vaccines.

1 The virus that causes a disease is isolated. The virus is then weakened or killed by heat, and a vaccine is prepared from it.

2 During vaccination, the weakened virus is injected into the body.

3 The body prepares defenses against the virus.

4 The body can now resist infection by the disease-causing virus.

Disease-causing virus

Weakened virus

Defenses

Weakened virus

apply it!

Viruses can cause disease around the world. Use the world map below to answer the questions about dengue (DEN gay) fever, a viral disease.

1 Interpret Maps Which continents have outbreaks of dengue fever?

North America, South America, Africa, Asia, Australia

2 Draw Conclusions Why do you think dengue fever only occurs in warm places?

Mosquitos reproduce in only warm places.

3 Infer Suppose people in South America are getting sick with an influenza virus. A few days earlier, there were reports of the same virus infecting people in Africa. How could the influenza virus have spread so quickly?

Maybe people with the disease in South America and spread it. Also the virus might have went to Africa in ships.

Dengue Fever
The virus is spread by mosquitoes. Mosquitoes cannot spread the virus in temperatures below 16°C.

Arctic Ocean

NORTH AMERICA

EUROPE

ASIA

Atlantic Ocean

AFRICA

Equator

SOUTH AMERICA

Pacific Ocean

Indian Ocean

AUSTRALIA

Lab zone® Do the Quick Lab
How Viruses Spread.

🔑 Assess Your Understanding

got it? ....

O **I get it!** Now I know that viruses interact in the living world by both _____

O **I need extra help with** _____

Go to MY SCIENCE ⑤ COACH online for help with this subject.

Bacteria

🔑 **What Are Bacteria?**

🔑 **How Do Bacteria Get Food, Get Energy, and Reproduce?**

🔑 **What Is the Role of Bacteria in Nature?**

my planet Diary

"Good" Germs

Misconception: All bacteria are harmful.

Many bacteria are harmless or even good for you! Your intestines are full of good bacteria. Some types of helpful bacteria, often called probiotics, are found in foods like yogurt, smoothies, and even cereal! Scientists have found that eating foods that contain probiotics puts good bacteria into your body and helps fight off the harmful bacteria that can cause disease.

MISCONCEPTION

Communicate Discuss these questions with a classmate. Write your answers below.

1. Why do people often think all bacteria are bad for you?

_____

_____

2. Can you think of some products you have used at home or at school to kill harmful bacteria?

_____

_____

_____

_____

▶ **PLANET DIARY** Go to **Planet Diary** to learn more about bacteria.

Lab zone® Do the Inquiry Warm-Up *How Quickly Can Bacteria Multiply?*

What Are Bacteria?

They thrive in your cup of yogurt. They coat your skin and swarm inside your nose. You cannot escape them because they live almost everywhere—under rocks, in the ocean, and all over your body. In fact, there are more of these organisms in your mouth than there are people on Earth! You don't notice them because they are very small. These organisms are bacteria.

Vocabulary

- bacteria
- cytoplasm
- ribosome
- flagellum
- cellular respiration
- binary fission
- conjugation
- endospore
- pasteurization
- decomposer

Skills

- Read
- Inqu

Cell Structures Bacteria were first discovered in the late 1600s by a Dutch merchant named Anton von Leeuwenhoek (LAY vun hook). He made microscopes as a hobby. One day, while looking at scrapings of his teeth, he noticed small wormlike organisms. If Leeuwenhoek had owned a modern high-powered microscope, he would have seen that the single-celled organisms were **bacteria** (singular *bacterium*). 🔑 **Bacteria are prokaryotes. The genetic material in their cells is not contained in a nucleus.** In addition to lacking a nucleus, the cells of bacteria also lack many other structures that are found in the cells of eukaryotes. Recall that eukaryotes include protists, fungi, and animals.

Figure 1 shows the structures in a typical bacterial cell. Most bacterial cells are surrounded by a rigid cell wall that protects the cell. Just inside the cell wall is the cell membrane, which controls what materials pass in and out of the cell. The region inside the cell membrane, called the **cytoplasm** (SY toh plaz um), contains a gel-like fluid that moves structures throughout the cell. Located in the cytoplasm are tiny structures called **ribosomes** (RY bo sohmz), chemical factories where proteins are produced. The cell's genetic material, which looks like a tangled string, is also found in the cytoplasm. It contains the instructions for all of the cell's functions. A bacterial cell may also have a **flagellum** (fluh JEL um; plural *flagella*), a long, whiplike structure that helps a cell to move.

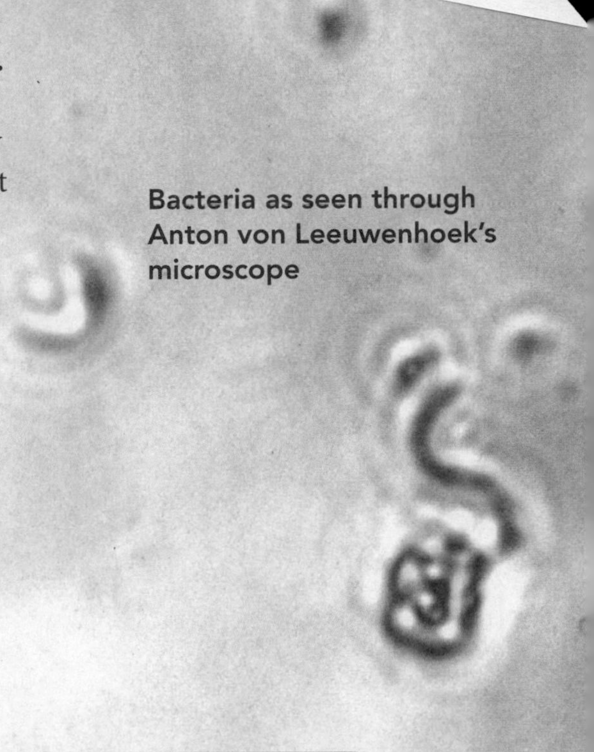

Bacteria as seen through Anton von Leeuwenhoek's microscope

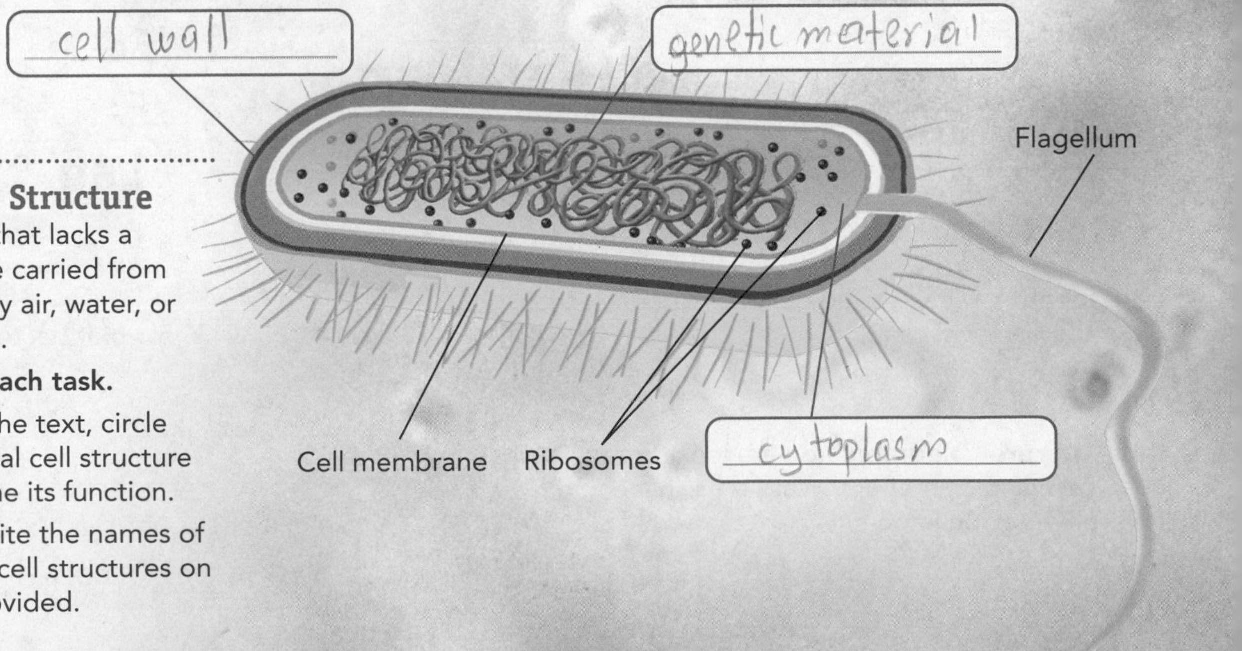

FIGURE 1 ·······

Bacterial Cell Structure

A bacterial cell that lacks a flagellum can be carried from place to place by air, water, or other organisms.

✏️ **Complete each task.**

1. **Review** In the text, circle each bacterial cell structure and underline its function.

2. **Identify** Write the names of the missing cell structures on the lines provided.

cell wall

genetic material

Flagellum

Cell membrane   Ribosomes

cytoplasm

Cell Shapes If you were to look at bacteria under a microscope, you would notice that most bacterial cells have one of three basic shapes: spherical, rodlike, or spiral. The chemical makeup of the cell wall determines the shape of a bacterial cell. The shape of the cell helps scientists identify the type of bacteria.

Cell Sizes Bacteria vary greatly in size. The largest known bacterium is about as big as the period at the end of this sentence. An average bacterium, however, is much smaller. For example, the spherical strep throat bacteria are about 0.5 to 1 micrometer in diameter. A micrometer is one millionth of a meter.

FIGURE 2 ·······················

Bacteria Shapes and Names

Bacteria are sometimes named for their shape.

✎ **Classify** Use the key to match the scientific names in the word bank to the correct bacteria. Write your answers in the boxes.

Word Bank
Leptospira interrogans   *Bacillus anthracis*
Stella vacuolata   *Streptococcus thermophilus*

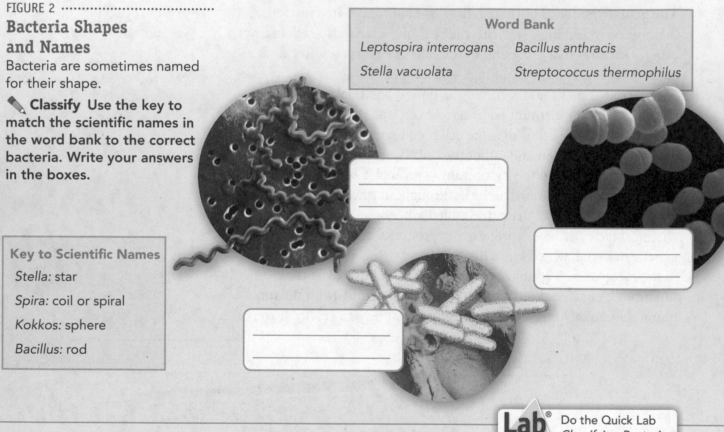

Key to Scientific Names

Stella: star

Spira: coil or spiral

Kokkos: sphere

Bacillus: rod

 Do the Quick Lab *Classifying Bacteria.*

🔑 Assess Your Understanding

1a. Identify Where is the genetic material located in a bacterial cell?

_____

b. Interpret Diagrams You are looking at a *Stella vacuolata* bacterium. What is its shape and how do you know?

_____

_____

got it?

○ **I get it!** Now I know that bacteria are _____

_____

_____

○ **I need extra help with** _____

Go to MY SCIENCE ⓢ COACH *online for help with this subject.*

How Do Bacteria Get Food, Get Energy, and Reproduce?

From the bacteria that live in soil to those that live in the pores of your skin, all bacteria need certain things to survive and reproduce. **Bacteria get energy by either making food or eating other organisms, and can reproduce asexually or sexually.**

Obtaining Food Some bacteria are autotrophs, meaning they make their own food. Some capture and use the sun's energy as plants do. Others, such as bacteria that live deep in mud, do not use the sun's energy. Instead, these bacteria use the energy from chemical substances in their environment to make their food.

Some bacteria are heterotrophs, and cannot make their own food. These bacteria must consume other organisms or the food that other organisms make. Heterotrophic bacteria consume a variety of foods—from milk and meat, which you might also eat, to decaying leaves on a forest floor.

Compare and Contrast How do autotrophic and heterotrophic bacteria differ in the way they obtain food?

_____

_____

_____

_____

_____

_____

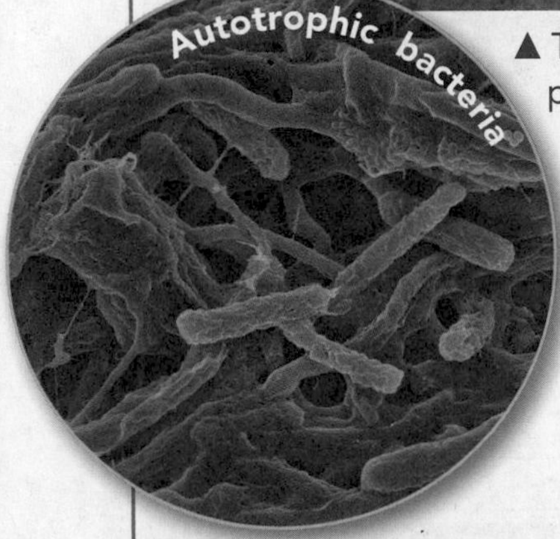

FIGURE 3 ·····················

Obtaining Food

Autotrophic bacteria in hot springs use chemical energy to make food. Heterotrophic bacteria in compost get energy from decaying food.

Compost ▼

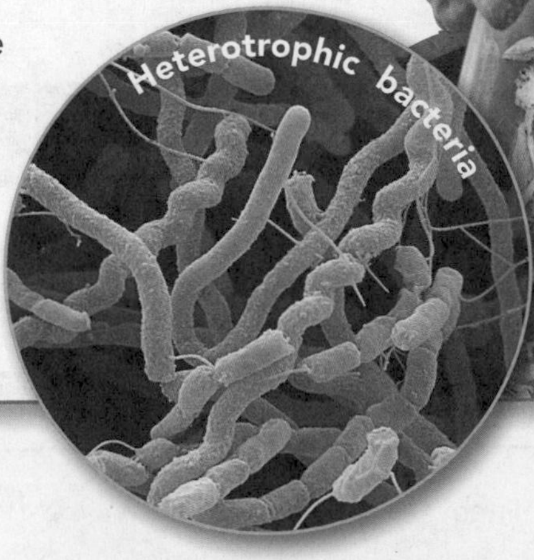

Autotrophic bacteria

▲ Trained researcher permitted to work at hot springs in Yellowstone National Park

Heterotrophic bacteria

FIGURE 4
Bacteria Buffet
These bacteria break down pollutants in this biopile to get energy.

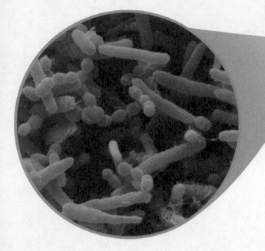

Respiration Like all organisms, bacteria need a constant supply of energy to carry out their functions. This energy comes from food. The process of breaking down food to release energy is called **cellular respiration.** Like many other organisms, most bacteria need oxygen to break down their food. But a few kinds of bacteria do not need oxygen for respiration. In fact, those bacteria die if oxygen is present in their surroundings. For them, oxygen is a poison that kills!

apply it!

Suppose you are a scientist studying disease-causing bacteria. You make a table that lists how the bacteria get energy and whether they need oxygen. One day, some of your data are accidentally erased.

❶ **Create Data Tables** Use what you know about bacteria to fill in the first two columns in the table.

❷ **Draw Conclusions** How would you destroy these dangerous bacteria? Use the information in the table to fill in the last column.

Food Source	Type of Bacterium	Need Oxygen?	How to Destroy
Decaying leaves	Hetotroph	Yes	take away oxygen
Sun	Autotrophic	No	block the sun
Chemicals	autotrophic	No	remove it

Reproduction One of the characteristics of living things is that they are able to reproduce, or make more copies of themselves. When bacteria have plenty of food, the right temperature, and other suitable conditions, they thrive and reproduce often. Bacteria can reproduce asexually or sexually.

FIGURE 5 ···

Bacterial Reproduction
Some bacteria are able to reproduce every 20 minutes.

✎ **Relate Text and Visuals** In the diagrams, label each reproductive process and answer the questions.

Asexual Reproduction

Bacteria sometimes reproduce asexually by a process called **binary fission,** in which one cell divides to form two identical cells. To prepare for binary fission, a bacterial cell grows to almost twice its size. Then it duplicates its genetic material and splits into two separate cells. Each new cell receives a complete copy of the parent's genetic material. As a result, the offspring are genetically identical to the parent. Binary fission increases the number of bacteria.

Why are all the bacteria the same color?

Asexual process called

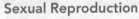

Bacteria undergoing conjugation

Sexual Reproduction

Sometimes bacteria reproduce sexually by a process called **conjugation.** During conjugation, one bacterium transfers some of its genetic material into another bacterium through a thin, threadlike bridge. After the transfer, the bacteria separate. Conjugation results in bacteria with new combinations of genetic material. When the bacteria divide by binary fission, the new genetic material passes to the offspring. Conjugation does not increase the number of bacteria, as binary fission does. However, it does result in bacteria that are genetically different from the parent cells.

Sexual process called

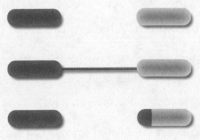

Why is the bacterium on the bottom right colored red and yellow?

Endospore Formation

Sometimes, conditions in the environment become unfavorable for the growth of bacteria. For example, food sources can disappear, water can dry up, or the temperature can fall or rise dramatically. Some bacteria can survive harsh conditions by forming endospores. An **endospore** is a small, rounded, thick-walled resting cell that forms inside a bacterial cell. It encloses the cell's genetic material and some of its cytoplasm.

Because endospores can resist freezing, heating, and drying, they can survive for many years in harsh conditions. Endospores are also light—a breeze can lift and carry them to new places. If an endospore lands in a place where conditions are suitable, it opens up. Then the bacterium can begin to grow and multiply.

FIGURE 6 ·······························

Endospore Formation
The panels below illustrate endospore formation.

✎ **Sequence** Based on the reading, draw and label the last panel.

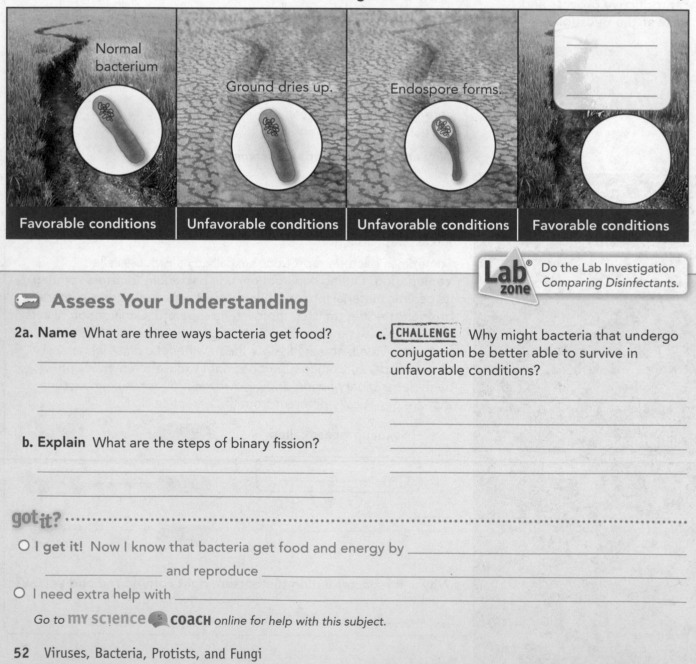

Increasing time ⟶

Normal bacterium

Ground dries up.

Endospore forms.

Favorable conditions | Unfavorable conditions | Unfavorable conditions | Favorable conditions

Lab® zone
Do the Lab Investigation
Comparing Disinfectants.

🔑 Assess Your Understanding

2a. Name What are three ways bacteria get food?

_____

_____

_____

b. Explain What are the steps of binary fission?

_____

_____

_____

c. CHALLENGE Why might bacteria that undergo conjugation be better able to survive in unfavorable conditions?

_____

_____

_____

_____

got**it?** ··

○ **I get it!** Now I know that bacteria get food and energy by _____

_____ and reproduce _____

○ I need extra help with _____

Go to MY SCIENCE ⑤ COACH online for help with this subject.

What Is the Role of Bacteria in Nature?

When you hear the word *bacteria*, you may think about getting sick. After all, strep throat, many ear infections, and other diseases are caused by bacteria. However, most bacteria are either harmless or helpful to people. In fact, in many ways, people depend on bacteria.  **Bacteria are involved in oxygen and food production, in health maintenance and medicine production, and in environmental cleanup and recycling.**

Oxygen Production Would it surprise you to learn that the air you breathe depends in part on bacteria? As autotrophic bacteria use the sun's energy to produce food, they release oxygen into the air. Billions of years ago, Earth had very little oxygen. Scientists think that autotrophic bacteria were responsible for first adding oxygen to Earth's atmosphere. Today, the distant offspring of those bacteria help keep oxygen levels in the air stable.

FIGURE 7 ....
Early Earth
Conditions on early Earth were very different than conditions today. There were frequent volcanic eruptions, storms, and earthquakes.

✎ **Infer** Could today's organisms have survived on early Earth? Why or why not?

_____

_____

_____

_____

apply it!

△ **Predict** Imagine you are growing a colony of autotrophic bacteria in the laboratory. What might happen to the level of oxygen as each of the three events listed below occurs? Read all three events, then draw your prediction on the graph.

❶ First event: The colony of autotrophic bacteria grows quickly under a sun lamp.

❷ Second event: The size of the bacterial colony stays stable.

❸ Third event: You accidentally put the bacteria in the shade.

Level of Oxygen

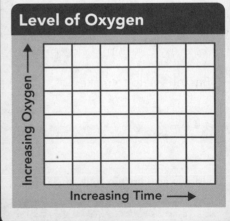

Increasing Oxygen →

Increasing Time →

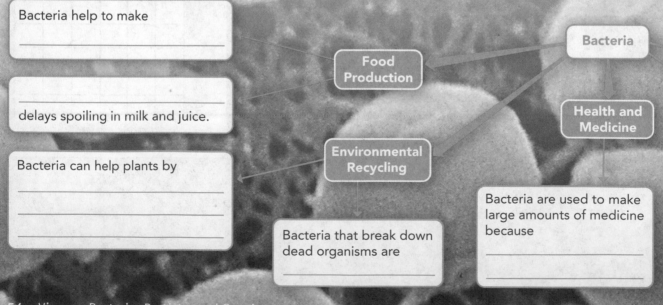

did you know?

Did you know that one to two kilograms of your body weight are bacteria in your digestive system? Up to 1,000 species of bacteria are crowded into your stomach and intestines.

FIGURE 8 ....

▶ **ART IN MOTION** **Bacteria and the Environment**
The *Deinococcus* bacteria pictured are named for their spherical shape.

✎ **Summarize** Fill in this graphic organizer to summarize the role of bacteria in nature.

Food Production

Do you like cheese, sauerkraut, or pickles? The activities of helpful bacteria produce all of these foods and more. For example, bacteria that grow in milk produce dairy products such as buttermilk, yogurt, sour cream, and cheeses.

However, some bacteria cause food to spoil when they break down the food's chemicals. Spoiled food usually smells or tastes foul and can make you very sick. Refrigerating and heating foods are two ways to slow down food spoilage. Another method, called pasteurization, is most often used to treat beverages such as milk and juice. During **pasteurization,** the food is heated to a temperature that is high enough to kill most harmful bacteria without changing the taste of the food. As you might have guessed, this process was named after Louis Pasteur, its inventor.

Health and Medicine

Did you know that many of the bacteria living in your body actually keep you healthy? In your digestive system, for example, your intestines teem with bacteria. Some help you digest your food. Some make vitamins that your body needs. Others compete for space with disease-causing organisms. They prevent the harmful bacteria from attaching to your intestines and making you sick.

Scientists use certain bacteria to make medicines and other substances. By manipulating the bacteria's genetic material, scientists can cause bacteria to produce human insulin. Although healthy people can make their own insulin, those with some types of diabetes cannot. Many people with diabetes need to take insulin daily. Thanks to bacteria's fast rate of reproduction, large numbers of insulin-making bacteria can be grown in huge vats. The human insulin they produce is then purified and made into medicine.

Bacteria help to make
_____

_____
delays spoiling in milk and juice.

Bacteria can help plants by
_____
_____
_____

Food Production

Bacteria

Health and Medicine

Environmental Recycling

Bacteria that break down dead organisms are
_____

Bacteria are used to make large amounts of medicine because
_____

Environmental Cleanup

Some bacteria help to clean up Earth's land and water. Certain bacteria can convert the poisonous chemicals in oil into harmless substances. Scientists have put these bacteria to work cleaning up oil spills in oceans and gasoline leaks in the soil under gas stations.

Environmental Recycling

Do you recycle? So do bacteria! Some bacteria that live in soil are **decomposers**—organisms that break down large, complex chemicals in dead organisms into small, simple chemicals.

Decomposers are "nature's recyclers." They return basic chemicals to the environment for other living things to reuse. For example, in autumn, the leaves of many trees die and drop to the ground. Decomposing bacteria spend the next months breaking down the chemicals in the dead leaves. The broken-down chemicals mix with the soil and can then be absorbed by the roots of nearby plants.

Another type of recycling bacteria, called nitrogen-fixing bacteria, help plants survive. Nitrogen-fixing bacteria live in the roots of certain plants, such as peanuts, peas, and soybeans. These helpful bacteria change nitrogen gas from the air into nitrogen products that plants need to grow. Plants are unable to make this conversion on their own. Therefore, nitrogen-fixing bacteria are vital to the plants' survival.

> Bacteria are able to convert poisons into harmless substances.

> _____
> _____

> _____
> _____

> Bacteria help provide oxygen for breathing.

Do the Quick Lab
Drawing Conclusions.

Assess Your Understanding

3a. Review How can certain bacteria in food make you sick?

_____

_____

b. List A friend says that all bacteria are harmful to people. List three reasons this statement is incorrect.

_____

_____

_____

c. Relate Cause and Effect How would life on Earth change if all autotrophic bacteria died off?

_____

_____

_____

_____

d. Apply Concepts How can bacteria acting as decomposers help plants grow?

My name is Sam and I am 13 year old

Hi my ng

got it? ....

O **I get it!** Now I know that the role of bacteria in nature includes _____

My name

_____

_____

O **I need extra help with** _____

_____

Go to MY SCIENCE COACH *online for help with this subject.*

3 Protists

UNLOCK
THE BIG
?

🔑 **What Are the Characteristics of Animal-Like Protists?**

🔑 **What Are the Characteristics of Plant-Like Protists?**

🔑 **What Are the Characteristics of Fungus-Like Protists?**

my pLaNeT DiaRY

PROFILE

Dancin' for a Cause

The protist *Plasmodium* causes malaria, a disease of the blood that can kill people. *Plasmodium* is carried by mosquitoes and is spread by their bites.

Malaria claims the life of a child in Africa every 30 seconds. Nets like these may help to prevent malaria infections.

When Allyson Brown from Melbourne, Florida, learned about malaria, she took action. She turned a school dance into a fundraiser, named Stayin' Alive, to buy mosquito nets for people in Africa. The nets keep mosquitoes away while people sleep. Since then, Allyson has teamed with the organization, *Malaria No More*, to help other schools to do the same.

Communicate Discuss these questions with a classmate. Write your answers below.

1. Why did Allyson donate mosquito nets to people in Africa?

_____

_____

_____

2. How could you raise awareness about malaria at your school?

_____

_____

_____

> PLANET DIARY Go to **Planet Diary** to learn more about protists.

Lab zone® Do the Inquiry Warm-Up *What Lives in a Drop of Pond Water?*

Vocabulary
- protist
- protozoan
- pseudopod
- contractile vacuole
- cilia
- algae
- pigment
- spore

Skills
- ↻ Reading: Summarize
- △ Inquiry: Graph

What Are the Characteristics of Animal-Like Protists?

The beautiful and diverse organisms in **Figure 1** below are protists. **Protists** are eukaryotes that cannot be classified as animals, plants, or fungi. The word that best describes protists is *diverse*. For example, most protists are unicellular, but some are multicellular. Some are heterotrophs, some are autotrophs, and others are both. Some protists cannot move, while others zoom around their habitats. However, all protists are eukaryotes, and all protists live in moist surroundings. Recall that eukaryotes are cells in which the genetic material is contained in a nucleus.

Because protists are so different from each other, scientists divide them into three categories based on characteristics they share with organisms in other kingdoms. These categories are: animal-like protists, plant-like protists, and fungus-like protists.

What image pops into your head when you think of an animal? Most people immediately associate animals with movement. In fact, movement is often involved with an important characteristic of animals—obtaining food. All animals that obtain food by eating other organisms are heterotrophs.

🔑 **Like animals, animal-like protists are heterotrophs, and most can move to get food.** But unlike animals, animal-like protists, or **protozoans** (proh tuh ZOH unz), are unicellular.

Vocabulary Prefixes The Greek word *proton* means "first" or "early." If the Greek word *zoia* means "animal," what do you think *protozoan* means?

FIGURE 1
Diversity of Protists
Protists come in many sizes and forms. Slime molds, amoebas, and euglenoids are just some of the many types of protists.

Slime mold ▼

◀ Amoeba

Euglenoid ▶

The Four Groups of Protozoans—How They Move and Live

Protozoans With Pseudopods

The amoeba in **Figure 2** belongs to the first group of protozoans called sarcodines. Sarcodines move and feed by forming **pseudopods** (SOO duh pahdz)—temporary bulges of the cell. The word *pseudopod* means "false foot." Pseudopods form when cytoplasm flows toward one location and the rest of the organism follows. Pseudopods enable sarcodines to move away from bright light. Sarcodines also use pseudopods to trap food by extending one on each side of a food particle. When the two pseudopods join together, the food is trapped inside the cell, as shown in **Figure 2.** Protozoans that live in fresh water have a problem. If excess water builds up inside the cell, the amoeba will burst. But amoebas have a **contractile vacuole** (kun TRAK til VAK yoo ohl), a structure that collects and expels excess water from the cell.

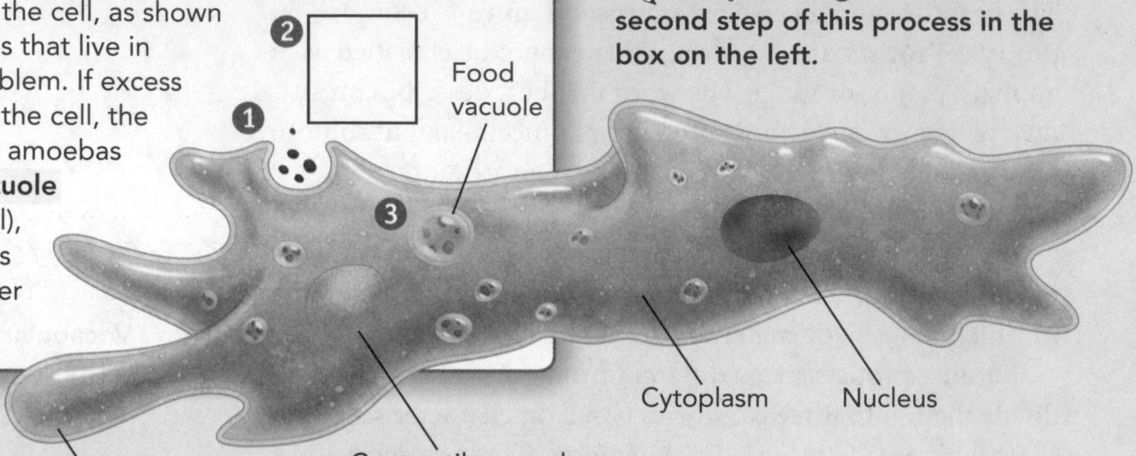

FIGURE 2

Amoeba
This amoeba's pseudopods surround and trap a food particle.

✏️ **Interpret Diagrams** Draw the second step of this process in the box on the left.

Food vacuole

Cytoplasm   Nucleus

Contractile vacuole

Pseudopod

Protozoans With Flagella

The second group of protozoans are the flagellates. Flagellates (FLAJ uh lits) are protozoans that use long, whiplike flagella to move. Some live inside the bodies of other organisms. One type of flagellate lives in the intestines of termites. When the termite eats wood, the flagellate breaks it down into sugars that the termite can eat. In return, the termite protects the flagellate. Sometimes, however, a protozoan harms its host. For example, the parasite *Giardia,* shown in **Figure 3,** is deposited in fresh water in the wastes of wild animals. When people drink water containing *Giardia,* these flagellates attach to their intestines, where they feed and reproduce. The people develop an intestinal condition commonly called hiker's disease.

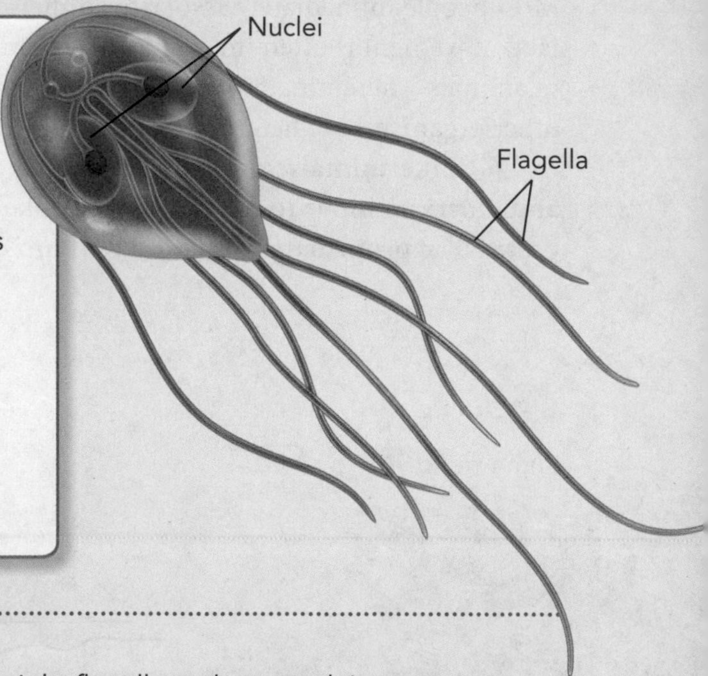

Nuclei

Flagella

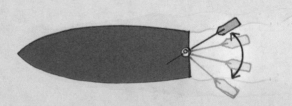

FIGURE 3

Giardia
Giardia has eight flagella and two nuclei.

✏️ **Make Models** How is the movement of the oar on this boat similar to the movement of a flagellum?

Protozoans With Cilia

The third group of protozoans are the ciliates. Ciliates have structures called **cilia** (SIL ee uh). These hairlike projections beat with a wavelike motion, moving the organism. The cilia also sweep food into the organism. Notice that the paramecium in **Figure 4** has two contractile vacuoles that collect and expel water from the cell. It also has two nuclei. The large nucleus controls the everyday tasks of the cell. The small nucleus functions in reproduction. Paramecia usually reproduce asexually by binary fission. But sometimes paramecia reproduce by conjugation. This occurs when two paramecia join together and exchange some of their genetic material.

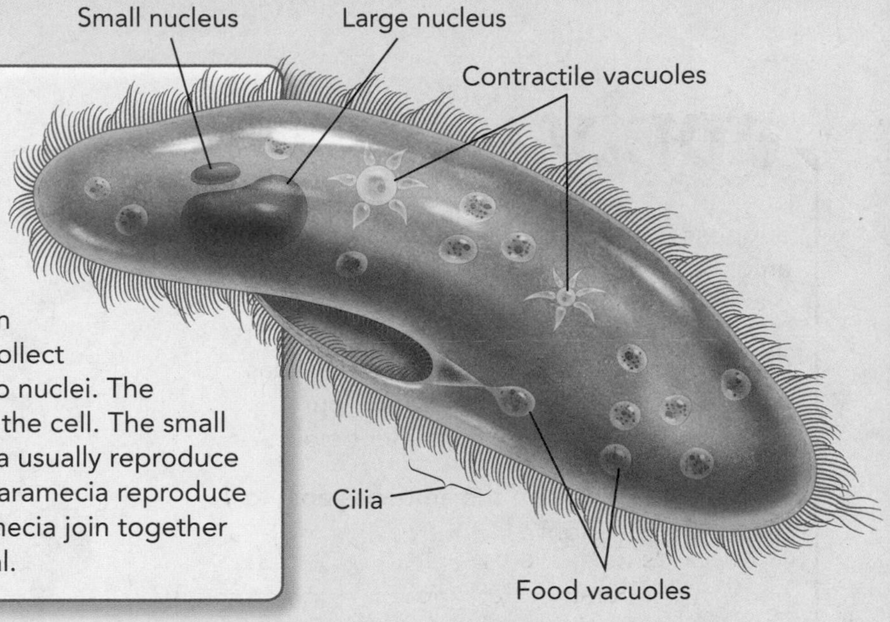

Small nucleus

Large nucleus

Contractile vacuoles

Cilia

Food vacuoles

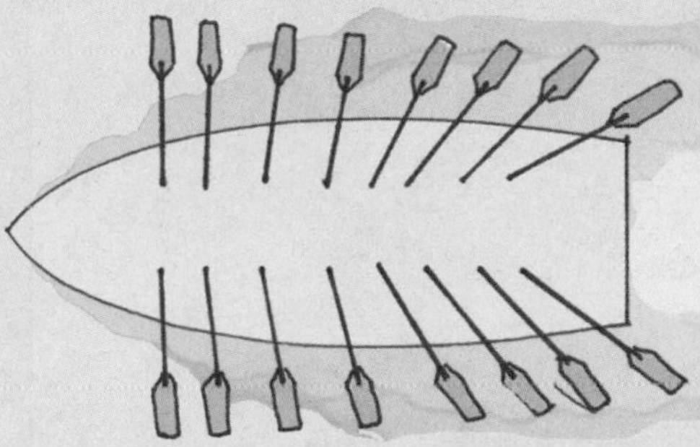

FIGURE 4 ···

▶ **INTERACTIVE ART** **Paramecium**
Paramecia use cilia to move through water.

✎ **Make Models** How is the movement of oars on this boat similar to the movement of cilia?

Protozoans That Are Parasites

The fourth group of protozoans are characterized more by the way they live than by the way they move. They are all parasites that feed on the cells and body fluids of their hosts. These protozoans move in a variety of ways. Some have flagella, and some depend on hosts for transport. One even produces a layer of slime that allows it to slide from place to place! Many of these parasites have more than one host. *Plasmodium,* shown in **Figure 5,** is a protozoan that causes malaria, a disease of the blood. Two hosts are involved in *Plasmodium's* life cycle—humans and a species of mosquitoes found in tropical areas. The disease spreads when a mosquito bites a person with malaria, becomes infected, and then bites a healthy person. Symptoms of malaria include high fevers that alternate with severe chills. These symptoms can last for weeks, then disappear, only to reappear a few   months later. Malaria can be fatal.

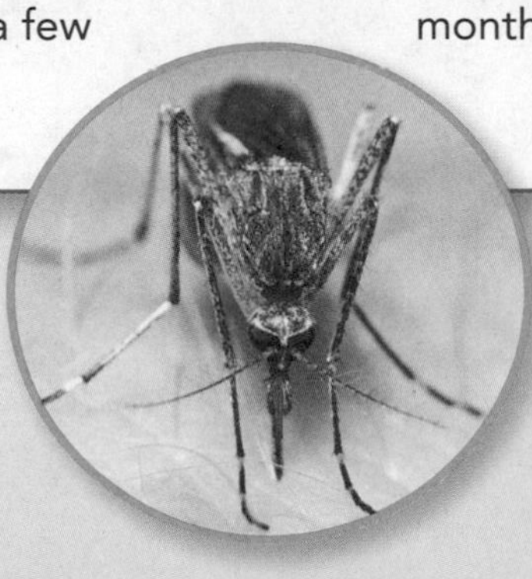

FIGURE 5 ···

Plasmodium
Plasmodium is transmitted through mosquito saliva.

✎ **Apply Concepts** If you lived in a tropical area, how could you reduce the risk of being infected with malaria?

apply it!

Suppose you fill a container with a culture of amoebas. Then you shine a bright light on one half of the container.

1 Predict How do you think the amoebas will respond to bright light? Draw your prediction in the empty container below.

2 Explain How were the amoebas able to respond to the light?

They will move away

3 Infer Why do you think it is important for amoebas to respond to bright light?

so they don't die

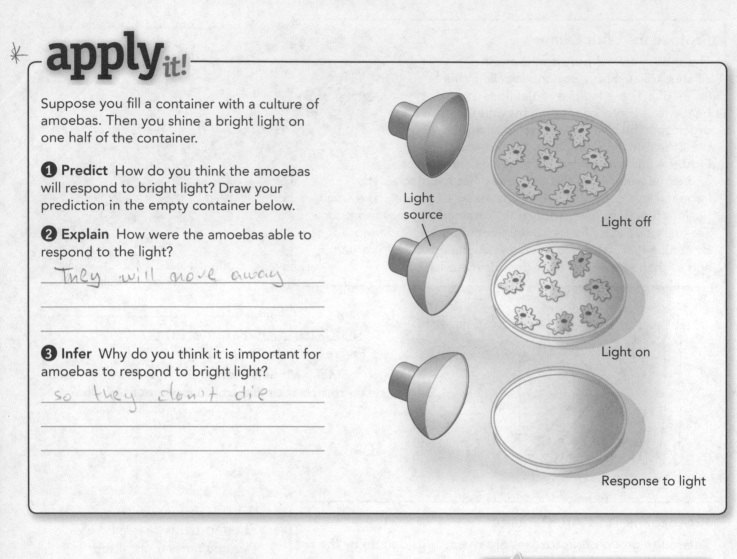

Light source

Light off

Light on

Response to light

 Do the Quick Lab *Observing Pseudopod Movement.*

🔑 Assess Your Understanding

1a. Review What are the three ways that animal-like protists move?

pseudopods

b. Classify You observe a protist under a microscope. It moves by forming temporary bulges of the cytoplasm. What type of protist is it? Explain your answer.

pseudopods because it forms larger cells

c. Draw Conclusions Why should you filter water from a stream before drinking it?

It has bacteria inside that will make you sick.

got it?

○ **I get it!** Now I know that the characteristics of animal-like protists are _____

_____

_____

_____

_____

○ **I need extra help with** _____

_____

Go to MY SCIENCE ⓢ COACH online for help with this subject.

What Are the Characteristics of Plant-Like Protists?

Plant-like protists, which are commonly called **algae** (AL jee; singular *alga*), are extremely diverse. **Algae are autotrophs, can be unicellular or multicellular, and use pigments to capture the sun's energy.** Most are able to use the sun's energy to make their own food.

Algae play a significant role in many environments. For example, algae that live near the surface of ponds, lakes, and oceans are an important food source for other organisms. In addition, much of the oxygen in Earth's atmosphere is made by these algae.

Algae vary greatly in size and color. Some algae are unicellular, while others are multicellular. Still others are groups of unicellular organisms that live together in colonies. Algae exist in a wide variety of colors because they contain many types of **pigments**— chemicals that produce color. Depending on their pigments, algae can be green, yellow, red, brown, orange, or even black.

Summarize Read the text about plant-like protists. Then summarize three characteristics of algae on the lines below.

_____

_____

_____

_____

Euglenoids

Euglenoids (yoo GLEE noydz) are green, unicellular algae that are usually found in fresh water. Most euglenoids are autotrophs that produce food using the sun's energy. However, when sunlight is not available, euglenoids will act as heterotrophs and obtain food from their environment. Some euglenoids move using a long, whiplike flagellum. The euglena on the right is a common euglenoid. Locate the red eyespot. The eyespot is not really an eye, but it contains pigments that are sensitive to light. It helps the euglena recognize the direction of a light source. Think how important this response is to an organism that needs light to make food.

Dinoflagellates

Dinoflagellates (dy noh FLAJ uh lits) are unicellular algae surrounded by stiff plates that look like a suit of armor. Dinoflagellates exist in a variety of colors because they have different amounts of green, orange, and other pigments. All dinoflagellates have two flagella held in grooves between their plates. When the flagella beat, the dinoflagellates twirl like toy tops as they move through the water. Many glow in the dark. They can light up an ocean's surface when disturbed by a passing boat or swimmer at night.

Diatoms

Diatoms are unicellular protists with beautiful glasslike cell walls. Some float near the surface of lakes or oceans or attach to rocks in shallow water. Diatoms are also a source of food for heterotrophs in the water. Many diatoms can move by oozing chemicals out of slits in their cell walls and gliding in the slime. When diatoms die, their cell walls collect on the bottoms of oceans and lakes. Over time, they form layers of a coarse substance called diatomaceous (dy uh tuh MAY shus) earth. Diatomaceous earth makes a good polishing agent and is used in household scouring products. It is even used as an insecticide—the diatoms' sharp cell walls puncture the bodies of insects.

Red Algae

Almost all red algae are multicellular seaweeds. Divers have found red algae growing more than 260 meters below the ocean's surface. Their red pigments are especially good at absorbing the small amount of light that is able to reach deep ocean waters. People use red algae in a variety of ways. Substances extracted from red algae, such as carrageenan (ka ruh JEE nun) and agar, are used in products such as ice cream and hair conditioner. Red algae is a nutrient-rich food that is eaten fresh, dried, or toasted by many people in Asian cultures.

Brown Algae

Many of the organisms that are commonly called seaweeds are brown algae. In addition to their brown pigment, brown algae also contain green, yellow, and orange pigments. A typical brown alga has many plant-like structures. For example, structures called holdfasts anchor the alga to rocks much as roots do for plants. Stalks support the blades, which are the leaflike structures of the alga. Many brown algae also have gas-filled sacs called bladders that allow the algae to float upright in ocean water. Some people eat brown algae. In addition, substances called algins are extracted from brown algae and used as thickeners in puddings and other foods.

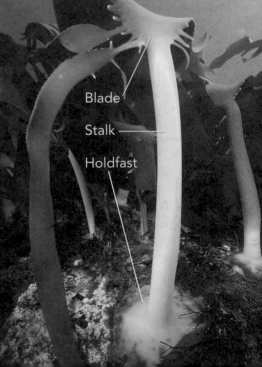

Blade

Stalk

Holdfast

FIGURE 6 ··

Functions of Algae

Algae play important roles in the environment.

✎ **Complete each task.**

1. **Classify** Label the type of algae in each of these photos.

2. **Explain** Check off the functions for each type of algae in the table below.

red algae   piatoms

Dinoflagellates   Brown algae   Eugleneids

Function	Type of Algae				
	Euglenoids	Dinoflagellates	Diatoms	Red Algae	Brown Algae
Produce oxygen					
Food source for other aquatic organisms					
Eaten by people					
Used in insecticides					
Used in polishing products					
Used in hair conditioner					

 Lab zone Do the Quick Lab Predicting.

🔑 Assess Your Understanding

2a. Review Why is sunlight important to plant-like protists?

_____

_____

b. Compare and Contrast What are some ways that algae are different from each other?

_____

_____

c. CHALLENGE How are euglenoids similar to animal-like protists?

_____

got it?

○ **I get it!** Now I know that the characteristics of plant-like protists are _____

_____

_____

_____

○ **I need extra help with** _____

Go to MY SCIENCE COACH online for help with this subject.

What Are the Characteristics of Fungus-Like Protists?

You can think of the fungus-like protists as the "sort of like" organisms. Fungus-like protists are sort of like animals because they are heterotrophs. They are sort of like plants because their cells have cell walls. 🔑 **Fungus-like protists are heterotrophs, have cell walls, and use spores to reproduce.** A **spore** is a tiny cell that is able to grow into a new organism. All fungus-like protists are able to move at some point in their lives. Three types of fungus-like protists are slime molds, water molds, and downy mildews.

Slime Molds
Slime molds are often brilliantly colored. They live in moist, shady places like forest floors. They ooze along the surfaces of decaying materials, feeding on bacteria and other microorganisms. Some slime molds are so small that you need a microscope to see them. Others may span several meters!

Slime molds begin their life cycle as tiny, amoeba-like individual cells. The cells use pseudopods to feed and creep around. If food is scarce, the cells grow bigger or join together to form a giant, jellylike mass. In some species, the giant mass is multicellular. In others, the giant mass is actually one giant cell with many nuclei.

The mass oozes along as a single unit. When environmental conditions become harsh, spore-producing structures grow out of the mass, as shown in **Figure 8,** and release spores. Eventually the spores develop into a new generation of slime molds.

Water Molds and Downy Mildews
Most water molds and downy mildews live in water or moist places. These organisms often grow as tiny threads that look like fuzz.

Water molds and downy mildews attack many food crops, such as potatoes, corn, and grapes. A water mold impacted history when it destroyed the Irish potato crops in 1845 and 1846. The loss of these crops led to a famine. More than 1 million people in Ireland died.

FIGURE 7 ·······························

A Slime Mold
This colorful slime mold, *Diachea leucopodia,* is producing spores.

✎ **Interpret Photos** What conditions might have changed in the slime mold's environment to cause spore production?

_____

_____

_____

_____

_____

_____

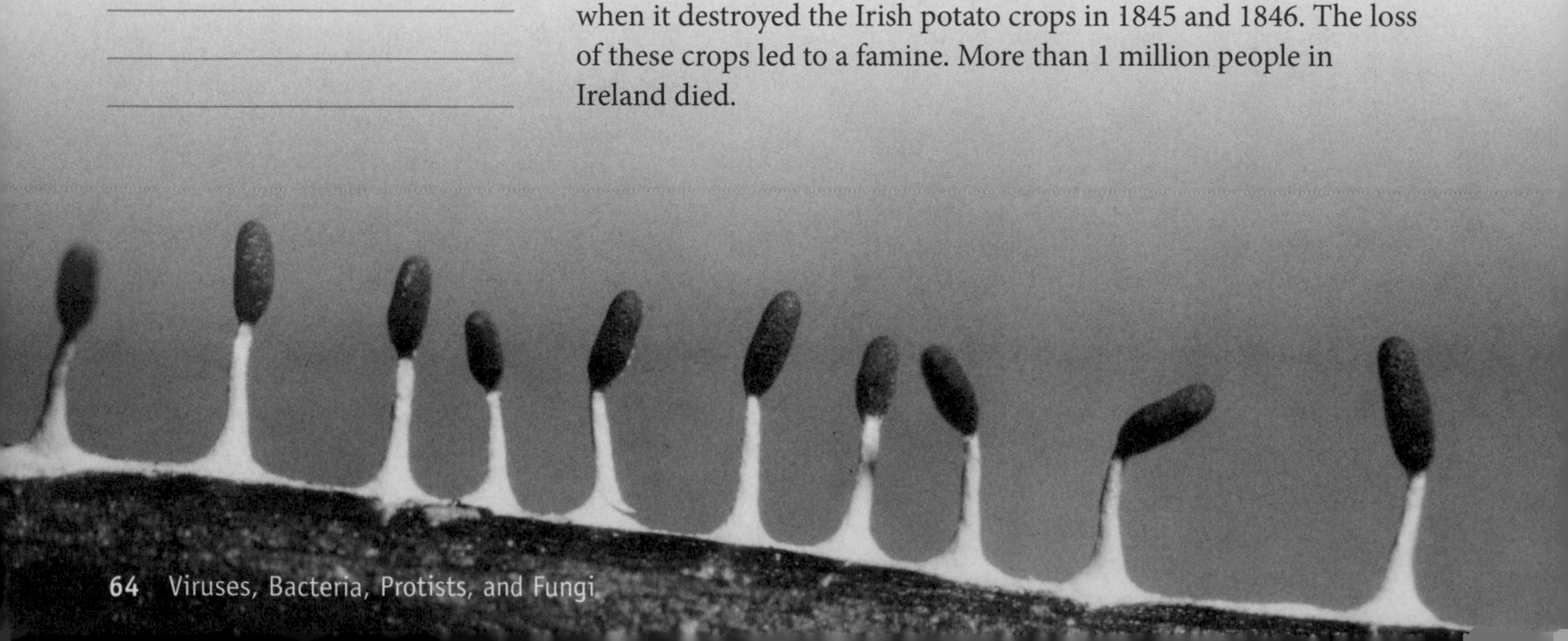

do the math! Analyzing Data

Soybean Crop Loss

Soybean plants can be infected and ruined by a water mold called *Phytophthora sojae*. The graph shows crop loss in metric tons in the United States between 2002 and 2005.

1 **Graph** Create a title for the graph. Then label the vertical axis.

2 **Read Graphs** In which year were the most soybeans lost?

_____

3 **Read Graphs** Describe how the soybean crop loss changed between 2002 and 2005.

_____

_____

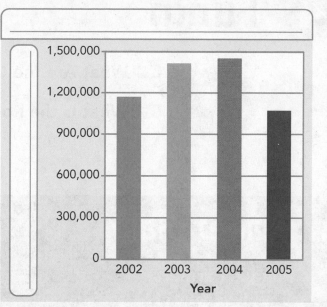

Year

Lab zone Do the Quick Lab *Observing Slime Mold.*

🔑 Assess Your Understanding

3a. List What are three types of fungus-like protists?

Slime Molds, Water Molds, and Downy Mildews

b. Describe What are two ways that fungus-like and animal-like protists are similar?

_____

_____

c. Apply Concepts A forest loses its trees and the forest floor dries up. How would slime molds be affected?

_____

_____

_____

_____

got it? ....

○ **I get it!** Now I know that the characteristics of fungus-like protists are _____

_____

○ **I need extra help with** _____

Go to my science **coach** *online for help with this subject.*

Fungi

UNLOCK THE BIG ?

🔑 **What Are the Characteristics of Fungi?**

🔑 **What Is the Role of Fungi in Nature?**

MY PLANET DIARY

Fungus Farmers

You may have heard of an "ant farm," but have you ever heard of ant farmers? Leafcutter ants act like farmers, growing fungus for food. First, the ants cut pieces of leaves from trees. Then the ants carry the leaves to an underground nest, where the leaves are crushed and chewed to make a mulch. Surprisingly, the ants don't eat the mulched leaves. They place them in a special growing chamber or "garden." Then they move strands of fungus from an existing garden to the new chamber, where it grows on the leaves. The ants help the fungus grow by removing harmful bacteria and mold. Finally, the ants eat the fungus!

FUN FACTS

Write your answer to each question below.

1. How do the ants act like farmers?

_____

_____

_____

2. How do the leafcutter ants and the fungus benefit from their relationship?

_____

_____

_____

_____

▶ **PLANET DIARY** Go to **Planet Diary** to learn more about fungi.

Lab zone® Do the Inquiry Warm-Up *There's a Fungus Among Us.*

What Are the Characteristics of Fungi?

You accidentally left an orange in your backpack. When you find it, it is covered in white fuzz! The orange is being digested by a mold, which is a type of fungus. You may be familiar with other kinds of fungi, too. For example, the molds that grow on stale bread and the mushrooms that sprout in forests are also fungi.

Vocabulary
- fungus • hyphae • fruiting body
- budding • lichen

Skills
⟳ Reading: Identify Supporting Evidence
△ Inquiry: Observe

Most **fungi** (singular *fungus*) share several important characteristics. ⟞ **Fungi are eukaryotes that have cell walls, are heterotrophs that feed by absorbing their food, and use spores to reproduce.** In addition, fungi need moist, warm places in which to grow. They thrive on damp tree barks, moist foods, lawns coated with dew, damp forest floors, and even wet bathroom tiles.

Cell Structure

Fungi range in size from tiny unicellular yeasts to large multicellular fungi. The cells of all fungi are surrounded by cell walls. Except for the simplest fungi, such as unicellular yeasts, the cells of most fungi are arranged in structures called **hyphae** (HY fee; singular *hypha*), shown in **Figure 1**. Hyphae are the branching, threadlike tubes that make up the bodies of multicellular fungi. The hyphae of some fungi are continuous threads of cytoplasm that contain many nuclei. Substances move quickly and freely through the hyphae. What a fungus looks like depends on how its hyphae are arranged. In fuzzy-looking molds, the threadlike hyphae are loosely tangled. In other fungi, the hyphae are packed tightly together.

Obtaining Food

Although fungi are heterotrophs, they do not take food into their bodies as you do. Instead, fungi absorb food through hyphae that grow into the food source.

First, the fungus grows hyphae into a food source. Then digestive chemicals ooze from the hyphae into the food. The chemicals break down the food into small substances that can be absorbed by the hyphae. Some fungi feed on dead organisms. Other fungi are parasites that break down the chemicals in organisms.

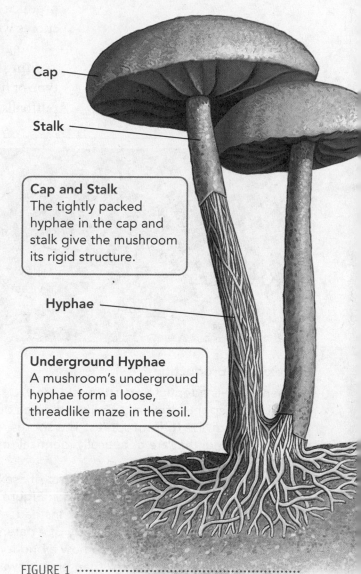

Cap

Stalk

Cap and Stalk
The tightly packed hyphae in the cap and stalk give the mushroom its rigid structure.

Hyphae

Underground Hyphae
A mushroom's underground hyphae form a loose, threadlike maze in the soil.

FIGURE 1 ⋯⋯⋯⋯⋯⋯⋯⋯⋯⋯⋯⋯⋯

Structure of a Mushroom
The largest known organism on Earth is an underground fungus that is larger than a thousand football fields.

✎ **Infer** What function might the underground hyphae in this mushroom perform?

_____

_____

_____

Reproduction in Fungi The way that fungi reproduce guarantees their survival and spread. Most fungi reproduce both asexually and sexually. Fungi usually reproduce by making spores. The lightweight spores are surrounded by a protective covering and can be carried easily through air or water to new sites. Fungi produce millions of spores, more than can ever survive. Only a few spores will fall where conditions are right for them to grow.

Fungi produce spores in reproductive structures called **fruiting bodies.** The appearance of a fruiting body varies from one type of fungus to another. In some fungi, such as mushrooms and puffballs, the visible part of the fungus is the fruiting body. In other fungi, such as bread molds, the fruiting bodies are tiny, stalklike hyphae that grow upward from the other hyphae. A knoblike spore case at the tip of each stalk contains the spores.

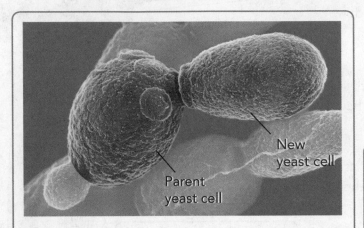

Asexual Reproduction

When there is adequate moisture and food, fungi make spores asexually. Cells at the tips of the hyphae divide to form spores. The spores grow into fungi that are genetically identical to the parent.

Unicellular yeast cells undergo a form of asexual reproduction called **budding,** shown in **Figure 2.** In budding, no spores are produced. Instead, a small yeast cell grows from the body of a parent cell in a way somewhat similar to how a bud forms on a tree branch. The new cell then breaks away and lives on its own.

FIGURE 2 ⋯⋯⋯⋯⋯⋯⋯⋯⋯⋯⋯⋯⋯⋯⋯⋯⋯⋯⋯
Yeast Reproduction
The smaller structure in the photo above is a new yeast cell budding from its parent.

✎ **Interpret Photos** How is this new yeast cell similar to its parent?

_____

_____

Sexual Reproduction

Most fungi can also reproduce sexually, especially when growing conditions become unfavorable. In sexual reproduction, the hyphae of two fungi grow together and genetic material is exchanged. Eventually, a new reproductive structure grows from the joined hyphae and produces spores. The spores develop into fungi that differ genetically from either parent.

FIGURE 3 ⋯⋯⋯⋯⋯⋯⋯⋯⋯⋯⋯⋯⋯⋯⋯⋯⋯⋯⋯
Bread Mold Reproduction
Two hyphae in this bread mold have joined together to undergo sexual reproduction. The round object between the hyphae will eventually produce spores.

Classification of Fungi

Three major groups of fungi are the club, sac, and zygote fungi. These groups are classified by the appearance of their reproductive structures. Additional groups include water species that produce spores with flagella and those that form tight associations with plant roots. **Figure 4** shows an example from one of the major groups of fungi.

FIGURE 4

Club Fungus

The reproductive structures of this chanterelle look like tiny clubs. You can see spherical spores forming at the end of one of the club-shaped reproductive structures.

Predict What will happen after these spores are released?

_____

_____

_____

_____

Do the Quick Lab *Do All Molds Look Alike?*

🔑 Assess Your Understanding

1a. Define What are hyphae?

_____

b. Review What role do spores play in the reproduction of fungi?

_____

_____

c. Sequence Outline the steps by which fungi produce spores during sexual reproduction.

_____

_____

_____

_____

_____

got it? ....

○ **I get it!** Now I know that the characteristics of fungi are _____

_____

○ **I need extra help with** _____

Go to MY SCIENCE ⬡ COACH online for help with this subject.

What Is the Role of Fungi in Nature?

Fungi affect humans and other organisms in many ways. 🔑 **Fungi may act as decomposers and recyclers, or provide foods for people. Fungi may help fight or cause disease. Some fungi live in a beneficial relationship with other organisms.**

Environmental Recycling Like bacteria, many fungi are decomposers—organisms that break down the chemicals in dead organisms. For example, many fungi live in the soil and break down the chemicals in dead plant matter. This process returns important nutrients to the soil. Without fungi and bacteria, Earth would be buried under dead plants and animals!

Food and Fungi When you eat a slice of bread, you benefit from the work of yeast, a type of fungus. Bakers add yeast to bread dough to make it rise. Yeast cells use the sugar in the dough for food and produce carbon dioxide gas as they feed. The gas forms bubbles, which cause the dough to rise. You see these bubbles as holes in a slice of bread. Without yeast, bread would be flat and solid. Yeast is also used to make wine from grapes. Yeast cells feed on the sugar in the grapes and produce carbon dioxide and alcohol.

Other fungi are also important sources of foods. The blue streaks in blue cheese, for example, are actually growths of mold. People enjoy eating mushrooms in salads and soups and on pizza. Because some mushrooms are extremely poisonous, however, you should never pick or eat wild mushrooms.

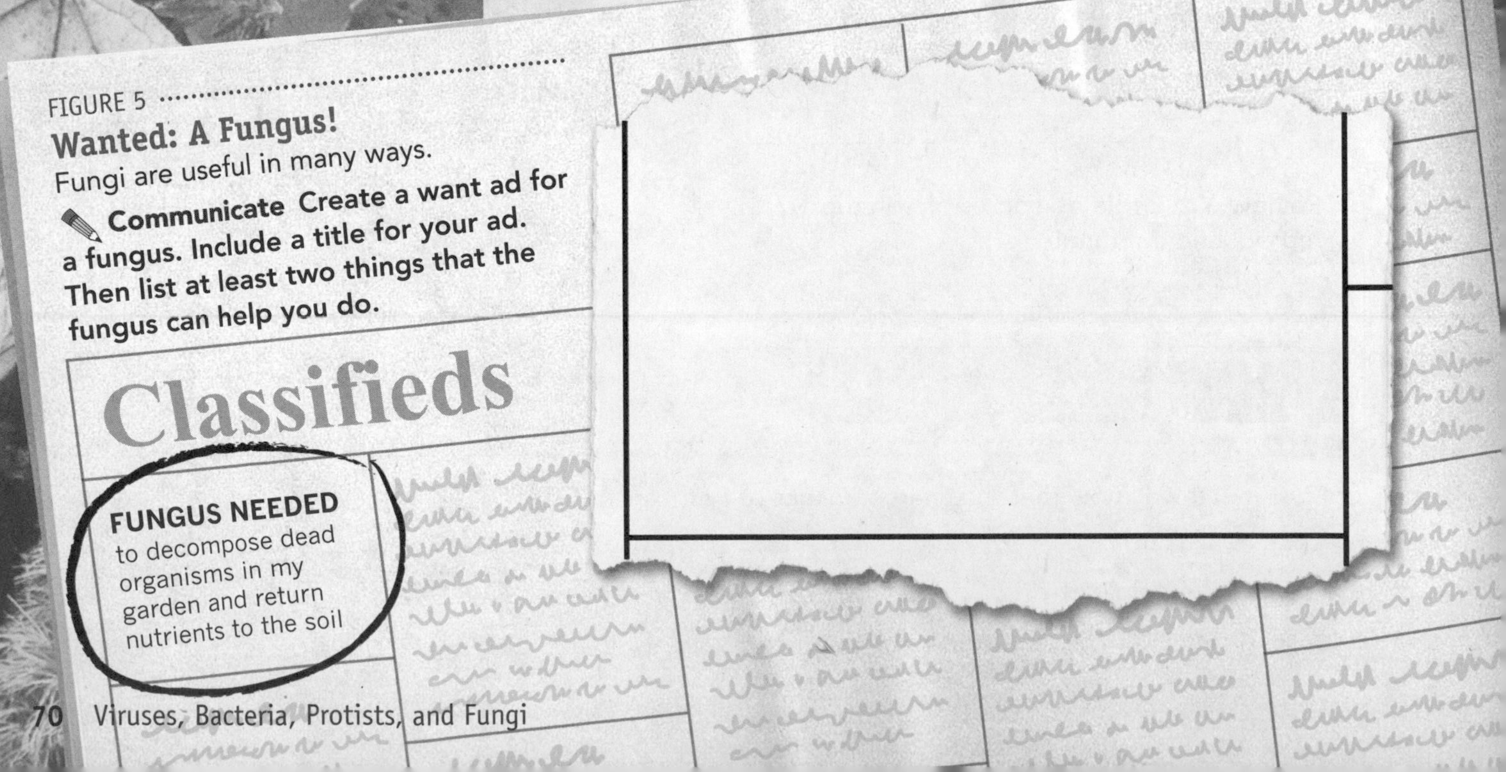

FIGURE 5 ·····················
Wanted: A Fungus!
Fungi are useful in many ways.

✏️ **Communicate** Create a want ad for a fungus. Include a title for your ad. Then list at least two things that the fungus can help you do.

Classifieds

FUNGUS NEEDED
to decompose dead organisms in my garden and return nutrients to the soil

Disease-Fighting Fungi

In 1928, a Scottish biologist named Alexander Fleming was examining petri dishes in which he was growing bacteria. To his surprise, Fleming noticed a spot of bluish green mold growing in one dish. Curiously, no bacteria were growing near the mold. Fleming hypothesized that the mold, a fungus named *Penicillium*, produced a substance that killed the bacteria near it.

Fleming's work contributed to the development of the first antibiotic, penicillin. It has saved the lives of millions of people with bacterial infections. Since the discovery of penicillin, many other antibiotics have been isolated from both fungi and bacteria.

Disease-Causing Fungi

Many fungi are parasites that cause serious diseases in plants. The sac fungus that causes Dutch elm disease is responsible for killing millions of elm trees in North America and Europe. Corn smut and wheat rust are two club fungi that cause diseases in important food crops. Fungal plant diseases also affect other crops, including rice, cotton, and soybeans, resulting in huge crop losses every year.

Some fungi cause diseases in humans. Athlete's foot is an itchy irritation in the damp places between toes. Ringworm shows up as a circular rash on the skin. Because the fungus that causes these diseases produces spores at the site of infection, the diseases spread easily from person to person. Both diseases can be treated with antifungal medications.

Identify Supporting Evidence Underline the evidence in the text that supports the conclusion that *Penicillium* mold kills bacteria.

apply it!

Suppose you are a scientist studying two dishes of the same bacteria. One day, you notice that two dots of mold have started growing in the middle of each dish. The next day you observe what happened.

1 Observe How were the two dishes of bacteria affected by the mold?

_____

_____

2 CHALLENGE Are the two dots of mold the same type of fungus? Explain your answer.

_____

_____

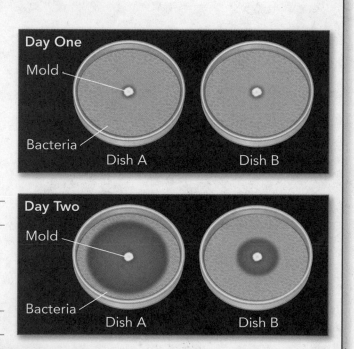

Day One
Mold
Bacteria
Dish A   Dish B

Day Two
Mold
Bacteria
Dish A   Dish B

Fungus-Plant Root Associations Some fungi help plants grow larger and healthier when their hyphae grow into, or on, the plants' roots. The hyphae spread out underground and absorb water and nutrients from the soil for the plant. With more water and nutrients, the plant grows larger than it would have grown without its fungal partner. The plant is not the only partner that benefits. The fungus gets to feed on the extra food that the plant makes and stores.

Most plants have fungal partners. Many plants are so dependent on the fungi that they cannot survive without them. For example, orchid seeds cannot develop without their fungal partners.

Rico arrives at a dairy factory in Europe. How are bacteria and fungi being used to make dairy products?

_____

_____

_____

_____

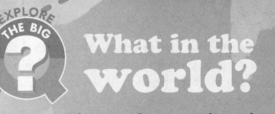

Before he starts his trip, Rico receives a vaccine. What will this vaccine protect him against?

_____

_____

_____

During Rico's first stop in South America, he steps over a rotting tree trunk. What are the roles of bacteria and fungi?

_____

_____

_____

EXPLORE THE BIG ?

What in the world?

How are living things other than plants and animals important to Earth?

FIGURE 6 ·······························

▶ **REAL-WORLD INQUIRY** Rico is taking a trip around the world. Follow him as he encounters viruses, bacteria, protists, and fungi in the environment.

✎ **Interpret Photos** Answer the question in each box on the lines provided.

Lichens A **lichen** (LY kun) consists of a fungus and either algae or autotrophic bacteria that live together in a relationship that benefits both organisms. You have probably seen some familiar lichens—irregular, flat, crusty patches that grow on tree barks or rocks. The fungus benefits from the food produced by the algae or bacteria. The algae or bacteria, in turn, obtain shelter, water, and minerals from the fungus.

 Do the Quick Lab *Considering Fungi as Decomposers.*

Next, Rico travels to the coast of Africa. He sees people gathering red and brown algae. How might they use the algae?

_____

_____

_____

On his way home, Rico sees lichens growing on a rock in Australia. How do the algae and fungus in this lichen help each other?

_____

_____

_____

Assess Your Understanding

2a. Name What are some foods that are made with fungi?

_____

b. Explain How can fungi be used to treat disease?

_____

_____

_____

c. ANSWER THE BIG ? How are living things other than plants and animals important to Earth?

_____

_____

_____

_____

got it? ....

○ **I get it!** Now I know the roles of fungi in

the environment are _____

_____

_____

_____

○ **I need extra help with** _____

_____

Go to **MY SCIENCE COACH** online for help with this subject.

2 Study Guide

_____ are nonliving. Some protists, such as _____, produce oxygen. Bacteria and fungi both play roles as _____.

LESSON 1 Viruses

🔑 Viruses are nonliving, have a protein coat that protects an inner core of genetic material, and cannot reproduce on their own.

🔑 Though viruses can cause disease, they can also be used to treat and prevent illnesses.

Vocabulary
• virus • host • parasite • vaccine

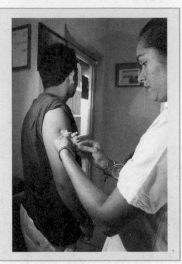

LESSON 2 Bacteria

🔑 Bacteria are prokaryotes. The genetic material in their cells is not contained in a nucleus.

🔑 Bacteria get energy by either making food or eating other organisms, and can reproduce asexually or sexually.

🔑 Bacteria are involved in oxygen and food production, in health maintenance and medicine production, and in environmental cleanup and recycling.

Vocabulary
• bacteria • cytoplasm • ribosome • flagellum • cellular respiration
• binary fission • conjugation • endospore • pasteurization • decomposer

LESSON 3 Protists

🔑 Like animals, animal-like protists are heterotrophs, and most can move to get food.

🔑 Algae are autotrophs, can be unicellular or multicellular, and use pigments to capture the sun's energy.

🔑 Fungus-like protists are heterotrophs, have cell walls, and use spores to reproduce.

Vocabulary
• protist • protozoan • pseudopod • contractile vacuole • cilia • algae • pigment • spore

LESSON 4 Fungi

🔑 Fungi are eukaryotes that have cell walls, are heterotrophs that feed by absorbing their food, and use spores to reproduce.

🔑 Fungi may act as decomposers and recyclers, or provide foods for people. Fungi may help fight or cause disease. Some fungi live in a beneficial relationship with other organisms.

Vocabulary
• fungus • hyphae • fruiting body
• budding • lichen

Review and Assessment

LESSON 1 Viruses

1. Bacteriophages are viruses that attack and destroy

    a. plants.   (**b.**) bacteria.

    c. humans.   **d.** other viruses.

2. A ___parasite___ is an organism that lives on or in a host and causes it harm.

3. Interpret Diagrams Label the following structures in the diagram below: protein coat, surface proteins, and genetic material.

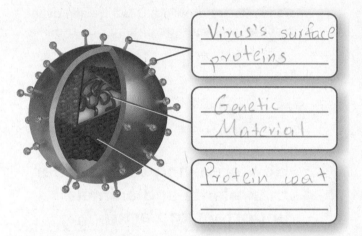

Virus's surface proteins

Genetic Material

Protein coat

4. Predict Chickenpox is a disease caused by a virus. The chickenpox vaccine began to be recommended for children in 1995. How do you think the rate of chickenpox infections changed after 1995?

There are less people with chickenpox because there is a vaccine.

5. **Write About It** Bacteria will grow in agar, a substance containing nutrients. Viruses do not grow in agar. If you needed to grow viruses in the laboratory, what kind of substances would you have to use? Explain your reasoning.

LESSON 2 Bacteria

6. Which process is used to kill bacteria in foods such as milk and juice?

    a. conjugation   (**b.**) pasteurization

    c. binary fission   **d.** decomposition

7. Bacteria reproduce sexually through

    conjugation

8. Classify Look at the photos below. Classify the bacteria according to their shape.

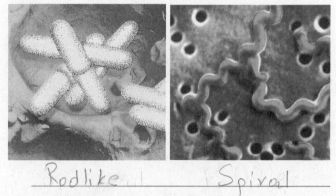

Rodlike   Spiral

9. Compare and Contrast Fill in the chart below to describe how bacteria obtain energy.

Type of Bacteria	Methods of Obtaining Energy	
Autotrophic	Sun	Use chemical energy to make food
Heterotrophic	Consume decaying leaves	consume other organisms

10. Infer How do bacteria "recycle" Earth's nutrients?

They break down complex chemicals into simple chemicals.

Protists

11. Protozoans, such as ciliates and flagellates, are
(a.) animal-like protists. **b.** plant-like protists.
c. fungus-like protists. **d.** bacteria-like protists.

12. Algae may be green, orange, red, yellow, brown, or black depending on the ___pigments___ they contain.

13. Make Generalizations Four different groups of protists are classified as "animal-like." What characteristics do these groups share?

They can move and eat food. They are heterotrophs.

14. Predict If all algae suddenly disappeared from Earth's waters, how would other living things be affected? Explain your answer.

Living things will die because
___
___
___

15. Write About It Write a pamphlet describing how homeowners can prevent the growth of slime molds in their basements. Be sure to explain why the suggested action will be effective.

Fungi

16. Which of the following is a characteristic of fungi?
a. They are autotrophic.
b. They lack cell walls.
(c.) They are eukaryotes.
d. They reproduce with seeds.

17. Spores are produced in reproductive structures called ___fruiting bodies___

18. Apply Concepts A fungicide is a substance that kills fungi and may be used in crop fields where plants are growing. Describe an advantage and a disadvantage of fungicide use.
Advantage: The fruits won't be destroyed.
Disadvantage: some plants might die.

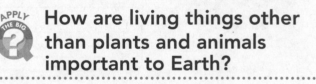

How are living things other than plants and animals important to Earth?

19. Viruses, bacteria, protists, and fungi are neither plants nor animals. In fact, viruses are not even alive! Still, each plays important roles on Earth. Describe at least three ways in which viruses, bacteria, protists, or fungi are important in your daily life.
Example-we eat mushrooms
-medicine
- help bodies
-earth's recyclers
-produce oxygen
___
___
___

Standardized Test Prep

Multiple Choice

Circle the letter of the best answer.

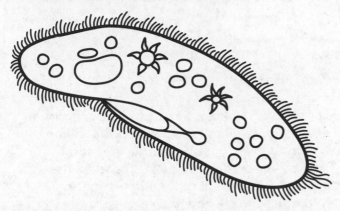

1. Identify the organism shown above and the structure it uses to move.

   A paramecium; cilia
   B protozoan; flagella
   C amoeba; pseudopod
   D parasite; contractile vacuole

2. Which of the following statements about fungus reproduction is true?

   A Fungi only reproduce asexually.
   B Fungi can reproduce by making spores.
   C Fungi reproduce sexually by budding.
   D Fungi reproduce asexually by joining hyphae and exchanging genetic material.

3. Which part of a virus determines which host cell it can infect?

   A nucleus   B protein coat
   C ribosomes   D surface proteins

4. Which statement is correct about plant-like and fungus-like protists?

   A Plant-like protists are all parasitic, while fungus-like protists are not.
   B Plant-like protists are unicellular, while fungus-like protists are multicellular.
   C Plant-like protists are usually autotrophs, while fungus-like protists are heterotrophs.
   D Plant-like protists live on land, while fungus-like protists live on land and in water.

5. Yogurt is produced with the help of _____ while bread rises because of _____.

   A viruses; fungi.   B fungi; protists.
   C bacteria; fungi.   D protists; bacteria.

Constructed Response

Use the diagram below and your knowledge of science to help you answer Question 6. Write your answer on a separate piece of paper.

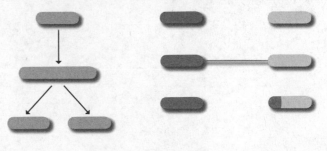

6. Name each process in the drawings of bacteria shown above. Then describe the main differences between these processes.

VIRUS TRACKERS

When an illness breaks out and affects an unusual number of people in an area, most people want to be as far away as possible. However, some scientists, called epidemiologists, travel to the front lines of these breakouts to investigate. Epidemiologists study how diseases spread. They identify a breakout or epidemic's cause, locate its source, and track how it is spreading. Then they help health officials develop strategies to slow or stop the spread of the disease.

An epidemiologist wearing a hazardous materials (hazmat) "bunny suit," which insulates the wearer from infectious diseases ▽

Some of an epidemiologist's most dangerous work occurs in labs, where teams of scientists study disease-causing organisms called pathogens. There are only six labs in the world where epidemiologists can study deadly pathogens such as the Ebola and Marburg viruses. These labs feature multiple airlocks, which prevent unfiltered, infected air from leaving the lab. Epidemiologists must wear pressurized suits and use oxygen tanks. This type of work is dangerous, but epidemiologists are helping us to understand how to protect groups of people from deadly infectious diseases.

Research It Find out more about the history of epidemiology. Learn about the spread of one major disease. What have epidemiologists learned about that disease? Create a timeline showing the first reported cases, the major events in the epidemic, and major events in the treatment of the disease.

Experimenting With Human Subjects

Sometimes researchers need to use human subjects in order to understand how a new treatment will work on people. How do they weigh whether a decision is appropriate? The research must be unlikely to hurt the subjects. The subjects must also understand the risks and join the study voluntarily.

Debate It Newspapers, buses, and the radio often have advertisements for research studies. These studies may offer volunteers money to try an experimental medicine, such as pain medicine, during recovery from surgery. These advertisements often appeal to college students and unemployed people. With a group of three or four classmates, discuss any ethical issues in advertising for research subjects. With your group, organize a debate about the ethics of these advertisements and studies.

page 3

January 1, 2009   The Science Daily

MUSHROOMS WORTH THEIR WEIGHT IN GOLD

A mushroom that attracts wild pigs? That's a delicacy? Absolutely! One of these mushrooms even sold for $330,000 at a charity auction.

Truffles live on the roots of certain trees. They feed on the trees, and in turn help the roots of the trees absorb minerals. Animals such as rodents or wild pigs eat the truffles, and their spores are spread around in the animals' feces. Some truffles release an odor that pigs find irresistible. Truffle hunters use pigs to sniff for these tasty underground fungi.

Evaluate It Research efforts to farm truffles using trees that have had truffle spores pumped into them. Were the sources written for young students, scientists, or someone else? Write a paragraph or two explaining your conclusion.

WHAT'S UNUSUAL ABOUT THESE TREES?

THE BIG ?

How do you know a plant when you see it?

With its wide trunk and short stubby branches, the baobab tree looks like a sweet potato or an upside-down tree. Seen for miles across the dry African savannah, the baobab can live for over 1,000 years and can grow to over 23 meters high and 27 meters around the trunk. It would take about 18 teenagers with arms spread wide and fingertips touching to encircle a tree that wide!

Draw Conclusions Why do you think the baobab tree has such a wide trunk and short branches only at the very top?

_____

_____

_____

_____

_____

▶ **UNTAMED SCIENCE** Watch the **Untamed Science** video to learn more about plants.

CHAPTER
Plants 3

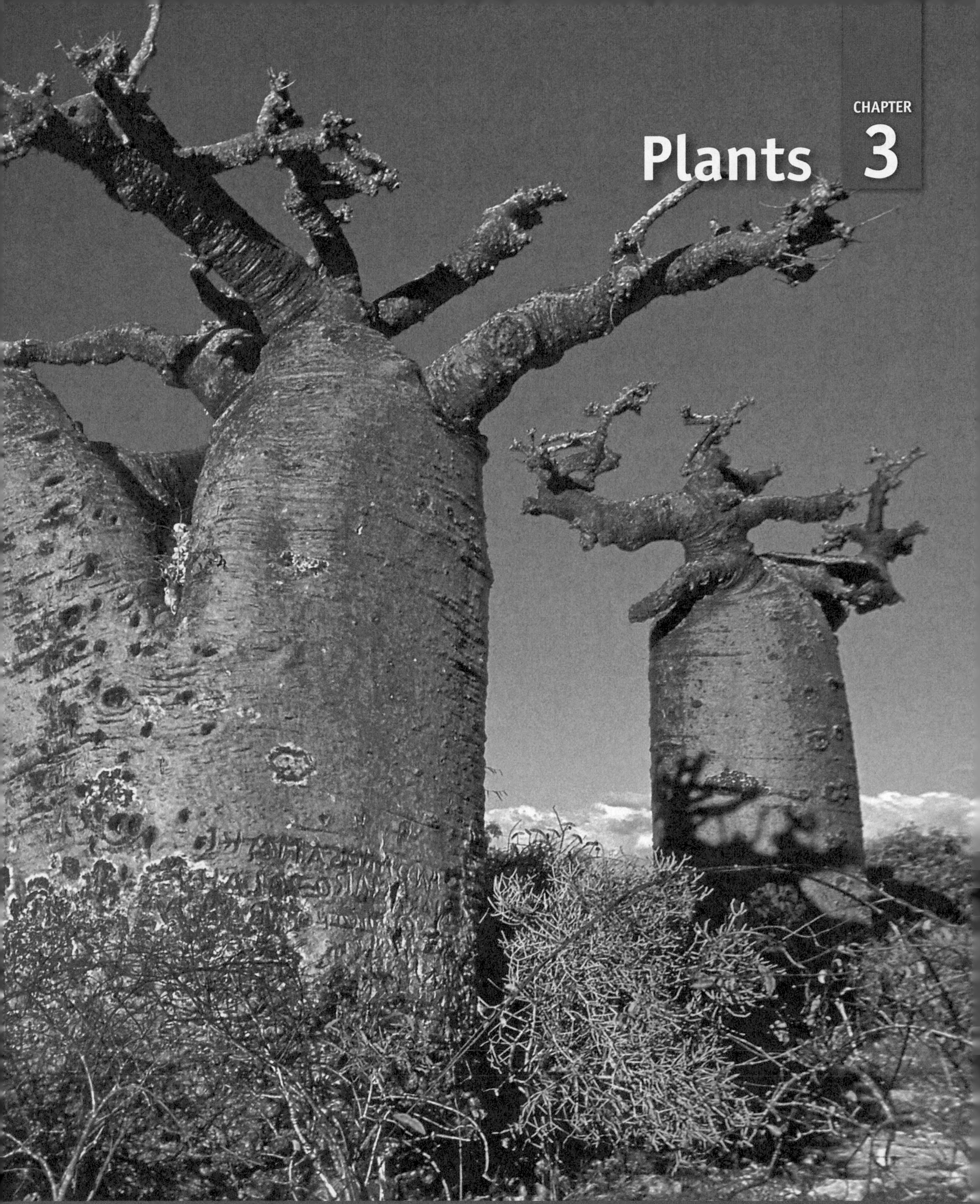

3 Getting Started

Check Your Understanding

1. **Background** Read the paragraph below and then answer the question.

Rahim and Malika were in the park after school. "Plants are such cool **organisms**," said Rahim. "Can you imagine if humans had green **pigment** in their skin?" "Yeah," said Malika. "If we were **autotrophs**, I'd never have to get up early to pack my lunch!"

> An **organism** is a living thing.
>
> A **pigment** is a colored chemical compound that absorbs light.
>
> An **autotroph** is an organism that makes its own food.

- Give an example of an autotrophic organism that has green pigment.

_____

_____

> MY READING WEB If you had trouble completing the question above, visit **My Reading Web** and type in *Plants.*

Vocabulary Skill

Greek Word Origins Many science words come to English from ancient Greek. Learning the Greek word parts can help you understand some of the vocabulary in this chapter.

Greek Word Part	Meaning	Example Word
chloros	pale green	chloroplast, *n.* green cellular structure in which photosynthesis occurs
petalon	leaf	petal, *n.* colorful, leaflike flower structure

2. **Quick Check** *Chlorophyll* is a pigment found in plants. Which part of the word *chlorophyll* tells you that it is a green pigment?

_____

chloroplast

monocot

sepal

fruit

Chapter Preview

LESSON 1
- chlorophyll • photosynthesis
- tissue • chloroplast • vacuole
- cuticle • vascular tissue
- ⟳ Compare and Contrast
- △ Predict

LESSON 2
- nonvascular plant • rhizoid
- vascular plant • phloem
- xylem • frond • pollen • seed
- gymnosperm • angiosperm
- cotyledon • monocot
- dicot
- ⟳ Outline
- △ Communicate

LESSON 3
- root cap • cambium • stoma
- transpiration • embryo
- germination • flower
- pollination • sepal • petal
- stamen • pistil • ovary
- ⟳ Relate Cause and Effect
- △ Observe

LESSON 4
- sporophyte • gametophyte
- annual • biennial • perennial
- fertilization • zygote
- cone • ovule • fruit
- ⟳ Summarize
- △ Infer

LESSON 5
- tropism • hormone
- auxin • photoperiodism
- critical night length
- short-day plant • long-day plant
- day-neutral plant • dormancy
- ⟳ Relate Text and Visuals
- △ Draw Conclusions

LESSON 6
- peat
- ⟳ Identify the Main Idea
- △ Pose Questions

1 What Is a Plant?

🔑 **What Characteristics Do All Plants Share?**

🔑 **What Do Plants Need to Live Successfully on Land?**

my planet Diary

How Does Your Garden Grow?

Students at The Hilldale School in Daly City, California, get to play in the dirt during class. The students planted and maintain a garden filled with native species. Native plants, or plants that have been in an area for a long time, can struggle to survive if new plants are introduced. This creates problems for the insects, animals, and other organisms that rely on the native plants. The students spent three months removing nonnative plants before creating a garden that will help local organisms right outside their school.

Communicate Discuss the question with a group of classmates. Write your answer below.

Describe a plant project you would like to do at your school.

_____

_____

_____

_____

_____

_____

_____

▶ **PLANET DIARY** Go to **Planet Diary** to learn more about plants.

Lab zone ® Do the Inquiry Warm-Up *What Do Leaves Reveal About Plants?*

What Characteristics Do All Plants Share?

Which organisms were the ancestors of today's plants? In search of answers, biologists studied fossils, the traces of ancient life forms preserved in rock and other substances. The oldest plant fossils are about 400 million years old. These fossils show that even at that early date, plants already had many adaptations for life on land.

Vocabulary

- chlorophyll
- photosynthesis
- tissue
- chloroplast
- vacuole
- cuticle
- vascular tissue

Skills

↩ Reading: Compare and Contrast

△ Inquiry: Predict

Better clues to the origin of plants came from comparing the chemicals in modern plants to those in other organisms. Biologists studied a pigment called chlorophyll. **Chlorophyll** (KLAWR uh fil) is a green pigment found in the chloroplasts of plants, algae, and some bacteria. Land plants and green algae contain the same forms of chlorophyll. Further comparisons of genetic material clearly showed that plants and green algae are very closely related. Today, green algae are classified as plants.

Members of the plant kingdom share several characteristics. 🔑 **Nearly all plants are autotrophs, organisms that produce their own food. With the exception of some green algae, all plants contain many cells. In addition, all plant cells are surrounded by cell walls.**

Plants Are Autotrophs

You can think of a typical plant as a sun-powered, food-making factory. Sunlight provides the energy for this food-making process, called **photosynthesis**. During photosynthesis, a plant uses carbon dioxide gas and water to make food and oxygen.

↩ **Compare and Contrast**
How do you think the ancient environment of the leaf in the fossil differed from that of the modern leaf in the pictures below?

_____

_____

_____

_____

_____

_____

_____

_____

Plants Are Multicellular
Except for some green algae, all plants are made of many cells. No matter how large or small a plant is, its cells are organized into **tissues.** Tissues are groups of similar cells that perform a specific function in an organism.

Plant Cells
Unlike the cells of animals, a plant's cells are enclosed by a cell wall. See **Figure 1.** The cell wall surrounds the cell membrane and separates the cell from the environment. Plant cell walls contain cellulose, a material that makes the walls rigid. Because their cell walls are rigid, plant cells look like small boxes. Cell walls make apples and carrots crunchy. Plant cells also contain many other structures. **Chloroplasts** (KLAWR uh plasts), which look like green jelly beans, are the structures in which food is made. A **vacuole** is a large storage sac that can expand and shrink. The vacuole stores many substances, including water, wastes, and food. A plant wilts when too much water has left its vacuoles.

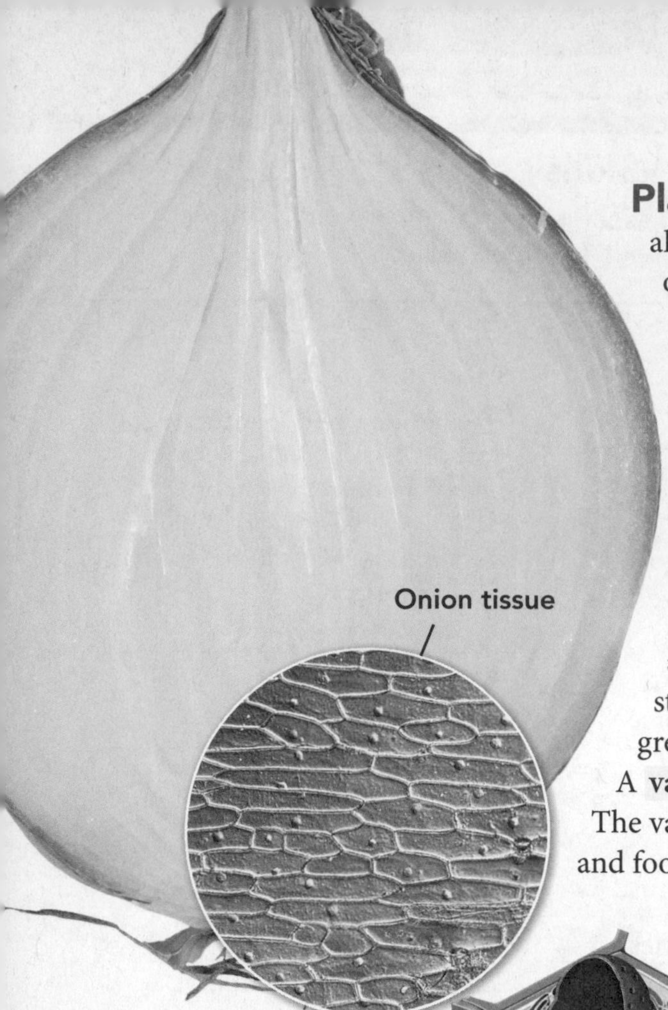

Onion tissue

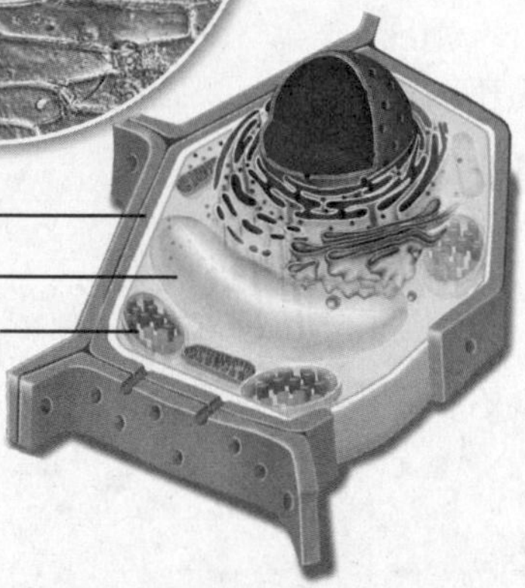

Cell wall
Vacuole
Chloroplast

FIGURE 1 ··

> INTERACTIVE ART **Plant Cells**

Plant cells are different from animal cells. Cell walls make onions crunchy.

✎ **Infer** How does having cell walls affect a plant's ability to grow tall?

_____

_____

 Lab ® Do the Quick Lab
zone *Algae and Other Plants.*

🔑 Assess Your Understanding

1a. Review Almost all plants (make/do not make) their own food.

b. Explain What is the function of the cell wall in a plant cell?

_____

_____

c. Infer What do you think happens to a plant cell if the plant is given too much water?

_____

_____

_____

got it? ···

○ **I get it!** Now I know that nearly all plants _____

_____

○ **I need extra help with** _____

Go to MY SCIENCE 🔵 COACH online for help with this subject.

What Do Plants Need to Live Successfully on Land?

Imagine multicellular algae floating in the ocean. The algae obtain water and other materials directly from the water around them. They are held up toward the sunlight by the water. Now imagine plants living on land. What adaptations would help them meet their needs without water all around them? **For plants to survive on land, they must have ways to obtain water and other nutrients from their surroundings, retain water, support their bodies, transport materials, and reproduce.**

Obtaining Water and Other Nutrients
Recall that all organisms need water to survive. Obtaining water is easy for algae because water surrounds them. To live on land, plants need adaptations for obtaining water from the soil. One adaptation is the way the plant produces its roots, as shown in **Figure 2.** Plants must also have ways of obtaining other nutrients from the soil.

Saguaro cactus

Acacia tree

FIGURE 2 ....
Getting Water in the Desert
The saguaro cactus and the acacia tree both live in deserts with limited water. Saguaro roots spread out horizontally. When it rains, the roots quickly absorb water over a wide area. Acacia trees in the Negev Desert of Israel get their water from deep underground instead of at the surface.

✎ **Interpret Diagrams** Draw the roots of the acacia tree. Then describe how the growth of the roots differs between the plants.

_____

_____

_____

FIGURE 3 ....

Waterproof Leaves

The waxy cuticle of many leaves, like the one below, looks shiny under light.

Retaining Water When there is more water in plant cells than in the air, the water leaves the plant and enters the air. The plant could dry out if it cannot hold onto water. One adaptation that helps a plant reduce water loss is a waxy, waterproof layer called the **cuticle.** You can see the cuticle on the leaf in **Figure 3.**

Support A plant on land must support its own body. It's easier for small, low-growing plants to support themselves. In larger plants, the food-making parts must be exposed to as much sunlight as possible. Cell walls and tissue strengthen and support the large bodies of these plants.

Transporting Materials A plant needs to transport water, minerals, food, and other materials from one part of its body to another. In general, water and minerals are taken up by the bottom part of the plant, while food is made in the top part. But all of the plant's cells need water, minerals, and food.

In small plants, materials can simply move from one cell to the next. Larger plants need a more efficient way to transport materials from one part of the plant to another. These plants have tissue for transporting materials called vascular tissue. **Vascular tissue** is a system of tubelike structures inside a plant through which water, minerals, and food move. See vascular tissue in action in **Figure 4.**

apply it!

This graph shows how much water a plant loses during the day. Give the graph a title.

1 **Interpret Graphs** During what part of the day did the plant lose the most water?

_____

2 **Predict** How might the line in the graph look from 10 P.M. to 8 A.M.? Why?

_____

_____

_____

_____

_____

_____

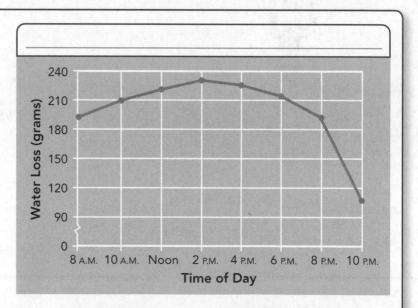

3 CHALLENGE Do you think this graph would be the same for plants all around the world? Why?

_____

_____

_____

_____

Reproduction For algae and some other plants, reproduction can only occur if there is water in the environment. This is because the sperm cells of these plants swim through the water to the egg cells. Land plants need to have adaptations that make reproduction possible in dry environments.

FIGURE 4 ·······················
Colorful Carnations

These three carnations were left overnight in glasses of water. Blue dye was added to the glass in the middle. The stem of the flower on the right was split in half. Part of the stem was placed in water with blue dye and the other part was placed in water with red dye.

✏ **Draw Conclusions** Why did the flowers in the glasses with dye change color?

_____

_____

_____

_____

_____

_____

Lab zone® Do the Quick Lab *Local Plant Diversity.*

🔑 Assess Your Understanding

2a. Define What is a cuticle?

_____

_____

_____

b. Apply Concepts Describe the pros and cons of being a tall land plant.

_____

_____

_____

_____

_____

got it?

○ **I get it!** Now I know that to live on land, plants need to _____

_____

_____

_____

_____

○ **I need extra help with** _____

_____

_____

Go to **MY SCIENCE** Ⓢ **COACH** *online for help with this subject.*

Classifying Plants

🔑 **What Are the Characteristics of Nonvascular Plants?**

🔑 **What Are the Characteristics of Seedless Vascular Plants?**

🔑 **What Are the Characteristics of Seed Plants?**

my planet Diary

CAREER

The Moss Is Greener on the Other Side

Tired of mowing the lawn? Never want to pull out another weed? Hire a moss landscaper! Landscapers design beautiful yards, usually planting trees, flowers, bushes, and grasses. These plants need a lot of care. Moss doesn't. Moss grows in the shade where other plants can't. Landscapers can use moss to cover an entire yard if the conditions are right. Mosses are also better for the environment. People don't have to put toxic chemicals on their moss lawns to kill weeds or keep it green.

Write your answer below.

Do you think people should use moss instead of grass for their lawns? Why?

_____

_____

_____

_____

▶ **PLANET DIARY** Go to **Planet Diary** to learn more about plant classification.

Lab zone® Do the Inquiry Warm-Up *Will Mosses Absorb Water?*

What Are the Characteristics of Nonvascular Plants?

Plants that lack vascular tissue for transporting materials are known as **nonvascular plants**. 🔑 **Nonvascular plants are low-growing, have thin cell walls, and do not have roots for absorbing water from the ground.** Instead, they obtain water and materials directly from their surroundings. The materials then pass from one cell to the next. This means that materials do not travel far or quickly. This slow method helps explain why most nonvascular plants live in damp, shady places. The thin cell walls are why these plants cannot grow more than a few centimeters tall.

Vocabulary

- nonvascular plant • rhizoid • vascular plant • phloem
- xylem • frond • pollen • seed • gymnosperm
- angiosperm • cotyledon • monocot • dicot

Skills

- Reading: Outline
- Inquiry: Communicate

Mosses Have you ever seen mosses growing in the cracks of a sidewalk or in a shady spot? With more than 10,000 species, mosses are by far the most diverse group of nonvascular plants.

If you were to look closely at a moss, you would see a plant that looks something like **Figure 1.** Structures that look like tiny leaves grow off a small, stemlike structure. Thin, rootlike structures called **rhizoids** anchor the moss and absorb water and nutrients. Moss grows a long, slender stalk with a capsule at the end. The capsule contains spores for reproduction.

FIGURE 1 ·····························

Moss Structure

Diagrams can be easier to read than photographs, but photographs are more realistic.

✏ **Relate Diagrams and Photos** Label the capsule, stalk, and leaflike structure in the photo. Draw lines from your labels to the structure itself, like in the diagram below.

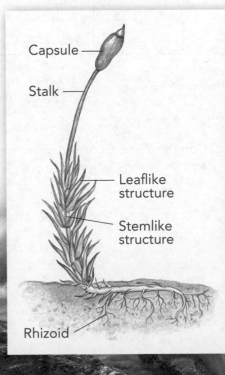

- Capsule
- Stalk
- Leaflike structure
- Stemlike structure
- Rhizoid

Capsule

Stalk

Leaflike structure

Liverwort ▲

Liverworts and Hornworts

Liverworts and hornworts are two other groups of nonvascular plants. There are more than 8,000 species of liverworts. This group of plants is named for the shape of the plant's body, which looks somewhat like a human liver. *Wort* is an old English word for "plant." Liverworts are often found growing as a thick crust on moist rocks or soil along the sides of a stream. There are fewer than 100 species of hornworts. If you look closely at a hornwort, you can see slender, curved structures that look like horns growing out of the plant. Unlike mosses or liverworts, hornworts are seldom found on rocks or tree trunks. Instead, hornworts usually live in moist soil, often mixed in with grass plants.

✏️ **Outline** Fill in the table to the right with what you have learned about liverworts and hornworts.

Hornwort ▶

Nonvascular Plants

Plant	Identifiable Physical Characteristic	Where Found
Mosses	Fuzzy appearance	Shady spots, rocks, tree trunks
Liverworts	looks like a human liver	thick crust on moist rocks or soil along the sides of a stream
Hornworts	slender, curved structure that look like horns growing out of a plant	rocks or tree trunks moist soil and often in gross plants

 Do the Quick Lab *Masses of Mosses.*

🗝️ Assess Your Understanding

1a. Review (Vascular tissues/Rhizoids) anchor moss and absorb water and nutrients.

b. Explain Why are most nonvascular plants short?

_____

_____

c. Compare and Contrast How are liverworts and hornworts different?

_____

_____

_____

_____

got it? ....

○ **I get it!** Now I know the characteristics of nonvascular plants are _____

_____

○ **I need extra help with** _____

Go to **MY SCIENCE COACH** online for help with this subject.

What Are the Characteristics of Seedless Vascular Plants?

If you could have walked through the ancient forests that existed long before the dinosaurs lived, they would have looked very strange to you. You might have recognized the mosses and liverworts that carpeted the moist soil, but you would have seen very tall, odd-looking trees. Among the trees grew huge, tree-sized ferns. Other trees resembled giant sticks with leaves up to one meter long. The odd-looking plants in the ancient forests are the ancestors of the ferns, clubmosses, and horsetails of today.

🔑 **Ferns, club mosses, and horsetails share two characteristics. They have vascular tissue and they do not produce seeds. Instead of seeds, these plants reproduce by releasing spores.**

Vascular Tissue Ancient trees were vascular plants. **Vascular plants** are plants with true vascular tissue. Vascular plants can grow tall because their vascular tissue provides an effective way of transporting materials throughout the plant. The vascular tissue also strengthens the plants' bodies. You can see vascular tissue in **Figure 2.** The cells making up the vascular tissue have strong cell walls. Imagine a handful of drinking straws bundled together with rubber bands. The bundle of straws is stronger and more stable than a single straw would be. Arranged similarly, the strong, tubelike structures in vascular plants give the plants strength and stability.

There are two types of vascular tissue. **Phloem** (FLOH um) is the vascular tissue through which food moves. After food is made in the leaves, it enters the phloem and travels to other parts of the plant. Water and minerals, on the other hand, travel in the vascular tissue called **xylem** (ZY lum). The roots absorb water and minerals from the soil. These materials enter the root's xylem and move upward into the stems and leaves.

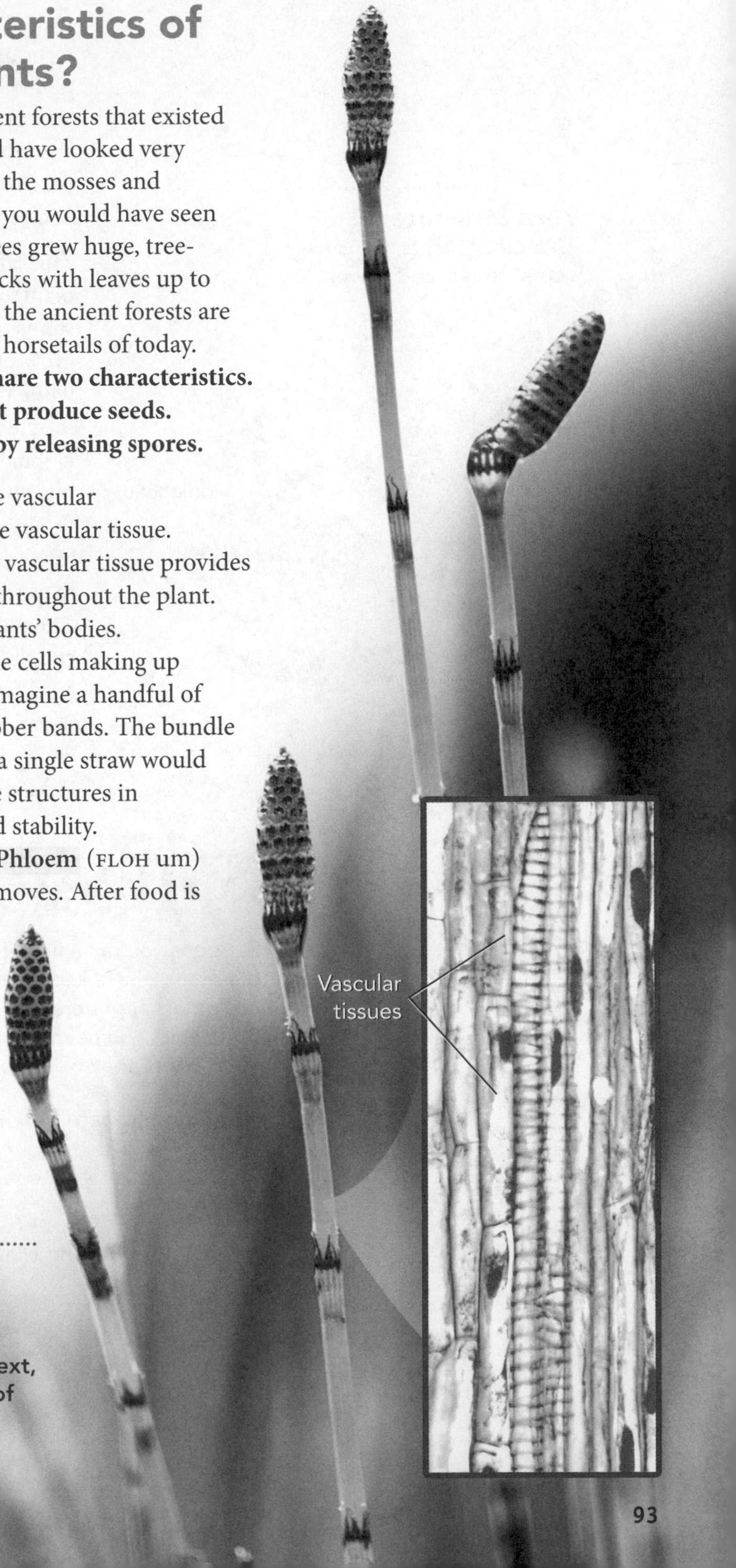

Vascular tissues

FIGURE 2 ·························
Vascular Tissue
Vascular plants have xylem and phloem.

✏️ **Identify** In the text, underline the roles of vascular tissue.

93

Ferns There are more than 12,000 species of ferns alive today. They range in size from tiny plants about the size of this letter *M* to tree ferns that grow up to five meters tall. Ferns thrive in shaded areas with moist soil. Some remain green year-round while others turn brown in the fall and regrow in spring.

The Structure of Ferns Like other vascular plants, ferns have stems, roots, and leaves. The stems of most ferns are underground. Leaves grow upward from the top side of the stems, while roots grow downward from the bottom of the stems. Water and nutrients enter the root's vascular tissue and travel through the tissue into the stems and leaves.

Figure 3 shows a fern's structure. Notice that the fern's leaves, or **fronds,** are divided into many smaller parts that look like small leaves. The upper surface of each frond is coated with a cuticle that helps the plant retain water. In many ferns, the developing leaves are coiled at first. Because they resemble the top of a violin, these young leaves are often called fiddleheads. Fiddleheads uncurl as they mature.

FIGURE 3 ·······························

Fern Structure
Like other plants, ferns have roots, stems, and leaves.

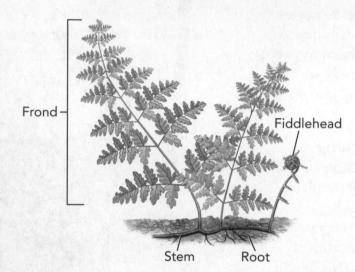

Frond

Fiddlehead

Stem   Root

apply it!

Suppose you ran a flower shop that sold cut flowers and potted plants. You have just received a shipment of potted ferns and several customers are interested in purchasing them. Before they are ready to be sold, you need to make sure your customers can take care of the ferns so they won't regret their purchase.

1 **Communicate** On the tag at left, write the care instructions that will be given to your customers who buy potted ferns. Include the conditions that the fern needs for light and water.

2 **CHALLENGE** Florists recommend not putting plants like ferns in south- or west-facing windows. Why?

_____

_____

_____

_____

Caring for Your Fern

_____

_____

_____

_____

_____

_____

◄ Horsetail

Club moss ▼

Club Mosses and Horsetails
Like ferns, club mosses and horsetails have true stems, roots, and leaves. However, there are relatively few species of club mosses and horsetails alive today.

Do not be confused by the name *club moss*. Unlike true mosses, club mosses have vascular tissue. You may be familiar with the club moss in **Figure 4.** The plant, which looks a little like a small branch of a pine tree, is sometimes called ground pine or princess pine. Club mosses usually grow in moist woodlands and near streams.

There are about 30 species of horsetails on Earth today. The whorled pattern of growth somewhat resembles the appearance of a horse's tail. The stems contain silica, a gritty substance also found in sand. During colonial times, Americans used the plants to scrub their pots and pans. Another common name for horsetails is scouring brushes.

FIGURE 4 ·····························

Moss Imposter?
A club moss is pictured at left.

✏ **Describe** Why is a club moss not a true moss?

_____
_____
_____
_____
_____

 Do the Quick Lab
Examining a Fern.

🔑 Assess Your Understanding

2a. Identify In plants, water moves through (phloem/xylem). Food moves through (phloem/xylem).

b. Infer Why do you think the developing leaves of a fern are coiled?

_____
_____

c. Develop Hypotheses Why do you think there are more ferns than club mosses?

_____
_____
_____
_____

got it? ·····························

○ **I get it!** Now I know the characteristics of seedless vascular plants include _____
_____

○ I need extra help with _____

Go to MY SCIENCE Ⓢ COACH *online for help with this subject.*

What Are the Characteristics of Seed Plants?

Seed plants outnumber seedless plants by more than ten to one. You eat many seed plants—rice, peas, and squash, for example. You wear clothes made from seed plants, such as cotton and flax. You may live in a home built from seed plants—oak, pine, or maple trees. In addition, seed plants produce much of the oxygen you breathe.

Seed plants share two important characteristics. 🔑 **Seed plants have vascular tissue, and they use pollen and seeds to reproduce.** In addition, the bodies of all seed plants have roots, stems, and leaves. Most seed plants live on land. Recall that land plants face many challenges, including standing upright and supplying all their cells with food and water. Like ferns, seed plants meet these two challenges with vascular tissue.

Pollen and Seeds
Unlike seedless plants, seed plants can live in a wide variety of environments. Recall that seedless plants need water in their surroundings for fertilization to occur. Seed plants do not need water for sperm to swim to the eggs. Instead, seed plants produce **pollen,** tiny structures that contain the cells that will later become sperm cells. Pollen deliver sperm cells directly near the eggs. After sperm cells fertilize the eggs, seeds develop. A **seed** is a structure that contains a young plant inside a protective covering. Seeds protect the young plant from drying out.

Gymnosperms
The giant sequoia trees belong to the group of seed plants known as gymnosperms. A **gymnosperm** (JIM noh spurm) is a seed plant that produces naked seeds. The seeds of gymnosperms are referred to as "naked" because they are not enclosed by a protective fruit.

Many gymnosperms have needlelike or scalelike leaves and deep-growing root systems. Gymnosperms are the oldest type of seed plant. According to fossil evidence, gymnosperms first appeared on Earth about 360 million years ago. Fossils also indicate that there were many more species of gymnosperms on Earth in the past than there are today. Four types of gymnosperms exist today, as shown in **Figure 5.**

Vocabulary Greek Word Origins The word *gymnosperm* comes from the Greek words *gumnos*, meaning "naked," and *sperma*, meaning "seed." Why are the seeds of gymnosperms considered to be naked?

_____

_____

_____

_____

GYMNOSPERM	DESCRIPTION/FUNCTION
Cycads 	About 175 million years ago, the majority of plants were cycads (SY kadz). Today, cycads grow mainly in tropical and subtropical areas. Cycads look like palm trees with cones that can grow as large as a football!
Conifers	Conifers (KAHN uh furz), or cone-bearing plants, are the largest and most diverse group of modern gymnosperms. Most conifers are evergreens, meaning they keep their leaves or needles year-round.
Ginkgoes 	Ginkgoes (GING kohz) also grew hundreds of millions of years ago. Today, only one species, *Ginkgo biloba*, exists. It probably survived because the Chinese and Japanese cared for it in their gardens. Today, ginkgo trees are planted along city streets because they can tolerate air pollution.
Gnetophytes 	Gnetophytes (NEE tuh fyts) live in hot deserts and in tropical rain forests. Some are trees, some are shrubs, and others are vines. The *Welwitschia* (shown at left) of West Africa can live for more than 1,000 years!

FIGURE 5 ·············

Types of Gymnosperms

The chart describes the four main groups of gymnosperms.

✎ **Answer these questions.**

1. **Name** Which group of gymnosperms has the most species?

   _____

2. **Apply Concepts** What could have happened to the ecosystem the *Ginkgo biloba* tree lived in if the tree had become extinct?

   _____

   _____

   _____

   _____

   _____

   _____

dicot

monocot

Angiosperms

You probably associate the word *flower* with a sweet-smelling plant growing in a garden. You certainly wouldn't think of something that smells like rotting meat. That's exactly what the corpse flower, or rafflesia, smells like. This flower, which grows in Asia, produces a meat smell, which attracts flies that spread the flower's pollen. You won't be seeing rafflesia in your local florist shop any time soon! Rafflesia belongs to the group of seed plants known as angiosperms (AN jee uh spurmz). **Angiosperms,** or flowering plants, share two important characteristics. First, they produce flowers. Second, in contrast to gymnosperms, which produce uncovered seeds, angiosperms produce seeds that are enclosed in fruits.

Angiosperms live almost everywhere on Earth. They grow in frozen areas in the Arctic, tropical jungles, and barren deserts. A few angiosperms, such as mangrove trees, live at the ocean's edge.

Types of Angiosperms

Angiosperms are divided into two major groups: monocots and dicots. "Cot" is short for cotyledon (kaht uh LEED un). The **cotyledon,** or seed leaf, provides food for the embryo. *Mono-* means "one" and *di-* means "two." **Monocots** are angiosperms that have only one seed leaf. Grasses, including corn, wheat, and rice, and plants such as lilies and tulips, are monocots. **Dicots,** on the other hand, produce seeds with two seed leaves. Dicots include plants such as roses and violets, as well as dandelions. Both oak and maple trees are dicots, as are food plants such as beans and apples. **Figure 6** shows the characteristics of monocots and dicots.

FIGURE 6 ·····················

VIRTUAL LAB **Monocots and Dicots**
Use the table below to find your answers.

✎ **Interpret Photos** Label the rafflesia (top) and the other flowers on this page as *monocots* or *dicots*.

dicot

Characteristics of Monocots and Dicots					
	Seeds	**Leaves**	**Flowers**	**Stems**	**Roots**
Monocots	Single cotyledon	Parallel veins	Floral parts often in multiples of 3	Vascular tissue bundles scattered throughout stem	Many roots spread out
Dicots	Two cotyledons	Branched veins	Floral parts often in multiples of 4 or 5	Vascular tissue bundles arranged in a ring	One main root

do the math!

Use the graph of known plant species to answer the questions.

1 **Interpret Graphs** Which plant group has the fewest species?

_____

2 **Calculate** Figure out the percentage that each of the following plant groups represents. Round your answer to the nearest tenth.

Green algae _____

Ferns and relatives _____

Angiosperms _____

3 **CHALLENGE** Why do you think angiosperms are the largest group?

_____
_____
_____
_____
_____

Major Groups of Known Plants

Green Algae: 7,000 species

Mosses and Relatives: 18,500 species

Ferns and Relatives: 12,000 species

Gymnosperms: 800 species

Angiosperms: 260,000 species

Lab zone® Do the Quick Lab
Common Characteristics.

Assess Your Understanding

3a. Define What are pollen?

_____
_____
_____
_____

b. Draw Conclusions Why do you think angiosperms enclose their seeds in fruits?

_____
_____
_____
_____

got it? ....

○ **I get it!** Now I know the characteristics of seed plants include _____

_____

○ **I need extra help with** _____

Go to **MY SCIENCE** Ⓢ **COACH** *online for help with this subject.*

Plant Structures

UNLOCK
THE BIG
?

🔑 **What Are the Functions of Roots, Stems, and Leaves?**

🔑 **How Do Seeds Become New Plants?**

🔑 **What Are the Structures of a Flower?**

my planeT DiaRY

SCIENCE STATS

Plant Giants

- The aroid plant (as shown here) on the island of Borneo in Asia has leaves that can grow three meters long! These are the largest undivided leaves on Earth!

- The rafflesia flower can grow up to one meter wide and weigh seven kilograms.

- The jackfruit can weigh up to 36 kilograms. That's the world's largest fruit that grows on trees!

Write your answer below.
Why do you think the aroid plant has such big leaves?

_____

_____

_____

▷ **PLANET DIARY** Go to **Planet Diary** to learn more about plant structures.

Lab zone® Do the Inquiry Warm-Up *Which Plant Part Is It?*

What Are the Functions of Roots, Stems, and Leaves?

Each part of a plant plays an important role in its structure and function. Roots, stems, and leaves are just three structures we will look into further.

Roots Have you ever tried to pull a dandelion out of the soil? It's not easy, is it? That is because most roots are good anchors. Roots have three main functions. 🔑 **Roots anchor a plant in the ground, absorb water and minerals from the soil, and sometimes store food.** The more root area a plant has, the more water and minerals it can absorb.

Vocabulary

- root cap • cambium • stoma • transpiration
- embryo • germination • flower • pollination
- sepal • petal • stamen • pistil • ovary

Skills

⟳ Reading: Relate Cause and Effect
△ Inquiry: Observe

Types of Roots The two main types of root systems are shown in **Figure 1.** A fibrous root system consists of many similarly sized roots that form a dense, tangled mass. Plants with fibrous roots take a lot of soil with them when you pull them out of the ground. Lawn grass, corn, and onions have fibrous root systems. In contrast, a taproot system has one long, thick main root. Many smaller roots branch off the main root. A plant with a taproot system is hard to pull out of the ground. Carrots, dandelions, and cacti have taproots.

FIGURE 1 ·························

Root Systems and Structure

There are two main root systems with many structures.

✎ **Interpret Photos** Label the taproot *T* and the fibrous roots *F*.

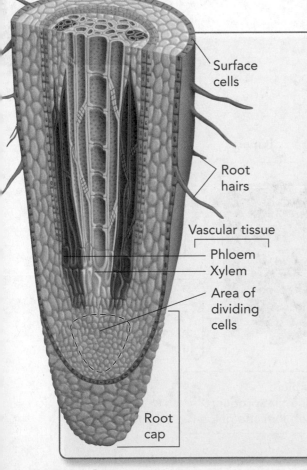

Surface cells

Root hairs

Vascular tissue
├ Phloem
├ Xylem
├ Area of dividing cells

Root cap

Root Structure

In **Figure 2,** you can see the structure of a typical root. The tip of the root is rounded and is covered by the root cap. The **root cap** protects the root from injury as the root grows through the soil. Behind the root cap are the cells that divide to form new root cells.

Root hairs grow out of the root's surface. These tiny hairs can enter the spaces between soil particles, where they absorb water and minerals. The root hairs also help to anchor the plant in the soil.

Locate the vascular tissue in the center of the root. The water and nutrients that are absorbed from the soil quickly move into the xylem. From there, these substances are transported upward to the plant's stems and leaves. Phloem transports food manufactured in the leaves to the root. The root tissues then use the food for growth or store it for future use by the plant.

FIGURE 2 ··

Root Structure

Roots have many structures.

✎ **Define** What is the function of the root cap?

_____

_____

Stems The stem of a plant has two main functions. 🔑 **The stem carries substances between the plant's roots and leaves. The stem also provides support for the plant and holds up the leaves so they are exposed to the sun.** In addition, some stems, such as those of asparagus, store food.

The Structure of a Stem Stems can be either woody or herbaceous (hur BAY shus). Woody stems are hard and rigid, such as in maple trees. Herbaceous stems contain no wood and are often soft. Plants with herbaceous stems include daisies, ivy, and asparagus (pictured left).

Herbaceous and woody stems consist of phloem and xylem tissue as well as many other supporting cells. As you can see in **Figure 3,** a woody stem contains many layers of tissue. The outermost layer is bark. Bark includes an outer protective layer and an inner layer of living phloem, which transports food through the stem. Next is a layer of cells called the **cambium** (KAM bee um), which divides to produce new phloem and xylem. It is xylem that makes up most of what you call "wood." Sapwood is active xylem that transports water and minerals through the stem. The older, darker, heartwood is inactive but provides support.

FIGURE 3 ....

Stem Structure
The woody stem of a tree contains many different structures.

✎ **Interpret Diagrams** Label the active xylem and phloem on the tree trunk below.

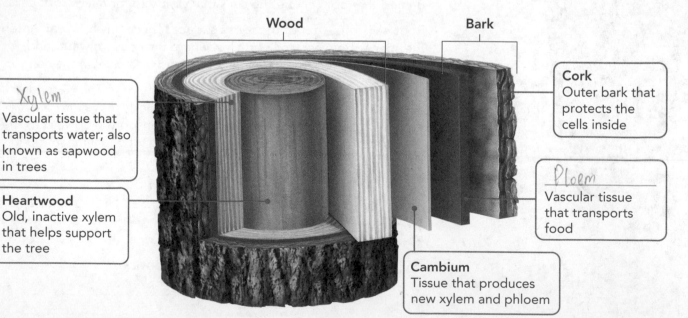

Wood   Bark

Xylem
Vascular tissue that transports water; also known as sapwood in trees

Heartwood
Old, inactive xylem that helps support the tree

Cambium
Tissue that produces new xylem and phloem

Cork
Outer bark that protects the cells inside

Ploem
Vascular tissue that transports food

Annual Rings Have you ever looked at a tree stump and seen a pattern of circles that looks something like a target? These circles are called annual rings. They represent a tree's yearly growth. Annual rings are made of xylem. Xylem cells that form in the spring are large and have thin walls because they grow rapidly. They produce a wide, light brown ring. Xylem cells that form in the summer grow slowly and, therefore, are small and have thick walls. They produce a thin, dark ring. One pair of light and dark rings represents one year's growth. You can estimate a tree's age by counting its annual rings.

The width of a tree's annual rings can provide important clues about past weather conditions, such as rainfall. In rainy years, more xylem is produced, so the tree's annual rings are wide. In dry years, rings are narrow. By examining annual rings from some trees in the southwestern United States, scientists were able to infer that severe droughts occurred in the years 840, 1067, 1379, and 1632.

◄ The annual rings in a tree reveal the tree's history.

apply it!

1 Calculate How old was the tree when it was cut down?

_____

2 ⚠ Observe The area at Area C is blackened from a fire that affected one side of the tree. Describe how the tree grew after the fire.

_____

_____

_____

_____

3 CHALLENGE Areas A and B both represent four years of growth. What might account for their difference in size?

_____

_____

_____

_____

_____

_____

Vocabulary Greek Word
Origins The Greek word *stoma*
means "mouth." How are the
stomata of a plant like mouths?

_____

_____

_____

_____

_____

_____

_____

Leaves
Leaves vary greatly in size and shape. Pine trees have needle-shaped leaves. Birch trees have small rounded leaves with jagged edges. Regardless of their shape, leaves play an important role in a plant. 🔑 **Leaves capture the sun's energy and carry out the food-making process of photosynthesis.**

The Structure of a Leaf If you were to cut through a leaf and look at the edge under a microscope, you would see the structures in **Figure 4.** The leaf's top and bottom surface layers protect the cells inside. Between the layers of cells are veins that contain xylem and phloem.

The surface layers of the leaf have small openings, or pores, called **stomata** (stoh MAH tuh; *singular* stoma). The stomata open and close to control when gases enter and leave the leaf. When the stomata are open, carbon dioxide enters the leaf, and oxygen and water vapor exit.

Upper Leaf Cells
Tightly packed cells trap the energy in sunlight.

Lower Leaf Cells
Widely spaced cells allow carbon dioxide to reach cells for photosynthesis and oxygen to escape into the air.

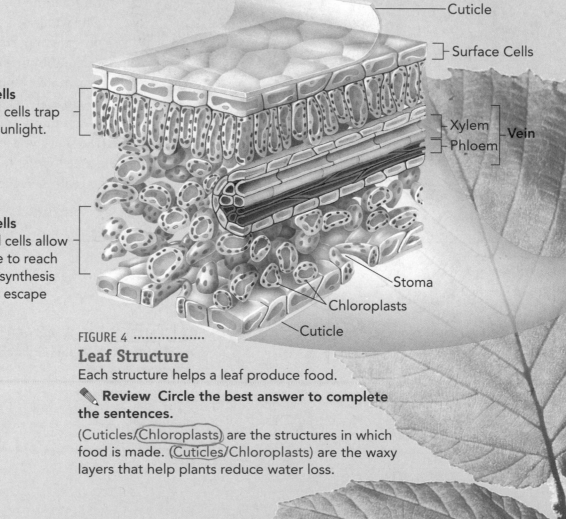

Cuticle

Surface Cells

Xylem

Phloem

Vein

Stoma

Chloroplasts

Cuticle

FIGURE 4 ·················
Leaf Structure
Each structure helps a leaf produce food.

✏️ **Review Circle the best answer to complete the sentences.**

(Cuticles/(Chloroplasts)) are the structures in which food is made. ((Cuticles)/Chloroplasts) are the waxy layers that help plants reduce water loss.

The Leaf and Photosynthesis The structure of a leaf is ideal for carrying out photosynthesis. The cells that contain the most chloroplasts are located near the leaf's upper surface, where they get the most light. The chlorophyll in the chloroplasts traps the sun's energy.

Carbon dioxide enters the leaf through open stomata. Water, which is absorbed by the plant's roots, travels up the stem to the leaf through the xylem. During photosynthesis, sugar and oxygen are produced from the carbon dioxide and water. Oxygen passes out of the leaf through the open stomata. The sugar enters the phloem and then travels throughout the plant.

Controlling Water Loss Because such a large area of a leaf is exposed to the air, water can quickly evaporate from a leaf into the air. The process by which water evaporates from a plant's leaves is called **transpiration.** A plant can lose a lot of water through transpiration. A corn plant, for example, can lose almost 4 liters of water on a hot summer day. Without a way to slow down the process of transpiration, a plant would shrivel up and die.

Fortunately, plants have ways to slow down transpiration. One way plants retain water is by closing the stomata. The stomata often close when leaves start to dry out.

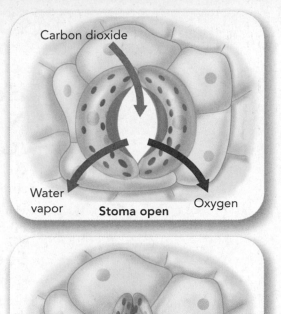

FIGURE 5 ·····································
Stomata
Stomata can slow water loss.

✏️ **Name** What three substances enter and leave a plant through stomata?

_____

_____

 ® Do the Lab Investigation *Investigating Stomata.*

🔑 **Assess Your Understanding**

1a. List What are the functions of a stem?

_____

_____

_____

_____

b. Infer If you forget to water a houseplant for a few days, would its stomata be open or closed? Why?

_____

_____

_____

got it? ···

○ I get it! Now I know that roots, stems, and leaves perform functions like _____

_____

○ I need extra help with _____

Go to MY SCIENCE 💬 COACH *online for help with this subject.*

How Do Seeds Become New Plants?

Many plants begin their life cycle as a seed. You can follow the cycle from seed to plant in **Figure 6.** All seeds share important similarities. 🔑 **Inside a seed is a partially developed plant. If a seed lands in an area where conditions are favorable, the plant sprouts out of the seed and begins to grow.**

Seed Structure A seed has three main parts—an embryo, stored food, and a seed coat. The young plant that develops from the zygote, or fertilized egg, is called the **embryo.** The embryo already has the beginnings of roots, stems, and leaves. In the seeds of most plants, the embryo stops growing when it is quite small. When the embryo begins to grow again, it uses the food stored in the seed until it can make its own food by photosynthesis. In all seeds, the embryo has one or more seed leaves, or cotyledons. In some seeds, food is stored in the cotyledons. In others, food is stored outside the embryo.

The outer covering of a seed is called the seed coat. The seed coat acts like plastic wrap, protecting the embryo and its food from drying out. This allows a seed to remain inactive for a long time. In many plants, the seeds are surrounded by a structure called a fruit.

FIGURE 6 ·······························

▶ INTERACTIVE ART **Story of a Seed**

Read the text on this page and the next page. Then complete the activities about seeds becoming new plants.

✎ **Complete each task.**

1. **Review** On the diagram, label the seed's embryo, cotyledons, and seed coat.

embryo

cotyledon

Stem and root

Stored food

coat

Seed Dispersal

After seeds form, they are usually scattered. The scattering of seeds is called seed dispersal. Seeds can be dispersed in many different ways. When animals eat fruit, the seeds inside the fruit pass through the animal's digestive system and are deposited in new areas. Other seeds are enclosed in barblike structures that hook onto fur or clothing. The seeds fall off in a new area. Water also disperses seeds that fall into oceans and rivers. Wind disperses lightweight seeds, such as those of dandelions and maple trees. Some plants eject their seeds. The force scatters the seeds in many directions. A seed that is dispersed far from its parent plant has a better chance of survival. Far away, a seed does not have to compete with its parent for light, water, and nutrients.

Germination

After a seed is dispersed, it may remain inactive for a while before it germinates. **Germination** (jur muh NAY shun) occurs when the embryo begins to grow again and pushes out of the seed. Germination begins when the seed absorbs water. Then the embryo uses stored food to begin to grow. The roots first grow downward. Then its stem and leaves grow upward.

⊙ Relate Cause and Effect
Underline a cause of seed dispersal and circle its effect in the text on this page.

2. **Explain** Give two reasons why this seed can be successfully dispersed by wind.

_____
_____
_____

B

3. [CHALLENGE] Which young plant, A or B, is more likely to grow into an adult plant? Why?

_____
_____
_____

A

Lab zone® Do the Quick Lab *The In-Seed Story.*

⊶ Assess Your Understanding

got it?

○ **I get it!** Now I know that a seed becomes a new plant when _____
_____

○ **I need extra help with** _____

Go to MY SCIENCE ⑤ COACH online for help with this subject.

What Are the Structures of a Flower?

Flowers come in all sorts of shapes, sizes, and colors. But, despite their differences, all flowers have the same function—reproduction. A **flower** is the reproductive structure of an angiosperm. 🔑 **A typical flower contains sepals, petals, stamens, and pistils.**

The colors and shapes of most flower structures and the scents produced by most flowers attract insects and other animals. These organisms ensure that pollination occurs. **Pollination** is the transfer of pollen from male reproductive structures to female reproductive structures. Pollinators, such as those shown in **Figure 7,** include birds, bats, and insects such as bees and flies. As you read, keep in mind that some flowers lack one or more of the parts. For example, some flowers have only male reproductive parts, and some flowers do not have petals.

Sepals and Petals
When a flower is still a bud, it is enclosed by leaflike structures called **sepals** (SEE pulz). Sepals protect the developing flower and are often green in color. When the sepals fold back, they reveal the flower's colorful, leaflike **petals.** The petals are generally the most colorful parts of a flower. The shapes, sizes, and number of petals vary greatly between flowers.

Stamens
Within the petals are the flower's male and female reproductive parts. The **stamens** (STAY munz) are the male reproductive parts. Locate the stamens inside the flower in **Figure 8.** The thin stalk of the stamen is called the filament. Pollen is made in the anther, at the top of the filament.

FIGURE 7 ·······························

Pollinator Matchup
Some pollinators are well adapted to the plants they pollinate. For example, the long tongue of the nectar bat helps the bat reach inside the agave plant, as shown below.

✎ **Apply Concepts** Write the letter of the pollinator on the plant it is adapted to pollinate.

Pistils The female parts, or **pistils** (PIS tulz), are found in the center of most flowers, as shown in **Figure 8.** Some flowers have two or more pistils; others have only one. The sticky tip of the pistil is called the stigma. A slender tube, called a style, connects the stigma to a hollow structure at the base of the flower. This hollow structure is the **ovary,** which protects the seeds as they develop. An ovary contains one or more ovules.

FIGURE 8 ·····················

> INTERACTIVE ART **Structures of a Typical Flower**
Flowers have many structures.

✎ **Relate Text and Visuals**
Use the word bank to fill in the missing labels.

_____ are the small, leaflike parts of a flower. They protect the developing flower.

_____ are usually the most colorful parts of a flower. Pollinators are attracted by their color and scent.

_____ are the male reproductive parts of a flower. Pollen is produced in the anther, at the top of the stalklike filament.

_____ are the female reproductive parts of a flower. They consist of a sticky stigma, a slender tube called the style, and a hollow structure called the ovary at the base.

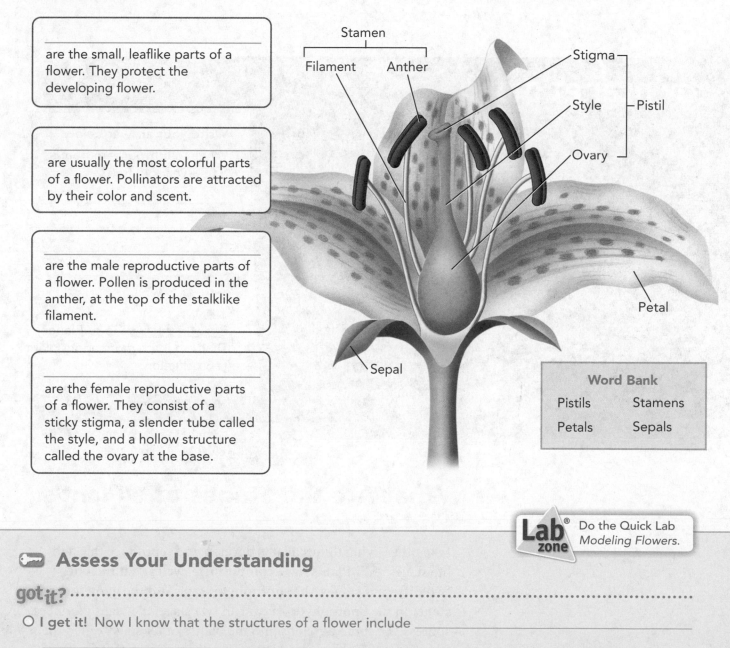

Word Bank

Pistils	Stamens
Petals	Sepals

Do the Quick Lab
Modeling Flowers.

🖝 **Assess Your Understanding**

got it? ···

○ **I get it!** Now I know that the structures of a flower include _____

_____

○ **I need extra help with** _____

Go to my science ⓢ coach *online for help with this subject.*

Plant Reproduction

UNLOCK
THE BIG
?

🔑 **What Are the Stages of a Plant Life Cycle?**

🔑 **How Do Plants Reproduce?**

MY PLANET DIARY

FUN FACT

If Trees Could Talk

Suppose you had been alive during the ancient Egyptian Empire, the Middle Ages, the American Revolution, and both World Wars. Think of the stories you could tell! Bristlecone pine trees can be this old. In 1964, a student got permission to cut down one of these trees. He counted the tree rings to see how old the tree was, and discovered it was 4,900 years old. He had just cut down the oldest living thing in the world! Today, Bristlecone pine forests are protected.

Write your answer below.
What could you learn from a 5,000-year-old tree?

_____

_____

_____

_____

_____

> PLANET DIARY   Go to **Planet Diary** to learn more about plant reproduction.

Lab zone®   Do the Inquiry Warm-Up
Make the Pollen Stick.

What Are the Stages of a Plant's Life Cycle?

Like other living things, plants develop and reproduce through life stages. 🔑 **Plants have complex life cycles that include two different stages, the sporophyte stage and the gametophyte stage.** In the **sporophyte** (SPOH ruh fyt) stage, the plant produces spores. The spore develops into the plant's other stage, called the gametophyte. In the **gametophyte** (guh MEE tuh fyt) stage, the plant produces two kinds of sex cells: sperm cells and egg cells. See **Figure 1.**

Vocabulary

- sporophyte • gametophyte • annual • biennial
- perennial • fertilization • zygote • cone
- ovule • fruit

Skills

↻ Reading: Summarize
△ Inquiry: Infer

FIGURE 1 ·······························

Plant Life Cycle

All plants go through two stages in their life cycle.

✎ **Interpret Diagrams** Label the sporophyte and gametophyte stages.

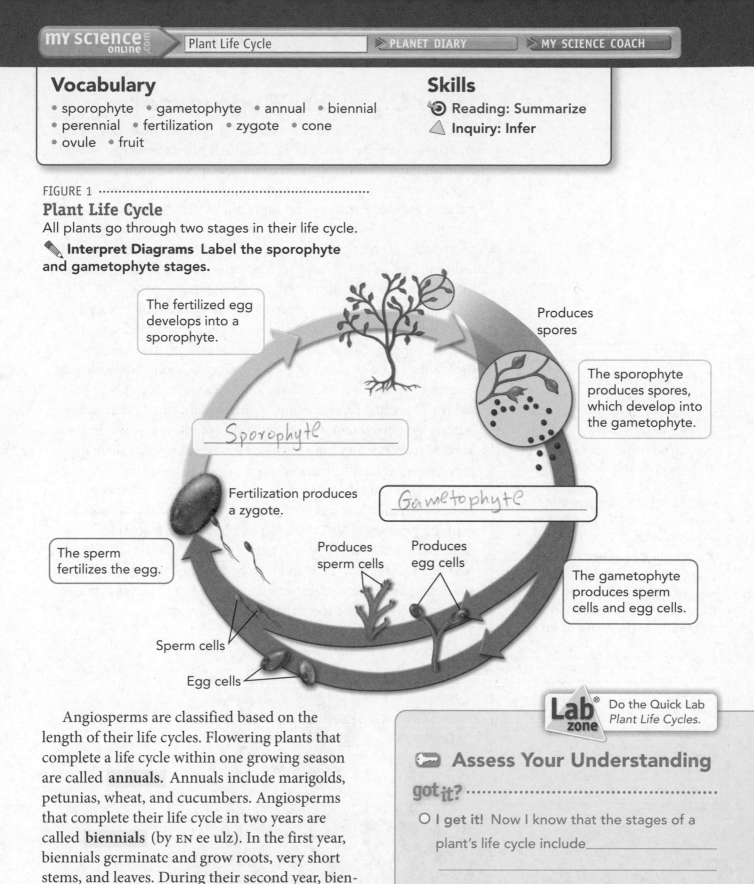

The fertilized egg develops into a sporophyte.

Produces spores

The sporophyte produces spores, which develop into the gametophyte.

Sporophyte

Fertilization produces a zygote.

Gametophyte

The sperm fertilizes the egg.

Produces sperm cells

Produces egg cells

The gametophyte produces sperm cells and egg cells.

Sperm cells

Egg cells

Angiosperms are classified based on the length of their life cycles. Flowering plants that complete a life cycle within one growing season are called **annuals.** Annuals include marigolds, petunias, wheat, and cucumbers. Angiosperms that complete their life cycle in two years are called **biennials** (by EN ee ulz). In the first year, biennials germinate and grow roots, very short stems, and leaves. During their second year, biennials lengthen their stems, grow new leaves, and then produce flowers and seeds. Parsley, celery, and foxglove are biennials. Flowering plants that live for more than two years are called **perennials.** Most perennials flower every year.

Lab zone ® Do the Quick Lab *Plant Life Cycles.*

⬚ Assess Your Understanding

got it? ·····························

○ **I get it!** Now I know that the stages of a plant's life cycle include_____

_____

_____

○ **I need extra help with** _____

_____

Go to my science ⑤ coach *online for help with this subject.*

How Do Plants Reproduce?

Plants reproduce in different ways depending on their structures and the environment they live in. 🔑 **All plants undergo sexual reproduction that involves fertilization.** Fertilization occurs when a sperm cell unites with an egg cell. The fertilized egg is called a **zygote.** For algae and some plants, fertilization can only occur if there is water in the environment. This is because the sperm cells of these plants swim through the water to the egg cells. Other plants, however, have an adaptation that makes it possible for fertilization to occur in dry environments.

Many plants can also undergo asexual reproduction. Recall that asexual reproduction includes only one parent and produces offspring that are identical to the parent. New plants can grow from the roots, leaves, or stems of a parent plant. Asexual reproduction does not involve flowers, pollination, or seeds, so it can happen faster than sexual reproduction. A single plant can quickly spread out in an environment if there are good conditions. However, asexual reproduction can reproduce unfavorable traits since there is no new genetic information being passed to offspring.

Scientists can take advantage of asexual reproduction in plants. A single plant can be used to create identical plants for experiments. Scientists can also copy plants with favorable characteristics. Grafting is one way of copying plants. In grafting, part of a plant's stem is cut and attached to another related plant species, such as a lemon tree and an orange tree. The plant matures and can then produce more than one kind of fruit.

FIGURE 2 ·································

Eyes on Potatoes

Did you know that a potato is actually the underground stem of the potato plant? If you have ever left a potato out long enough, you may have noticed it beginning to sprout. A potato can grow new potato plants from buds called eyes, as seen in this photo.

✏️ **Apply Concepts** Potato plants also produce flowers and reproduce sexually. How does being able to reproduce asexually benefit the plant?

_____

_____

_____

_____

_____

_____

_____

apply it!

A citrus farmer was able to graft a lemon tree branch onto an orange tree. Now the same tree produces lemons and oranges! The farmer plans to use branches from the same lemon trees to create other combined fruit trees.

1 Review The farmer used the lemon tree's ability to (sexually/asexually) reproduce.

2 Infer Name at least one negative effect of using the same lemon tree to create new trees the farmer should know about.

_____

_____

3 CHALLENGE Why might the public be opposed to using this method to create new fruit trees?

_____

_____

Nonvascular and Seedless Vascular Plants

Mosses, liverworts, hornworts, ferns, club mosses, and horsetails need to grow in moist environments. This is because the plants release spores into their surroundings, where they grow into gametophytes. When the gametophytes produce egg cells and sperm cells, there must be enough water available for the sperm to swim toward the eggs.

For example, the familiar fern, with its visible fronds, is the sporophyte stage of the plant. On the underside of mature fronds, spores develop in tiny spore cases. Wind and water can carry the spores great distances. If a spore lands in moist, shaded soil, it develops into a gametophyte. Fern gametophytes are tiny plants that grow low to the ground.

Spore cases on the fronds of a fern

Gymnosperms You can follow the process of gymnosperm reproduction in **Figure 3.**

1 Cone Production

Most gymnosperms have reproductive structures called **cones.** Cones are covered with scales. Most gymnosperms produce two types of cones: male cones and female cones. Usually, a single plant produces both male and female cones. In some types of gymnosperms, however, individual trees produce either male cones or female cones. A few gymnosperms produce no cones.

2 Pollen Production and Ovule Development

(A) Male cones produce pollen grains. Cells in the pollen will mature into sperm cells. (B) The female gametophyte develops in structures called ovules. An **ovule** (OH vyool) is a structure that contains an egg cell. Female cones contain at least one ovule at the base of each scale. The ovule later develops into the seed.

3 Egg Production

Two egg cells form inside each ovule on the female cone.

4 Pollination

The transfer of pollen from a male reproductive structure to a female reproductive structure is called pollination. In gymnosperms, wind often carries the pollen from the male cones to the female cones. The pollen collect in a sticky substance produced by each ovule.

5 Fertilization

Once pollination has occurred, the ovule closes and seals in the pollen. The scales also close, and a sperm cell fertilizes an egg cell inside each ovule. The zygote then develops into the embryo part of the seed.

6 Seed Development

Female cones remain on the tree while the seeds mature. As the seeds develop, the female cone increases in size. It can take up to two years for the seeds of some gymnosperms to mature. Male cones, however, usually fall off the tree after they have shed their pollen.

7 Seed Dispersal

When the seeds are mature, the scales open. The wind shakes the seeds out of the cone and carries them away. Only a few seeds will land in suitable places and grow into new plants.

FIGURE 3 ·······················

Gymnosperm Reproduction Cycle

The reproduction cycle of a gymnosperm is shown at right.

 Complete each task.

1. **Identify** Underline the sentence(s) on this page that use the vocabulary terms *cone* and *ovule*.

2. **Describe** What is the relationship between cones and ovules?

_____

_____

_____

_____

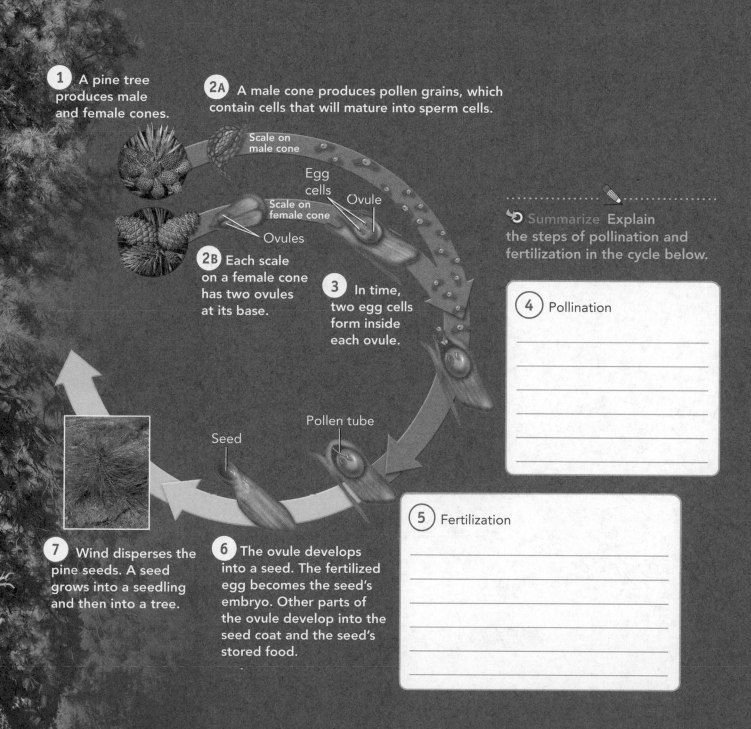

1 A pine tree produces male and female cones.

2A A male cone produces pollen grains, which contain cells that will mature into sperm cells.

Scale on male cone

Egg cells

Ovule

Scale on female cone

Ovules

2B Each scale on a female cone has two ovules at its base.

3 In time, two egg cells form inside each ovule.

Pollen tube

Seed

7 Wind disperses the pine seeds. A seed grows into a seedling and then into a tree.

6 The ovule develops into a seed. The fertilized egg becomes the seed's embryo. Other parts of the ovule develop into the seed coat and the seed's stored food.

↺ Summarize **Explain** the steps of pollination and fertilization in the cycle below.

4 Pollination

_____
_____
_____
_____
_____

5 Fertilization

_____
_____
_____
_____
_____
_____

FIGURE 4 ·······························

Angiosperm Reproduction

Reproduction in angiosperms begins with flowers.

✎ **Relate Text and Visuals**
Look back at the plant life and gymnosperm reproduction cycles in this lesson. What do the yellow and purple colors of the arrows represent?

_____

_____

_____

_____

Angiosperms

You can follow angiosperm reproduction in **Figure 4.** First, pollen fall on a flower's stigma. In time, the sperm cell and egg cell join together in the flower's ovule. The zygote develops into the embryo part of the seed.

Pollination A flower is pollinated when a grain of pollen falls on the stigma. Some angiosperms are pollinated by the wind, but most rely on other organisms. When an organism enters a flower to obtain food, it becomes coated with pollen. Some of the pollen can drop onto the flower's stigma as the animal leaves. The pollen can also be brushed onto the stigma of the next flower the animal visits.

Fertilization If the pollen fall on the stigma of a similar plant, fertilization can occur. A sperm cell joins with an egg cell inside an ovule within the ovary at the base of the flower. The zygote then begins to develop into the seed's embryo. Other parts of the ovule develop into the rest of the seed.

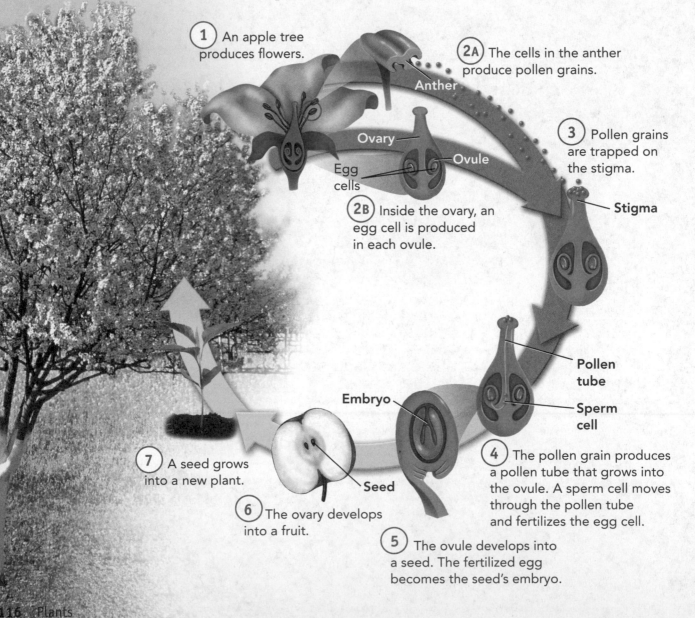

1 An apple tree produces flowers.

2A The cells in the anther produce pollen grains.

Anther

Ovary

Ovule

Egg cells

2B Inside the ovary, an egg cell is produced in each ovule.

3 Pollen grains are trapped on the stigma.

Stigma

Pollen tube

Sperm cell

4 The pollen grain produces a pollen tube that grows into the ovule. A sperm cell moves through the pollen tube and fertilizes the egg cell.

Embryo

Seed

5 The ovule develops into a seed. The fertilized egg becomes the seed's embryo.

6 The ovary develops into a fruit.

7 A seed grows into a new plant.

Fruit Development and Seed Dispersal As the seed develops, the ovary changes into a **fruit.** A fruit is the ripened ovary and other structures that enclose one or more seeds. Fruits include apples, cherries, tomatoes, squash, and many others. Fruits are the means by which angiosperm seeds are dispersed. Animals that eat fruits help to disperse their seeds by depositing them in new areas.

FIGURE 5 ·······

Flower to Fruit

Flowers eventually develop into fruit.

✎ **Sequence** Write the numbers 1 through 4 in the blank circles to show the progression from flower to fruit.

Lab zone Do the Quick Lab *Where Are the Seeds?*

🔑 Assess Your Understanding

1a. Review (Fertilization/Asexual reproduction) occurs when a sperm cell unites with an egg cell.

b. Explain Why do plants like liverworts need to live in moist environments?

So the sperm cells have enough water to swim to the eggs.

c. Relate Cause and Effect Underline the cause and circle the effect in the sentences below.

Pollination can occur when pollen on an insect is dropped onto the stigma.

Animals eating fruit is one way seeds are dispersed.

got it? ·······

○ **I get it!** Now I know that all of the major plant groups reproduce _____

○ **I need extra help with** _____

Go to **MY SCIENCE COACH** online for help with this subject.

Plant Responses and Growth

🔑 **What Are Three Stimuli That Produce Plant Responses?**

🔑 **How Do Plants Respond to Seasonal Changes?**

my planet diary

DISCOVERY

Flower Power

What makes a plant flower? Plants detect the amount of light each day. When there is just enough light, the plant sends a signal to the flower. But what is this signal? For almost 80 years, the answer remained a mystery. In 2008, scientists discovered the protein that was responsible. They linked the protein they thought controlled flowering to a fluorescent, or glowing, protein they obtained from a jellyfish. Then they watched the bright green protein travel with the flowering protein through the stem to make the plant bloom. Why does this experiment matter?

Global climate change is starting to hurt crops. Some places near the equator are becoming too warm to farm. Areas closer to Earth's poles may be needed to grow more crops as they warm. These areas, however, do not get as much sunlight. Scientists could use the flowering protein to encourage plants to flower without direct sunlight.

The green you see in these plant cells is from a fluorescent protein like the one used in the flowering experiment.

Communicate Discuss the question with a group of classmates. Then write your answer below.

In addition to getting the plants to flower with no light, what other challenges might scientists have to overcome when trying to get plants to succeed in a new area?

_____

_____

_____

_____

_____

▶ **PLANET DIARY** Go to **Planet Diary** to learn more about plant responses and growth.

 Do the Inquiry Warm-Up *Can a Plant Respond to Touch?*

Vocabulary

- tropism • hormone • auxin • photoperiodism
- critical night length • short-day plant • long-day plant
- day-neutral plant • dormancy

Skills

- Reading: Relate Text and Visuals
- Inquiry: Draw Conclusions

What Are Three Stimuli That Produce Plant Responses?

You may be one of those people who close their window shades at night because the morning light wakes you up. People respond to many stimuli each day. Did you know plants also respond to some of the same stimuli, including light?

Tropisms Animals usually respond to stimuli by moving. Unlike animals, plants usually respond by growing either toward or away from a stimulus. A plant's growth response toward or away from a stimulus is called a **tropism** (TROH piz um). If a plant grows toward the stimulus, it is said to show a positive tropism. If a plant grows away from a stimulus, it shows a negative tropism. 🔑 **Touch, gravity, and light are three important stimuli that trigger growth responses, or tropisms, in plants.**

Touch

Some plants show a response to touch called thigmotropism. The prefix *thigmo-* comes from a Greek word that means "touch." The stems of many vines, such as morning glories, sweet peas, and grapes, show a positive thigmotropism. As the vines grow, they coil around any object they touch.

FIGURE 1 ·················

Plant Responses to Stimuli

The stimuli in space are not always the same as those on Earth.

✎ **Develop Hypotheses** How might the roots of a plant grow in space without the influence of gravity?

_____

_____

_____

_____

Gravity

Plants can respond to gravity. This response is called gravitropism. Roots show positive gravitropism if they grow downward. Stems, on the other hand, show negative gravitropism. Stems grow upward against gravity.

119

⊙ **Relate Text and Visuals** Use what you have read to label the side of the plant with more auxin and the side with less auxin.

more auxin   less auxin

Light

All plants exhibit a response to light called phototropism. The leaves, stems, and flowers of plants grow toward light. This shows a positive phototropism. A plant receives more energy for photosynthesis by growing toward the light.

Plants are able to respond to stimuli because they produce hormones. A **hormone** produced by a plant is a chemical that affects how the plant grows and develops. One important plant hormone is named **auxin** (AWK sin). Auxin speeds up the rate at which a plant's cells grow and controls a plant's response to light. When light shines on one side of a plant's stem, auxin builds up in the shaded side of the stem. The cells on the shaded side begin to grow faster. The cells on the stem's shaded side are longer than those on its sunny side. The stem bends toward the light.

Lab **zone** Do the Quick Lab
Watching Roots Grow.

⚷ Assess Your Understanding

1a. Define What is a tropism?

_____

_____

_____

_____

b. Predict What do you think would happen if a plant did not create enough of the hormone that controlled flower formation?

_____

_____

_____

got it? ....

○ **I get it!** Now I know that plants respond to _____

_____

○ **I need extra help with** _____

Go to **MY SCIENCE** ⓢ **COACH** *online for help with this subject.*

How Do Plants Respond to Seasonal Changes?

People have long observed that plants respond to the changing seasons. Some plants bloom in early spring, while others don't bloom until summer. The leaves on some trees change color in autumn and then fall off by winter.

Photoperiodism What triggers a plant to flower? 🔑 **The amount of darkness a plant receives determines the time of flowering in many plants.** A plant's response to seasonal changes in the length of night and day is called **photoperiodism.**

Plants respond differently to the length of nights. Some plants will only bloom when the nights last a certain length of time. This length, called the **critical night length,** is the number of hours of darkness that determines whether or not a plant will flower. For example, if a plant has a critical night length of 11 hours, it will flower only when nights are longer than 11 hours. You can read more on how different plants respond to night length in **Figure 2.**

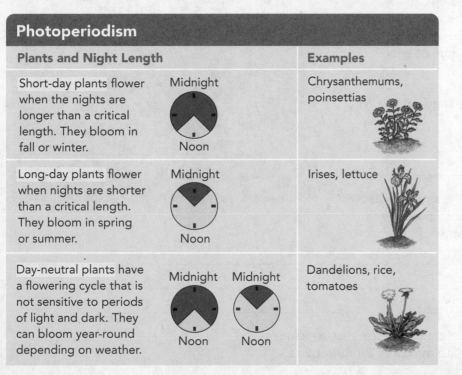

Photoperiodism

Plants and Night Length		Examples
Short-day plants flower when the nights are longer than a critical length. They bloom in fall or winter.	Midnight / Noon	Chrysanthemums, poinsettias
Long-day plants flower when nights are shorter than a critical length. They bloom in spring or summer.	Midnight / Noon	Irises, lettuce
Day-neutral plants have a flowering cycle that is not sensitive to periods of light and dark. They can bloom year-round depending on weather.	Midnight / Noon Midnight / Noon	Dandelions, rice, tomatoes

FIGURE 2 ·······················

Photoperiodism

Flowering plants can be grouped as short-day plants, long-day plants, and day-neutral plants.

✏️ **Infer** Suppose you are a farmer in a climate that supports plant growth all year-round but night length varies. Based on the categories in the chart, would you plant mostly one type of plant or a mixture of all three? Explain.

_____

_____

_____

_____

_____

Winter Dormancy Some plants prepare differently than others for certain seasons. As winter draws near, many plants prepare to go into a state of **dormancy.** Dormancy is a period when an organism's growth or activity stops. 🔑 **Dormancy helps plants survive freezing temperatures and the lack of liquid water.**

With many trees, the first visible change is that the leaves begin to turn color. Cooler weather and shorter days cause the leaves to stop making chlorophyll. As chlorophyll breaks down, yellow and orange pigments become visible. In addition, the plant begins to produce new red pigments. This causes the brilliant colors of autumn leaves. Over the next few weeks, sugar and water are transported out of the tree's leaves. When the leaves fall to the ground, the tree is ready for winter.

apply it!

One hundred radish seeds were planted in two identical trays of soil. One tray was kept at 10°C. The other tray was kept at 20°C. The trays received equal amounts of sun and water. The graph shows how many seeds germinated over time at each temperature.

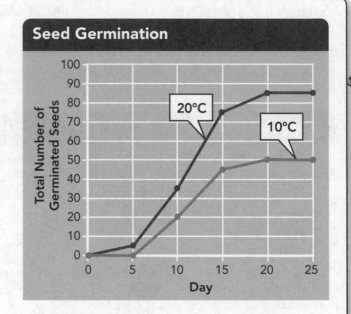

Seed Germination

❶ **Read Graphs** About how many seeds in the 20°C tray germinated on Day 13?

_____

_____

❷ **Draw Conclusions** Based on the graph, what can you conclude about the relationship between the two temperatures and germination?

_____

_____

_____

❸ [CHALLENGE] After the experiment, a fellow scientist concludes that more seeds will *always* germinate at higher temperatures. Is the scientist right? Why?

_____

_____

_____

_____

Roving for Life in Space

How do you know a plant when you see it?

FIGURE 3 ···

▶ ART IN MOTION You are a scientist researching distant planets. You have sent a rover to collect samples from one of the planets and you get some exciting results. The rover has found three living things, and one of them is a plant! But, on the way back to Earth, the rover has a rough landing and the samples get mixed up. You run some tests in your lab to find which sample is the plant. The results are shown below.

✏️ Circle the sample that is a plant. Then answer the question below.

Lab Findings on Rover Life-Form Samples

	Sample 1	Sample 2	Sample 3
Reproduces sexually	Yes	Yes	No
Cells have cell walls	No	Yes	Yes
Contains vascular tissue	Yes	No	No
Multicellular	Yes	Yes	Yes
Autotroph	No	Yes	No
Responds to light	Yes	Yes	No

Choose one of the samples you did not circle. Why is this sample not a plant?

_____

_____

_____

_____

 Do the Quick Lab Seasonal Changes.

🔑 Assess Your Understanding

2a. Review (Short-day/Long-day) plants flower when nights are shorter than a critical length.

b. Explain Why do the leaves of some trees change color in autumn?

_____

_____

c. ANSWER THE BIG ❓ How do you know a plant when you see it?

_____

_____

_____

_____

got it? ···

○ **I get it!** Now I know that plants respond to seasonal changes because_____

_____

○ **I need extra help with** _____

Go to MY SCIENCE Ⓢ COACH online for help with this subject.

Plants in Everyday Life

 UNLOCK THE BIG ?

🔑 **How Are Plants Important to Everyday Life?**

MY PLANET DiARY

BLOG

Posted by: George

Location: Tacoma, Washington

I never really thought much about how important trees are until my dad and I planted a plum tree in our yard. I've watched it grow over the last couple of years. The first year we didn't get any plums. The next year, we had tons of plums and they were good! This made me think more about all that we get from plants —food to eat, wood to build houses, and cotton to make clothes!

Communicate Discuss the question with a group of classmates. Then write your answer below.

Describe a plant that is important to your everyday life.

_____

_____

_____

_____

_____

▶ PLANET DIARY Go to **Planet Diary** to learn more about plants in everyday life.

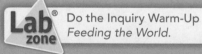 Lab zone® Do the Inquiry Warm-Up *Feeding the World.*

Vocabulary
• peat

Skills
↻ Reading: Identify the Main Idea
△ Inquiry: Pose Questions

How Are Plants Important to Everyday Life?

What did you have for breakfast today? Cereal? Toast? Orange juice? Chances are you have already eaten something today that came from plants. Besides providing food, plants play many roles on Earth. ⚷ **In addition to food, plants provide habitats. Plants can clean the water and protect the soil in an environment. Plants are also the base of many products important to human life, such as medicines, paper, and clothing.**

The Role of Plants in an Ecosystem Plants play many roles in an ecosystem. You can see some of these roles in **Figure 1.** Recall that an ecosystem contains living things and the nonliving surroundings. People are included in ecosystems too!

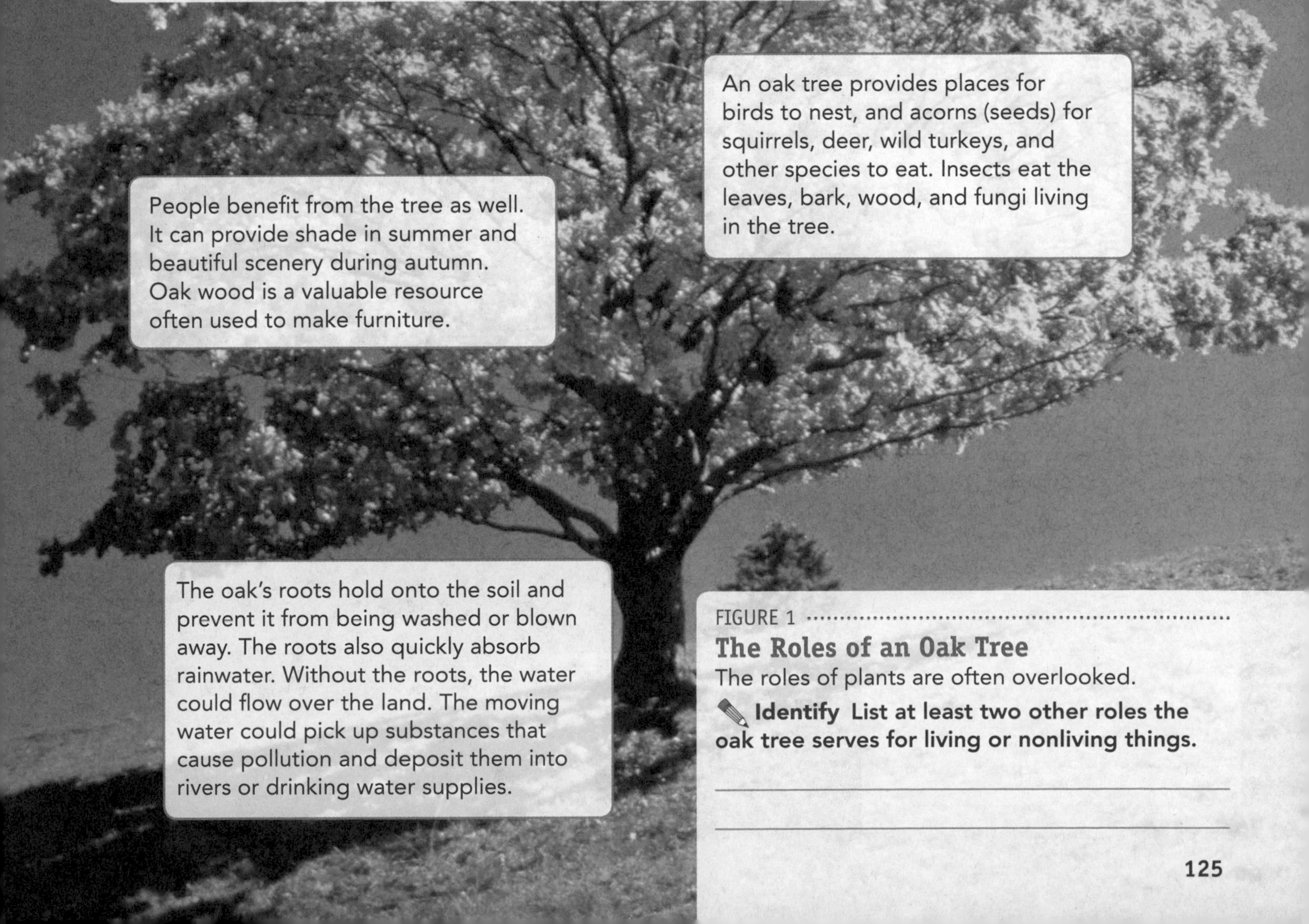

An oak tree provides places for birds to nest, and acorns (seeds) for squirrels, deer, wild turkeys, and other species to eat. Insects eat the leaves, bark, wood, and fungi living in the tree.

People benefit from the tree as well. It can provide shade in summer and beautiful scenery during autumn. Oak wood is a valuable resource often used to make furniture.

The oak's roots hold onto the soil and prevent it from being washed or blown away. The roots also quickly absorb rainwater. Without the roots, the water could flow over the land. The moving water could pick up substances that cause pollution and deposit them into rivers or drinking water supplies.

FIGURE 1 ································
The Roles of an Oak Tree
The roles of plants are often overlooked.

✎ **Identify** List at least two other roles the oak tree serves for living or nonliving things.

_____

_____

125

apply it!

You are at a grocery store buying cleaning products to clean your bathroom. You can choose a cleaner made from chemicals made in a lab or one made from plant-derived chemicals.

1 Pose Questions What questions should you ask before making your decision?

_____

_____

_____

_____

_____

_____

_____

2 CHALLENGE What could be some disadvantages of the plant-based cleaner?

_____

_____

_____

_____

_____

_____

How People Use Plants People have found ways to directly use almost all plants. Green algae is often used in scientific research and as a thickening agent in some foods. Liverworts, club mosses, and other plants are used in parts of the world to treat conditions from fevers to itchy skin.

Many people use moss in agriculture and gardening. The moss that gardeners use contains sphagnum (SFAG num) moss. Sphagnum moss grows in a type of wetland called a bog. The still water in a bog is so acidic that decomposers cannot live in the water. When the plants die, they do not decay. Instead, the dead plants accumulate at the bottom of the bog. Over time, the mosses become compressed into layers and form a blackish-brown material called **peat.** In some parts of Europe and Asia, people use peat as a fuel to heat homes and to cook food.

Peat drying after being extracted from a bog

Gymnosperms provide many useful products. Paper and the lumber used to build homes come from conifers. The rayon fibers in clothes as well as the cellophane wrappers on some food also come from conifers. Turpentine and the rosin used by baseball pitchers, gymnasts, and musicians are made from conifer sap.

Angiosperms are an important source of food, clothing, and medicine. People eat a variety of vegetables, fruits, and cereals, all of which are angiosperms. The seeds of cotton plants are covered with cotton fibers. The stems of flax plants provide linen fibers. The sap of rubber trees is used to make rubber for tires and other products. Furniture is often made from the wood of maple, cherry, and oak trees. Some important medications come from angiosperms, too. For example, the heart medication digitalis comes from the leaves of the foxglove plant.

FIGURE 2 ···

Plants in Your Life

You may not have realized how many things, like clothes and sports equipment, are made of plants!

✎ **Name** List at least five things in your everyday life that come from plants.

_____

_____

_____

_____

 Labzone® Do the Quick Lab *Everyday Plants.*

🗝 Assess Your Understanding

1a. List Give two uses of moss.

_____

b. Describe Why is conifer sap important?

_____

_____

_____

c. Make Judgments Should governments spend more money on plant research than they currently do? Why?

_____

_____

_____

_____

got it? ···

○ **I get it!** Now I know that plants provide many useful things, such as _____

_____

○ **I need extra help with** _____

Go to **MY SCIENCE COACH** online for help with this subject.

3 Study Guide

Nearly all plants have cells surrounded by _____, are _____ that photosynthesize, and are made of many cells.

LESSON 1 What Is a Plant?

🔑 Nearly all plants are autotrophs and contain many cells surrounded by cell walls.

🔑 For plants to survive on land, they must have ways to obtain water and nutrients, retain water, support their bodies, transport materials and reproduce.

Vocabulary
• chlorophyll
• photosynthesis • tissue
• chloroplast • vacuole
• cuticle • vascular tissue

LESSON 2 Classifying Plants

🔑 Nonvascular plants are low-growing, have thin cell walls, and do not have roots.

🔑 Seedless vascular plants have vascular tissue and produce spores.

🔑 Seed plants have vascular tissue and seeds.

Vocabulary
• nonvascular plant • rhizoid • vascular plant
• phloem • xylem • frond • pollen • seed
• gymnosperm • angiosperm
• cotyledon • monocot • dicot

LESSON 3 Plant Structures

🔑 A plant's roots, stems, and leaves anchor the plant, absorb water and minerals, capture the sun's energy, and make food.

🔑 A seed contains a partially developed plant.

🔑 A typical flower contains sepals, petals, stamens, and pistils.

Vocabulary
• root cap • cambium • stoma • transpiration
• embryo • germination • flower • pollination
• sepal • petal • stamen • pistil • ovary

LESSON 4 Plant Reproduction

🔑 Plants have complex life cycles that include a sporophyte stage and a gametophyte stage.

🔑 All plants undergo sexual reproduction that involves fertilization.

Vocabulary
• sporophyte • gametophyte • annual • biennial
• perennial • fertilization • zygote • cone
• ovule • fruit

LESSON 5 Plant Responses and Growth

🔑 Plants show growth responses, or tropisms, toward touch, gravity, and light.

🔑 The amount of darkness a plant receives determines the time of flowering in many plants. Dormancy helps plants survive winter.

Vocabulary
• tropism • hormone • auxin • photoperiodism
• critical night length • short-day plant
• long-day plant • day-neutral plant • dormancy

LESSON 6 Plants in Everyday Life

🔑 In addition to food, plants provide habitats, clean water, and protect soil. Plants are also the base of many products, including medicine, paper, and clothing.

Vocabulary
• peat

Review and Assessment

LESSON 1 What Is a Plant?

1. In which cellular structure do plants store water and other substances?

- **a.** cuticle
- **b.** vacuole ⃝
- **c.** cell wall
- **d.** chloroplast

2. The pigment _chloroplast_ is found in chloroplasts.

3. Make Generalizations Complete the table below to describe plant adaptions for life on land.

Structure	Function
Roots	Helps obtain water and nutrients
Cuticle	reduces a plant's water loss
Vascular tissue	where water, minerals, and food move

LESSON 2 Classifying Plants

4. Which of the following are seedless vascular plants?

- **a.** ferns ⃝
- **b.** liverworts
- **c.** gymnosperms
- **d.** angiosperms

5. Nonvascular plants have rootlike structures called _rhizoids_

6. Compare and Contrast How are gymnosperms and angiosperms alike and different?

Gymnospers and angiosperms produce flowers. Angiosperms produces enclosed seeds. Gymnospers produce naked seeds.

— have vascular tissues
— have seeds and pollen

LESSON 3 Plant Structures

7. A plant absorbs water and minerals through

- **a.** roots. ⃝
- **b.** stems.
- **c.** leaves.
- **d.** stomata.

8. Transpiration slows down when _stomata_ are closed.

9. Relate Cause and Effect When a strip of bark is removed all the way around the trunk of a tree, the tree dies. Explain why.

Bark protects the tree and transports food through the stem.

10. **Write About It** Plant structures do not look the same among all plants. For example, some leaves are short and others long. Explain why you think there is so much variation.

LESSON 4 Plant Reproduction

11. A zygote is the direct result of

- **a.** pollination.
- **b.** fertilization. ⃝
- **c.** biennial growth.
- **d.** the sporophyte stage.

12. _annuals_ complete their life cycles within one growing season.

13. Sequence Describe the major events in the plant life cycle. Use the terms _zygote_, _sperm_, _sporophyte_, _spores_, _gametophyte_, and _egg_.

The sperm fertilizes the egg. Fertilization produces the zygote. Fertilized egg develops into a sporophyte. Produces spores. Sporopyte produces spores, which develop into the gametophyte. Gametophyte produces sperm cells and egg cells.

LESSON 5 Plant Responses and Growth

14. A plant's response to gravity is an example of a

    a. dormancy.   **b.** hormone.

    (c.) tropism.   **d.** critical night length.

15. The plant hormone ___auxin___ affects the rate of cell growth.

16. Predict A particular short-day plant has a critical night length of 15 hours. Fill in the chart below to predict when this plant would flower.

Day Length	Night Length	Will It Flower?
9 h	15 h	Yes
10 h	14 h	No
7.5 h	16.5 h	Yes

17. Develop Hypotheses Suppose climate change alters the environment of an oak tree from one with cold and snowy winters to one with warmer winters. Will the tree still go into a state of dormancy? Explain.

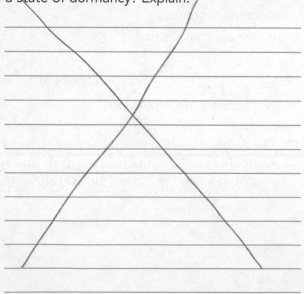

LESSON 6 Plants in Everyday Life

18. Which of the following is *not* a way that people use plants?

    a. for food   **b.** for clothing

    c. for medicines   **(d.)** for metal extracts

19. Over time, mosses may compact into ___peat___

20. Make Judgments Should the government put as much effort into protecting plants as they do animals? Why or why not?

Yes, because without plants, a lot of animals will lose their habitat and die. We also need plants to make furniture.

How do you know a plant when you see it?

21. Plants are all around us. Describe a plant that you see often and then explain what makes it a plant.

Standardized Test Prep

Multiple Choice

Circle the letter of the best answer.

1. The diagram below shows the parts of a flower. In which flower part does pollination take place?

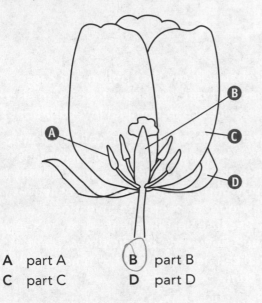

    A part A   **B** part B
    C part C   D part D

2. You examine plant cells under a microscope and notice many round, green structures within the cells. The structures are most likely

    A tissues.   B vacuoles.
    C cell walls.   **D** chloroplasts.

3. Most gymnosperms produce _____, while most angiosperms produce _____.

    A sperm, eggs   B pollen, cones
    C cones, flowers   D flowers, fruits

4. What kind of tropism do roots display when they grow downward into the soil?

    A gravitropism   B phototropism
    C thigmotropism   D photoperiodism

5. The vegetables, fruits, and cereals that people eat all come from

    A peat.   **B** angiosperms.
    C moss.   D nonvascular plants.

Constructed Response

Use the diagrams below to help you answer Question 6. Write your answer on a separate piece of paper.

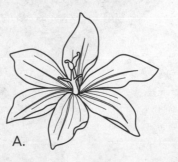
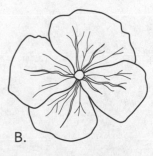

A.   B.

6. Which of the plants above is a monocot? Which is a dicot? Explain your answers.

A is a monocot because it has one seed leaf. B is a dicot because it has two seed leafs.

131

GRAINS OF EVIDENCE

You probably know that pollen can cause allergies, but did you know that it can also be used as evidence in criminal investigations?

A growing field of research, called forensic botany, is helping investigators use plant evidence to solve crimes. Forensic botany is the study of plant material, such as leaves, pollen, wood, or seeds, to investigate a crime. Because certain plants grow in specific areas and flower at specific times, plant material can help identify the time or place that a crime occurred.

Seeds or pollen found on a suspect's clothing can be used to link a suspect to a crime scene. Botanical evidence can also be found in a victim's stomach. Because certain plant parts cannot be digested, forensic botanists can even determine a victim's last meal!

Write About It Find out more about the life cycle of a plant described in this chapter. Draw a life cycle for the plant. Then describe how investigators could use knowledge of the plant's life cycle to solve a crime.

◀ Back in 1997 in New Zealand, pollen grains such as this one were used as the evidence to prove that a suspect was involved in a struggle at the crime scene.

PLANTING
ROOTS IN OUTER
SPACE

Far from farms and greenhouses on Earth, future space explorers will need to grow their own food, and recycle and purify their air and water. Astronauts from the National Aeronautics and Space Administration (NASA) have been experimenting with plants in space for many years.

Which Way Is Up?

On Earth, plant roots grow downward and outward in response to Earth's gravity, while plant shoots grow upward. In space, where there is no clear up or down, roots and shoots both grow toward the light! In order to grow with the roots at the bottom and the stems at the top, plants need gravity. So space stations need special plant chambers that rotate continuously to create artificial gravity for plants.

Tomatoes From Outer Space

To study whether radiation in space will affect the ability of seeds to grow, NASA scientists placed 12.5 million tomato seeds in a satellite that orbited Earth for six years! Students around the world then planted the seeds, which grew normally and produced normal tomatoes. So scientists now know that seeds will survive for a long time in orbit.

Design It Scientists are still learning about how to grow plants to support space travel. Find out about current NASA research on plants in space. Identify one question you have about plant growth in space. Then write a proposal for an experiment to investigate your question.

A researcher holds tiny *Arabidopsis* seedlings. *Arabidopsis* plants are related to the cabbage plant, and are often used as model plants in research projects.

HOW ARE THESE TWO LIVING THINGS DIFFERENT?

How do you know an animal when you see it?

These living things look alike and are both green. Each needs water and energy to grow. Yet one makes food, and the other has to find food.

⚠ Infer **What is different about these living things?**

_____

_____

_____

_____

_____

_____

_____

_____

▶ UNTAMED SCIENCE Watch the **Untamed Science** video to learn more about animals.

Introduction to Animals

4 Getting Started

Check Your Understanding

1. **Background** Read the paragraph below and then answer the question.

Mei's birthday present is a bird. She knows that to **survive,** an **organism** needs food, water, and oxygen. So at home she chooses a stable **environment** in a warm place, away from drafts. Here, she sets up a cage with dishes for food and paper for waste removal. Under Mei's care, her bird will have what it needs to live and grow.

> To **survive** is to manage to stay alive, especially in difficult situations.
>
> An **organism** is a living thing.
>
> An **environment** is all the surrounding factors that affect the organism's life.

• What does an organism need to survive?

_____

_____

> MY READING WEB If you had trouble completing the question above, visit **My Reading Web** and type in *Introduction to Animals.*

Vocabulary Skill

Prefixes A prefix is a word part that is added to the beginning of a word to change its meaning. The table below lists prefixes that will help you learn terms used in this chapter.

Prefix	Meaning of Prefix	Example
endo-	inner	endoskeleton, *n.* internal skeleton
exo-	outer	exoskeleton, *n.* outer skeleton

2. **Quick Check** Complete the following sentence with the correct terms from the table above.

• The _____ of a crab, which is a tough outer shell,

differs from the _____ of a cat, which is internal.

vertebrate

bilateral symmetry

mollusk

endotherm

Chapter Preview

LESSON 1
- homeostasis • adaptation
- vertebrate • invertebrate
- ↻ Relate Text and Visuals
- △ Classify

LESSON 2
- tissue • organ • radial symmetry
- bilateral symmetry
- ↻ Relate Cause and Effect
- △ Make Models

LESSON 3
- cnidarian • mollusk
- arthropod • exoskeleton
- echinoderm • endoskeleton
- ↻ Identify the Main Idea
- △ Classify

LESSON 4
- chordate • notochord
- vertebra • ectotherm
- endotherm
- ↻ Summarize
- △ Draw Conclusions

LESSON 5
- fish • cartilage • amphibian
- reptile • bird • mammal
- mammary gland
- monotreme • marsupial
- placental mammal • placenta
- ↻ Compare and Contrast
- △ Interpret Data

▷ **VOCAB FLASH CARDS** For extra help with vocabulary, visit **Vocab Flash Cards** and type in *Introduction to Animals.*

What Is an Animal?

UNLOCK
THE BIG
?

🔑 What Are the Functions of Animals?

🔑 How Are Animals Classified?

my planet DiaRY

DISCOVERY

Animal Discoveries

What would a mammal never before seen look like? The answer lies in the mountains of Tanzania, Africa. There, scientists discovered a vertebrate, which is a mammal, in 2005. The animal, which has been named *Rhynochocyon udzungwensis*, is a species of giant elephant shrew. It weighs about 700 grams and measures about 30 centimeters in length, which is just a little longer than this book. This newly discovered mammal is larger than other elephant shrews, and it has its own distinctive color.

Other animals have also been discovered in the mountains of Tanzania. Unknown amphibians and reptiles have been discovered there as well. Each discovery reveals more of the diversity of the animals living on Earth.

Read the following question. Then write your answer below.

Do you think it is important to protect areas such as these mountains? Why?

It is important because there are new species and they need to live and reproduce.

▶ PLANET DIARY Go to **Planet Diary** to learn more about animals.

Lab zone® Do the Inquiry Warm-Up *Is It an Animal?*

What Are the Functions of Animals?

Like plants, animals live almost everywhere on Earth. Animals may have scales, feathers, shells, or fins. They may be brightly colored or completely see-through. Some animals do not have limbs. Others have too many limbs to count. You may wonder if animals have anything in common. Well, they do.

Vocabulary
- homeostasis
- adaptation
- vertebrate
- invertebrate

Skills
- ⟳ Reading: Relate Text and Visuals
- △ Inquiry: Classify

Functions All animals are multicellular organisms that feed on other organisms and perform the same basic functions. 🔑 The main functions of an animal are to obtain food and oxygen, keep internal conditions stable, move in some way, and reproduce. Keeping internal body conditions stable is called **homeostasis** (hoh mee oh stay sis).

Adaptations Structures and behaviors that allow animals to perform their functions are called **adaptations.** Teeth and limbs are adaptations that allow animals to obtain food and move. The pouch of a kangaroo is an adaptation for reproduction.

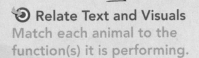

⟳ **Relate Text and Visuals**
Match each animal to the function(s) it is performing.

Obtaining Food B, D
Animals eat other organisms and raw materials for energy and for growth.

Reproducing C, D
Animals make new individuals like themselves.

Moving A
Animals move to perform other functions as well.

Do the Quick Lab
Get Moving.

🔑 Assess Your Understanding

got it? ....

○ I get it! Now I know that the functions of animals are _____

_____

○ I need extra help with _____

Go to **my science** ⓢ **coach** online for help with this subject.

How Are Animals Classified?

There are more than 1.6 million species of animals, and more are discovered each year. So far, biologists have classified animals into about 35 major groups. In **Figure 1,** you can see some of the major groups. Notice how the groups are arranged on branches. Animal groups on nearby branches are more closely related than groups on branches farther apart. For example, birds are more closely related to reptiles than they are to mammals.

🔑 **Animals are classified according to how they are related to other animals. These relationships are determined by an animal's body structure, the way the animal develops, and its DNA.** DNA is a chemical in cells that controls an organism's inherited characteristics.

All animals are either vertebrates or invertebrates. **Vertebrates** are animals with a backbone. **Invertebrates** are animals without a backbone.

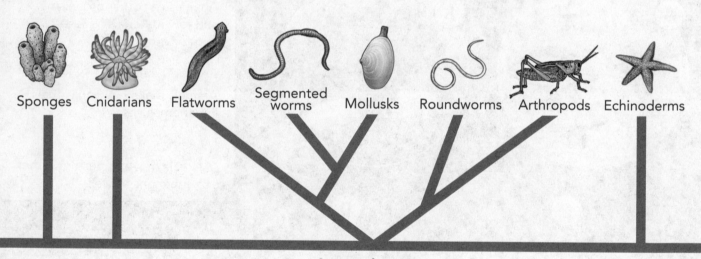

Sponges Cnidarians Flatworms Segmented worms Mollusks Roundworms Arthropods Echinoderms

Invertebrates

FIGURE 1 ···

▶ VIRTUAL LAB **Major Animal Groups**

✎ **Complete these tasks.**

1. **Interpret Diagrams** Are flatworms more closely related to segmented worms or to roundworms? Circle your answer on the diagram.

2. **CHALLENGE** What do you think the bird branch coming off of the reptile branch indicates?

_____

_____

_____

apply it!

Use the information in **Figure 1** to help you classify the animals at the right.

1 ☒ **Classify** Write the name of each animal's group in the box provided.

2 Identify Which animals are vertebrates? Which animals are invertebrates?

_____

_____

_____

_____

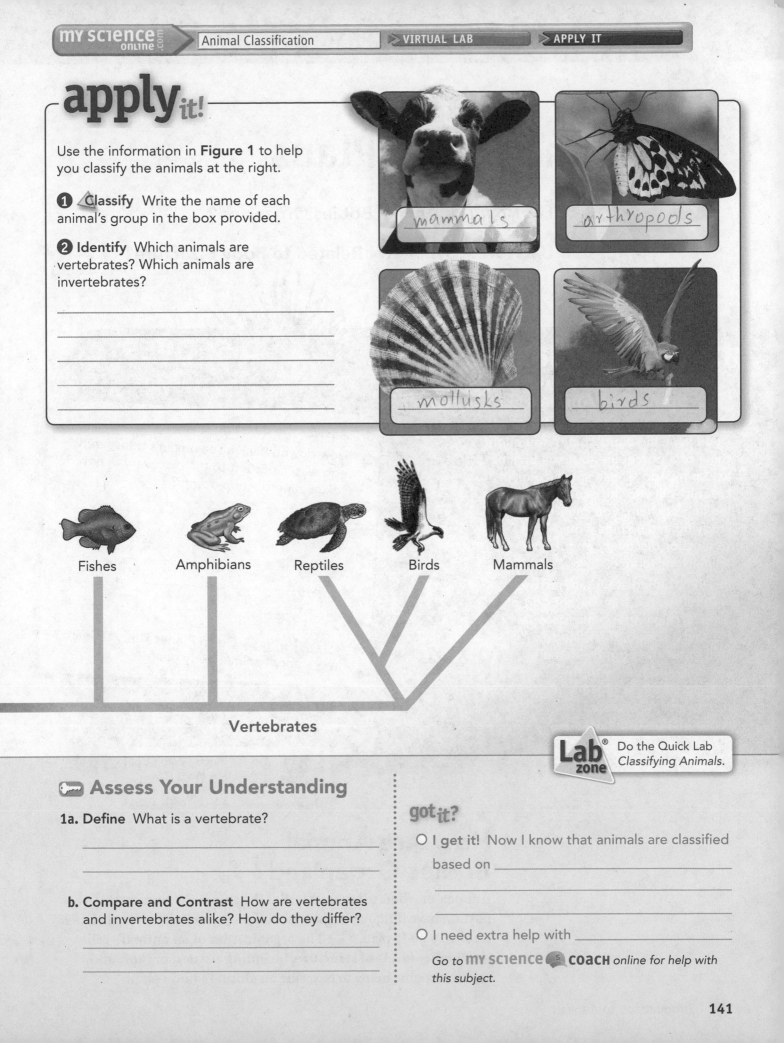

mammals

arthropods

mollusks

birds

Fishes   Amphibians   Reptiles   Birds   Mammals

Vertebrates

Lab ® zone Do the Quick Lab
Classifying Animals.

☞ Assess Your Understanding

1a. Define What is a vertebrate?

_____

_____

b. Compare and Contrast How are vertebrates and invertebrates alike? How do they differ?

_____

_____

got it?

○ **I get it!** Now I know that animals are classified based on _____

_____

○ **I need extra help with** _____

_Go to_ **my science** ⓢ **coach** _online for help with this subject._

141

Animal Body Plans

UNLOCK
THE BIG
?

🔑 How Are Animal Bodies Organized?

🔑 How Is Symmetry Related to Body Structure?

MY PLANET DIARY

DISCOVERY

Spiny Sea Animals

What animal do you think of when you hear the word *spiny*? You might think of a porcupine, but sea urchins are spiny, too. These small, colorful creatures live in the ocean. Just by looking at them, you can't tell that studying sea urchins would lead to a major discovery about how animals reproduce.

In 1875, biologist Oskar Hertwig was studying a transparent egg of a sea urchin under a microscope. He saw a sperm, the male sex cell, enter the egg, the female sex cell, and fuse with the nucleus of the egg. He had discovered how sexual reproduction occurs.

Answer the question below.

How do you think a sea urchin's transparent egg was important to the discovery of how sexual reproduction occurs?

You can see how they
reproduce

▷ PLANET DIARY Go to **Planet Diary** to learn more about animal body plans.

Lab® zone
Do the Inquiry Warm-Up *How Many Ways Can You Fold It?*.

How Are Animal Bodies Organized?

Animals are diverse organisms. But the animals within each phylum have uniquely organized body structures. This organization is called a body plan. 🔑 **The organization of an animal's cells into higher levels of structure, including tissues, organs, and organ systems, helps to describe an animal's body plan.**

Vocabulary
- tissue • organ • radial symmetry
- bilateral symmetry

Skills
↪ **Reading:** Relate Cause and Effect
△ **Inquiry:** Make Models

Cells and Tissues All animals are made up of many cells. Their cells are usually specialized and organized as tissues. A **tissue** is a group of similar cells that performs a specific function. Muscle tissue, nervous tissue, and connective tissue are all animal tissues. Bone and blood are examples of kinds of connective tissues.

Organs and Organ Systems In most animals, tissues combine to form organs and organ systems. An **organ** is made up of different tissues. For example, the leg bone of a frog shown in **Figure 1** is an organ composed of bone tissue, nervous tissue, and blood. An organ performs more complex functions than the tissues that make it up could perform alone. Groups of organs make up organ systems. These systems perform the animal's broadest functions.

FIGURE 1 ....

A Skeletal System's Organization
Different levels of organization are found in a frog's skeleton.

✎ **Describe** Tell what makes up each level of organization in this frog's skeletal system.

Organ System
made up of multiple organs

Tissue
group of similar cells that perform a specific function

Organ
made up of different tissues

Cell
A bone cell is the basic unit of structure in bone tissue.

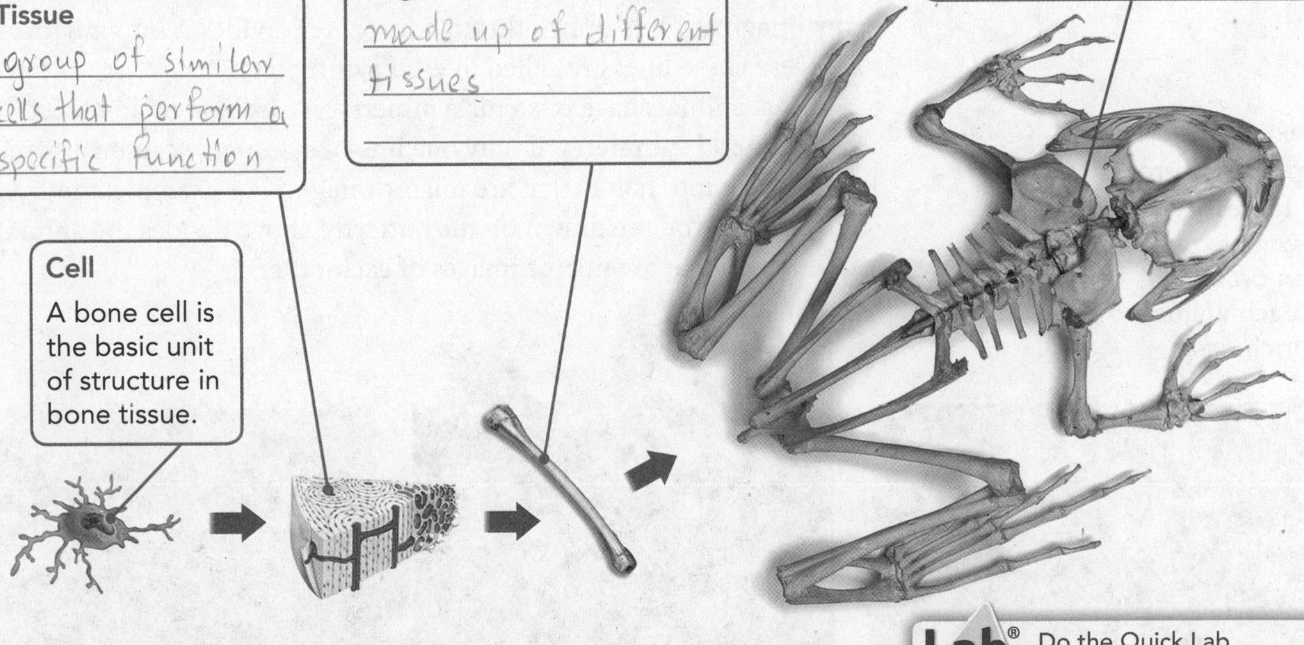

Lab zone ® Do the Quick Lab *Organizing Animal Bodies.*

⚷ Assess Your Understanding

got it? ....

○ I get it! Now I know that animal bodies are organized into _____

○ I need extra help with _____

Go to MY SCIENCE ⓢ COACH *online for help with this subject.*

How Is Symmetry Related to Body Structure?

A butterfly with bilateral symmetry

Have you ever noticed a butterfly perched on a flower? You probably saw its colors and wing patterns. Did you also see that the pattern on the left side is a mirror image of the pattern on the right side? Many organisms and objects have this balanced display of body parts called symmetry.

Types of Symmetry Animals have different types of symmetry, as you can see in **Figure 2.** Some animals have no symmetry, or are asymmetrical. For example, most sponges are asymmetrical. However, most animals have either radial symmetry or bilateral symmetry.

An animal has **radial symmetry** if many imaginary lines can be drawn through a central point to divide it into two mirror images. For example, from above, the shape of a jellyfish is circular. So any imaginary line drawn through its center divides it into mirror images. These lines are called lines of symmetry.

Most animals have bilateral symmetry. An animal or an object has **bilateral symmetry** if only one line of symmetry can be drawn to divide it into halves that are mirror images. For example, the dashed line you see drawn on the butterfly above divides the animal into halves that are mirror images of each other.

FIGURE 2 ·······················

Types of Symmetry
✎ **Identify** Write the type of symmetry each animal has. Then draw lines of symmetry on each animal to support your choice.

radial

asymmetrical

bilateral

Symmetry and Body Structure

The structures of animals are related to their symmetry. **The bodies of animals without symmetry are organized simply, with some specialized cells but no tissues. In contrast, animals with radial symmetry have complex body plans with tissues and usually with organ systems. Animals with bilateral symmetry have organ systems.**

Radial Symmetry All animals with radial symmetry live in water. Some creep slowly along the ocean floor. Others stay in one spot as adults. A few can move quickly. Most animals with radial symmetry do not have front or back ends. Also, they do not have heads with specialized sense organs. This kind of symmetry allows them to take in information about their surroundings from all directions. This is an advantage for animals that usually move slowly.

Relate Cause and Effect In the second paragraph, underline an effect of having radial symmetry.

apply it!

Many objects you see have symmetry, but some do not.

❶ **Interpret Photos** Under each picture, write the type of symmetry shown by the object.

❷ **Explain** Draw lines of symmetry on each object to support your choice.

❸ **Make Models** Draw a common object not pictured here that has radial symmetry. Draw lines of symmetry to support your choice.

bilateral

bilateral

radial

asymetrtrical

bilateral

CHALLENGE Why is it an advantage for an animal to have its head be the first part of its body to enter a new area?

_____

_____

_____

_____

Bilateral Symmetry In general, animals with bilateral symmetry are larger and more complex than animals with radial symmetry. They have complex organ systems that help them function efficiently. Also, most animals with bilateral symmetry have streamlined bodies, which help them move quickly.

Most animals with bilateral symmetry have heads at their front ends. Having a head is important to an animal. Most of an animal's specialized sense organs, such as its eyes, are in its head, as you can see in **Figure 3.** In addition, a concentration of nervous tissue is found in an animal's head. Nervous tissue processes information for the animal and coordinates the animal's responses. In fact, an animal usually moves into a new area with its head first.

FIGURE 3

A Coral Reef

Many animals with bilateral and radial symmetry live in coral reefs.

✎ **Compare and Contrast** In the Venn diagram, write how a sea star and a fish are alike and how they are different.

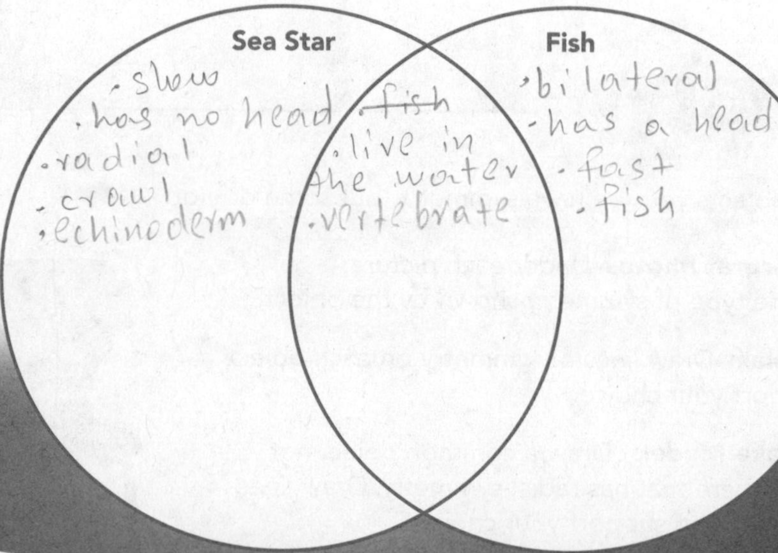

Sea Star
- slow
- has no head
- radial
- crawl
- echinoderm

(overlap) fish
- live in the water
- vertebrate

Fish
- bilateral
- has a head
- fast
- fish

Animal or Not?

How do you know an animal when you see it?

FIGURE 4 ···

All animals have functions they perform. Most animals have some type of symmetry and an organization that includes organ systems.

✎ **Apply Concepts** Answer the questions in the boxes.

2 What adaptations does this animal have for obtaining food?

· big fangs
· big body
· fast
· sense of smell

1 What are the functions of this animal?

obtain food and oxygen, be healthy, move, and re-produce

3 How is this animal organized and what type of symmetry does it have?

It's a vertebrate and it's a bilateral symmetry

Lab ® **zone** Do the Quick Lab Front-End Advantages.

🔑 Assess Your Understanding

1a. Infer Why do you think bilateral symmetry is an advantage for an animal?

_____
_____
_____

b. ANSWER THE BIG **?** How do you know an animal when you see it?

_____
_____
_____

got_it? ···

○ **I get it!** Now I know that symmetry relates to body structure because _____

_____
_____
_____

○ **I need extra help with** _____

Go to **MY SCIENCE** ⑤ **COACH** online for help with this subject.

147

LESSON
3

Introduction to Invertebrates

UNLOCK THE BIG Q?

🔑 **What Are Invertebrates?**

my planeT DiaRY

FUN FACTS

Ready, Aim, Fire!

To *bombard* is to "attack with materials that explode." This action is exactly what the bombardier beetle does. This incredible insect sprays predators with an explosion of deadly chemicals from its own body!

Why don't the chemicals kill the beetle? The chemicals needed for the spray are stored in different places in the beetle's body. When the beetle defends itself, the chemicals are combined into a deadly mixture. The mixture is sprayed on a predator at a temperature of 100°C!

Communicate Discuss the following question with a partner. Then write your answer below.

What other animals do you know about that have unique forms of self defense? Describe their defenses.

_____

_____

_____

▶ **PLANET DIARY** Go to **Planet Diary** to learn more about invertebrates.

Lab zone® Do the Inquiry Warm-Up *How Do Natural and Synthetic Sponges Compare?*

What Are Invertebrates?

At dusk near the edge of a meadow, a grasshopper leaps through the grass. Nearby, a hungry spider waits in its web. The grasshopper leaps into the web. It's caught! The spider bites the grasshopper to stun it and quickly wraps it in silk. The grasshopper will soon become a tasty meal for the spider.

Vocabulary

- cnidarian • mollusk • arthropod • exoskeleton
- echinoderm • endoskeleton

Skills

↻ Reading: Identify the Main Idea

△ Inquiry: Classify

Invertebrate Characteristics A grasshopper and a spider are both invertebrates. 🗝 **Animals that do not have backbones are invertebrates. The main invertebrate groups are sponges, cnidarians, flatworms, roundworms, segmented worms, mollusks, arthropods, and echinoderms.** About 96 percent of known animals are invertebrates. They live in every climate.

Sponges Sponges, such as the one shown in **Figure 1,** are asymmetrical invertebrates. They have some specialized cells but no tissues or organs. Unlike most animals you know, adult sponges stay in one place, like plants. But, like other animals, sponges take food into their bodies to get energy.

Cnidarians Jellyfishes and corals are examples of **cnidarians** (ny DEHR ee unz), invertebrates that have stinging cells and take food into a central body cavity. Cnidarians have radial symmetry. Although they lack organs, they do have some tissues.

FIGURE 1 ·······················

▶ INTERACTIVE ART **Sponges and Cnidarians**
Both sponges and cnidarians are animals that live in water.

✎ **Interpret Photos Based on symmetry, label these animals as sponges or cnidarians. Then write how sponges and cnidarians are alike and different.**

_____

_____

_____

_____

_____

_____

_____

cnidarians

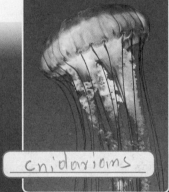

cnidarians

sponges

149

Worms

Worms If you have ever worked in a garden, you have probably seen some worms. The three major phyla of worms are flatworms, roundworms, and segmented worms, which you can see in **Figure 2.** All worms have bilateral symmetry, with head and tail ends. They also have tissues, organs, and organ systems. Flatworms have flat, soft bodies. Some have eye spots on their heads that detect light. Roundworms look like smooth, thin tubes. They have two body openings: a mouth and an anus. Segmented worms have bodies made up of many linked sections called segments. They are the simplest animals with a brain. Their brains help them detect food and predators.

FIGURE 2 ···

Worms

The three major phyla of worms are flatworms, roundworms, and segmented worms.

✎ **Classify** In the boxes, write the phylum of each worm. Then write notes that describe each worm.

Phylum: roundworm
_____
_____
_____

Phylum: segmented worms
_____
_____
_____
_____

Hookworm

Earthworm

Planarian

Phylum: flat worms
_____
_____
_____
_____

Mollusks Have you ever picked up seashells on the beach? Those seashells probably belonged to a mollusk. Invertebrates with soft, unsegmented bodies that are often protected by a hard shell are called **mollusks.** All mollusks have a thin layer of tissue called a mantle that covers their internal organs and an organ called a foot. Depending on the type of mollusk, the foot might be used for crawling, digging, or catching prey. **Figure 3** shows some mollusks.

The three major groups of mollusks are gastropods, bivalves, and cephalopods (SEF uh luh pahdz). Gastropods, such as snails, have a single shell or no shell, and a distinct head. Bivalves, such as clams, have two shells and a simple nervous system. Cephalopods may have an external or internal shell or no shell at all. They have good vision and large brains to help them remember what they've learned. A squid is a cephalopod with an internal shell.

Identify the Main Idea
Underline the main idea in the second paragraph. Then circle the supporting details.

FIGURE 3

Mollusks
A snail, clam, and squid do not look alike, but they have the same basic structure.

Summarize Fill in each box in the chart for each organism. Then write a title for the chart.

Characteristics	Gastropod	Bivalve	Cephalopod
	Snail	Clam	Squid
	Foot	Foot	Foot
Number of Shells	1	2	0
Internal or External Shells	external	external	internal
Uses Foot to ...	crawling	digging	catching prey

151

did you know?

Smaller than a paper clip, honeybees are important insects. They collect nectar from flowers to make honey and pollinate some plants. Without the honey bee, an apple tree might not produce the apples you eat.

do the math! Analyzing Data

This circle graph shows a distribution of animal groups.

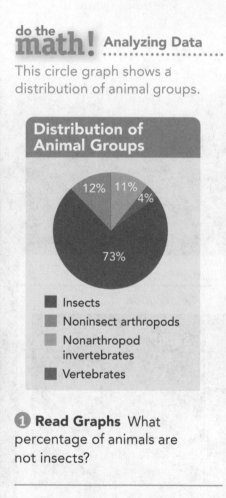

Distribution of Animal Groups

12% 11%
4%

73%

■ Insects
■ Noninsect arthropods
■ Nonarthropod invertebrates
■ Vertebrates

❶ **Read Graphs** What percentage of animals are not insects?

_____

_____

❷ [CHALLENGE] What percentage of animals are invertebrates that are not insects?

_____

_____

_____

Arthropods At first you may not think that a crab and a spider have anything in common. But look at the spider and crab in **Figure 4.** Crabs and spiders are **arthropods,** or invertebrates that have hard outer coverings, segmented bodies, and pairs of jointed appendages. Legs, wings, and antennae are appendages. The outer covering is called an **exoskeleton,** or outer skeleton. At times, the exoskeleton is shed and replaced as the animal grows. One arthropod group, crustaceans, includes animals such as crabs. A second group, arachnids, includes animals such as spiders. A third group includes centipedes, millipedes, and insects, such as bees and ants.

Insect

Arachnid

FIGURE 4 ·······························
Arthropods
Members of the three arthropod groups have different characteristics.

✎ **Observe** Tell how the number of pairs of legs of a spider and a bee differ.

_____

_____

_____

_____

_____

_____

Crustacean

Echinoderms An **echinoderm** is an invertebrate that has an internal skeleton and a system of fluid-filled tubes. An internal skeleton is called an **endoskeleton.** Echinoderms, shown in **Figure 5,** have radial symmetry. They use their system of tubes to move and obtain food and oxygen. Sea cucumbers, sea stars, sea urchins, and brittle stars are the major echinoderm groups.

Sea cucumber

Sea star

Sea urchins

Brittle stars

FIGURE 5 ·······························

▶ ART IN MOTION **Echinoderms**

Echinoderms are diverse animals, but all live in salt water.

✏ **Compare and Contrast** In the chart, write a brief description of the shape and symmetry of each echinoderm.

	Sea Cucumber	Sea Star	Sea Urchin	Brittle Star
Shape	Oval	Star	hair	star
Symmetry	radial	radial	radial	radial

 Do the Lab Investigation
Earthworm Responses.

🔑 **Assess Your Understanding**

1a. Identify How are all cnidarians alike?

_____

_____

b. Explain If you saw a worm, how would you identify its phylum?

_____

_____

got it?

○ **I get it!** Now I know that invertebrates _____

_____

_____

○ I need extra help with _____

Go to MY SCIENCE ⓢ COACH *online for help with this subject.*

Introduction to Vertebrates

🔑 **What Are the Characteristics of Chordates and Vertebrates?**

🔑 **How Do Vertebrates Control Body Temperature?**

my planet Diary

BRRRR! It's Freezing!

How can anything survive in Antarctica, the coldest and windiest place on Earth? Emperor penguins have many physical characteristics that help them live there. For example, they have a layer of fat that helps them stay warm. They also have short, stiff feathers that help to insulate and protect them from the freezing air.

However, the penguins' physical characteristics are not enough to stay warm in Antarctica during the winter. Emperor penguins cooperate to keep warm. They huddle together in groups and take turns standing on the outside of the huddle where it is the coldest. This way, every penguin gets a chance to stand in the middle of the huddle where it is the warmest. Now that's teamwork!

FUN FACTS

Read the following questions. Then write your answers below.

1. Why don't emperor penguins freeze to death in Antarctica?

_____
_____
_____

2. What are other ways you know about that animals use to stay warm?

_____
_____
_____

▶ PLANET DIARY Go to **Planet Diary** to learn more about vertebrates.

 Lab zone Do the Inquiry Warm-Up *How Is an Umbrella Like a Skeleton?*

Vocabulary
- chordate • notochord • vertebra
- ectotherm • endotherm

Skills
⟳ Reading: Summarize
△ Inquiry: Draw Conclusions

What Are the Characteristics of Chordates and Vertebrates?

The animals you are probably most familiar with are members of the phylum Chordata. Members of this phylum are called chordates (KAWR dayts). Most chordates, including all fishes, amphibians, reptiles, birds, and mammals, are vertebrates. A few chordates, such as sea squirts and lancelets, do not have backbones.

Chordate Characteristics 🔑 **At some point in their lives, all chordates have three characteristics: a notochord, a nerve cord, and pouches in the throat area. Most chordates also have a backbone.**

Notochord A notochord is a flexible rod that supports a chordate's back. The name *Chordata* comes from this structure's name.

Nerve Cord All chordates have a nerve cord that runs down their back. Your spinal cord is such a nerve cord. The nerve cord connects the brain to nerves in other parts of the body.

Throat Pouches At some point in their lives, chordates have pouches in their throat area. In fishes and lancelets, like the one shown in **Figure 1,** grooves between these pouches become gill slits. In most other vertebrates, the pouches disappear before birth.

FIGURE 1 ·············
Chordates
Lancelets show the three characteristics shared by all chordates at some point in their lives.

✎ **Relate Text and Visuals**
Circle the labels of the three chordate characteristics. Then explain how a lancelet is different from a fish.

_____

_____

_____

_____

_____

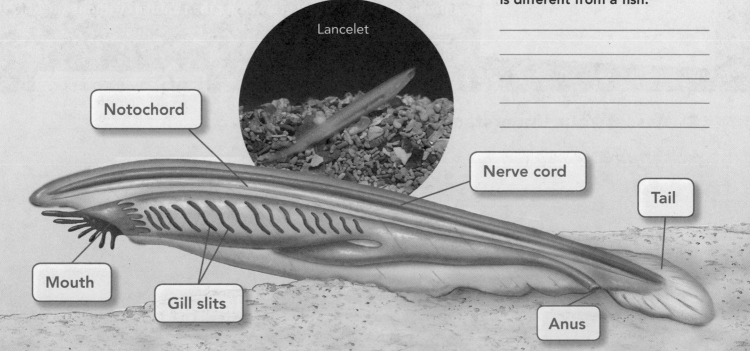

Lancelet

Notochord

Nerve cord

Tail

Mouth

Gill slits

Anus

skull backbone

ribs

FIGURE 2 ··
▶ **INTERACTIVE ART** **A Seal Skeleton**
A seal has an endoskeleton that helps it move through water.

🖉 Label the three key parts of the seal skeleton.

··················· 🖉 ·······················
↺ **Summarize** On the notebook below, write the organ that each key part of an endoskeleton protects.

Backbones In addition to a notochord, a nerve cord, and throat pouches, most chordates have a backbone. The backbone, or spine, runs down the center of the back and replaces the notochord. The backbone is made up of a stack of many small bones called **vertebrae** (singular *vertebra*). Each vertebra has a hole in it. The holes form a tunnel that a bundle of nerve tissue, or spinal cord, passes through. A pad of soft tissue separates each vertebra, giving the spine flexibility.

The backbone is a key part of a vertebrate's endoskeleton. It protects the spinal cord. The skull and ribs are other key parts of an endoskeleton. The skull protects the brain. The ribs protect the heart and lungs. An endoskeleton, such as the one you can see in Figure 2, shapes a body and provides muscles with places to attach. It also forms an internal frame that supports the body and allows it to move easily. An endoskeleton grows with the animal. Vertebrates often grow larger than animals without an endoskeleton.

Lab ® Do the Quick Lab
zone *Characteristics of Vertebrates.*

🔑 **Assess Your Understanding**

1a. Define What is a notochord?

_____

_____

b. Relate Cause and Effect What allows a backbone to be flexible?

_____

_____

_____

got it?

○ **I get it!** Now I know that chordates and vertebrates _____

_____

_____

_____

○ **I need extra help with** _____

Go to MY SCIENCE Ⓢ COACH *online for help with this subject.*

How Do Vertebrates Control Body Temperature?

The major groups of vertebrates differ in how they control body temperature. **Some vertebrates do not produce much internal heat. Therefore, their body temperatures change with the environment. Other vertebrates control their internal heat and maintain a constant body temperature.**

Amphibians, reptiles, and most fishes are ectotherms. An animal that produces little internal body heat is called an **ectotherm.** Its body temperature changes with temperature changes in its environment.

Birds and mammals are endotherms. An **endotherm** is an animal that controls the internal heat it produces and regulates its own temperature. An endotherm's body temperature is always fairly constant. Endotherms have adaptations such as sweat glands, fur, and feathers for maintaining body temperature.

Vocabulary Prefixes The prefix *ecto-* means "outside." What do you think the prefix *endo-* means?

_____

apply it!

Animals control body temperature in different ways.

❶ **Draw Conclusions** Write whether you think each animal is an endotherm or ectotherm.

❷ **CHALLENGE** Would it be more difficult for a penguin to live in a desert or a snake to live in a polar region? Explain.

_____
_____
_____
_____

ectotherm   endotherm

endotherm   ectotherm

Do the Quick Lab
Keeping Warm.

Assess Your Understanding

got it? ....

○ I get it! Now I know that vertebrates' body temperature _____

_____

○ I need extra help with _____

Go to **my science** ⑤ **coach** online for help with this subject.

Vertebrate Diversity

UNLOCK
THE BIG
?

🔑 **What Are the Major Groups of Vertebrates?**

my planet Diary

FUN FACTS

Sending Messages

Have you ever felt like stomping your feet to show your frustration? People aren't the only ones who stomp their feet to express themselves. Researchers think that elephants communicate by stomping. For example, they think elephants stomp their feet to greet one another and send warnings.

What if an animal has no feet to stomp? It can sing! Many species of whales communicate with one another through song. They make different sounds to communicate different messages. Who knows what else researchers will discover about animal communication!

Communicate Discuss the following question with a partner. Then write your answers below.

What are three ways you communicate with others without using words?

_____

_____

_____

_____

_____

▷ **PLANET DIARY** Go to **Planet Diary** to learn more about vertebrate diversity.

Lab zone® Do the Inquiry Warm-Up *Exploring Vertebrates.*

What Are the Major Groups of Vertebrates?

Vertebrates, like all other animals, are diverse. They live in almost all types of environments on Earth and vary in shape, size, and color. 🔑 **There are five major groups of vertebrates. They are fishes, amphibians, reptiles, birds, and mammals.** Members of each group share certain characteristics.

Vocabulary

- fish • cartilage • amphibian • reptile • bird
- mammal • mammary gland • monotreme • marsupial
- placental mammal • placenta

Skills

↻ **Reading:** Compare and Contrast
△ **Inquiry:** Interpret Data

Fishes A **fish** is a vertebrate that lives in water and uses fins to move. Most fishes are ectotherms. They have scales and obtain oxygen through gills. They make up the largest group of vertebrates. Based on certain characteristics, fishes are organized into three major groups, which are shown in **Figure 1.**

Jawless fishes have no jaws or scales. They scrape, suck, and stab their food. Their skeletons are made of **cartilage,** a tissue more flexible than bone. Fish with jaws, scales, and skeletons made of cartilage are cartilaginous fishes (kahr tuh LAJ uh nuhs). Bony fishes have jaws, scales, and a pocket on each side of the head that holds the gills. Their skeletons are made of hard bone.

FIGURE 1 ·······························

Types of Fishes

The three groups of fishes are jawless fishes, cartilaginous fishes, and bony fishes.

✎ **Summarize** Write on the notebook the characteristics of each group of fishes.

Lamprey

Lamprey's mouth

Jawless fish

Gray reef shark

Cartilaginous fish

Bony fish

Goldfish

Gill pocket

Amphibians You may know that some amphibians such as frogs can be noisy neighbors. Frogs, toads, and salamanders are examples of amphibians. An **amphibian** is a vertebrate that is ectothermic and spends its early life in water and its adult life on land. In fact, the word *amphibian* means "double life." Most amphibians spend their adult lives on land. But they return to water to lay eggs and reproduce. Look at the amphibians in **Figure 2**.

FIGURE 2 ···

Amphibian Diversity

Adult salamanders have tails, but almost all adult frogs and toads do not.

✎ **Interpret Photos** Label each type of amphibian. Explain the evidence in each picture that helped you decide.

_____

_____

_____

_____

_____

_____

_____

_____

do the
math!

Vertebrate Diversity

The table shows the estimated number of species in each vertebrate group. Use the table to answer the questions.

1 Calculate About how many vertebrate species are there in all?

_____

2 Interpret Data Which group has the greatest number of species? The least?

_____

_____

Estimated Number of Species of Vertebrates	
Vertebrate Group	**Number of Species**
Fishes	30,700
Amphibians	6,347
Reptiles	8,734
Birds	9,990
Mammals	5,488

Reptiles The alligator, snake, and chameleon shown in **Figure 3** are all reptiles. A **reptile** is an ectothermic vertebrate that has scaly skin and lungs and lays eggs on land. Some reptiles, such as sea turtles, live in water but still breathe air. Most reptiles live on land even though some swim a lot. To live on land, an animal must have adaptations that keep water in its cells. The skin of reptiles is thick and helps keep water inside their bodies. Reptiles also have organs called kidneys that conserve water. Most young reptiles develop inside tough-shelled eggs. The eggshell helps keep water inside the egg.

Chameleon

FIGURE 3 ···

Reptile Diversity

Reptiles are adapted to life on land.

✎ **Complete these tasks.**

1. **Draw Conclusions** In each box, describe how you know that the animal is a reptile.

2. CHALLENGE Explain how a shell keeps water inside an egg.

_____

_____

Snake

Alligator

This ibis wades through water with its tall, thin legs. It uses its long bill to find small prey.

Birds

If you have ever watched birds at a feeder, you know how fascinating they are. A **bird** is an endothermic vertebrate that lays eggs and has feathers and a four-chambered heart. Birds are adapted for flight. They have wings and lightweight, nearly hollow bones. Shown in **Figure 4,** birds are the only modern animals with feathers.

FIGURE 4 ·····························
Birds
Different adaptations allow birds to live in different environments.

✎ **Make Generalizations** In each box, underline adaptations the bird has that help it survive. Then explain how you think feathers help birds survive.

_____

_____

_____

This rainbow bee-eater uses its pointed bill to feed on bees and other insects, which it catches as it flies.

Sharp vision and keen hearing help owls like this tawny owl hunt at night. They use razor-sharp claws to grab prey.

✎ **Compare and Contrast**
In the Venn diagram, list how reptiles and birds are alike and different.

Birds

Reptiles

· wings
· feathers
· leight weight

· lay eggs
· vertebrate
· get oxygen from the air

· ectothermic
· scales
· live in water

Mammals There are three main groups of mammals. **Mammals** are endothermic vertebrates that have skin covered with fur or hair, and a four-chambered heart. The young are fed with milk produced by organs, called **mammary glands,** in the mother's body.

The mammal groups differ in how their young develop. **Monotremes** lay eggs. **Marsupials** are born at an early stage of development, and they usually continue to develop in a pouch on the mother's body. A **placental mammal** develops inside its mother's body until its body systems can function independently. Materials are exchanged between the mother and the embryo through an organ called the **placenta.**

Giraffe

Placental Mammal

get food from their mother

FIGURE 5 ....

Mammals
The main groups of mammals are monotremes, marsupials, and placental mammals.

✎ **Review** In each box, write a note about how the young of the group develops.

Kangaroo

Marsupial

stay in their mother's pouch

Platypus

Monotreme

live in the eggs

Lab zone® Do the Quick Lab
It's Plane to See.

🗝 Assess Your Understanding

1a. Name Name the three groups of fishes.

_____

_____

b. Relate Cause and Effect Why can mammals live in colder environments than reptiles?

_____

got it? ....

○ **I get it!** Now I know that the major groups of vertebrates are _____

_____

○ **I need extra help with** _____

Go to **MY SCIENCE** 🔵 **COACH** *online for help with this subject.*

4 Study Guide

I would know an animal by its _____, _____,
and _____.

LESSON 1 What Is an Animal?

🔑 The main functions of an animal are to obtain food and oxygen, keep internal conditions stable, move in some way, and reproduce.

🔑 Animals are classified according to how they are related to other animals. These relationships are determined by an animal's body structure, the way the animal develops, and its DNA.

Vocabulary
- homeostasis • adaptation
- vertebrate • invertebrate

LESSON 2 Animal Body Plans

🔑 The organization of an animal's cells into higher levels of structure helps to describe an animal's body plan.

🔑 Animals without symmetry have no tissues. Animals with radial symmetry have tissues and usually have organ systems. Animals with bilateral symmetry have organ systems.

Vocabulary
- tissue • organ • radial symmetry
- bilateral symmetry

LESSON 3 Introduction to Invertebrates

🔑 Animals that do not have backbones are invertebrates.

Vocabulary
- cnidarian
- mollusk
- arthropod
- exoskeleton
- echinoderm
- endoskeleton

LESSON 4 Introduction to Vertebrates

🔑 At some point in their lives, all chordates have three characteristics: a notochord, a nerve cord, and pouches in the throat area.

🔑 The body temperatures of some vertebrates change with the environment. Other vertebrates maintain a constant body temperature.

Vocabulary
- chordate • notochord
- vertebra • ectotherm
- endotherm

LESSON 5 Vertebrate Diversity

🔑 There are five major groups of vertebrates. They are fishes, amphibians, reptiles, birds, and mammals.

Vocabulary
- fish • cartilage • amphibian
- reptile • bird
- mammal • mammary gland
- monotreme • marsupial
- placental mammal
- placenta

Review and Assessment

LESSON 1 What Is an Animal?

1. The process that the body uses to maintain a stable internal environment is called

a. adaptation. **b.** endothermic.

c. homeostasis. **d.** sweating.

2. The presence of a ___back bone___ determines whether an animal is a vertebrate or an invertebrate.

3. Identify the Main Idea What are the five main functions of animals?

obtain food and oxygen, keep internal conditions stable, move in some way, and reproduce

4. Draw Conclusions Suppose a book titled *Earth's Animals* is about vertebrates. Is its title a good one? Explain your answer.

No, because not all animals are vertebrates.

5. Apply Concepts Some insects and birds can fly. Despite this similarity, why are insects and birds classified as different groups?

Insects are invertebrates and birds are vertebrates.

6. Write About It Choose an animal that you know well and describe a day in its life. Include the functions it carries out and the adaptations it uses to survive in its environment.

LESSON 2 Animal Body Plans

7. What is the highest level of organization an animal can have?

a. cells **b.** organ systems

c. organs **d.** tissues

8. An animal with many lines of symmetry has ___radial___ symmetry.

9. Compare and Contrast Describe how the symmetry of a sea star, a sponge, and a fish differ.

A sea star is radial and sponge assymetrical and fishes are bilateral symmetry

LESSON 3 Introduction to Invertebrates

10. Mollusks with two shells are called

a. cephalopods. **b.** sea stars.

c. bivalves. **d.** gastropods.

11. An ___echinoderm___ has a system of fluid-filled tubes for obtaining food and oxygen.

12. Make Generalizations Suppose you see an animal. You wonder if it is an arthropod. What characteristics would you look for?

Has an outer cover, segmented bodies, and legs, wings or antennas

13. Write About It Explain whether a snail or a sponge has a higher level of organization and how this organization helps the invertebrate.

165

Introduction to Vertebrates

14. All vertebrates are

(a.) chordates.　　　**b.** invertebrates.

c. fishes.　　　**d.** reptiles.

15. A ___notochord___ is replaced by a backbone in many vertebrates.

16. Make Generalizations Why is the endoskeleton important?

It protects the spinal cord.
· allows you to move
· shapes body

17. Relate Cause and Effect Whales, polar bears, and seals are endotherms. How might their thick layer of fat help them?

Their thik layer of fat helps them be warm in cold places. good swimmers

18. Infer Would an ectotherm or an endotherm be more active on a cold night? Explain.

An endotherm beause it can make itself warmer.

19. [Write About It] Your friend has both a hamster and a lizard as pets. She wants to buy a heat lamp for each of them to keep them warm. Tell her whether each pet needs a heat lamp to stay warm. Include the two ways animals maintain their body temperatures in your answer.

Vertebrate Diversity

20. A reptile

a. is an endotherm.　　　**b.** lives only in water.

c. has gills.　　　(d.) has scaly skin.

21. ___birds___ are the only animals with feathers.

22. Classify Into which group of fishes would you classify a fish with jaws and a skeleton made of cartilage?

Cartilaginous Fish

23. Summarize What is the main difference between the three mammal groups?

Monotherms lay eggs, marsupials develop in mother's pouch, placentall mammals develop inside mother's body

APPLY THE BIG Q

How do you know an animal when you see it?

24. Look at the squid below. Describe how you know it is an animal. Include details about its functions and its adaptations to survive.

· internal skeleton
· brain
· eyes
· feet to kill
· biolateral

Standardized Test Prep

Multiple Choice

Circle the letter of the best answer.

1. A lancelet is shown below. Which of its characteristics belong to a chordate?

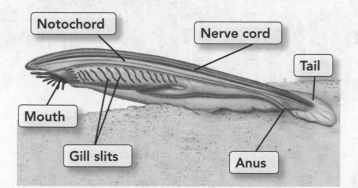

Notochord

Nerve cord

Tail

Mouth

Gill slits

Anus

   A   the mouth, gill slits, and nerve cord
   B   the gill slits, notochord, and nerve cord
   C   the notochord, nerve cord, and tail
   D   the gill slits, notochord, and mouth

2. Which characteristics do birds and mammals have in common?

   A   Both are endothermic vertebrates.
   B   Both have fur or hair.
   C   Both have a three-chambered heart.
   D   Both are vertebrates that produce milk.

3. Which of the following best describes the function of the placenta?

   A   delivers oxygen to the body's cells
   B   stores food inside the body before swallowing and digesting it
   C   directs and coordinates a mammal's complex movements
   D   passes materials between a mother and her offspring before it is born

4. What kind of evidence is used to determine the relationships between animals?

   A   evidence from the way an animal develops
   B   evidence from an animal's DNA
   C   evidence from an animal's body structure
   D   all of the above

5. Which describes an ectothermic animal?

   A   an animal that has a thick coat of fur
   B   an animal that sweats when the environment is too hot
   C   an animal that depends on the sun to raise its body temperature
   D   an animal that maintains its body temperature when walking through snow

Constructed Response

Use the photos below and your knowledge of science to help you answer Question 6. Write your answer on a separate sheet of paper.

· chidariariorb
· radial

· mollusk
· biolateral

· sponges
· assymetrial

Jellyfish

Clam

Sponge

6. Invertebrates are animals without a backbone. Identify the group each of the invertebrates above belongs to. Then, for each group, name three characteristics that all its members share.

167

JUNIOR ZOOKEEPERS

What is a lemur's favorite snack? Are baboons grumpy when they wake up in the morning? What, exactly, goes on behind the scenes at a zoo? If you want to know the answers to these questions, find out about Junior Zookeeper programs.

Many zoos throughout the country have volunteer programs for teenagers. Junior Zookeepers' tasks can include caring for zoo animals and assisting in zoo research. At some zoos, volunteers even help design and run educational programs. These volunteers serve as guides to help the public learn more from the zoo exhibits.

Some jobs are a little messy. You might have to help clean up the elephant cages! But the rewards can be just as big—taking care of animals can be a life-changing experience.

Design It Find out more about how zoo habitats are designed. How do zookeepers simulate an animal's habitat? How do they design exhibits that educate the public? Then choose an animal and design a model zoo exhibit that simulates its habitat and educates the public about the animal.

A Slimy Defense

If there were a contest for the most disgusting animal in the sea, the hagfish would probably win. This eel-like creature is almost blind, and it feeds by burrowing into the flesh of dead animals on the ocean floor. If a hagfish is attacked, it releases large amounts of thick slime, which can suffocate any predator foolish enough to attack! This thick gooey slime contains threads that are almost as strong as spider silk. Studies of hagfish slime may one day help scientists make materials that are stronger than the fabric we now use in bulletproof vests!

Write About It Find examples of how biological research has inspired the development of technology. Then make a poster that describes three examples. Explain how the technology affected society.

SUPERCOOLING FROGS

When you think of animals in Alaska, you probably think of caribou, arctic foxes, polar bears, and lynx. But what about frogs? Alaska is also home to a species of frog that freezes completely during the winter. When the temperatures warm again, the frog will thaw and be completely fine!

The wood frog has several adaptations that allow it to freeze. Much of the water from the frog's cells moves into its body cavity before the water freezes. This prevents the ice from damaging tissues. High levels of glucose protect the frog's cells from freezing. Finally, the wood frog may even ingest bacteria that allow it to control the rate at which freezing occurs!

Research It Find out about other animals that have adapted to live in extreme conditions. Then create an illustrated guide that shows how three of these animals survive in extreme environments.

WHAT MAKES A BAT AGILE IN FLIGHT?

THE BIG ? How do animals move?

Bats are the only mammals that can truly fly. The wings of a bat are made of a thin skin that stretches from its shoulders to the tips of its long, flexible finger bones. When the bat moves its wings up and down, the skin billows out like a balloon. As a bat flies, its wings are more flexible than your hand waving because the wing bones bend. This little brown bat can reach speeds of 35 km/h as it flies, swoops, or dives after a moth.

▲ **Develop Hypotheses** **How can a bat alter its course so quickly?**

_____

_____

_____

_____

> **UNTAMED SCIENCE** Watch the **Untamed Science** video to learn more about how animals move.

Getting Around

5 Getting Started

Check Your Understanding

1. **Background** Read the paragraph below and then answer the question.

Why can you not leap like a frog? Like a frog, you are a **vertebrate.** But frogs have **adaptations** for leaping. A frog's powerful hind legs and sturdy **endoskeleton** allow it to leap and land without injury.

> An animal that has a backbone is a **vertebrate.**
>
> An **adaptation** is a characteristic that enables an animal to live successfully in its environment.
>
> An **endoskeleton** is an internal skeleton.

• What adaptations do frogs have that enable them to leap?

_____

_____

_____

_____

> **MY READING WEB** If you had trouble completing the question above, visit **My Reading Web** and type in *Getting Around.*

Vocabulary Skill

Identify Multiple Meanings Some words have different meanings in science and in everyday use. The table below lists the multiple meanings for some words in this chapter.

Word	Everyday Meaning	Scientific Meaning
impulse	*n.* a sudden desire, urge, or inclination	*n.* an electrical message that moves from one neuron to another
stimulus	*n.* something that encourages an activity to begin	*n.* a change that an animal detects in its environment

2. **Quick Check** In the table above, circle the meaning of the word *stimulus* as it is used in the following sentence.

• The smell of pancakes was the *stimulus* that made Theo's mouth water.

molting

joint

response

water vascular system

Chapter Preview

LESSON 1
- molting
- cartilage
- joint
- muscle

⊙ **Compare and Contrast**
△ **Infer**

LESSON 2
- nervous system
- stimulus
- response
- neuron
- impulse
- sensory neuron
- interneuron
- motor neuron
- brain

⊙ **Identify Supporting Evidence**
△ **Draw Conclusions**

LESSON 3
- water vascular system
- swim bladder

⊙ **Relate Text and Visuals**
△ **Calculate**

▷ VOCAB FLASH CARDS For extra help with vocabulary, visit **Vocab Flash Cards** and type in *Getting Around.*

Skeletons and Muscles

UNLOCK
THE BIG
?

🔑 **What Supports and Protects Animal Bodies?**

🔑 **What Is the Role of Muscles?**

my planet Diary

Fast Felines

Which animal is the fastest sprinter? It is a cheetah. The cheetah's body structure and muscles allow it to reach speeds of up to 112 km/h in only three seconds. Its flexible spine enables the cheetah to extend its limbs to great lengths. This ability allows the cheetah to cover as much ground in one stride as a racehorse. The cheetah also has a high percentage of fast-twitch muscle fibers. These fibers provide power and allow the cheetah to reach its incredible speed faster than a race car can reach the same speed. It's no wonder that the cheetah holds the title of "World's Fastest Land Animal."

Lab zone ® Do the Inquiry Warm-Up *Will It Bend and Move?*

FUN FACTS

Read the following questions. Then write your answers below.

1. What are two parts of a cheetah's body that help it run fast?

_____

_____

_____

2. Why do you think a cheetah's speed is an advantage to the animal?

_____

_____

_____

_____

> **PLANET DIARY** Go to **Planet Diary** to learn more about skeletons and muscles.

Vocabulary
- molting • cartilage
- joint • muscle

Skills
↻ Reading: Compare and Contrast
△ Inquiry: Infer

What Supports and Protects Animal Bodies?

Imagine you are watching lions moving slowly through tall grass. They are surrounding a young zebra that has wandered away from its mother. Flies buzz, and beetles chew on grass blades. Buzzards circle in the distance. Nearby, a snake slithers away from one of the lions. Unaware, the zebra continues to graze.

Think about all these different animals. Do they have anything in common? The answer is yes. All of their bodies are supported by skeletons, which have similar functions. 🔑 **A skeleton is a framework that shapes and supports an animal, protects its internal organs, and allows it to move in its environment.**

Types of Skeletons Most animals have one of three types of skeletons: skeletons without hard parts, exoskeletons, and endoskeletons. An exoskeleton is a hard outer covering, while an endoskeleton is a framework inside the body. Some animals, such as sponges, do not have skeletons. However, most sponges have hard, spikelike structures scattered among their cells. These structures help support and protect them.

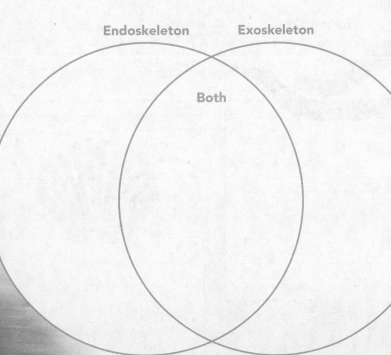

Endoskeleton   **Exoskeleton**

Both

✏️
↻ **Compare and Contrast**
Complete the Venn diagram to show how endoskeletons and exoskeletons are alike and how they are different.

175

Skeletons Without Hard Parts Have you ever seen blobs that look like clear gelatin washed up on beach sand? These blobs are the bodies of jellyfish. They still have some shape because of their skeleton. Jellyfish and other cnidarians, as well as earthworms and some other annelids, have skeletons without hard parts. These skeletons have fluid-filled cavities surrounded by muscle, a tissue used in movement. Like all skeletons, this type of skeleton helps an animal keep its shape and move about.

Exoskeletons Mollusks and arthropods have exoskeletons. Clam and scallop shells are mollusk exoskeletons made of calcium-containing compounds. The exoskeletons of arthropods are made of a different substance. Exoskeletons have some disadvantages. First, exoskeletons have no cells, so they cannot grow the way organisms grow. A mollusk's shell does get larger over time as the animal secretes calcium. But to grow, arthropods must shed their exoskeletons periodically and produce new ones in a process called **molting.** Second, an exoskeleton can be heavy. This weight prevents an animal from growing very large. Look at the skeletons in **Figure 1.**

FIGURE 1 ·······················
> INTERACTIVE ART **Two Types of Skeletons**
Some animals have skeletons without hard parts, while others have exoskeletons.

✎ **Relate Text and Visuals** In each box, write a description of the type of the animal's skeleton.

Earthworm

Cicada

Old skeleton

Scallop

Endoskeletons Echinoderms and vertebrates have endoskeletons. Like exoskeletons, endoskeletons may contain different materials. For example, a sea star's endoskeleton is made of plates that contain calcium. Sharks and some other fishes have endoskeletons made of **cartilage,** a tissue that is more flexible than bone. The endoskeletons of most other vertebrates are made of mostly bone with some cartilage.

Bone and cartilage contain living cells. As a result, a vertebrate's endoskeleton can grow. In addition, because endoskeletons are relatively light, vertebrates with endoskeletons can grow larger than animals with exoskeletons. Some animals with endoskeletons are shown in **Figure 2.**

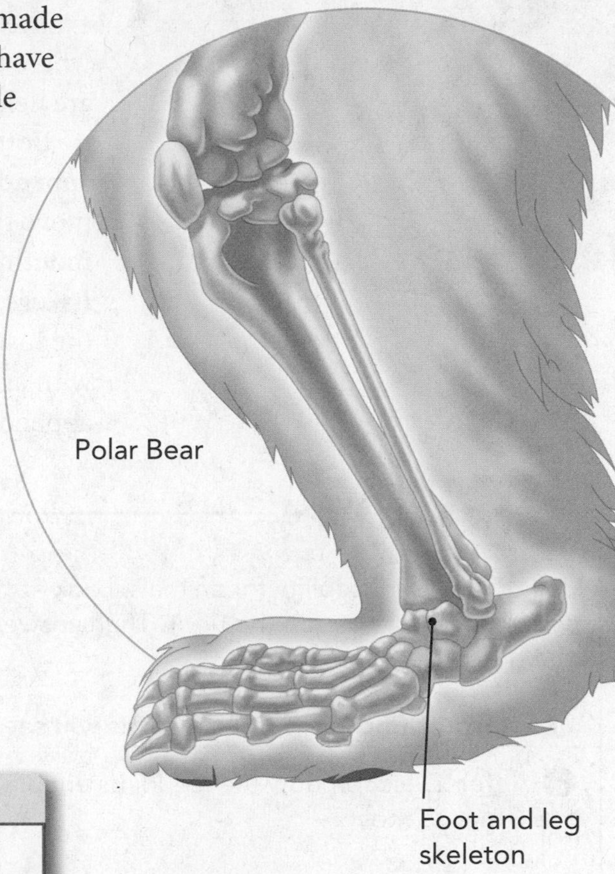

FIGURE 2 ·····

Endoskeletons

Endoskeletons are made of different materials.

✎ **Complete these tasks.**

1. **Relate Text and Visuals** In the table, identify the material that each animal's endoskeleton is made of.

Animal	Material in Endoskeleton
Sea Star	
Shark	
Bear	

2. **Draw Conclusions** Why is having an endoskeleton an advantage to a bird?

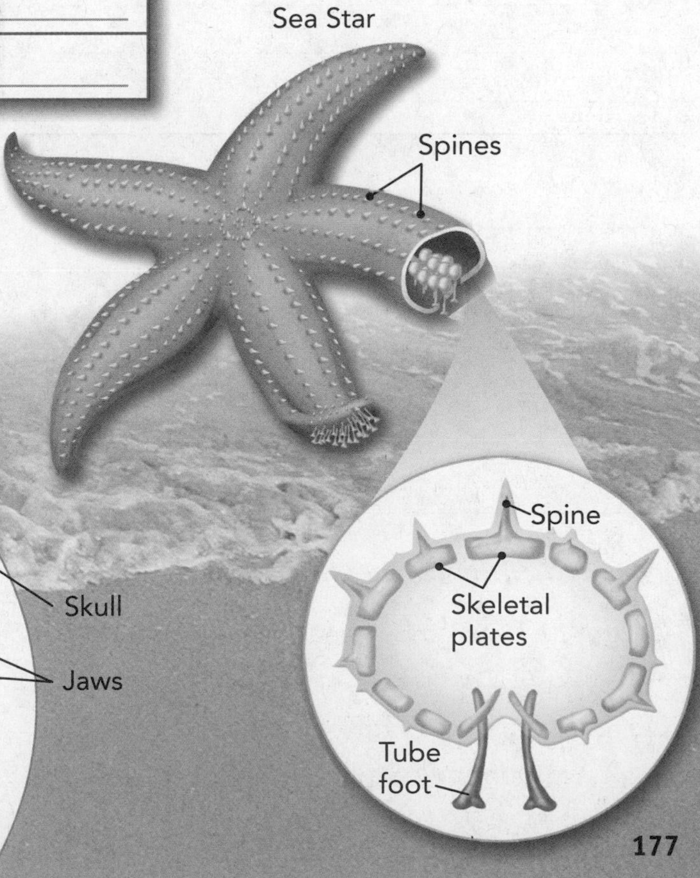

_____

_____

Polar Bear

Foot and leg skeleton

Sea Star

Spines

Great White Shark

Skull

Jaws

Spine

Skeletal plates

Tube foot

177

Joint

Costa Rican Spider

Joints Have you ever tried to run without bending your legs? If you have, then you know it is difficult. Fortunately, most exoskeletons and endoskeletons have joints. A **joint** is a place where two or more parts of a skeleton meet. The way the parts are held together in a joint determines how the joint can move.

Both arthropods and vertebrates have joints. An arthropod's appendages, or jointed attachments, enable the arthropod to move these appendages in different ways. For example, an insect's mouthparts may move from side to side and crush blades of grass. Its legs, however, may move forward and backward, enabling the insect to crawl. Vertebrates also have jointed appendages. As with arthropods, different joints enable vertebrates to move their appendages in different ways.

apply it!

Joints provide flexibility for animals. Look at the picture of the lemur on the right. Then answer the questions.

1 **Interpret Photos** Circle the joints you see.

2 **Infer** Describe how the leg joints enable the lemur to move.

_____

_____

_____

_____

Lab zone Do the Quick Lab *Comparing Bone and Cartilage.*

🔑 Assess Your Understanding

1a. Define What is cartilage?

_____

_____

b. **CHALLENGE** Why is a lobster more vulnerable to predators when it molts?

_____

_____

_____

got it? ....

○ **I get it!** Now I know that a skeleton is a framework that _____

_____

○ **I need extra help with** _____

Go to **MY SCIENCE COACH** *online for help with this subject.*

What Is the Role of Muscles?

Muscles help animals move their body parts. Tissues that contract or relax to create movement are **muscles.** Some muscles are part of an organ. For example, muscles make up most of the walls of some blood vessels. When these muscles contract, or get shorter, they squeeze blood through the vessels.

Other muscles attach to parts of skeletons. Muscles attach to the inside of exoskeletons. In an endoskeleton, muscles attach to the outsides of the bones or cartilage. For both types of skeletons, movement occurs when muscles pull on skeletons.

Muscles attached to skeletons always work in pairs, as shown in **Figure 3.** When one muscle contracts, the other muscle relaxes, or returns to its original length. The contracted muscle pulls on the skeleton and causes it to move in a certain direction. Then, as the contracted muscle relaxes, the relaxed muscle contracts. This action causes the skeleton to move in the opposite direction.

FIGURE 3 ······································

Muscle Pairs

✎ **Complete these tasks.**

1. **Use Context to Determine Meaning** In the text above, underline key phrases that help you understand the terms *relaxed* and *contracted*.

2. **Interpret Diagrams** Label each muscle as *relaxed* or *contracted* for both types of skeletons.

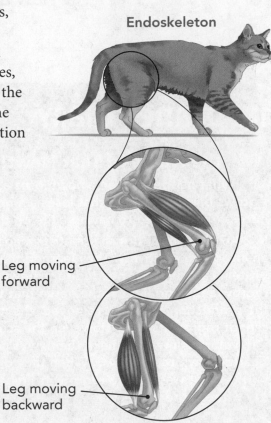

Endoskeleton

Leg moving forward

Leg moving backward

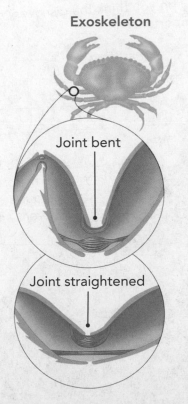

Exoskeleton

Joint bent

Joint straightened

Lab zone® Do the Quick Lab
What Do Muscles Do?

🔑 Assess Your Understanding

got **it?** ·······································

○ **I get it!** Now I know that muscles help animals _____

_____

○ **I need extra help with** _____

Go to MY SCIENCE COACH *online for help with this subject.*

UNLOCK
THE BIG
?

🔑 **What Is the Role of the Nervous System?**

🔑 **How Do Nervous Systems Differ?**

my planeT DiaRY

DISCOVERY

The Nerve of That Newt!

What happens when a newt loses a limb? It grows back! So a newt that loses a limb is not necessarily doomed to having a life on three legs.

In 2007, a team of British scientists made an intriguing discovery. They learned that a protein called nAG is needed for a newt to regrow a missing limb. If the nerve that triggers the production of nAG is removed, the newt cannot regrow its limb. However, the scientists developed a way to make the newt's cells artificially produce nAG. When they did this, the newt was able to regrow its limbs, even without the nerve.

Read the following questions. Write your answers below.

1. What role does a nerve play in the newt's ability to regrow a missing limb?

_____

_____

_____

_____

2. Why do you think the discovery of nAG is important?

_____

_____

_____

_____

▶ PLANET DIARY Go to **Planet Diary** to learn more about the nervous system of different animals.

Lab zone Do the Inquiry Warm-Up *Sending Signals.*

Vocabulary

- nervous system
- stimulus
- response
- neuron
- impulse
- sensory neuron
- interneuron
- motor neuron
- brain

Skills

➲ Reading: Identify Supporting Evidence

△ Inquiry: Draw Conclusions

What Is the Role of the Nervous System?

You are in the yard studying. Your dog, Rugger, is lying beside you. Suddenly, Rugger lifts his head and perks his ears. A few seconds later, a car pulls into the driveway.

Interactions Rugger's actions resulted from interactions of his nervous system. A **nervous system** receives information from the environment and coordinates a response. In this way, it acts like the body's control panel. ⬤ **A nervous system allows animals to detect signals in their environments, process the signals, and react to them.**

A signal that causes an animal to react in some way is called a **stimulus** (plural *stimuli*). Touch, sound, and the things animals smell, taste, or see are stimuli. After a nervous system detects a stimulus, it processes the information. For animals like Rugger, this process happens in the brain. Processing information results in a response. A **response** is an animal's reaction to a stimulus. Rugger's response to hearing the car was to lift his head and perk his ears. Rugger could have also responded by barking or running.

apply it!

A chameleon eats insects. When it sees an insect, a chameleon snaps out its long, sticky tongue, which traps the insect on the end.

❶ Identify What is the stimulus for this chameleon? What is the response?

_____

_____

❷ △ Draw Conclusions Why is this response important to the chameleon?

_____

_____

Types of Cells
Animals often respond to a stimulus in fractions of seconds. If they didn't, they might not eat, or they might be eaten. The basic unit of the nervous system, a neuron, enables speedy responses. A **neuron** is a nerve cell with a unique structure for receiving and passing on information. In a nerve cell, information travels as an electrical message called an **impulse.**

Complex animals have three kinds of neurons that work together to take in information, process it, and enable an animal to respond. **Sensory neurons** are nerve cells that detect stimuli. Organs, such as eyes and ears, contain many sensory neurons. **Interneurons** are nerve cells that pass information between neurons. **Motor neurons** are nerve cells that carry response information to muscles and other organs.

⊙ **Identify Supporting Evidence** In the second paragraph, underline three examples of supporting evidence for the statement, "Complex animals have three kinds of neurons."

apply it!

In complex animals, different kinds of neurons work together to transfer information.

❶ **Classify** Under each picture, write the type of neuron the mouse is using.

❷ **Describe** Based on these pictures, what stimulus is the mouse receiving? What is its response?

_____
_____
_____

Lab zone® Do the Quick Lab *Design a Nervous System.*

🔑 Assess Your Understanding

1a. Review What is a stimulus?

_____
_____

b. Apply Concepts What kind of stimulus would produce a response from a hungry animal?

_____
_____

got it?

○ **I get it!** Now I know that a nervous system allows animals to _____

_____

○ **I need extra help with** _____

Go to MY SCIENCE ⊙ₛ COACH online for help with this subject.

How Do Nervous Systems Differ?

It is hard to imagine an animal without a nervous system. This is because most familiar animals have complex nervous systems. But sponges don't have a nervous system, and many other animals have very simple ones. **The simplest nervous systems are a netlike arrangement of neurons throughout the body. The most complex systems have a nerve cord and a brain.**

Types of Nervous Systems A cnidarian's nervous system consists of neurons arranged like a net, as you can see in **Figure 1.** This type of nervous system is called a nerve net. Animals with nerve nets have no specialized neurons. Therefore, a stimulus to one neuron sends impulses in all directions.

Many animals have more organized nervous systems than those of cnidarians. For example, a planarian's nervous system has nerve cords formed from groups of interneurons. Arthropods, mollusks, and vertebrates have nervous systems with brains. A **brain** is an organized grouping of neurons in the head of an animal with bilateral symmetry. A brain receives information, interprets it, and controls an animal's response. A complex animal with a brain and nerve cord may have billions of neurons.

A hydra has a nerve net with no specialized neurons.

Cnidarian

Neurons

FIGURE 1 ·····················

> ART IN MOTION **Nervous Systems**
Different types of nervous systems have different functions.

✎ **Identify** In the table, write the structures that make up each animal's nervous system.

Nerve cord

Groups of interneurons

Flatworm

A planarian has two small structures in its head that are formed from groups of interneurons.

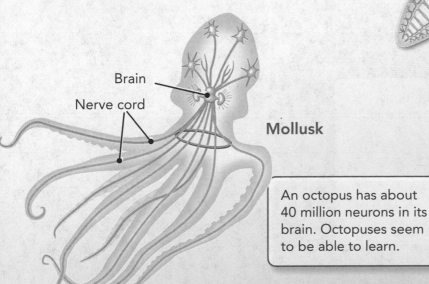

Brain

Nerve cord

Mollusk

An octopus has about 40 million neurons in its brain. Octopuses seem to be able to learn.

Nervous System Structures	
Cnidarian	
Flatworm	
Mollusk	

183

Sense Organs The more complex an animal's nervous system is, the more specialized its sense organs are. Sense organs such as ears, eyes, and noses detect stimuli in the form of sound, light, odor, and touch. Many, but not all, sense organs are located in the head. For example, a grasshopper has compound eyes and antennae on its head, which detect chemicals and touch. It also has membranes on its body that detect vibrations.

Animals with many sense organs can process many stimuli at the same time. This is because different areas of the brain respond to different stimuli at the same time. For example, when an animal such as your dog is around food, its brain processes messages about the food's color, smell, taste, and temperature all at the same time. Look at **Figure 2** to learn about some animals' sense organs.

While under water, a platypus uses its bill to detect the movements of other animals.

_____
_____
_____
_____

FIGURE 2 ···
Sense Organs
✏️ **Read about each animal. Then answer the questions below.**

1. **Infer** Write in the boxes how the sense organ might help the animal.

2. CHALLENGE Where are the sense organs located on most animals with bilateral symmetry? Why?

_____
_____

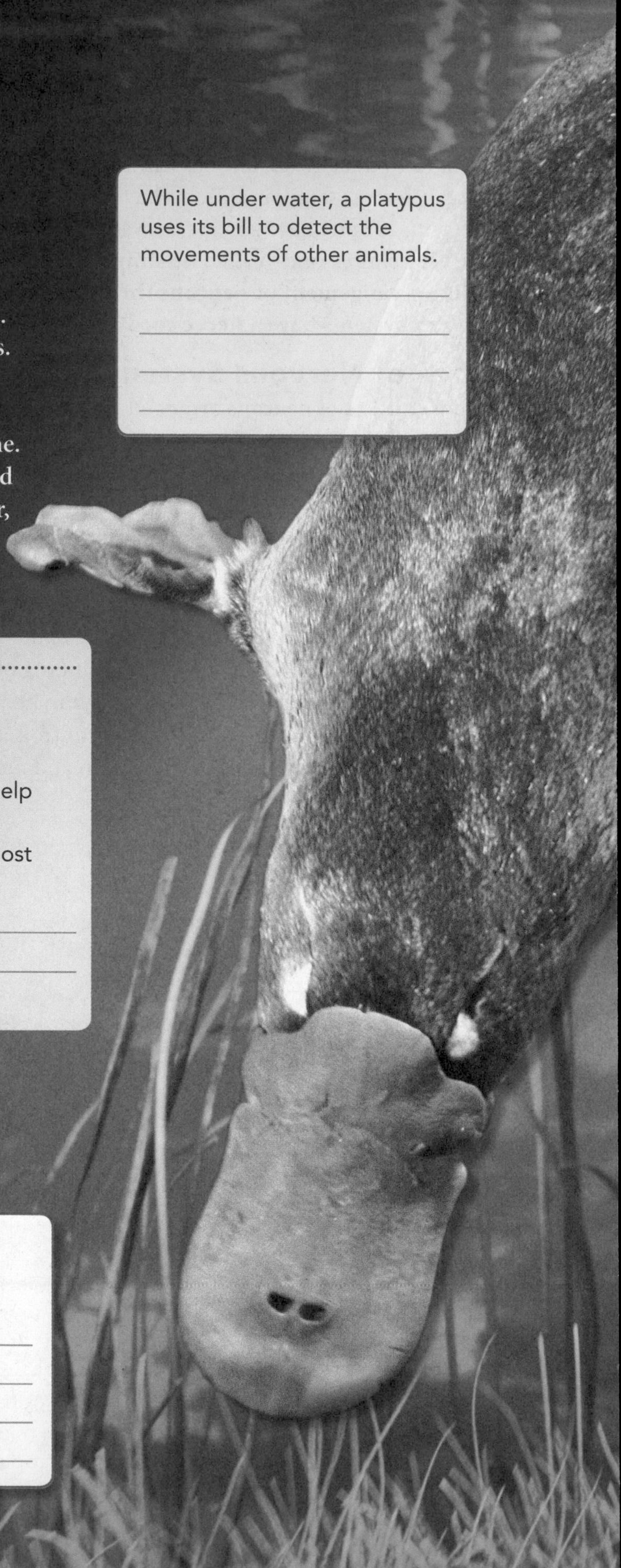

A frog detects vibrations in the air with its tympanic membrane.

_____
_____
_____
_____

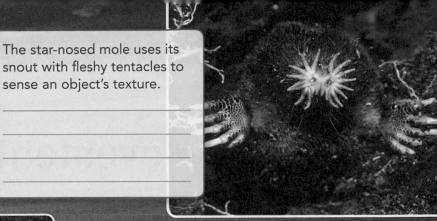

The star-nosed mole uses its snout with fleshy tentacles to sense an object's texture.

_____

_____

_____

_____

A shark uses cells in its nasal passages to detect tiny amounts of blood in sea water.

_____

_____

_____

Most insects detect some colors and movement with their compound eyes.

_____

_____

_____

_____

Lab zone® Do the Quick Lab
Compare Nervous Systems.

🔑 Assess Your Understanding

2a. Define What is a brain?

_____

_____

_____

_____

b. Infer Why is having many sense organs an advantage for an animal?

_____

_____

_____

got it? ....

○ **I get it!** Now I know that structures in a simple nervous system differ from those in a complex nervous

system in that they have a _____

_____

○ I need extra help with _____

Go to **my science** ⑤ **coach** *online for help with this subject.*

UNLOCK THE BIG ?

🔑 **What Causes Animals to Move?**

🔑 **How Do Adaptations for Movement Compare?**

my planet diary

BLOG

Posted by: Dylan

Location: Newton, Massachusetts

Often in the summer when I am walking down the beach, I think of myself running and taking off, soaring into the open sky and looking down at the coastline. Being able to fly is a dream of mine because it seems like a quick way to travel. Also, I want to be the first person in the world that can fly. I want to fly for leisure, not "fight evil with my powers" like superheroes do in the movies. I think many people dream of being able to fly. Who knows, maybe someday that dream will come true.

Communicate Discuss the following questions with a partner. Then write your answers below.

1. In what ways can people fly today?

_____

_____

_____

2. Would it affect your life in a positive or negative way if people could fly unassisted? Why?

_____

_____

_____

_____

▶ **PLANET DIARY** Go to **Planet Diary** to learn more about animal movement.

 Do the Inquiry Warm-Up *Hydra Doing?*

Vocabulary
- water vascular system
- swim bladder

Skills
- Reading: Relate Text and Visuals
- Inquiry: Calculate

What Causes Animals to Move?

All animals move about in certain ways during their lives. They may swim, walk, slither, crawl, run, hop, fly, soar, jump, or swing through trees. However, all animal movements have something in common. **An animal moves about when its nervous system, muscular system, and skeletal system work together to make movement happen.** First, an animal's nervous system receives a signal from the environment. Second, its nervous system processes the signal. Finally, its nervous system signals the muscles, which contract, causing the skeleton to move.

Animals move for many reasons. They move to obtain food, defend and protect themselves, maintain homeostasis, and find mates.

Relate Text and Visuals For each photo, write a reason why the animal might be moving.

Raccoon

Hermit Crab

Peacock

Lab zone — Do the Lab Investigation *A Snail's Pace.*

Assess Your Understanding

got it?

O **I get it!** Now I know that animals move about _____

O **I need extra help with** _____

Go to MY SCIENCE COACH online for help with this subject.

How Do Adaptations for Movement Compare?

Animals live nearly everywhere on Earth. 🔑 **Animals that live in water, on land, or in the air have different adaptations for movement.**

Moving in Water If you have ever tried to walk in a swimming pool, you know that moving in water is more difficult than moving on land. This is because water is resistant to movement through it. Many animals that swim, such as fishes, dolphins, and penguins, have streamlined bodies that help them move through water. They also have appendages for swimming. Fishes have fins, dolphins have flippers, and penguins have wings.

Some animals that live in water do not swim but move through water in other ways. For example, sea stars and other echinoderms have a **water vascular system,** a system of fluid-filled tubes. The tubes produce suction, which enables an echinoderm to grip surfaces and move along. Look at **Figure 1** to see some different animal adaptations for moving in water.

FIGURE 1 ···

▶ **INTERACTIVE ART** **Moving Through Water**
✏ **Complete the activity and then answer the question.**

1. **Summarize** In the table on the next page, identify each animal's adaptation for moving. Then describe how the animal moves.

2. **Make Judgments** How is a fish helped by staying at a certain depth without using a lot of energy?

_____

_____

_____

Fins for Balance These fins help the fish stay upright in the water.

Bony fish

Tail Fin The tail fin, along with the fish's side muscles, provide swimming power.

Swim Bladder A **swim bladder** is an internal, gas-filled sac. By adjusting the gas level, a fish can stay at a certain depth without using much energy.

Sea Star

Penguin

Water Vascular System A sea star has tube feet on the under sides of its arms. They are part of the water vascular system and grip surfaces with suction.

Streamlined Bodies A penguin has a streamlined body and wings.

Frog

Jet Propulsion A squid moves by jet propulsion. It uses muscles to pull water into its body, and then shoots it out through a narrow tube. This shoots the squid in the opposite direction.

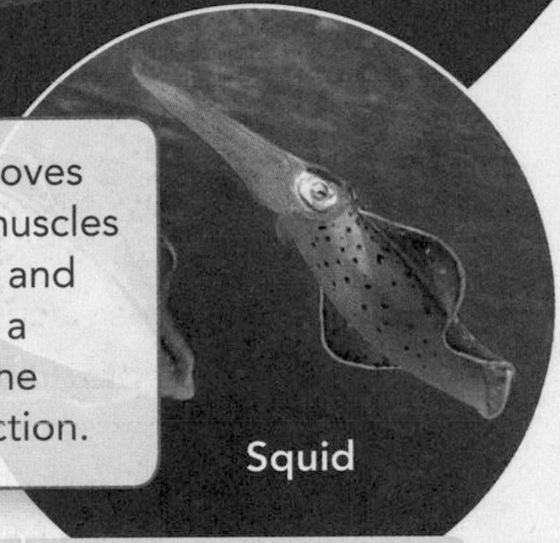

Squid

Webbed Feet Webbed feet help a frog push itself through water.

Animal	Movement Adaptations	How It Moves
Bony Fish		
Penguin		
Sea Star		
Frog		
Squid		

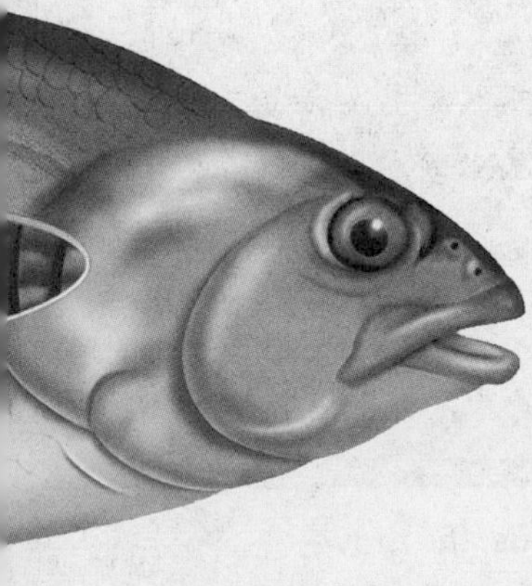

Muscles and Bristles
A segmented worm, such as this fireworm, has muscles that contract to extend the worm forward. It also has bristles that grip the soil.

Moving on Land Have you ever watched a snake slither through the grass? Perhaps you've watched ants walk across the ground. Both snakes and ants move on land, but their adaptations for moving on land are different. A snake contracts its muscles and pushes against the ground with its body. An ant uses its jointed appendages to walk. **Figure 2** shows some of the many adaptations that animals have for moving on land.

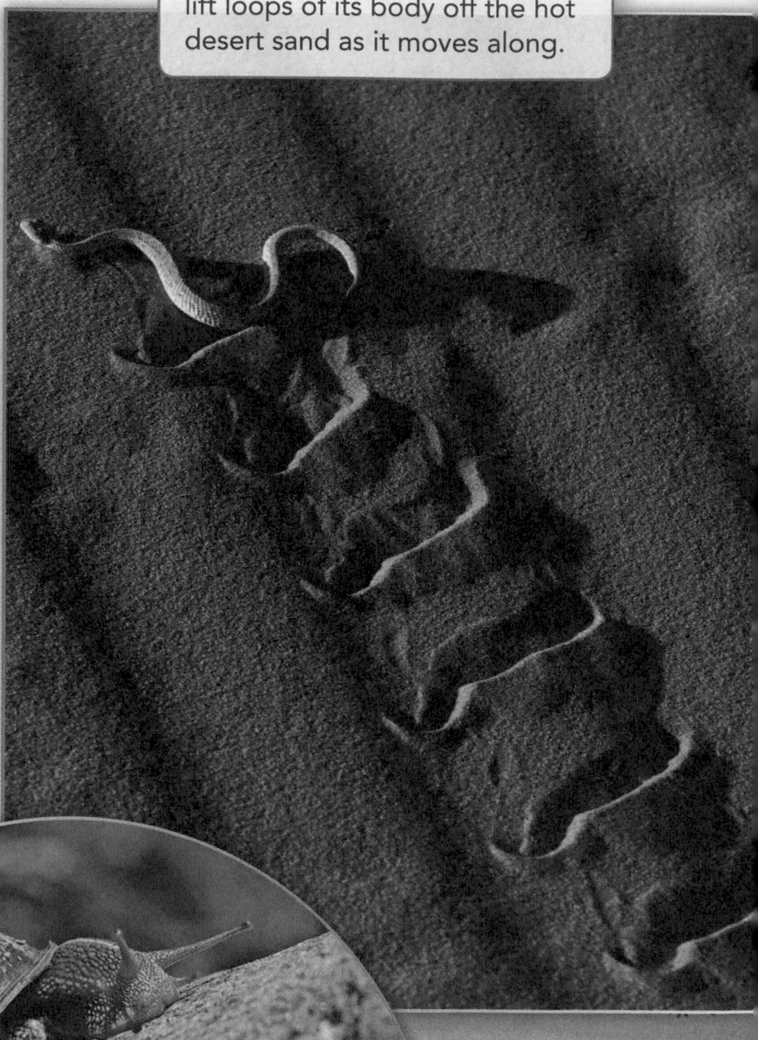

Body Muscles This sidewinding adder snake uses its muscles to lift loops of its body off the hot desert sand as it moves along.

FIGURE 2 ·······························
Moving on Land
The different adaptations of these animals allow them to move in different ways.

✎ **Complete these activities.**

1. **Apply Concepts** In the graphic organizer on the next page, describe an adaptation for moving that three other animals you know have.

2. CHALLENGE Describe the adaptations that a kangaroo has for movement.

_____

_____

_____

_____

✎

Vocabulary Identify Multiple Meanings The word *foot* has other meanings besides appendage. Write another meaning for *foot* below.

_____

_____

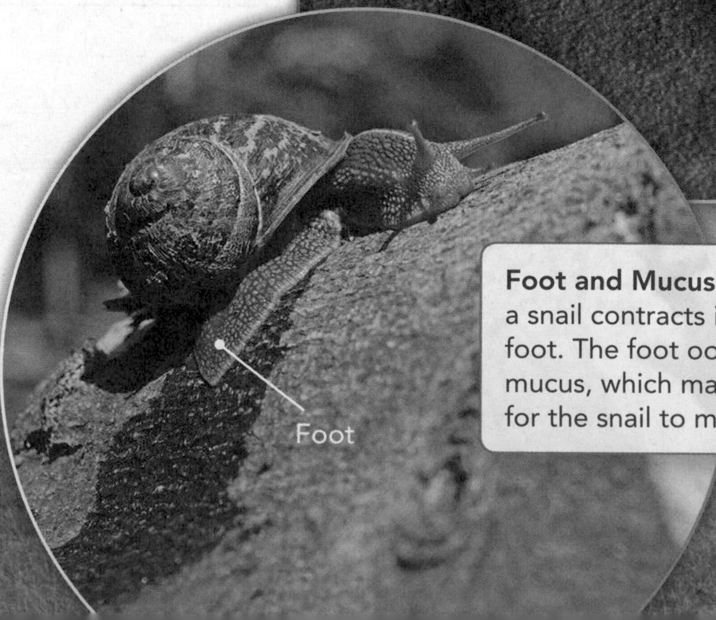

Foot

Foot and Mucus To move, a snail contracts its muscular foot. The foot oozes slippery mucus, which makes it easier for the snail to move along.

Long Arms An orangutan grasps branches with its long arms and swings from place to place.

Muscular Legs A grasshopper's muscular hind legs enable it to push off a surface. An adult grasshopper can travel 20 times its body length in a single jump!

Land Animal Movements

Long Legs and Two Toes An ostrich has long legs with only two toes on each foot. These traits help it run as fast as 60 km/h.

Moving in Air What do beetles, birds, and bats have in common? The answer, of course, is that they can fly. When you think of animals that fly, you probably first think about birds. Birds are uniquely adapted for flight, as shown in **Figure 3.** But many insects are also flight experts. Their wings grow from their exoskeletons and can move up, down, forward, and backward. A few insects can even twist their wings. Some insects warm up their flight muscles before flying by vibrating their wings, much like a pilot warms up an airplane's engines before taking off.

Skin and Bones A bat is the only mammal that flies. A bat wing is made of thin skin stretched over the bat's long finger bones.

Feathers This hawk's long, broad wing feathers provide lift, enabling it to fly very high. Also, the large surface area of its feathers help the hawk soar.

FIGURE 3 ·······························

> INTERACTIVE ART Moving Through Air

✏ **Compare and Contrast** Choose two animals on these pages. Then, in the table, write how their wings are alike and different.

Wings	Animals
Alike	
Different	

Paired Wings A dragonfly has two wings on each side of its body. The wings enable it to fly a long time and change direction quickly.

Wings for Hovering The small, narrow wings of this hummingbird can flap rapidly. This allows hummingbirds to fly forward, backward, and even hover like a helicopter.

Short, Round Wings Some forest birds, such as this pheasant, have short, rounded wings that enable them to take off rapidly.

Front and Hind Wings Butterflies have front and hind wings that are linked by a thin layer of cells. This helps the butterfly flap both pairs of wings at the same time.

do the
math! ....

Different insects beat their wings at different rates, which are measured in beats per second (bps).

Insect	Wing bps
Housefly	190
Horsefly	96
Large white butterfly	12

1 Interpret Data How many times does a housefly beat its wings in one minute?

_____

_____

2 Calculate How many times faster does a horsefly beat its wings than a large white butterfly?

_____

_____

EXPLORE THE BIG Q

A MOVING STORY

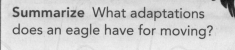

How do animals move?

FIGURE 4

REAL-WORLD INQUIRY A raccoon scurries over rocks as a bald eagle soars above it looking for a meal. Nearby, dragonflies skim over a stream where trout surface to snatch a meal. Movement is everywhere.

Answer the questions in the boxes.

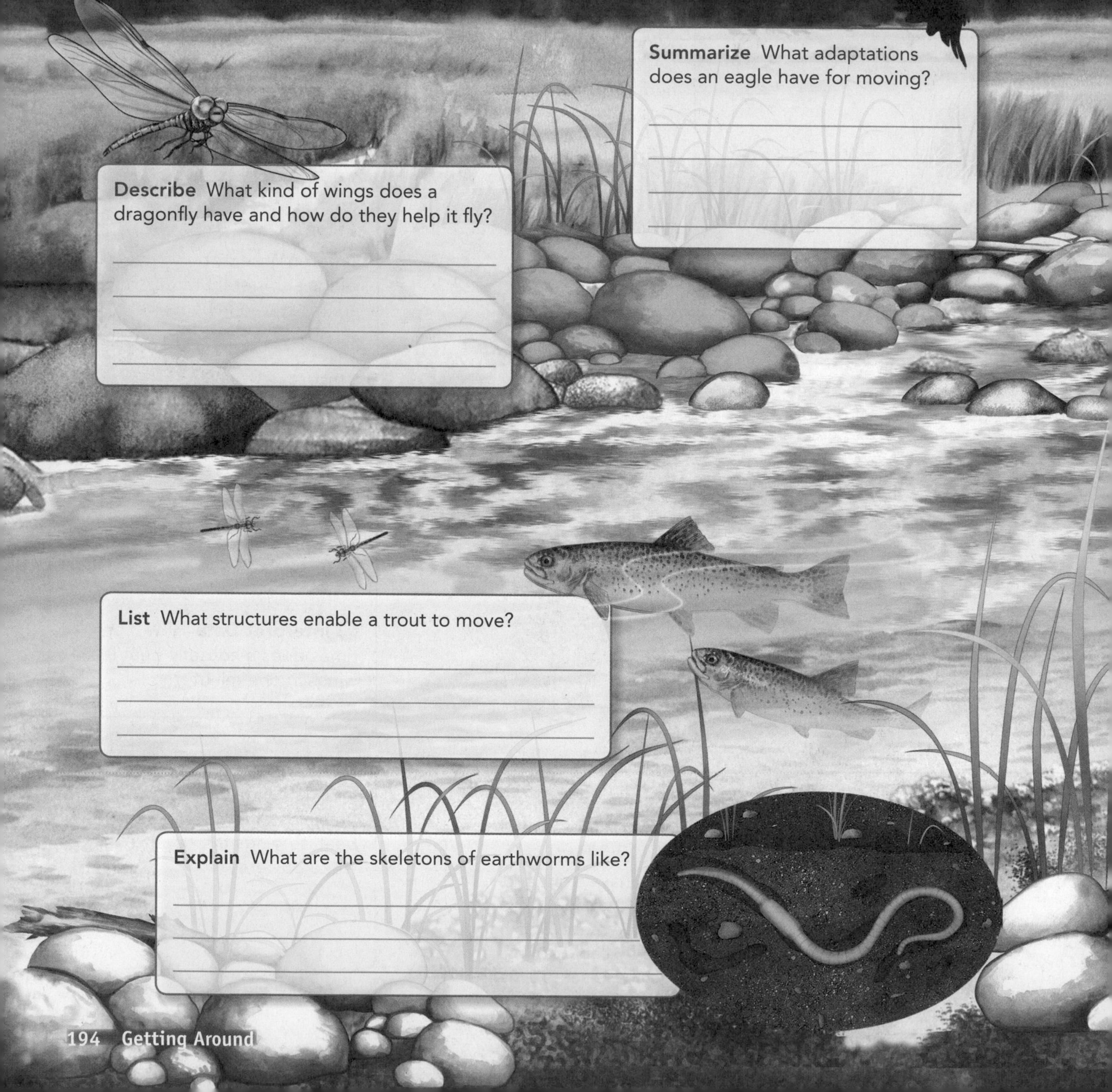

Summarize What adaptations does an eagle have for moving?

Describe What kind of wings does a dragonfly have and how do they help it fly?

List What structures enable a trout to move?

Explain What are the skeletons of earthworms like?

Summarize How does a raccoon's nervous system work with its muscular system to escape an eagle?

_____

_____

_____

_____

Identify When a moose smells a leafy plant, what kinds of neurons are involved? What roles do the neurons serve?

_____

_____

_____

_____

_____

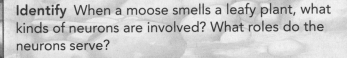

Lab zone® Do the Quick Lab *Webbing Along.*

🔑 Assess Your Understanding

1a. Explain What adaptation does a grasshopper have to move on land?

_____

_____

_____

b. ANSWER THE BIG **?** How do animals move?

_____

_____

_____

got it? ....

○ **I get it!** Now I know that animals have different adaptations for movement depending on _____

_____

○ I need extra help with _____

Go to **MY SCIENCE ⑤ COACH** online for help with this subject.

Study Guide

An animal's _____, _____, and _____ work together to help the animal move.

LESSON 1 Skeletons and Muscles

🔑 A skeleton is a framework that shapes and supports an animal, protects its internal organs, and allows it to move in its environment.

🔑 Muscles help animals move their body parts.

Vocabulary
• molting
• cartilage
• joint
• muscle

LESSON 2 The Nervous System

🔑 A nervous system allows animals to detect signals in their environments, process the signals, and react to them.

🔑 The simplest nervous systems are a netlike arrangement of neurons throughout the body. The most complex systems have a nerve cord and a brain.

Vocabulary
• nervous system • stimulus • response • neuron
• impulse • sensory neuron • interneuron
• motor neuron • brain

LESSON 3 Animal Movement

🔑 An animal moves about when its nervous system, muscular system, and skeletal system work together to make movement happen.

🔑 Animals that live in water, on land, or in the air have different adaptations for movement.

Vocabulary
• water vascular system
• swim bladder

Review and Assessment

LESSON 1 Skeletons and Muscles

1. What type of skeleton is shown in the diagram below?

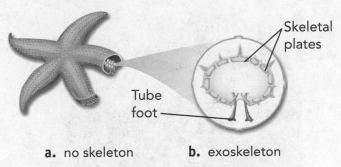

Skeletal plates

Tube foot

a. no skeleton

b. exoskeleton

c. a skeleton without hard parts

d. endoskeleton

2. A _____ is a place where two or more parts of a skeleton meet.

3. Make Generalizations List three functions of a skeleton.

_____

_____

_____

4. Relate Cause and Effect How might an endoskeleton affect the size of an animal?

_____

_____

_____

5. Sequence Describe how your muscles work to help you kick a ball.

_____

_____

_____

_____

_____

_____

LESSON 2 The Nervous System

6. A signal that causes an animal to react in some way is called a

a. response.

b. neuron.

c. stimulus.

d. impulse.

7. The most complex nervous systems have a nerve cord and a _____

8. Communicate Describe the nervous system of a cnidarian.

_____

_____

_____

_____

_____

Use the diagrams below to answer Question 9.

A   B

9. Interpret Diagrams Explain the stimulus in diagram A and the toad's response in diagram B.

_____

_____

_____

_____

10.  **Write About It** Write a paragraph in which you describe a complex animal's response to a specific stimulus. Explain how the three kinds of neurons work together to transfer information in your example.

197

LESSON 3 Animal Movement

11. An animal that moves using a water vascular system is a

　a. sea star.

　b. penguin.

　c. squid.

　d. shark.

12. A fish can use its _____

to help it stay at a certain depth without

using much energy.

13. Draw Conclusions What are three reasons why an animal might need to move about?

_____

_____

_____

_____

_____

_____

_____

14. Apply Concepts Why is it easier for a dolphin to move through water than it is for a horse?

_____

_____

_____

_____

_____

15. **Write About It** Write a paragraph in which you describe a different adaptation that rabbits, bats, and snakes each have that enables them to move as they do.

How do animals move?

16. Suppose this ostrich's nervous system was not receiving signals properly. How might it be dangerous for the ostrich?

_____

_____

_____

_____

_____

_____

_____

_____

_____

_____

_____

_____

_____

_____

_____

_____

_____

_____

Standardized Test Prep

Multiple Choice

Circle the letter of the best answer.

1. Which is true of the skeleton shown below?

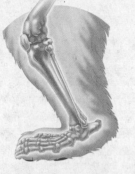

   A It grows with the animal.
   B It molts as the animal grows.
   C It does not have hard parts.
   D It is mostly cartilage.

2. A rock hits a turtle on its shell. Then the turtle hides inside its shell. What is the stimulus?

   A the turtle hiding
   B the turtle's shell
   C a rock hitting the shell
   D the turtle walking

3. What adaptation does a sea star have for moving in water?

   A a water vascular system
   B a streamlined body
   C fins
   D a swim bladder

4. What enables an animal's endoskeleton to grow?

   A The animal molts.
   B The animal's joints become dislocated.
   C The animal's nervous system gets larger.
   D The animal's bone and cartilage contain living cells.

5. Animals with nerve nets have

   A no specialized neurons.
   B sensory neurons, but no interneurons.
   C interneurons, but no sensory neurons.
   D only motor neurons.

Constructed Response

Use the diagram below and your knowledge of science to help you answer Question 6. Write your answer on a separate sheet of paper.

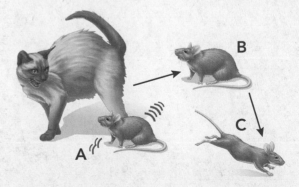

6. Describe how the mouse's nervous system is functioning in this diagram. Include the roles of the sensory neurons, interneurons, and motor neurons.

LIGHTS, CÁMERA, SHARK ACTION!

In movies, sharks are often scary, toothy costars. Although many people know that sharks have a mean reputation, there is a lot that we don't know about them.

To discover more about these mysterious creatures, Fabien Cousteau and his team created a shark submarine. The one-person submarine has a steel skeleton and a thick rubber skin that makes it look like a great white shark. The 4.25-meter shark sub moves through the water as quietly and quickly as a real shark, and can even wiggle its tail!

In the sub, Cousteau was able to observe shark behavior up close. He saw sharks' feeding habits, how they investigated new things, and how they prepared to attack. He also saw real sharks trying to communicate with the fake one by rolling their eyes and puffing their gills. The submarine's cameras recorded hours of shark action, which will help us understand these creatures better.

Research It Find three articles describing Cousteau's interaction with the sharks. Write your own article comparing and reviewing the science presented in the articles. Describe any new information you learned from each article, and evaluate any bias in the articles. How was the information presented in each article? Did the authors balance their discussions of the risks and benefits of shark research?

Museum of Science

"feet" of engineering

Geckos are tiny lizards that live in warm climates all over the world, including the southwestern United States. If you've ever seen one, you've probably watched it scale a wall in about the time it takes for you to blink. Or you may have seen a gecko hang from one foot.

How do geckos hang from one foot? The answer is their hair! The gecko's feet are covered in millions of tiny hairs. Molecules in the hairs are attracted to molecules in the wall or on any other surface. These forces of attraction, called van der Waals forces, affect every form of matter, but they are usually so weak that you can't feel them. However, there are so many tiny hairs on a gecko's feet that geckos can cling to nearly any surface!

Gecko feet have inspired scientists to design artificial super-sticky materials that use the same principle. Maybe someday these materials could be used for surgical bandages, wall-crawling robots, or even shoes with incredible grip. For now, scientists will have to see which designs stick!

Design It Technological design inspired by biology is called biomimetic design. Research a few other examples of biomimetic design, and choose a simple problem that one of your examples could solve. Make or draw a model of your solution.

HOW CAN THIS SNAKE DIGEST A FROG?

How do animals get and use energy?

You might wonder how a snake can swallow a frog that is much bigger than the snake's mouth. A snake's jaws can stretch open, allowing the snake to spread its jaws around the frog. The snake's teeth are curved backward to hold the frog, as parts of the jaw, throat, and cheek muscles work the frog into the snake's food tube, or esophagus. All the while, digestion begins in the snake's mouth as its saliva drenches the frog.

Predict What do you think happens after the frog reaches the snake's esophagus?

_____

_____

_____

▶ **UNTAMED SCIENCE** Watch the **Untamed Science** video to learn more about how animals get and use energy.

Obtaining Energy

6 Getting Started

Check Your Understanding

1. Background Read the paragraph below and then answer the question.

After Amy's dog ate, he curled up and fell asleep. Sleeping after eating is his normal **behavior.** His chest slowly rose and fell with each breath. The blood pumping through his heart's **chambers** helped the dog's lungs **exchange** oxygen and carbon dioxide.

> **Behavior** is the actions an animal performs.
>
> A **chamber** is an enclosed space.
>
> To **exchange** is to trade one thing for another.

- What was happening inside the dog's body as his chest rose and fell?

_____

_____

_____

> MY READING WEB If you had trouble completing the question above, visit **My Reading Web** and type in *Obtaining Energy.*

Vocabulary Skill

Suffixes A suffix is a word part that is added to the end of a word to change its meaning. The table below lists suffixes that will help you learn key terms in this chapter.

Suffix	Meaning of Suffix	Example
-ory	relating to	circulatory, *adj.* relating to the movement of blood through the body
-sion	process of	diffusion, *n.* the process in which particles move from an area of high concentration to an area of low concentration

2. Quick Check Fill in the blank with the correct term.

- The _____ system includes blood, vessels, and a heart.

Chapter Preview

LESSON 1
- carnivore
- herbivore
- omnivore
- filter feeder
- radula
- digestion
- digestive system
- anus
- crop
- gizzard
- intestine
- esophagus
- stomach

◐ **Identify the Main Idea**
△ **Classify**

LESSON 2
- cellular respiration
- diffusion
- respiratory system
- gill
- lung

◐ **Compare and Contrast**
△ **Predict**

LESSON 3
- circulatory system
- heart
- open circulatory system
- closed circulatory system
- capillary
- atrium
- ventricle
- excretory system
- kidney
- urine

◐ **Summarize**
△ **Draw Conclusions**

> VOCAB FLASH CARDS For extra help with vocabulary, visit **Vocab Flash Cards** and type in *Obtaining Energy.*

How Animals Obtain and Digest Food

🔑 How Do Animals Obtain Food?

🔑 How Do Animals Digest Food?

my planet diary

Owl Pellets

You chew your food before you swallow it using your teeth. Owls, however, do not have teeth. They swallow their food whole. Their food includes mice and insects. After an owl swallows, the food travels into its digestive system to be digested.

What happens to the body parts that an owl cannot digest? Any bones, teeth, and fur travel to the gizzard, a part of an owl's digestive system. Then the owl regurgitates, or spits up, the undigested parts as a pellet. Scientists can examine a pellet to find out what an owl eats.

Owl pellet

FUN FACTS

Read the following questions. Write your answers below.

1. What happens to the food that an owl eats?

_____

_____

_____

2. What might you learn about an owl's environment by looking at its pellet?

_____

_____

_____

> PLANET DIARY Go to **Planet Diary** to learn more about how animals obtain and digest food.

Lab zone® Do the Inquiry Warm-Up How Do Snakes Feed?

How Do Animals Obtain Food?

Think about the last time you had pizza and how good it tasted. That pizza was more than just a great meal. It also gave you the energy you needed to ride a bike or use a computer. All animals—including you—need food to provide the raw materials and energy that their cells need to carry out their functions.

Vocabulary
- carnivore • herbivore • omnivore • filter feeder
- radula • digestion • digestive system • anus
- crop • gizzard • intestine • esophagus • stomach

Skills
↻ Reading: Identify the Main Idea
△ Inquiry: Classify

Caterpillar

What Animals Eat 🔑 The different ways that an animal obtains food depends on what it eats and its adaptations for getting food. Animals may be grouped based on what type of food they eat. Most animals, like those in **Figure 1,** are carnivores, herbivores, or omnivores. Animals that eat only other animals are **carnivores.** Animals that eat only plant material are **herbivores.** Animals that eat both plant material and other animals are **omnivores.** A few types of animals—such as earthworms, snails, and crabs—eat decaying plants and animals.

FIGURE 1 ....

Animal Diets
All animals need food, but they differ in what they eat and how they get it.

✎ **Infer** Choose one animal from each of the three groups and write in the box what you think it eats.

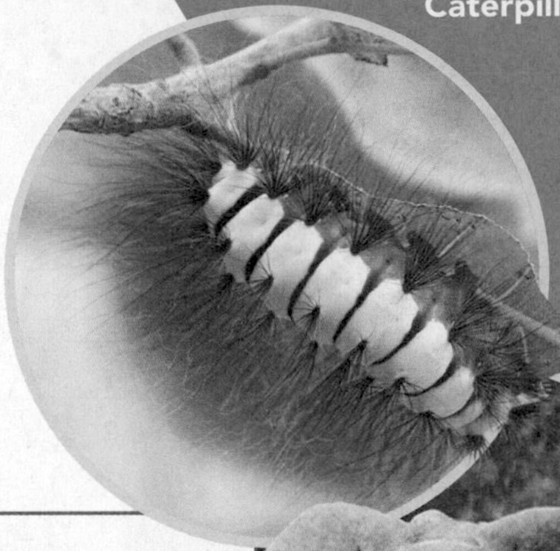

Herbivores
_____
_____
_____

Raccoon

Lion

Elephant

Omnivores
_____
_____
_____

Carnivores
_____
_____
_____

Bear

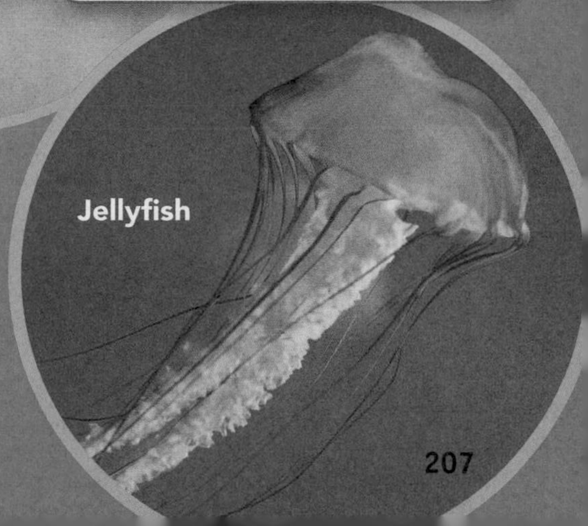

Jellyfish

207

Animal Mouthparts

Animal Mouthparts Have you ever watched animals eating? If you have, you may have noticed some of the many different adaptations that animals have for eating. Depending on their mouthparts, animals may eat by tearing, chewing, sucking, or filtering their food.

Animals That Tear, Chew, and Suck Food Some animals have mouthparts that are specialized for tearing, chewing, or sucking food. For example, grasshoppers have sharp mouthparts that tear and chew leaves. Hummingbirds and some arthropods, such as butterflies, have mouthparts that enable them to suck plant juices from flowers, stems, and leaves.

Many other animals have teeth. Animal teeth are specialized for eating certain types of food. Carnivores, such as wolves, have pointed teeth used for tearing meat. Herbivores, such as rabbits, have flat teeth for grinding plant material. Omnivores usually have both pointed and flat teeth for eating their food.

A butterfly's strawlike mouthpart

apply it!

Many animals use teeth to eat.

1 Classify Look at the teeth of each animal. Based on its teeth, classify each animal as a carnivore, herbivore, or omnivore.

2 Relate Evidence and Explanation In each box, explain why you classified the animal as you did.

Animals That Filter Food Some animals that live in water strain their food from the water. They are called filter feeders. Most **filter feeders** trap and eat microscopic organisms that live in the water. They have netlike structures for doing this. Filter feeders vary in size from the largest animals on Earth, blue whales, to small barnacles. You can see some filter feeders in **Figure 2.**

FIGURE 2 ....
Filter Feeders
✎ **Compare and Contrast** Write on the line below how all these animals are alike. Then write in the chart below how they are different.

_____

_____

Clams

Clams have siphons that draw water into their bodies. The water passes over their gills, which filter out the microorganisms that they eat.

do the
math! ....
Sponges are filter feeders. They have specialized cells for filtering food particles from the water that moves through their bodies. To find how much water flows through a sponge in a given time, use the formula below.

$$\text{Flow rate} = \frac{\text{Volume of water}}{\text{Time}}$$

Calculate A tiny, marble-sized sponge filters 78 liters of water in five days. How many liters does it filter per day?

_____

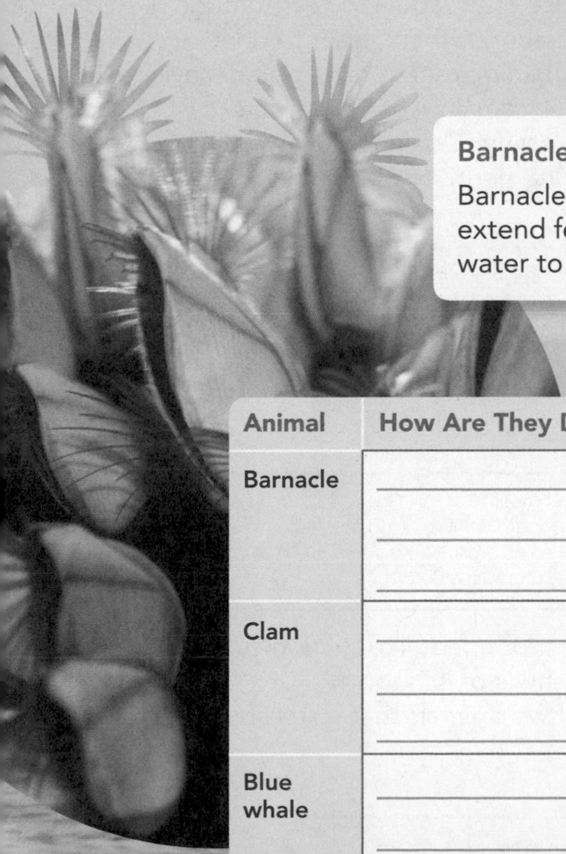

Blue Whale

Comblike structures called baleen filter out tiny organisms from the water that the blue whale sucks through its mouth. The whale then licks off the food and swallows it.

Barnacles

Barnacles open their plates and extend featherlike legs into the water to filter out their food.

Animal	How Are They Different?
Barnacle	
Clam	
Blue whale	

Adaptations for Obtaining Food

Animals have an amazing variety of adaptations for obtaining food. These adaptations include structures and behaviors. For example, animals have an opening through which food enters their bodies. This opening is usually called a mouth. Structures such as beaks and claws enable animals to get food into their mouths. Behaviors also help animals obtain food. For example, most spiders make webs that help them capture their prey. In **Figure 3,** you can see some adaptations that animals have for obtaining food.

FIGURE 3 ···

> **INTERACTIVE ART** **Obtaining Food**

Adaptations help organisms such as a grasshopper and a spider obtain food.

✎ **Study the photos and read the description about how each animal obtains food. Then answer the questions in the boxes.**

Snail

Mouth

Radula

Radula teeth

A snail has a **radula,** or a flexible, tonguelike ribbon of tiny teeth. Some snails use their radula to tear through plant tissues. Others use it to drill through animal shells or scrape decaying material from surfaces of objects.

✎ **Classify** Do you think a snail is a carnivore, herbivore, or omnivore? Why?

_____
_____
_____
_____
_____

Grasshopper   **Spider**

Insects have different mouthparts. Grasshoppers have mouthparts for chewing grass.

✎ **Develop Hypotheses** This spider is a carnivore. Describe how you think it uses its fangs.

_____
_____

Sea Star

A sea star uses its tube feet like suction cups to pry open the shells of its food.

✎ **Infer** Name two animals that a sea star might eat.

_____
_____

Hawk

A coral has stinging cells on its tentacles that stun its prey.

✎ **Interpret Photos** Identify how corals move their food into their mouths.

_____

_____

Silversides Fish

Birds use their beaks to obtain food. The shapes of beaks are specialized for eating different kinds of food.

✎ **Communicate** Look at the beaks of the hawk and pileated woodpeckers. With a partner, decide which beak shape is best for probing soft material and which is best for eating meat.

_____

_____

_____

_____

Cup Coral

 Do the Quick Lab
Planarian Feeding Behavior.

🔑 **Assess Your Understanding**

1a. Review What types of food do carnivores, herbivores, and omnivores eat?

_____

_____

Pileated Woodpeckers

b. Compare and Contrast How are the teeth of carnivores and herbivores alike and different?

_____

_____

_____

_____

_____

This type of snake stretches its jaws, opens its mouth very wide, and swallows its food whole.

✎ **CHALLENGE** Explain how this adaptation might help this type of snake survive.

_____

_____

gotit? ....

○ **I get it!** Now I know that the way an animal gets food depends on _____

_____

Egg-Eating Snake

○ **I need extra help with** _____

Go to **MY SCIENCE COACH** *online for help with this subject.*

211

How Do Animals Digest Food?

You already know that the food animals eat provides needed materials to their cells. However, the food that animals eat is too large to enter the cells. It must be broken down first. The process that breaks down food into small molecules is called **digestion**. 🔑 **Some types of animals digest food mainly inside their cells, but most animals digest food outside their cells.**

Digestion Inside Cells Sponges and a few other animals digest food inside specialized cells in their bodies. The digested food then diffuses into other cells, where it is used. This process is called intracellular digestion. **Figure 4** shows how intracellular digestion occurs in sponges.

FIGURE 4 ···

Intracellular Digestion
Structures surrounding the central cavity of a sponge are adapted for digestion.

✏ **Sequence** Read each box carefully. Then write a number in each circle to show the order in which intracellular digestion occurs in sponges.

Pore
Water containing food particles enters the sponge's body cavity through pores in its body wall.

Collar Cell
Collar cells filter out food particles and then start to digest them.

Jellylike Cell
Specialized jellylike cells complete digestion. Then they carry digested food to the other cells of the sponge.

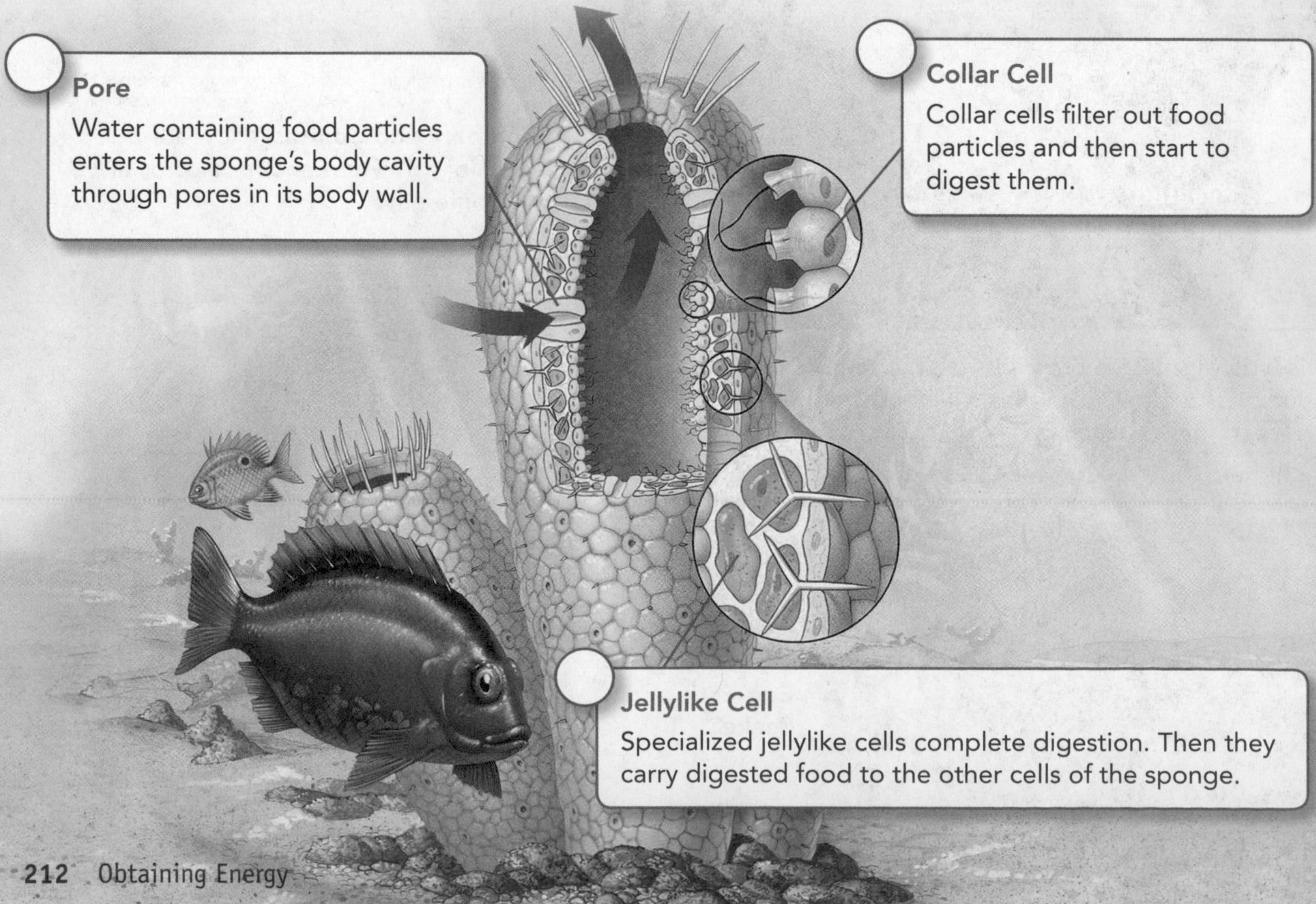

Digestion Outside Cells

Most animals digest their food outside their cells. This process is called extracellular digestion. Digestion outside cells occurs in a digestive system. A **digestive system** is an organ system that has specialized structures for obtaining and digesting food. Most carnivores, herbivores, and omnivores have digestive systems.

Internal Body Cavity The simplest kind of digestive system has only one opening. Food enters the body and wastes exit the body through the same opening. Cnidarians and flatworms have this type of digestive system, which you can see in **Figure 5.**

FIGURE 5 ·······································

Extracellular Digestion

Corals are a type of cnidarian. Planarians are a type of flatworm. Both have extracellular digestion and an internal body cavity with one opening.

✎ **Compare and Contrast** Write in the Venn diagram how intracellular digestion and extracellular digestion are alike and different.

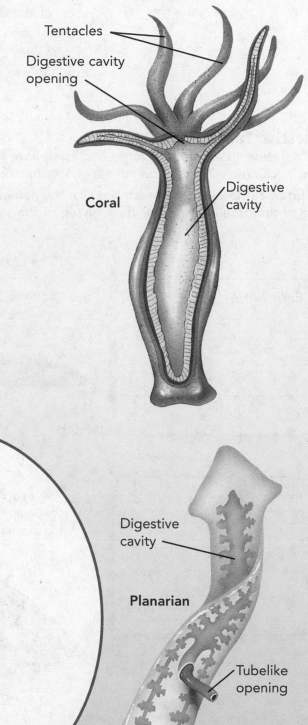

Tentacles

Digestive cavity opening

Coral

Digestive cavity

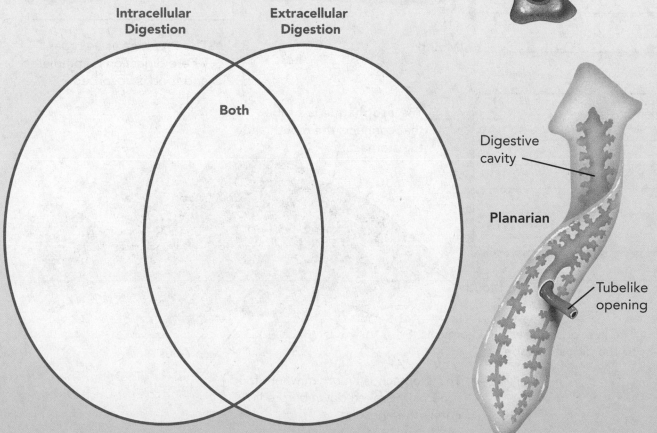

Intracellular Digestion

Extracellular Digestion

Both

Digestive cavity

Planarian

Tubelike opening

● Identify the Main Idea
Underline the main idea in the
Digestive Tube section. Then
circle the supporting details.

Digestive Tube Complex animals have digestive systems that consist of a tube with two openings. One opening is a mouth for taking in food. The other opening is an **anus** through which wastes leave. A digestive tube has specialized areas where food is processed for digestion, digested, and absorbed. You can see the specialized areas of an earthworm's and a fish's digestive tubes in **Figure 6**. A digestive system with two openings is more efficient than a system with one opening. This efficiency is because digested food does not mix with undigested food.

FIGURE 6 ·····································

Digestive Tubes
The digestive tubes of earthworms and fishes have specialized areas in common. These areas have the same functions.

✎ **Interpret Diagrams** In each box, list the names of each area of the tube in the order through which food passes.

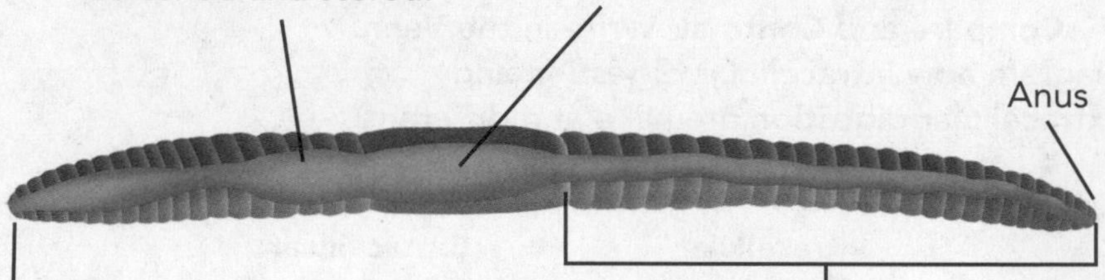

The **crop** is an organ where food is softened and stored.

The **gizzard** is a muscular organ where food is ground up.

Earthworm _____
_____
_____
_____
_____
_____

Anus

Mouth

The **intestine** is an organ where digestion is completed and food is absorbed.

Fish _____
_____
_____
_____
_____
_____
_____

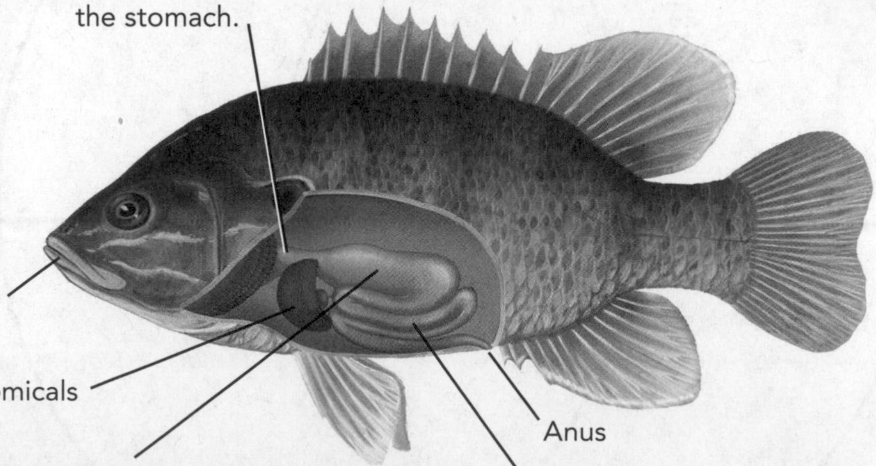

The **esophagus** is a tube that connects the mouth and the stomach.

Mouth

The liver adds digestive chemicals to the digestive tube.

Anus

The **stomach** is an organ where food is partially broken down before it enters the intestine.

Intestine

Specialized Digestive Systems Some animals have specialized digestive systems that meet their needs. For example, birds have a crop where they can store food for long flights. A cow's stomach has four parts, each with a special function. The largest part of the cow's stomach is called the rumen. Bacteria in the rumen produce chemicals that help the cow digest plant material. The cow's digestive system is shown in **Figure 7**.

Rumen

FIGURE 7 ....

Specialized Digestive System of a Cow

The rumen is the first and largest chamber in a cow's stomach.

✎ **Complete these tasks.**

1. **Identify** Label the parts of a cow's digestive system in the diagram.

2. **Summarize** In the box, write how its rumen helps a cow digest grass.

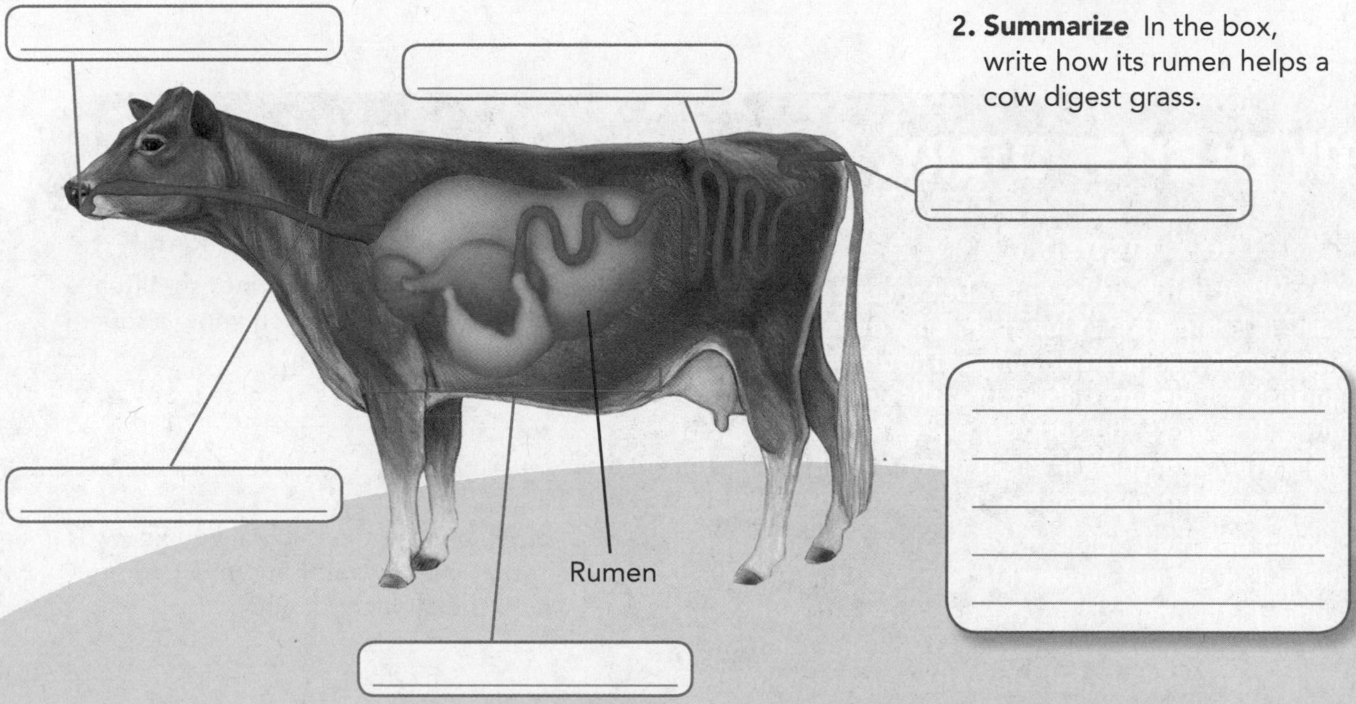

Lab zone Do the Lab Investigation
Looking at an Owl's Leftovers.

🔑 **Assess Your Understanding**

2a. Explain What is extracellular digestion?

_____

_____

_____

b. Draw Conclusions How is it an advantage for an animal to have a long intestine?

_____

_____

_____

got it? ....

○ **I get it!** Now I know that the two ways animals can digest food are _____

_____

○ I need extra help with _____

Go to **MY SCIENCE COACH** online for help with this subject.

215

How Animals Obtain Oxygen

🔑 **How Do Animals Obtain Oxygen?**

🔑 **How Do Animal Respiratory Systems Compare?**

my PLANET DiARY

The Lungfish

What fish lives in water but must come up for air? It is the African lungfish. Like many fish, it has gills. But it also has two lungs. Though the African lungfish can use its gills, it breathes mostly with its lungs. It rises to the surface, pokes its mouth out of the water, and gulps in air. If it cannot obtain air this way, it can drown. Imagine that—a fish drowning!

Sometimes the bodies of water that African lungfish live in can dry up. When this happens, the fish digs a hole in the mud. Then mucus oozes out of its body and lines the hole. The mucus keeps the fish from drying out. The lungfish clears the area around its nostrils so it can still breathe. Lungfish can survive this way for months until the area fills with water again.

FUN FACTS

Answer the following questions.

1. What are two ways lungfish differ from other fishes you know about?

_____

_____

_____

2. What is another animal you know that lives in water and must come to the surface for air?

_____

_____

_____

▶ **PLANET DIARY** Go to **Planet Diary** to learn more about how animals obtain oxygen.

 Lab zone Do the Inquiry Warm-Up *How Does Water Flow Over a Fish's Gills?*

Vocabulary
- cellular respiration
- respiratory system
- diffusion
- gill
- lung

Skills
> Reading: Compare and Contrast
△ Inquiry: Predict

How Do Animals Obtain Oxygen?

What happens when you try to hold your breath? It is not easy after a while, is it? It is difficult because you must breathe to exchange two important gases with your surroundings. Your body cannot function without constantly taking in oxygen and getting rid of carbon dioxide.

Why Animals Need Oxygen Just like you, all other animals need a constant supply of oxygen. Animals need oxygen for a process called cellular respiration. **Cellular respiration** is the process in which cells use oxygen and digested food molecules to release the energy in food. Cellular respiration occurs in every cell in an animal's body. Carbon dioxide is a waste product of the process.

Breathing and cellular respiration are not the same process. Some animals breathe to get oxygen into their bodies. But other animals do not breathe. Instead, they get oxygen into their bodies in different ways. Cellular respiration cannot occur until oxygen is inside an animal's cells. All animals have cellular respiration, but not all animals breathe.

Breathing   Cellular Respiration

Both

> **Compare and Contrast**
In the Venn diagram, compare and contrast breathing and cellular respiration.

Exchanging Gases Animals exchange oxygen and carbon dioxide with their surroundings by diffusion. In the process of **diffusion,** particles move from an area of high concentration to an area of low concentration. 🔑 **Animal cells exchange oxygen and carbon dioxide with their surroundings by diffusion across the outer coverings, or membranes, of cells.** Cell membranes are moist and thin, which enable efficient diffusion.

Cells use oxygen in the process of cellular respiration. Therefore, the concentration of oxygen inside cells is usually lower than it is outside cells. So, oxygen tends to diffuse into cells. Because cellular respiration produces carbon dioxide, there is usually a higher concentration of carbon dioxide inside cells than outside cells. As a result, carbon dioxide tends to diffuse out of cells.

apply it!

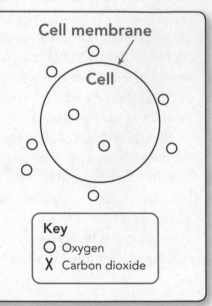

Cell membrane

Cell

Use this model of an animal's muscle cell to complete the activity.

❶ Identify Is the concentration of oxygen greater inside or outside the cell?

_____

❷ Predict Draw X's to represent the concentration of carbon dioxide inside and outside the cell. Explain what you drew.

_____

_____

Key
O Oxygen
X Carbon dioxide

Do the Quick Lab
How Do Animals Get Oxygen?

🔑 **Assess Your Understanding**

1a. Review What does breathing do for an animal?

_____

_____

b. Relate Cause and Effect Why does oxygen tend to diffuse into cells?

_____

_____

got it? ....

○ **I get it!** Now I know that animals exchange oxygen and carbon dioxide with their surroundings _____

○ **I need extra help with** _____

Go to MY SCIENCE 🅢 COACH online for help with this subject.

How Do Animal Respiratory Systems Compare?

The structures that an animal uses to exchange gases with its surroundings make up the **respiratory system**. 🔑 **Respiratory systems include structures such as skin, gills, and lungs. The type of respiratory system an animal has depends on how complex the animal is and where it lives.**

Animals that exchange gases across their skin live in water or in moist places on land. However, most animals that live in water, which contains dissolved oxygen, have gills. **Gills** are featherlike structures where gases are exchanged between water and blood. In contrast, most animals that breathe air, which contains oxygen, have lungs. **Lungs** are saclike structures made up of a thin layer of cells where gases are exchanged between air and blood. Lungs are located inside the body where they can stay moist. Animals with these structures can be seen in **Figure 1**.

FIGURE 1 ....

> ART IN MOTION **Respiratory Structures**
Animals exchange gases with their environment through gills, lungs, or skin.

✎ **Make Generalizations** Explain what you think is different about where dolphins are found and where lobsters are found in the water.

_____

_____

_____

_____

A lobster is an arthropod that has gills under its body near its legs.

A dolphin is a mammal that has lungs inside its body.

A frog is an amphibian that exchanges gases through the skin that covers its body.

Animals Living in Water Think about animals that live in water, such as jellyfishes, clams, sharks, and whales. Just as these animals are diverse, so are their respiratory structures. Most of these animals use either their outer body coverings or gills as respiratory structures, as shown in **Figure 5**. For example, cnidarians use their outer body coverings for gas exchange. Fishes, mollusks, and arthropods use their gills. However, some animals that live in water have lungs and get oxygen from the air. Whales, dolphins, and alligators breathe air at the surface and hold their breath when they dive.

FIGURE 5 ·······························

Respiration Without Lungs

Animals that live in water and do not have lungs use their outer body covering or gills to exchange gases.

✎ **Relate Text and Visuals** In each box, identify the animal's respiratory structure.

This fish is a bony fish.
_____

This reef squid is a mollusk.
_____

A coral is a cnidarian.
_____

Animals Living on Land You might think that all animals living on land use their lungs to exchange gases. Some animals do use lungs, but others do not. For example, amphibians may use their skin as their main respiratory structure. Arthropods and other invertebrates have some unique respiratory structures. Although the respiratory structures of land-dwelling animals are diverse, they do have something in common. They all are made up of thin layers of moist cells. In addition, in more complex animals, the layers have folds or pockets that increase the surface area for gas exchange. The respiratory structures of invertebrates and vertebrates are different.

Invertebrate Structures Just a few of the invertebrates that live on land are shown in **Figure 3**. Their respiratory structures include skin, book lungs, and tracheal tubes.

FIGURE 3 ··

Invertebrate Respiration
Skin, book lungs, and tracheal tubes are respiratory structures of invertebrates.

✎ **Summarize** In the chart, list each animal shown, and write the name of its respiratory structure.

Earthworms exchange gases through their moist skin.

Spiders have structures called book lungs, which are made of thin, stacked cell layers.

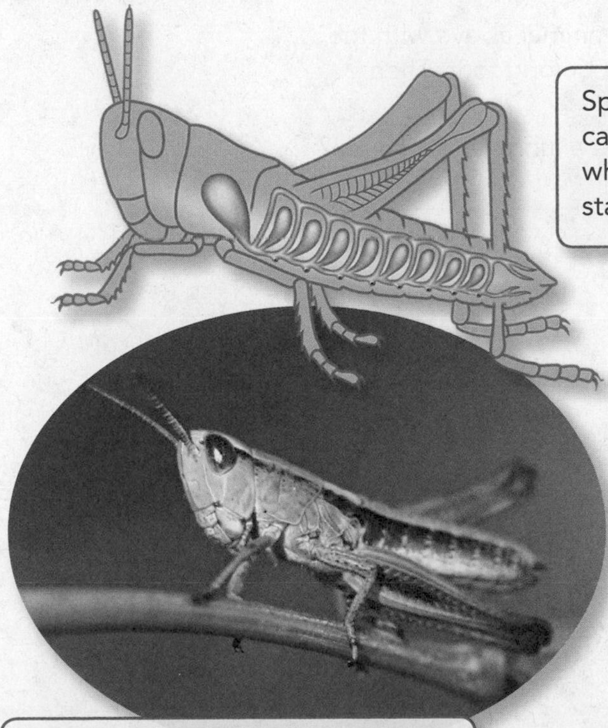

Grasshoppers have tracheal tubes, which have openings for gases to enter and leave the body.

Animal	Respiratory Structure
_____	_____
_____	_____
_____	_____

Vertebrate Structures Most vertebrates, including reptiles, birds, mammals, and most adult amphibians, use lungs to breathe. However, as you can see in **Figure 4,** lungs are not all the same. Because some lungs have more pockets or folds than others, the amount of surface area for gas exchange differs. For example, adult amphibian lungs are small and do not have many pockets. Therefore, the main respiratory structure for an adult amphibian is its skin. In contrast, the lungs of mammals are large. A mammal's lungs have many more pockets than those of reptiles and adult amphibians. Additional pockets make the lungs of mammals very efficient.

FIGURE 4 ···

Lungs

✎ Complete these tasks.

1. **Relate Text and Visuals** Label each animal above with the correct letter of the lungs below that belong to it. Then answer the question.

2. **CHALLENGE** How do pockets increase a lung's surface area?

_____

_____

_____

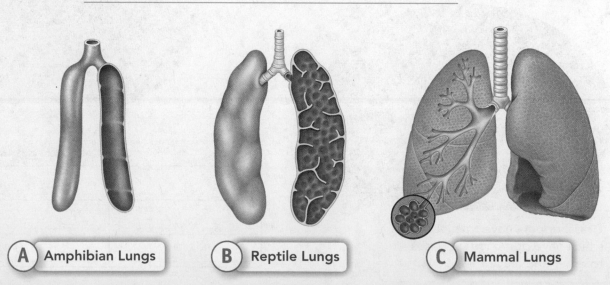

A Amphibian Lungs   **B** Reptile Lungs   **C** Mammal Lungs

Specialized Respiratory Structures Birds require a lot of energy to fly. Therefore, their cells must receive plenty of oxygen to release the energy contained in food. To obtain more oxygen from each breath of air, birds have a system of air sacs in their bodies. Most birds have nine air sacs. As you can see in **Figure 5**, air sacs connect to the lungs.

FIGURE 5 ....

A Bird's Lungs

In this simplified diagram, you can see how the fresh air a bird inhales flows through a long tube into the lower air sacs. It then flows into the lungs. From there, it flows into the upper air sacs until it is exhaled.

✎ **Observe** On the diagram, draw arrows to trace the path of air through the bird's respiratory structures.

Upper air sac

Lung

Lower air sac

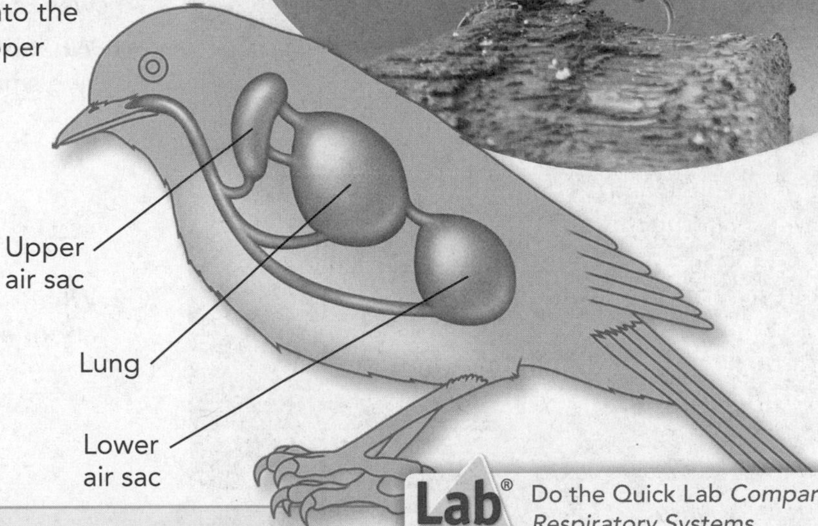

Lab zone ® Do the Quick Lab *Comparing Respiratory Systems.*

☞ Assess Your Understanding

2a. Explain What do all respiratory structures have in common?

_____

_____

_____

b. Apply Concepts Why is having several air sacs an advantage for a bird?

_____

_____

_____

got it? ....

○ **I get it!** Now I know that the type of respiratory structure an animal has depends on _____

_____

○ **I need extra help with** _____

Go to **MY SCIENCE COACH** *online for help with this subject.*

Circulation and Excretion

🗝 **What Are the Two Types of Circulatory Systems?**

🗝 **How Do Vertebrate Circulatory Systems Differ?**

🗝 **How Do Animals Get Rid of Wastes?**

my planet Diary

DISCOVERY

Octopus Hearts

How many hearts do you think an octopus has? One? Two? No, it has three! An octopus has one main heart and two smaller hearts, one for each gill. The two smaller hearts pump blood through each gill, where the blood picks up oxygen. The main heart then pumps this oxygen-rich blood through the rest of the body of the octopus. To make things even stranger, all this blood pumping through the octopus is not red, it is blue!

Answer the questions below.

1. What is the function of the octopus's two smaller hearts?

_____

_____

_____

2. What other facts do you know about an octopus?

_____

_____

_____

_____

> **PLANET DIARY** Go to **Planet Diary** to learn more about circulation and excretion.

Lab zone® Do the Inquiry Warm-Up *Getting Oxygen.*

Vocabulary

- circulatory system • heart • open circulatory system • closed circulatory system • capillary • atrium • ventricle • excretory system • kidney • urine

Skills

↻ Reading: Summarize

△ Inquiry: Draw Conclusions

What Are the Two Types of Circulatory Systems?

You have probably seen ants coming and going from their nest. Did you know that ants work as a team? Each ant has a specific job. While worker ants are out searching for food, other ants are protecting the nest. A soldier ant may even put its head in the nest's opening to stop enemies from entering. By working together, these ants are able to get food and stay safe. What teamwork!

Getting materials to an animal's cells and taking away wastes also takes teamwork. The circulatory system must work with both the digestive and respiratory systems to do so. The **circulatory system** transports needed materials to cells and takes away wastes.

🔑 **Complex animals have one of two types of circulatory systems: open or closed.** Both types of systems include blood, vessels, and a heart. A **heart** is a hollow, muscular structure that pumps blood through vessels. Blood vessels are a connected network of tubes that carries blood. Blood transports digested food from the digestive system and oxygen from the respiratory system to the cells. In addition, blood carries carbon dioxide and other wastes from cells to the organs that eliminate them from the body.

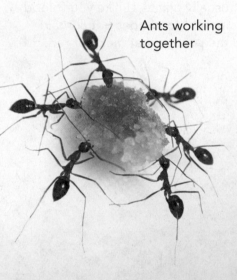

Ants working together

↻ **Summarize** On the clipboard, write in your own words how the digestive, respiratory, and circulatory systems work as a team.

Swallowtail Caterpillar

Open Circulatory Systems

Open Circulatory Systems Many invertebrates, including arthropods and most mollusks, have open circulatory systems. In an **open circulatory system,** blood does not always travel inside vessels. One or more hearts pump blood to the head and organs. Then the blood flows into the spaces around the animal's organs. There, food particles, oxygen, water, and wastes are exchanged between the blood and cells directly. Eventually, the blood moves back into the heart or hearts to be pumped out to the body again. You can see this type of circulatory system in the grasshopper shown in **Figure 1.**

FIGURE 1 ·······································

An Open Circulatory System

Grasshoppers have several hearts that pump blood into short vessels. These vessels open into the body spaces containing the internal organs. The blood washes over the organs and eventually returns to the hearts.

✎ **Sequence** In the graphic organizer, describe the flow of blood in the grasshopper's body. Start with blood in the hearts.

Hearts

Blood vessels

Step 1	Step 2	Step 3	Step 4

Closed Circulatory Systems

Closed Circulatory Systems Segmented worms, some mollusks, and all vertebrates have closed circulatory systems. In a **closed circulatory system,** blood always stays inside vessels and the heart. Large vessels lead away from the heart to the organs. In the organs, vessels called capillaries surround the cells. **Capillaries** are tiny, thin-walled blood vessels where the blood and body cells exchange substances. Digested food molecules and oxygen in the blood pass through the capillary walls into the cells. At the same time, carbon dioxide and other wastes pass from the cells into the capillaries. The capillaries merge and form large vessels that lead back to the heart. You can see an earthworm's closed circulatory system in **Figure 2.**

CHALLENGE Why is an earthworm's circulatory system more efficient than that of an insect?

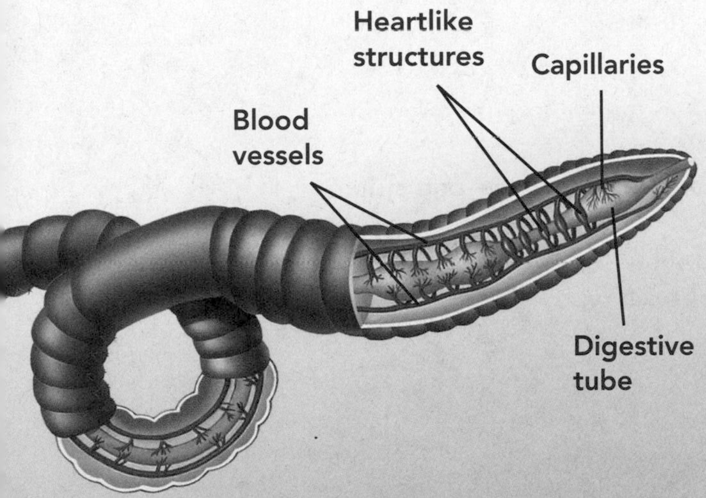

_____
_____
_____
_____
_____

FIGURE 2 ······················

A Closed Circulatory System
An earthworm's body is divided into more than 100 segments. The earthworm's circulatory system runs through all of the segments.

✎ **Compare and Contrast** On the notebook page, write how open and closed circulatory systems are alike and different.

Heartlike structures

Capillaries

Blood vessels

Digestive tube

 Do the Quick Lab *Comparing Circulatory Systems.*

🔑 Assess Your Understanding

1a. Describe What are the parts of a circulatory system?

_____
_____
_____

b. Draw Conclusions What happens in a circulatory system if the heart stops functioning?

_____
_____
_____

got it? ·······················

○ **I get it!** Now I know that the two types of circulatory systems are _____
_____

○ **I need extra help with** _____

Go to **MY SCIENCE** ⓢ **COACH** *online for help with this subject.*

227

How Do Vertebrate Circulatory Systems Differ?

All vertebrates have closed circulatory systems. However, these circulatory systems are not all the same. There are two patterns for circulating blood in a closed circulatory system. **Some closed systems have a single-loop circulation pattern. Others have a double-loop circulation pattern.**

Both circulation patterns rely on a heart to pump blood through the body. All vertebrate hearts have two types of hollow areas called chambers. One type of chamber is called an atrium (plural *atria*). An **atrium** receives blood from the body. The other type of chamber is called a ventricle. A **ventricle** receives blood from an atrium and pumps it to the body. You can see the two chambers of a fish's heart in **Figure 3.**

Vocabulary Suffixes The suffix *-tion* means "process of." Use this meaning to write a definition of *circulation* in your own words.

_____

_____

_____

_____

FIGURE 3 ···

Heart Chambers
In fishes, the heart has two chambers—one atrium and one ventricle.

Summarize In the boxes, write the function of each type of heart chamber.

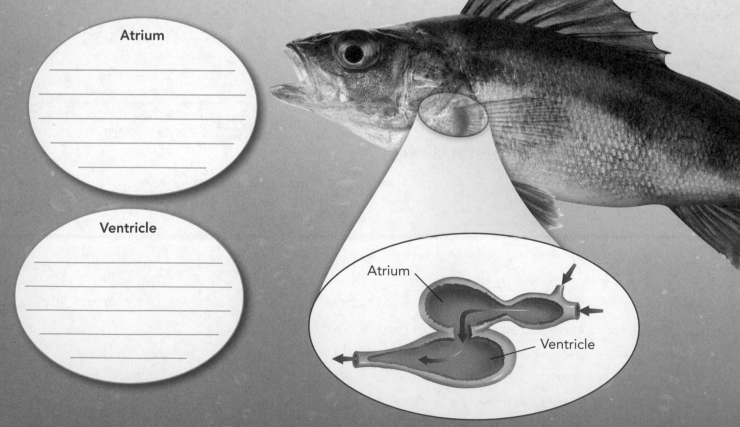

Atrium

Ventricle

Atrium

Ventricle

A Single-Loop Pattern Sharks, some of Earth's most fearsome hunters, have a single-loop circulation pattern, as do most vertebrates with gills. A single-loop circulation pattern forces blood around an animal's body in one direction. The ventricle of a two-chambered heart pumps blood to capillaries in the gills. Here, carbon dioxide diffuses out of the blood and oxygen diffuses into the blood. The oxygen-rich blood moves into vessels that lead to capillaries in the animal's organs. There, oxygen diffuses from the blood into the cells, and waste products diffuse from the cells into the blood. The oxygen-poor blood flows from the organs back to the heart's atrium. Then the blood moves from the atrium to the ventricle, completing the pattern. The pattern is shown in **Figure 4.**

Sequence Underline the text that describes the steps involved in blood flow in a single-loop pattern. Number the steps.

FIGURE 4 ....
A Single-Loop Pattern
Water flows into the mouth of this fish and then over its gills. Oxygen moves into the blood and is delivered to the cells of the fish. Blood is pumped around the body in one direction.

✎ **Interpret Diagrams** Label the atrium and ventricle. In the boxes, write what happens to oxygen and carbon dioxide in the gills and body organs.

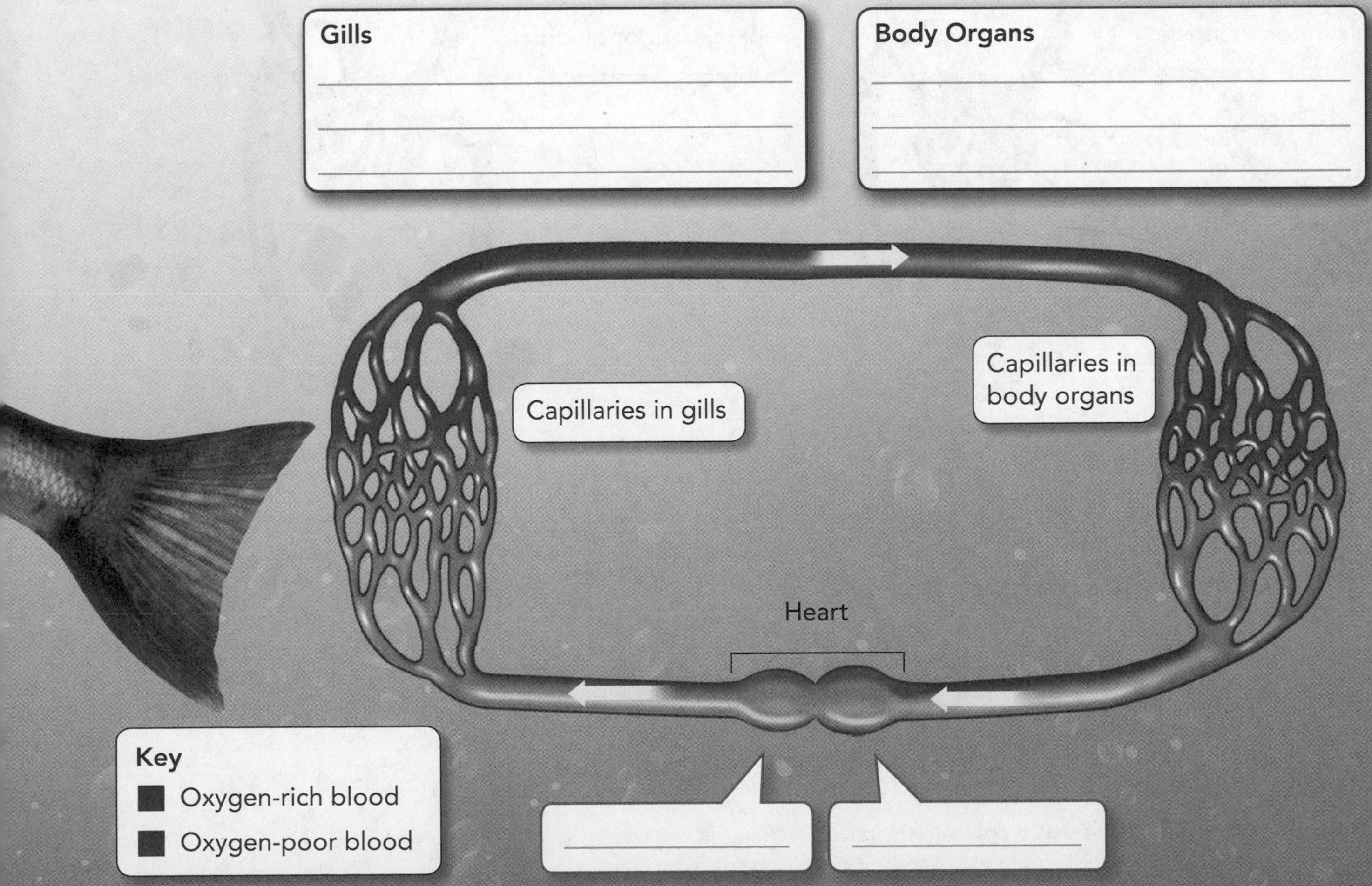

Gills
_____
_____
_____

Body Organs
_____
_____
_____

Capillaries in gills

Capillaries in body organs

Heart

Key
■ Oxygen-rich blood
■ Oxygen-poor blood

_____   _____

229

A Double-Loop Pattern Most vertebrates that live on land have a double-loop circulation pattern. In the first loop, the right side of the heart pumps oxygen-poor blood to the lungs. The blood picks up oxygen and drops off carbon dioxide in the lungs and then returns to the heart. In the second loop, the left side of the heart pumps the oxygen-rich blood out to the rest of the body. In **Figure 5,** you can see that adult amphibians and most reptiles have a three-chambered heart, while birds and mammals have a four-chambered heart.

Sloth

FIGURE 5 ···

> **INTERACTIVE ART** **A Double-Loop Pattern**

✎ **Classify** Look at the key. On the lines, write an *R* or a *P* to describe the type of blood in each heart chamber. If blood is mixed, use both letters. The first one is done for you.

Key

■ Oxygen-rich blood (R)

■ Oxygen-poor blood (P)

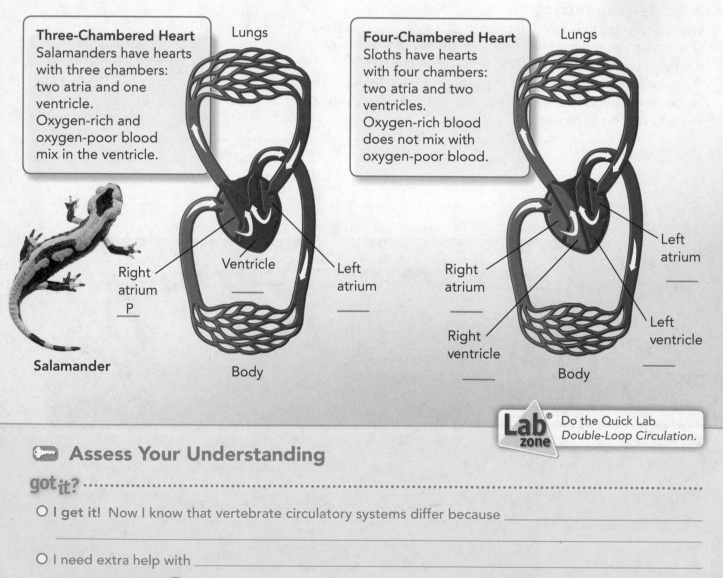

Three-Chambered Heart
Salamanders have hearts with three chambers: two atria and one ventricle.
Oxygen-rich and oxygen-poor blood mix in the ventricle.

Lungs

Right atrium
P

Ventricle

Left atrium

Salamander

Body

Four-Chambered Heart
Sloths have hearts with four chambers: two atria and two ventricles.
Oxygen-rich blood does not mix with oxygen-poor blood.

Lungs

Right atrium

Right ventricle

Left atrium

Left ventricle

Body

Lab zone® Do the Quick Lab *Double-Loop Circulation.*

⊸ **Assess Your Understanding**

got it? ···

○ **I get it!** Now I know that vertebrate circulatory systems differ because _____
_____

○ **I need extra help with** _____

Go to **MY SCIENCE** ⓢ **COACH** online for help with this subject.

How Do Animals Get Rid of Wastes?

Many animals have specialized structures to get rid of wastes. As you know, most animals use their respiratory systems to take in oxygen and to get rid of carbon dioxide. However, cells produce other wastes that the respiratory system cannot eliminate. For example, breaking down certain foods during cellular respiration produces wastes that contain nitrogen. Some animals also have excess water or salt in their bodies, depending on where they live or what they eat. For example, planarians live in fresh water and have excess water in their cells. Fishes that live in oceans have excess salt in their cells.

In animals, the **excretory system** is the system that rids a body of nitrogen-containing wastes, and excess salt and water. Depending on the animal, this system includes different structures. In vertebrates, **kidneys** are the main organs that filter nitrogen-containing wastes from the blood. They produce **urine,** a watery fluid that holds those wastes.

apply it!

A marine iguana spends hours feeding in ocean water every day. It has a specialized structure in its nose that helps it "sneeze out" the excess salt that gets into its body.

1 Identify What other wastes does a marine iguana need to get rid of?

_____

_____

_____

2 Draw Conclusions Look at the marine iguana. What do you think the white crusty material is on its head? Explain.

_____

_____

_____

_____

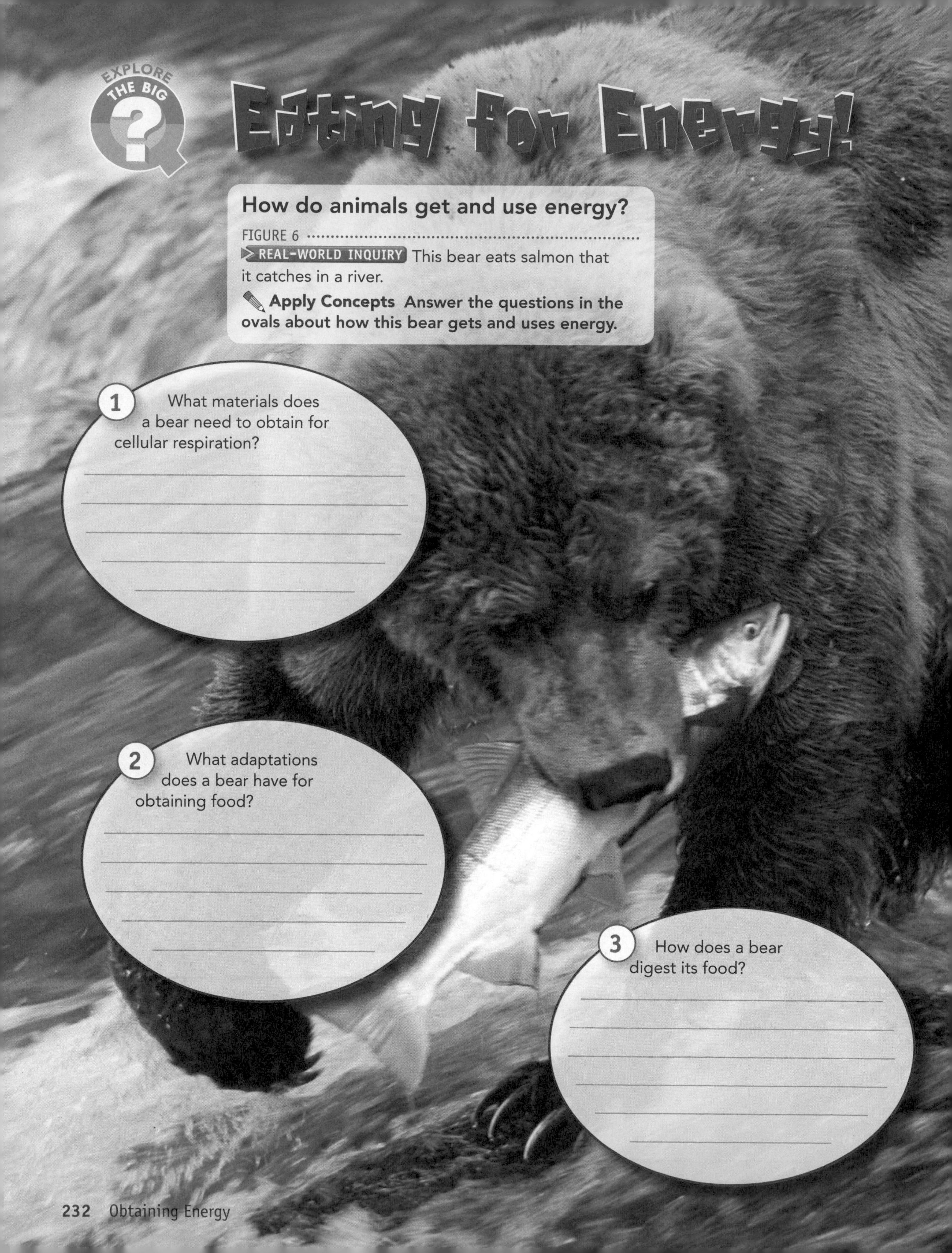

EXPLORE THE BIG Q

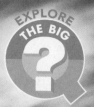

Eating for Energy!

How do animals get and use energy?

FIGURE 6

REAL-WORLD INQUIRY This bear eats salmon that it catches in a river.

Apply Concepts **Answer the questions in the ovals about how this bear gets and uses energy.**

1 What materials does a bear need to obtain for cellular respiration?

2 What adaptations does a bear have for obtaining food?

3 How does a bear digest its food?

6 What structures does a bear have to get rid of wastes?

_____

_____

_____

_____

_____

5 How does a bear's circulatory system work?

_____

_____

_____

_____

_____

_____

4 How does a bear obtain oxygen?

_____

_____

_____

_____

_____

Lab zone® Do the Quick Lab
Modeling a Kidney.

Assess Your Understanding

2a. List What are three types of wastes an animal may need specialized excretory structures for?

_____

_____

b. **ANSWER THE BIG ?** How do animals get and use energy?

_____

_____

_____

_____

_____

_____

_____

got it? ....

○ **I get it!** Now I know that to get rid of wastes animals have _____

_____

○ **I need extra help with** _____

_Go to_ **MY SCIENCE** 🔵 **COACH** _online for help with this subject._

233

Study Guide

REVIEW THE BIG ?

An animal's _____, _____, and _____ systems help it obtain food and use the food as _____.

LESSON 1 How Animals Obtain and Digest Food

🔑 The different ways that an animal obtains food depends on what it eats and its adaptations for getting food.

🔑 Some types of animals digest food mainly inside their cells, but most animals digest food outside their cells.

Vocabulary
- carnivore • herbivore
- omnivore • filter feeder
- radula • digestion • digestive system
- anus • crop • gizzard • intestine
- esophagus • stomach

LESSON 2 How Animals Obtain Oxygen

🔑 Animal cells exchange oxygen and carbon dioxide with their surroundings by diffusion across the outer coverings, or membranes, of cells.

🔑 Respiratory systems include structures such as skin, gills, and lungs. The type of respiratory system an animal has depends on how complex the animal is and where it lives.

Vocabulary
- cellular respiration • diffusion
- respiratory system • gill • lung

LESSON 3 Circulation and Excretion

🔑 Complex animals have one of two types of circulatory systems: open or closed.

🔑 Some closed systems have a single-loop circulation pattern. Others have a double-loop circulation pattern.

🔑 Many animals have specialized structures to get rid of wastes.

Vocabulary
- circulatory system • heart • open circulatory system
- closed circulatory system • capillary • atrium
- ventricle • excretory system • kidney • urine

Review and Assessment

LESSON 1 How Animals Obtain and Digest Food

1. Animals that eat only plant material are

    a. omnivores.   **b.** filter feeders.

    c. carnivores.   **d.** herbivores.

2. The process of breaking down food into small

molecules is called _____

3. Compare and Contrast How are the digestive systems of a flatworm and an earthworm alike? How are they different?

_____

_____

_____

_____

_____

_____

4. Relate Cause and Effect Explain how a butterfly uses its mouthparts to obtain food.

_____

_____

_____

5. Make Generalizations What type of teeth would you expect an omnivore to have? How do they help the animal eat its food?

_____

_____

_____

_____

_____

_____

LESSON 2 How Animals Obtain Oxygen

6. The process in which an animal's cells use oxygen and digested food molecules to release the energy in food is

    a. breathing.   **b.** cellular respiration.

    c. diffusion.   **d.** gas exchange.

7. When particles move from an area of high

concentration to an area of low concentration,

_____ occurs.

8. Apply Concepts Describe the function of the main respiratory structure of the dolphin shown below.

_____

_____

_____

9. Draw Conclusions How is having moist skin an advantage for a frog?

_____

_____

_____

_____

10. **Write About It** Describe three structures that an animal's respiratory system may have. Name one animal that has each structure.

6 Review and Assessment

LESSON 3 Circulation and Excretion

11. A heart chamber that receives blood from body structures is called

    a. a capillary.   **b.** a ventricle.

    c. an atrium.   **d.** a vessel.

12. Blood always stays inside the heart and blood vessels in a _____ circulatory system.

13. Predict What would happen if a kidney stopped functioning?

_____

_____

_____

_____

_____

14. Interpret Diagrams How does blood move in a fish's circulatory system shown below?

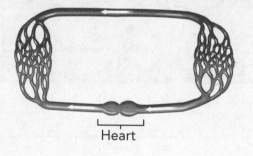

Heart

_____

_____

_____

_____

15. (Write About It) When visiting a pond, you see a fish and a frog. Describe how the single-loop circulation pattern of the fish is similar to and different from the double-loop circulation pattern of the frog.

 How do animals get and use energy?

16. This pileated woodpecker eats insects that live in trees. Explain how its beak helps it obtain its food. Then describe how its body digests the food into molecules, obtains oxygen, and transports these materials to body cells. Include how the body cells use the materials.

_____

_____

_____

_____

_____

_____

_____

_____

_____

_____

_____

_____

_____

_____

_____

_____

_____

_____

Standardized Test Prep

Multiple Choice

Circle the letter of the best answer.

1. Based on the type of teeth you see in the diagram below, make an inference about what type of animal it is.

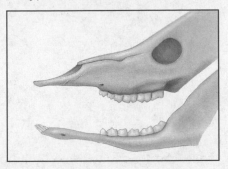

   A omnivore   B herbivore
   C carnivore   D filter feeder

2. Which organs do mollusks use to obtain oxygen from their environments?

   A radula
   B lungs
   C gills
   D legs

3. Of the following digestive tube structures, which one stores food?

   A bill
   B crop
   C gizzard
   D stomach

4. Animals get rid of nitrogen-containing wastes through the

   A respiratory system.
   B digestive system.
   C circulatory system.
   D excretory system.

5. What is an adult amphibian's main respiratory structure?

   A skin
   B gills
   C lungs
   D tracheal tubes

Constructed Response

Use the diagrams below and your knowledge of science to help you answer Question 6. Write your answer on a separate sheet of paper.

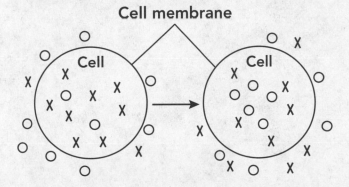

6. The diagram above shows a process that occurred in the same cell. The Os represent oxygen particles. The Xs represent carbon dioxide particles. Identify the process. Describe how the concentrations of particles changed.

A FREE LUNCH?

A *Sacculina* infection looks like a white lump on a crab's body. But it's more than a lumpy infection.

Is there really "no free lunch"? All animals are consumers. They eat other organisms. This usually means that they have to gather or hunt their food. That's a lot of work! But you could say the parasite *Sacculina* gets its lunch for free.

Sacculina begins its life as a tiny organism that drifts in the ocean. Eventually, it finds its host, a crab. It injects itself into the crab's body and absorbs nutrients from the crab's bloodstream.

Many animals, including crabs, produce hormones. These hormones, produced in the brain, control the animals' behavior and development. Over time, *Sacculina* alters the way its host produces hormones. At first, the crab is not affected. As the hormone levels change, the crab's behavior and development change. In fact, the crab behaves as if the eggs of the *Sacculina* parasite are crab eggs.

When the parasite eggs are ready to hatch, the crab releases the larvae in pulses. The crab will even wave its claws to help the *Sacculina* parasite larvae spread out to find other victims!

Think About It *Sacculina* and other parasites often make their hosts very sick. But they do not usually kill the host. In one or two paragraphs, describe your hypothesis for why this might be true.

SKIN OR GILLS?

Like most other living things, tiger salamanders need oxygen to get energy from food stored in their cells. Cells use this energy to function. But unlike most living things, tiger salamanders can change the way they get oxygen.

Tiger salamanders breed and lay eggs in water. Their larvae also live in water and have large, feathery external gills that absorb oxygen from the water. When a larva matures, it goes through a change, or metamorphosis. Normally, the larva loses its gills and becomes a land-dweller. The adult salamander absorbs oxygen from the air through its moist skin and mouth.

Sometimes, though, a tiger salamander keeps its gills into adulthood. It stays under water and never becomes a land dweller. How might keeping its gills benefit the adult salamander? The answer is in its environment.

Tiger salamanders eat insects and other small animals. Salamander larvae find food in the ponds in which they live. Adult salamanders eat insects that they find on land. In very dry areas, there may be very few insects on land. So, in these areas, tiger salamanders do not go through metamorphosis. The larvae keep their gills and continue to live in the water, where they can find food and reproduce.

▲ Adult tiger salamanders usually live on land. They absorb oxygen through their skin and mouth.

Research It Salamanders are known as "environmental indicator" species. This means that when there are dangerous chemicals, or toxins, in the environment, salamanders are among the first species to show ill effects. Find out what feature of salamanders makes them more likely to be harmed by toxins. Make a poster to tell people in your school about why it is important to monitor the health of salamander populations.

WHAT
BODY PARTS HELP THESE ARMADILLOS SURVIVE?

How does an animal's behavior help it survive and reproduce?

These nine-banded armadillo pups are well adapted to survive where they live. Armadillos have a great sense of smell, which they use to find insects. Armadillos dig into an insect nest using their sharp claws, and then scoop up the insects with their long tongues. If they are threatened by a predator, armadillos use their claws to defend themselves. They also have tough, scaly skin that acts like armor.

△Draw Conclusions **What body parts will help these young armadillos survive?**

_____

_____

_____

_____

> UNTAMED SCIENCE   Watch the **Untamed Science** video to learn more about behavior.

Animal Reproduction and Behavior

7 Getting Started

Check Your Understanding

1. **Background** Read the paragraph below and then answer the question.

Sal and Kai are at the zoo, trying to decide where to go. Sal wants to see the birds, reptiles, and **mammals**. Kai has a completely different plan. She doesn't understand why Sal only wants to see **vertebrates**. Kai would rather go directly to the **invertebrate** exhibit.

> **Mammals** are vertebrates whose body temperatures are regulated by their internal heat, and that have skin covered with hair or fur and glands that produce milk to feed their young.
>
> **Vertebrates** are animals with backbones.
>
> **Invertebrates** are animals without backbones.

- Circle the correct word to complete the following sentence. A bird is an example of a (vertebrate/invertebrate).

> **MY READING WEB** If you had trouble completing the question above, visit **My Reading Web** and type in *Animal Reproduction and Behavior.*

Vocabulary Skill

High-Use Academic Words High-use academic words appear frequently in textbooks and are often used in classrooms. As you read this chapter, look for the words in the table below.

Word	Definition	Example Sentence
aquatic	*adj.* related to or living in water	Caesar has a large tank filled with fish and other *aquatic* animals.
demonstrate	*v.* to show	Will you *demonstrate* how to ride that bicycle?

2. **Quick Check** Fill in the word that best completes the following sentence.

- Whales, sharks, and eels live in an _____ environment.

external fertilization

amniotic egg

instinct

courtship behavior

Chapter Preview

LESSON 1
- larva • polyp • medusa
- external fertilization
- internal fertilization
- gestation period
- ↻ Compare and Contrast
- △ Calculate

LESSON 2
- amniotic egg • placenta
- metamorphosis
- complete metamorphosis
- pupa
- incomplete metamorphosis
- nymph • tadpole
- ↻ Summarize
- △ Interpret Data

LESSON 3
- behavior • instinct • learning
- imprinting • conditioning
- trial-and-error learning
- insight learning
- ↻ Relate Cause and Effect
- △ Predict

LESSON 4
- pheromone • aggression
- territory • courtship behavior
- society • circadian rhythm
- hibernation • migration
- ↻ Identify the Main Idea
- △ Communicate

▷ VOCAB FLASH CARDS For extra help with vocabulary, visit **Vocab Flash Cards** and type in *Animal Reproduction and Behavior.*

Animal Reproduction and Fertilization

UNLOCK THE BIG

🔑 **How Do Animals Reproduce?**

🔑 **How Do External and Internal Fertilization Differ?**

my planet Diary

A Nutty Experiment

Did you know that moths have favorite foods? The navel orangeworm moth lays its eggs inside of nuts, such as pistachios, walnuts, and almonds. The young that hatch out of the eggs look like worms, and eat their way out of the nuts. This causes damage to crops on nut farms.

Navel orangeworm moths were thought to prefer almonds over other nuts—that is, until California middle school student Gabriel Leal found evidence to the contrary. Gabriel conducted a science project to investigate whether the young of navel orangeworm moths preferred pistachios, walnuts, or almonds. He put equal amounts of each type of nut into three different traps. A fourth trap was left empty. All four traps were placed into a cage with young navel orangeworms. Most worms went to the pistachio trap. No worms went to the empty trap. Gabriel's research could help scientists control worm damage to walnut and almond crops.

Control Variables Read the paragraphs and answer the questions below.

1. Write a one-sentence conclusion of Gabriel's research.

_____

_____

_____

2. What was the purpose of the empty trap in Gabriel's experiment?

_____

_____

_____

▶ PLANET DIARY Go to **Planet Diary** to learn more about animal reproduction and fertilization.

Lab zone® Do the Inquiry Warm-Up Making More.

Vocabulary
- larva • polyp • medusa • external fertilization
- internal fertilization • gestation period

Skills
- Reading: Compare and Contrast
- Inquiry: Calculate

How Do Animals Reproduce?

Whether they wiggle, hop, fly, or run, have backbones or no backbones—all animal species reproduce. Elephants make more elephants, grasshoppers make more grasshoppers, and sea stars make more sea stars. Some animals produce offspring that are identical to the parent. Most animals, including humans, produce offspring that are different from the parents. **Animals undergo either asexual or sexual reproduction to make more of their own kind or species.** Because no animal lives forever, reproduction is essential to the survival of a species.

Asexual Reproduction Imagine you are digging in the soil with a shovel, and accidentally cut a worm into two pieces. Most animals wouldn't survive getting cut in two—but the worm might. Certain kinds of worms can form whole new worms from each cut piece. This is one form of asexual reproduction. Another example of asexual reproduction is called budding. In budding, a new animal grows out of the parent and breaks off. In asexual reproduction, one parent produces a new organism identical to itself. This new organism receives an exact copy of the parent's set of genetic material, or DNA. Some animals, including sponges, jellyfish, sea anemones, worms, and the hydra in **Figure 1,** can reproduce asexually.

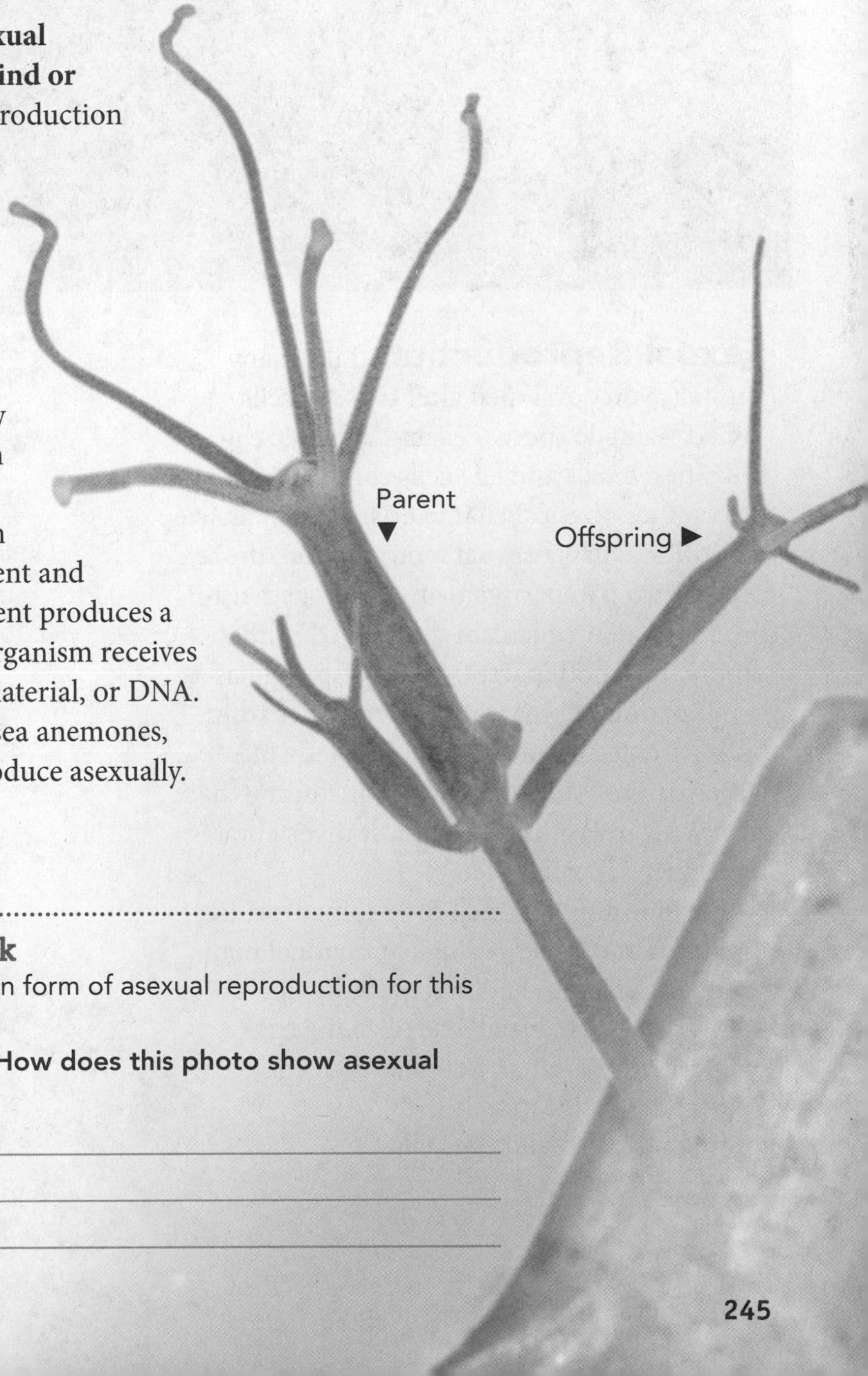

Parent ▼

Offspring ▶

FIGURE 1 ....

A Chip off the Old Block
Budding is the most common form of asexual reproduction for this hydra, a type of cnidarian.

✎ **Relate Text to Visuals** How does this photo show asexual reproduction?

_____

_____

_____

Sexual Reproduction

Like many animals, you developed after two sex cells joined—a male sperm cell and a female egg cell. Sperm cells and egg cells carry DNA that determines physical characteristics such as size and color. During sexual reproduction, the sex cells of two parent organisms join together to produce a new organism that has DNA that differs from both parents. The offspring has a combination of physical characteristics from both parents and may not look exactly like either parent. Most vertebrates, including the mammals in **Figure 2,** and most invertebrates reproduce sexually.

In some animals, including some worms, mollusks, and fishes, a single individual may produce both eggs and sperm. Individuals of these species will usually fertilize the eggs of another individual, not their own eggs. Recall that fertilization is the joining of sperm and egg cells.

FIGURE 2 ·····················

Sexual Reproduction

These wolf cubs and guinea pig pups are products of sexual reproduction.

✎ **Use the photos to answer the questions.**

1. **Interpret Photos** How do the offspring in each photo differ from their parent?

_____

_____

_____

2. **Explain** Why do the parent and the offspring look different?

_____

_____

_____

_____

_____

Comparing Asexual and Sexual Reproduction

Asexual and sexual reproduction are different survival methods. Each method has advantages and disadvantages. An advantage of asexual reproduction is that one parent can quickly produce many identical offspring. But a major disadvantage is that the offspring have the same DNA as the parent. The offspring have no variation from the parent and may not survive changes in the environment. In contrast, sexual reproduction has the advantage of producing offspring with new combinations of DNA. These offspring may have characteristics that help them adapt and survive changes in the environment. However, a disadvantage of sexual reproduction is that it requires finding a mate, and the development of offspring takes a longer time.

did you know?

Some fishes, such as this anemone clownfish, can change from male to female during their lifetime!

FIGURE 3

Asexual and Sexual Reproduction

Compare and Contrast Write an advantage and a disadvantage of each type of reproduction in the table.

	Asexual Reproduction	Sexual Reproduction
Advantage		
Disadvantage		

These aphids can reproduce asexually and sexually. They reproduce asexually when environmental conditions are favorable. If conditions worsen, they reproduce sexually.

▼

Reproductive Cycles Several aquatic invertebrates, such as sponges and cnidarians, have life cycles that alternate between asexual and sexual reproduction.

A Sponges

Sponges reproduce both asexually and sexually. Sponges reproduce asexually through budding. Small new sponges grow, or bud, from the sides of an adult sponge. Eventually, the buds break free and begin life on their own. Sponges reproduce sexually, too, but they do not have separate sexes. A sponge can produce both sperm cells and egg cells. After a sponge egg is fertilized by a sperm, a larva develops. A **larva** (plural *larvae*) is an immature form of an animal that looks very different from the adult. **Figure 4** shows sponge reproduction.

B Cnidarians

Many cnidarians alternate between two body forms: a **polyp** (PAHL ip) that looks like an upright vase and a **medusa** (muh DOO suh) that looks like an open umbrella. Some polyps reproduce asexually by budding. Other polyps just pull apart, forming two new polyps. Both kinds of asexual reproduction rapidly increase the number of polyps in a short time. Cnidarians reproduce sexually when in the medusa stage. The medusas release sperm and eggs into the water. A fertilized egg develops into a swimming larva. In time, the larva attaches to a hard surface and develops into a polyp that may continue the cycle. The moon jelly in **Figure 5** undergoes both asexual and sexual reproduction.

1 An adult sponge releases sperm.

2 Sperm enter another sponge and fertilize an egg.

3 A larva develops.

4 Water currents carry the larva away.

5 The larva settles on a hard surface. It develops into an adult sponge.

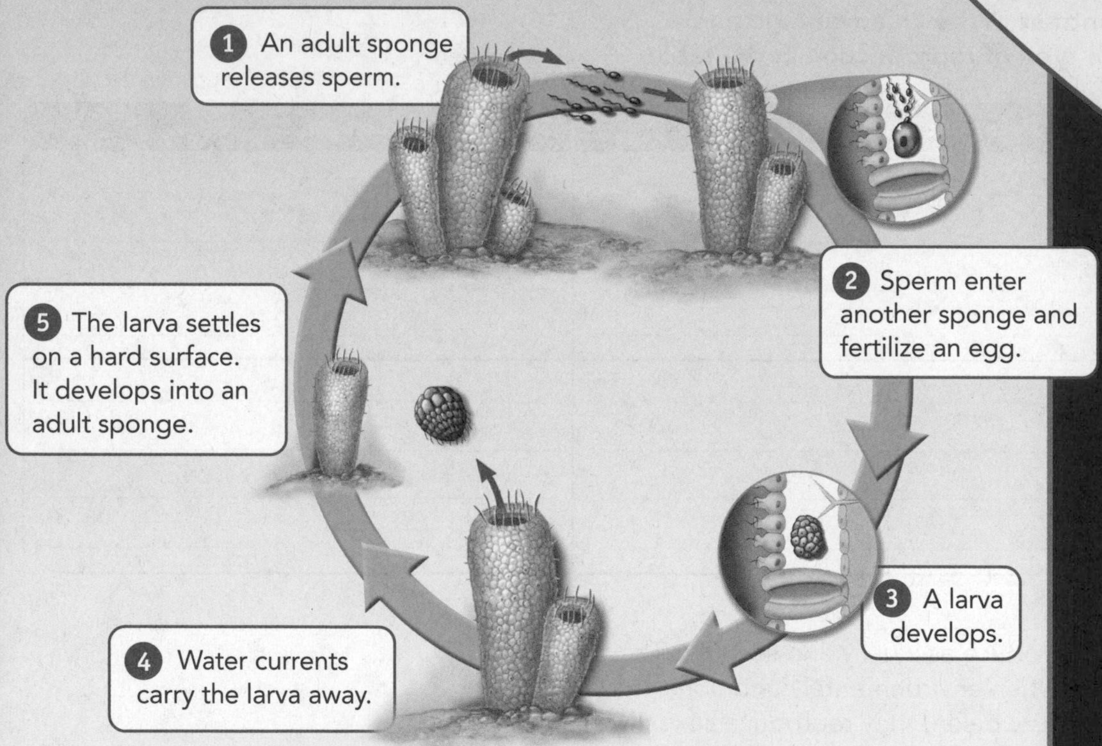

FIGURE 4

Reproduction of a Sponge

These sponges are reproducing sexually. ✎ **Complete these tasks.**

1. **Identify** A budded sponge is a product of (asexual/sexual) reproduction and a larva is a product of (asexual/sexual) reproduction.

2. **Interpret Diagrams** How do the sponge larva and adult differ?

_____

_____

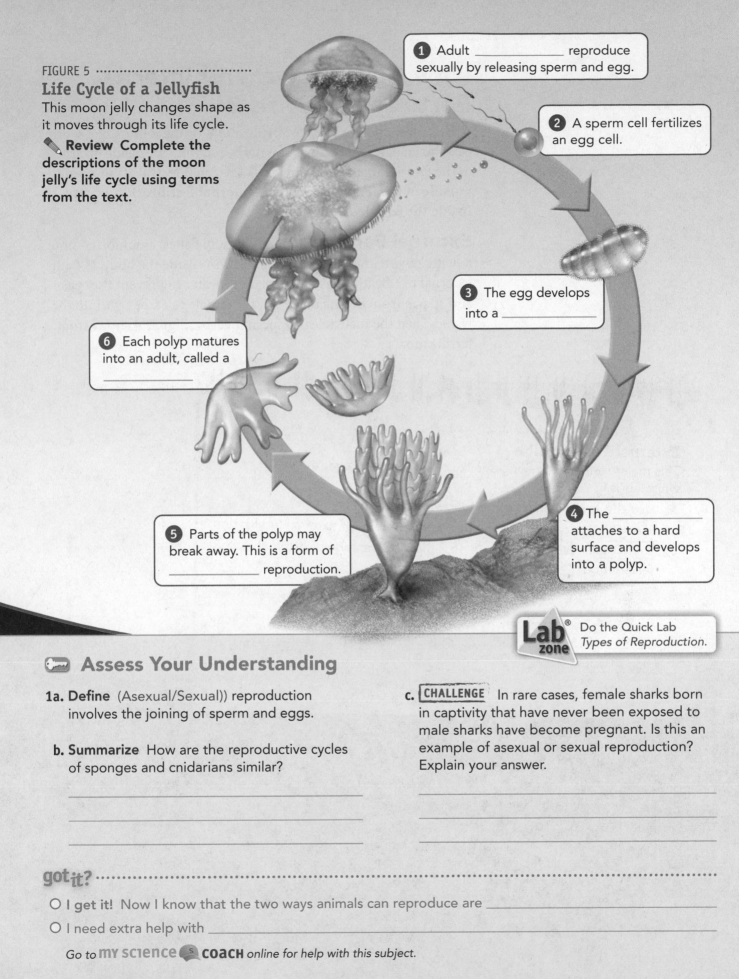

FIGURE 5 ·······························
Life Cycle of a Jellyfish
This moon jelly changes shape as it moves through its life cycle.

✏ **Review** Complete the descriptions of the moon jelly's life cycle using terms from the text.

1 Adult _____ reproduce sexually by releasing sperm and egg.

2 A sperm cell fertilizes an egg cell.

3 The egg develops into a _____

4 The _____ attaches to a hard surface and develops into a polyp.

5 Parts of the polyp may break away. This is a form of _____ reproduction.

6 Each polyp matures into an adult, called a _____

Lab ® Do the Quick Lab
zone *Types of Reproduction.*

🔑 **Assess Your Understanding**

1a. Define (Asexual/Sexual)) reproduction involves the joining of sperm and eggs.

b. Summarize How are the reproductive cycles of sponges and cnidarians similar?

_____

_____

_____

c. **CHALLENGE** In rare cases, female sharks born in captivity that have never been exposed to male sharks have become pregnant. Is this an example of asexual or sexual reproduction? Explain your answer.

_____

_____

_____

got it? ···

○ **I get it!** Now I know that the two ways animals can reproduce are _____

○ **I need extra help with** _____

Go to **MY SCIENCE** 🟦 **COACH** *online for help with this subject.*

249

How Do External and Internal Fertilization Differ?

Sexual reproduction involves fertilization, or the joining of a sperm cell and an egg cell. Fertilization may occur either outside or inside of the female organism's body. **External fertilization occurs outside of the female's body, and internal fertilization occurs inside the female's body.**

External Fertilization For many fishes, amphibians, and aquatic invertebrates, fertilization occurs outside the body. Usually external fertilization must take place in water to prevent the eggs and sperm from drying out. First, the female releases eggs into the water. Then the male releases sperm nearby. **Figure 6** shows trout fertilization.

FIGURE 6 ···

External Fertilization

This male trout is depositing a milky cloud of sperm over the round, white eggs.

✎ **Use the text to answer the following questions.**

1. **Identify** (Land/Water) is the best environment for external fertilization.

2. **CHALLENGE** What might be a possible disadvantage of external fertilization?

_____

_____

_____

_____

Internal Fertilization

Internal Fertilization Fertilization occurs inside the body in many aquatic animals and all land animals. The male releases sperm directly into the female's body, where the eggs are located.

Most invertebrates and many fishes, amphibians, reptiles, and birds lay eggs outside the parent's body. The offspring continue to develop inside the eggs. For other animals, including most mammals, fertilized eggs develop inside the female animal. The female then gives birth to live young. The length of time between fertilization and birth is called the **gestation period.** Opossums have the shortest gestation period—around 13 days. African elephants have the longest gestation period—up to 22 months.

✏️ **Compare and Contrast**
Describe how external and internal fertilization are alike and different.

_____

_____

_____

_____

_____

_____

_____

_____

do the math!

Study the graph and answer the questions below.

1 ⚠️ **Calculate** About how many days longer is the giraffe's gestation period than the fox's?

_____

2 **Make Generalizations** How do you think an animal's size relates to the length of its gestation period?

_____

_____

_____

_____

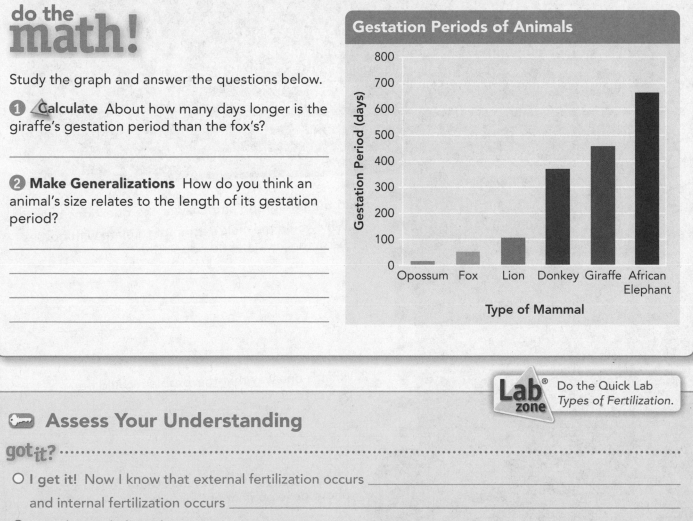

Gestation Periods of Animals

Gestation Period (days): 0, 100, 200, 300, 400, 500, 600, 700, 800

Type of Mammal: Opossum, Fox, Lion, Donkey, Giraffe, African Elephant

Lab zone Do the Quick Lab *Types of Fertilization.*

🔑 Assess Your Understanding

got it? ....

○ **I get it!** Now I know that external fertilization occurs _____

and internal fertilization occurs _____

○ **I need extra help with** _____

Go to **my science COACH** *online for help with this subject.*

Development and Growth

UNLOCK
THE BIG
?

🗝 **Where Do Embryos Develop?**

🗝 **How Do Young Animals Develop?**

🗝 **How Do Animals Care for Their Young?**

MY PLANET DiARY

DISCOVERY

Beware of Glass

Is that a beetle or a bottle? Australian jewel beetles seem to have trouble figuring out the difference. These large insects live in certain dry regions of Australia. Male beetles can fly, but the larger females cannot. As males fly around, they look for females. Males recognize females by the color and pattern of the female beetle's body. Researchers have discovered that male beetles are also attracted to something else with a similar color and pattern: glass bottles. Many beetles have been seen trying to mate with discarded glass bottles. Scientists are concerned that the jewel beetle population may be harmed—because mating with bottles does not produce jewel beetle offspring!

Read the paragraph and answer the questions below.

1. Why would the male's attempt to mate with bottles harm the jewel beetle population?

_____

_____

_____

_____

2. What is one way that this problem could be prevented?

_____

_____

> PLANET DIARY Go to **Planet Diary** to learn more about development and growth.

Lab® zone Do the Inquiry Warm-Up "Eggs-amination."

Vocabulary

- amniotic egg • placenta • metamorphosis
- complete metamorphosis • pupa
- incomplete metamorphosis • nymph • tadpole

Skills

- Reading: Summarize
- Inquiry: Interpret Data

Where Do Embryos Develop?

Turtles, sharks, and mice all reproduce sexually. But after fertilization occurs, the offspring of these animals develop in different ways. **The growing offspring, or embryo, may develop outside or inside of the parent's body.**

Egg-Laying Animals The offspring of some animals develop inside an egg laid outside of the parent's body. Most animals without backbones, including worms and insects, lay eggs. Many fishes, reptiles, and birds lay eggs, too. The contents of the egg provide all the nutrients that the developing embryo needs. The eggs of land vertebrates, such as reptiles and birds, are called **amniotic eggs.** Amniotic eggs are covered with membranes and a leathery shell while still inside the parent's body. **Figure 1** shows some of the structures of an amniotic egg.

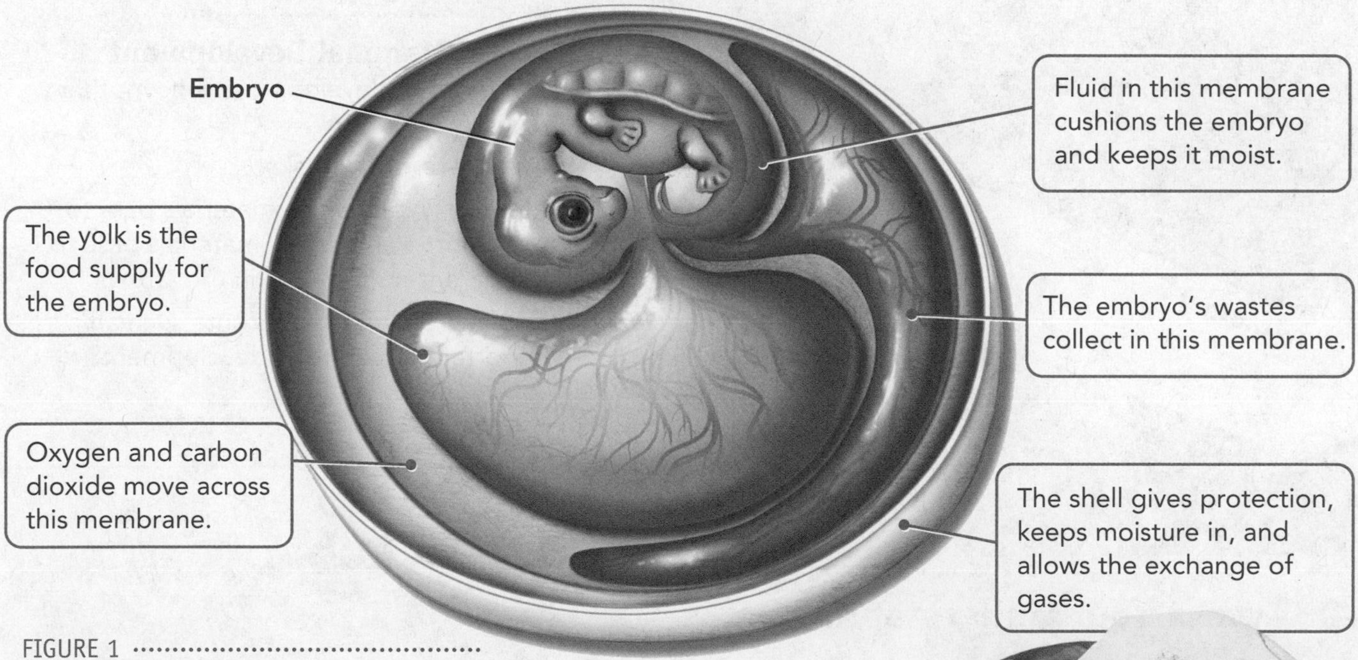

Embryo

Fluid in this membrane cushions the embryo and keeps it moist.

The yolk is the food supply for the embryo.

The embryo's wastes collect in this membrane.

Oxygen and carbon dioxide move across this membrane.

The shell gives protection, keeps moisture in, and allows the exchange of gases.

FIGURE 1 ·······················

Amniotic Egg

Reptiles, such as this tortoise, develop inside an amniotic egg. The amniotic egg is a unique adaptation for life on land.

✏ **Relate Text to Visuals** Circle the descriptions of the structures that keep the embryo from drying out.

Summarize Read the text about egg-retaining animals. Then summarize how the embryo develops in these animals.

_____

_____

_____

_____

Egg-Retaining Animals

In certain animals, an embryo develops inside an egg that is kept, or retained, within the parent's body. The developing embryo gets all its nutrients from the egg's yolk, just like the offspring of egg-laying animals. The young do not receive any extra nutrients from the parent. The egg hatches either before or after being released from the parent's body. This type of development is found in fishes, amphibians, and reptiles.

Placental Mammals

In dogs, horses, humans, and other placental mammals, the embryo develops inside the mother's body. The mother provides the embryo with everything it needs during development. Materials are exchanged between the embryo and the mother through an organ called the **placenta**, shown in **Figure 2**. Blood carrying food and oxygen from the mother flows to the placenta and then to the embryo. Blood carrying wastes and carbon dioxide from the embryo flows to the placenta and then to the mother. The mother's blood does not mix with the embryo's blood. A placental mammal develops inside its mother's body until its body systems can function on their own.

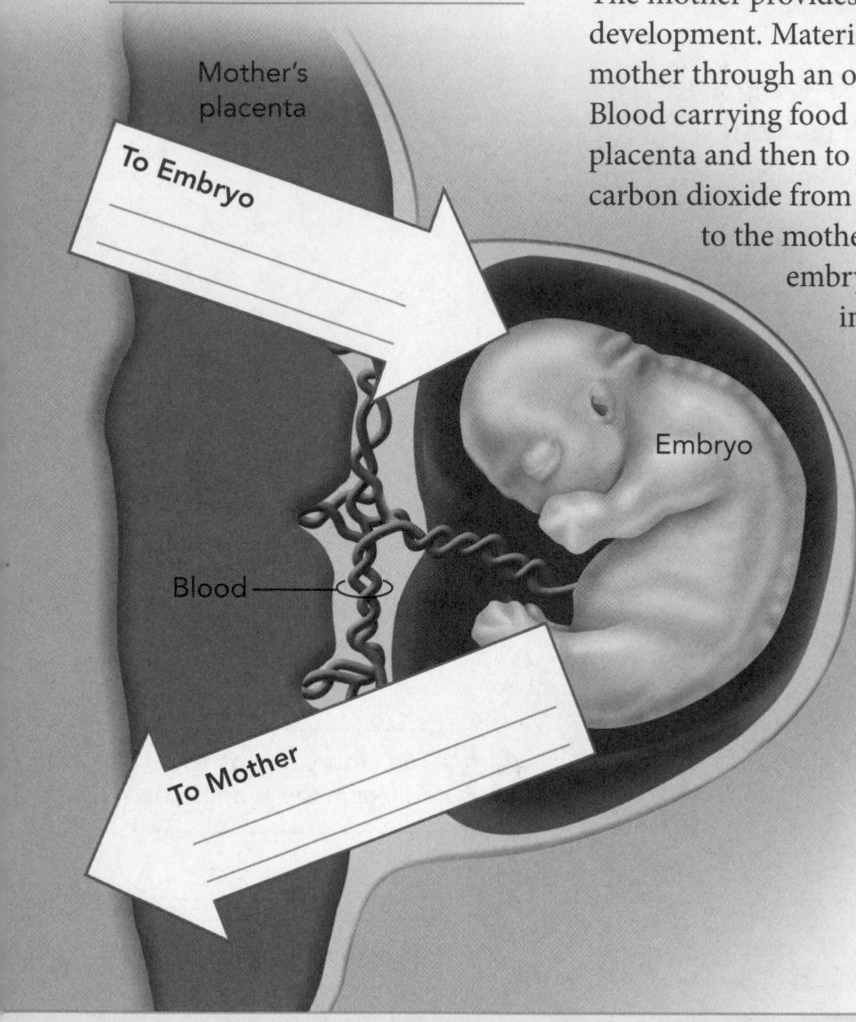

Mother's placenta

To Embryo

Blood

To Mother

Embryo

FIGURE 2 ·····················

Placental Mammal Development

This cat embryo develops inside its mother for about two months.

Complete these tasks.

1. **Identify** Write which materials pass to the embryo and which materials pass to the parent on the lines in the arrows.

2. **Explain** Why is the placenta such an important structure in development?

_____

_____

_____

 Do the Quick Lab "Eggs-tra" Protection.

Assess Your Understanding

got it? ···

○ **I get it!** Now I know that the places embryos can develop are _____

○ **I need extra help with** _____

Go to **MY SCIENCE COACH** online for help with this subject.

How Do Young Animals Develop?

Living things grow, change, and reproduce during their lifetimes. Some young animals, including most vertebrates, look like small versions of adults. Other animals go through the process of **metamorphosis,** or major body changes, as they develop from young organisms into adults. 🗝 **Young animals undergo changes in their bodies between birth and maturity, when they are able to reproduce.** As you read, notice the similarities and differences among the life cycles of crustaceans, insects, and amphibians.

Crustaceans Most crustaceans, such as lobsters, crabs, and shrimp, begin their lives as tiny, swimming larvae. The bodies of these larvae do not resemble those of adults. Larvae may swim or drift in the water as they grow and change. Eventually, through metamorphosis, crustacean larvae develop into adults. **Figure 3** shows three stages of a lobster's life cycle.

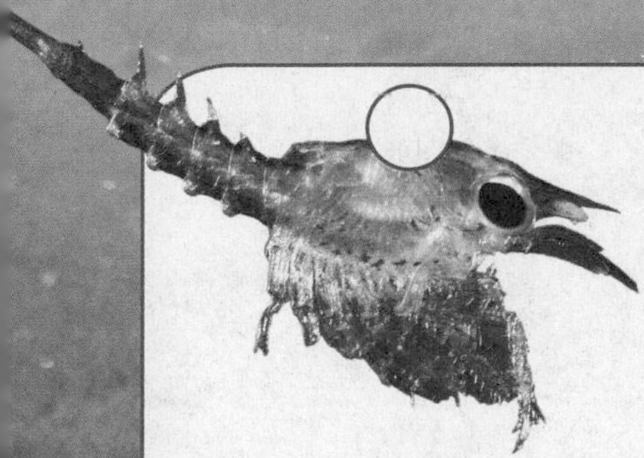

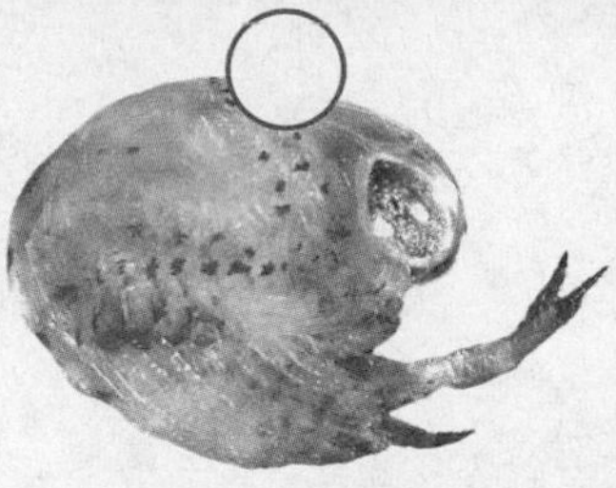

FIGURE 3 ·····

Lobster Metamorphosis
Lobster larvae are only 8 millimeters long. Adults can reach lengths of 1 meter!

✏️ **Use the photos to help you complete the tasks.**

1. **Sequence** Write the correct order of the lobster's development in the circles above each photo.

2. **Interpret Photos** Which structures changed as the lobster developed and grew?

_____

_____

_____

255

Insects Have you ever seen an insect egg? You might find one on the underside of a leaf. After an insect hatches from the egg, it begins metamorphosis as it develops into an adult. Insects such as butterflies, beetles, and grasshoppers undergo complete metamorphosis or incomplete metamorphosis.

Complete Metamorphosis The cycle to the right shows a ladybug going through **complete metamorphosis,** which has four different stages: egg, larva, pupa, and adult. An egg hatches into a larva. A larva usually looks something like a worm. It is specialized for eating and growing. After a time, a larva enters the next stage of the process and becomes a **pupa** (PYOO puh). As a pupa, the insect is enclosed in a protective covering. Although the pupa does not eat and moves very little, it is not resting. Major changes in body structure take place in this stage, as the pupa becomes an adult.

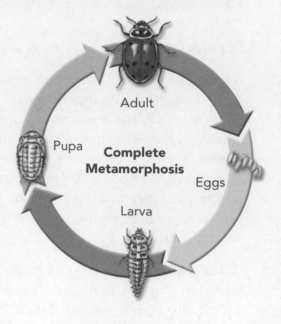

Adult

Pupa

Complete Metamorphosis

Eggs

Larva

A monarch butterfly egg develops on a milkweed plant.

A larva, or a caterpillar, hatches from the egg. The caterpillar grows larger as it feeds on plants. Then it enters the pupa stage.

Inside the pupa case, adult structures such as wings, antennae, and legs form.

Incomplete Metamorphosis In contrast, a second type of metamorphosis, called **incomplete metamorphosis,** has no distinct larval stage. Incomplete metamorphosis has three stages: egg, nymph, and adult. An egg hatches into a stage called a **nymph** (nimf), which usually looks like the adult insect without wings. As the nymph grows, it may shed its outgrown exoskeleton several times before becoming an adult. The chinch bug to the right is going through incomplete metamorphosis.

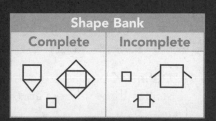

Adult

Nymph

Incomplete Metamorphosis

Eggs

Nymph

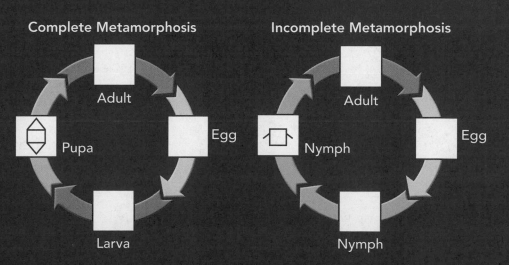

FIGURE 4 ·······························

> **INTERACTIVE ART**

Insect Metamorphosis
The photos show a monarch butterfly going through complete metamorphosis.

✎ **Sequence** In the cycles below, the shapes represent stages of complete or incomplete metamorphosis. Using the shape bank, draw the shapes that you think best represent the missing stages in each type of metamorphosis.

▲ An adult monarch butterfly

The adult butterfly comes out of the pupa case and the butterfly's wings expand as the blood flows into them.

Shape Bank	
Complete	**Incomplete**

Complete Metamorphosis

Adult

Pupa

Egg

Larva

Incomplete Metamorphosis

Adult

Nymph

Egg

Nymph

Amphibians Frogs begin their life cycle as fertilized eggs in water. After a few days, larvae wriggle out of the eggs and begin swimming. The larva of a frog is called a **tadpole.** Tadpoles look very different from adult frogs. You can follow the process of frog metamorphosis in **Figure 5.**

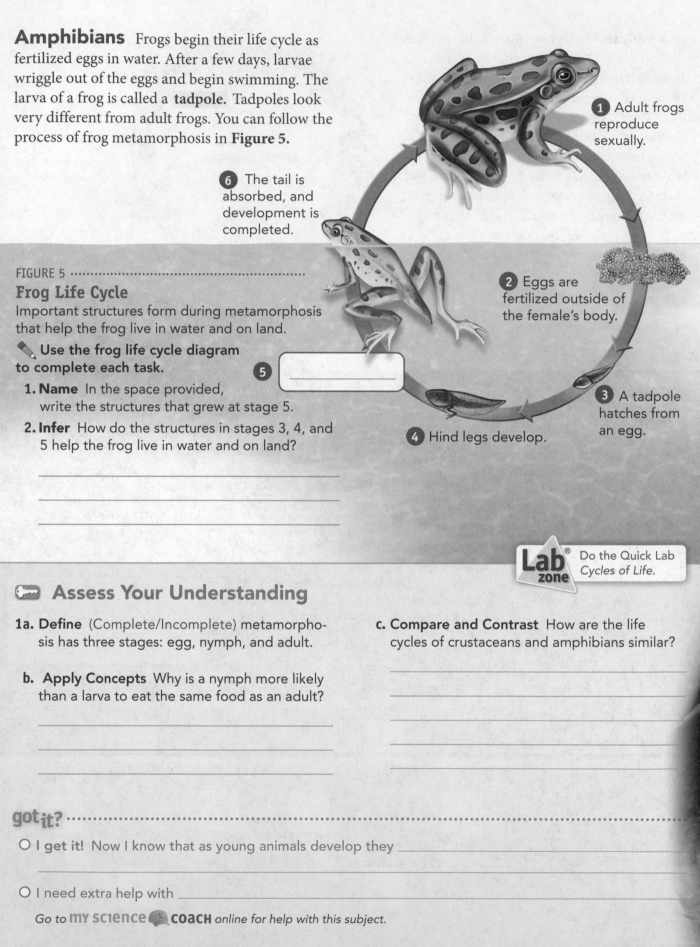

1 Adult frogs reproduce sexually.

6 The tail is absorbed, and development is completed.

FIGURE 5 ···
Frog Life Cycle
Important structures form during metamorphosis that help the frog live in water and on land.

🖉 **Use the frog life cycle diagram to complete each task.**

5 _____

1. **Name** In the space provided, write the structures that grew at stage 5.

2. **Infer** How do the structures in stages 3, 4, and 5 help the frog live in water and on land?

_____
_____
_____

2 Eggs are fertilized outside of the female's body.

3 A tadpole hatches from an egg.

4 Hind legs develop.

Lab ® Do the Quick Lab
zone *Cycles of Life.*

🔑 Assess Your Understanding

1a. Define (Complete/Incomplete) metamorphosis has three stages: egg, nymph, and adult.

b. Apply Concepts Why is a nymph more likely than a larva to eat the same food as an adult?

_____
_____
_____

c. Compare and Contrast How are the life cycles of crustaceans and amphibians similar?

_____
_____
_____
_____
_____

got it? ···

○ I get it! Now I know that as young animals develop they _____
_____

○ I need extra help with _____

Go to MY SCIENCE 💬 COACH online for help with this subject.

How Do Animals Care for Their Young?

Have you seen a caterpillar, tadpole, puppy, duckling, or other baby animal recently? You may have noticed that different animals care for their offspring in different ways. **Most amphibians and reptiles do not provide parental care, while most birds and mammals typically care for their offspring.**

No Parental Care Not all animals take care of their young. Most aquatic invertebrates, fishes, and amphibians release many eggs into water and then completely ignore them! Most amphibian larvae, or tadpoles, develop into adults without parental help. Similarly, the offspring of most reptiles, such as the snakes in **Figure 6,** are independent from the time they hatch. Offspring that do not receive parental care must be able to care for themselves from the time of birth.

FIGURE 6 ··

Checklist for Survival

These bushmaster snakes have just hatched from their eggs. They may stay inside the shell for several days for safety.

List Make a list of what you think these snakes must be able to do to survive their first few days of life.

Parental Care You've probably never seen a duckling walking by itself. That's because most birds and all mammals typically spend weeks to years under the care and protection of a parent.

Birds Most bird species lay their eggs in nests that one or both parents build. Then one or both parents sit on the eggs, keeping them warm until they hatch. Some species of birds can move around and find food right after they hatch. Others are helpless and must be fed by the parent, as shown in **Figure 7**. Most parent birds feed and protect their young until they are able to care for themselves.

Mammals Whether a monotreme, a marsupial, or a placental mammal, young mammals are usually quite helpless for a long time after they are born. After birth, all young mammals are fed with milk from the mother's body. One or both parents may continue caring for their offspring until the young animals are independent.

FIGURE 7 ···
Parental Care
The parent bird shown above cares for its hungry offspring until they are ready to fly. The mother polar bear at the right stays with her cubs for up to two years.

✎ **Answer each question.**

1. **Interpret Photos** How are the parents in these two photos caring for their young?

   _____

   _____

   _____

2. **Communicate** What is one way that a family member cares for you?

   _____

   _____

   _____

do the math! Analyzing Data

Suppose that you are a scientist researching how many fox and turtle offspring survive the first year of life. Foxes provide parental care, but turtles do not.

1 Calculate Using the information in the second and fourth columns of the table, calculate the number of offspring that survive the first year. Put your answer in the third column of the table.

2 Graph Use the data from the table to construct a double bar graph in the space provided. Label the vertical axis. Then provide a key for the data in the graph.

3 △ Interpret Data How do you think parental care is related to the percentage of offspring that survive the first year of life?

_____
_____
_____
_____

4 CHALLENGE Why do you think animals that provide parental care have fewer offspring?

_____
_____
_____
_____

Type of Animal	Number of Offspring	Number That Survive the First Year	Percentage That Survive the First Year
Fox	5	_____	60%
Turtle	20	_____	20%

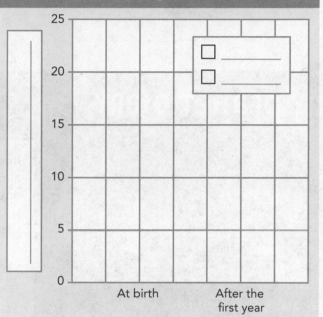

Survival of Offspring

(graph with vertical axis 0–25, horizontal axis labeled "At birth" and "After the first year")

Do the Quick Lab
To Care or Not to Care.

🔑 Assess Your Understanding

got it? ....

⭕ I get it! Now I know that parental care occurs _____
_____

⭕ I need extra help with _____

Go to **MY SCIENCE COACH** online for help with this subject.

What Is Behavior?

🔑 **What Causes Animal Behavior?**

🔑 **What Are the Types of Animal Behavior?**

my PLANET DiARY

BLOG

Posted by: Chris

Location: Brewerton, New York

When my dog was a puppy, my parents and I would train him. He didn't like to listen when he was young. He would try to take all of my socks and eat them. But as he got older, his behavior changed and he got more mature. Now he is two years old, and he is fully house trained.

Read the blog entry and then answer the question below.

How did the puppy's behavior change?

_____

_____

_____

_____

_____

_____

▷ **PLANET DIARY** Go to **Planet Diary** to learn more about behavior.

Lab ® **zone** Do the Inquiry Warm-Up
What Behaviors Can You Observe?

What Causes Animal Behavior?

Have you ever heard a bird call, or seen a dog bark at a stranger? These are examples of animal behavior. An animal's **behavior** consists of all the actions it performs. For example, behaviors include actions an animal takes to obtain food, avoid predators, and find a mate. Like body structures, the behaviors of animals are adaptations that have evolved over long periods of time.

Vocabulary
- behavior • instinct • learning • imprinting
- conditioning • trial-and-error learning • insight learning

Skills
↻ Reading: Relate Cause and Effect
△ Inquiry: Predict

FIGURE 1 ·······································

A Moth's "Eyes"
Certain moths have markings on their underwings that look like the eyes of an owl. When the moth is frightened by a predator, it raises its forewings to reveal the "eyes."

✎△ **Predict** How is this behavior important to the moth's survival?

_____

_____

_____

Most behavior is a complex process in which different parts of an animal's body work together. Consider what happens when a water current carries a small animal to a hydra's tentacles. After stinging cells on the tentacles catch the prey, the tentacles bend toward the hydra's mouth. At the same time, the hydra's mouth opens to receive the food.

Behavior as Response In the previous situation, the touch of the prey on the tentacles acts as a stimulus to the hydra. Recall that a stimulus (plural *stimuli*) is a signal that causes an organism to react in some way. The organism's reaction to the stimulus is called a response. The hydra's response to the prey is to sting it. 🔑 **All animal behaviors are responses to stimuli.**

Some stimuli, such as prey brushing a hydra's tentacles, are outside the animal. Other stimuli, such as hunger, come from inside. An animal's responses are either external actions or internal changes (such as a faster heartbeat), or both.

The Functions of Behavior Most behaviors help an animal survive or reproduce. When an animal looks for food or hides to avoid a predator, it is doing something that helps it stay alive. When animals search for mates and build nests for their young, they are behaving in ways that help them reproduce.

Lab zone | Do the Quick Lab *Animal Behavior.*

🔑 **Assess Your Understanding**

got it? ···

○ **I get it!** Now I know that animal behaviors are _____

_____

_____

○ **I need extra help with** _____

_____

Go to **my science** **COACH** *online for help with this subject.*

FIGURE 2 ··

Survival Instinct
This spider has trapped a butterfly in the sticky strands of its silky web.

✎ **Explain** Read the text below about instincts. Could the spider survive without the instinct to spin a web? Why or why not?

_____

_____

What Are the Types of Animal Behavior?

Animals perform some behaviors correctly without practice. Other behaviors are learned through experience. 🔑 **The types of animal behavior are instincts and learned behaviors.**

Instincts Animals perform some behaviors without being taught. An **instinct** is a response to a stimulus that is inborn and that an animal performs correctly the first time. For example, spiders, such as the one in **Figure 2,** spin complicated webs on their first try without making mistakes in the pattern. Most birds build their nests without ever being taught how.

Instincts are important for an animal's survival. For example, a newborn kangaroo crawls into its mother's pouch and attaches itself to a nipple. Without this instinct, baby kangaroos could not obtain the milk they need to live.

Hawks, which have short necks, prey on gull chicks. Geese, which have long necks, do not prey on gull chicks. Newly-hatched gull chicks instinctively crouch down when they see any bird's shadow. As the chicks become older, they still crouch when they see a hawk's shadow, but they learn not to crouch when they see a goose's shadow.

△ **Predict** Circle the bird shadows that will cause an older gull chick·to crouch when it sees them.

Learned Behaviors Think about the first time you rode a bicycle. It probably took a few tries before you did it well—you had to learn how. **Learning** is the process that leads to changes in behavior based on practice or experience. In general, the larger an animal's brain, the more the animal can learn. Because learned behaviors result from an animal's experience, they are not usually done perfectly the first time.

All learned behaviors depend in part on characteristics that have passed from parents to offspring. For example, the cheetah cubs in **Figure 1** were born with physical characteristics and instincts that are necessary for hunting. They have claws that help them capture prey. They also have an instinct to pounce on any object that attracts their attention. However, only through experience can they learn hunting skills. Learned behaviors include imprinting, conditioning, trial-and-error learning, and insight learning.

FIGURE 3 ···

Learned Behavior
These cheetah cubs are practicing their hunting skills on a young gazelle.

✎ **Interpret Photos** In this photo, what action shows instinct behavior, and what action shows learned behavior?

_____

_____

_____

····················· ✏ ·····················

⟳ **Relate Cause and Effect**
Underline why the birds
imprinted on Konrad Lorenz,
and circle the effect.

Imprinting Imprinting is a learned behavior. In **imprinting,**
certain newly hatched birds and newborn mammals recognize and
follow the first moving object they see. This object is usually the
parent. But imprinting also involves instinct. The young animal has
an instinct to follow a moving object, but is not born knowing what
its parent looks like. The young animal learns from experience
what object to follow.

Once imprinting takes place, it cannot be changed. That is
true even if the young animal has imprinted on something other
than its parent. Young animals have imprinted on moving toys and
even humans. Konrad Lorenz, an Austrian scientist, conducted
experiments in which he, rather than the parent, was the
first moving object that newly hatched birds saw. **Figure 4**
shows how young geese that had imprinted on Lorenz
followed him around.

For young animals, imprinting on a parent is
valuable for two reasons. First, it keeps offspring close
to their parents, who know where to find food and how
to avoid predators. Second, imprinting allows young
animals to learn what other animals of their own species
look like. This knowledge protects the animals while
they are young. In later life, this knowledge is important
when the animals search for mates.

FIGURE 4 ···
Follow the Leader
These geese ignored other members of their species and
trailed after Dr. Lorenz.

✏ **Answer the following questions.**

1. **Infer** What might happen if geese imprinted on the
wrong species?

_____

_____

_____

2. CHALLENGE Why might imprinting be important for the
offspring of animals that live in large groups?

_____

_____

_____

Two Stimuli Together

When a hungry dog sees or smells food, it produces saliva. Dogs do not usually salivate in response to other stimuli, such as the sound of a ringing bell.

For many days, the scientist Ivan Pavlov rang a bell every time he fed a dog. The dog learned to associate the ringing of the bell with the sight and smell of food.

New Stimulus Only

In time, when Pavlov rang a bell but did not feed the dog, the dog still produced saliva. The new stimulus produced the response that normally only food would produce.

FIGURE 5 ....

Teaching a Dog New Tricks

Pavlov conditioned a dog to salivate at the sound of a ringing bell.

✎ **Read the text about conditioning and complete each task.**

1. ↻ **Relate Cause and Effect** In the first panel, label the stimulus and the response.

2. ◣ **Predict** What might the dog do if the doorbell rang?

_____

Conditioning When a dog sees its owner approaching with a leash, the dog may jump up, eager to go for a walk. The dog has learned to associate the leash with a pleasant event—a brisk walk. Learning that a particular stimulus or response leads to a good or a bad outcome is called **conditioning**.

Pets are often trained using conditioning. At first, a puppy rarely comes when you call. But every now and then, the puppy runs to you in response to your call. Each time the puppy comes, you give it a dog biscuit. Your puppy will soon learn to associate the desired response—coming when called—with the good outcome of a food reward. After a while, the puppy will come to you even if you don't give it a dog biscuit.

During the early 1900s, the Russian scientist Ivan Pavlov performed experiments involving one kind of conditioning. **Figure 5** shows the steps that Pavlov followed in his experiments.

.... ✎ ....

Vocabulary High-Use Academic Words An *outcome* is defined as a result or as the way something turns out. What *outcome* did the puppy associate with training?

_____

_____

_____

_____

Trial-and-Error Learning Another type of learned behavior is **trial-and-error learning.** In trial-and-error learning, an animal learns to do a behavior through repeated practice. An animal learns to repeat behaviors that result in rewards and avoid behaviors that result in punishment. When you learned to ride a bicycle, you did it by trial and error. You may have wobbled at first, but eventually you got better. You learned to move in ways that adjusted your balance and kept you from falling over.

Many animals learn by trial and error which methods are best for obtaining food. They also learn which methods to avoid. Think of what happens when a predator tries to attack a skunk. The skunk sprays the predator with a substance that stings and smells awful. In the future, the predator is likely to avoid skunks. The predator has learned to associate the sight of a skunk with its terrible spray.

FIGURE 6 ....

A Tough Lesson
This dog has a mouthful of porcupine quills.

✎ **Infer** Why will this dog avoid porcupines in the future?

_____

_____

do the
math! Analyzing Data

A scientist conducted an experiment to find out if mice would learn to run a maze more quickly if they were given rewards. The scientist set up two identical mazes. She put a cheese reward at the end of one maze and not at the end of the other maze. Use the graph to answer the questions.

❶ Read Graphs On Day 1, how long on average did it take mice with a cheese reward to complete the maze?

_____

❷ Calculate On Day 4, how much faster did mice with a reward complete the maze than mice without a reward?

_____

❸ Interpret Data What was the manipulated variable in this experiment?

_____

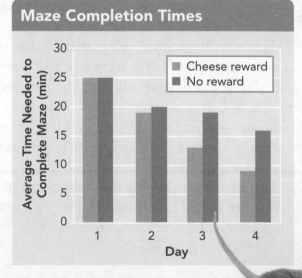

Maze Completion Times

■ Cheese reward
■ No reward

Average Time Needed to Complete Maze (min)

Day

Betty learned to use a curved wire to pull up a bucket of food from a narrow plastic tube.

A larger crow stole the curved wire. Betty found a straight wire and bent it into a curved shape.

Betty then used the curved wire to get the bucket of food.

Insight Learning The first time you try out a new video game, you may not need someone to explain how to play it. Instead, you may use what you already know about other video games to figure out how the new one works. When you solve a problem or learn how to do something new by applying what you already know, without a period of trial and error, you are using **insight learning.**

Insight learning is most common in primates, such as gorillas, chimpanzees, and humans. For example, chimpanzees use twigs to probe into the nests of termites and other insects that they eat. The chimps use insight to bend or chew their twig "tools" into a shape that will best fit the holes. Other animals, such as the crow in **Figure 7,** have also shown insight learning.

FIGURE 7 ·····················

> ART IN MOTION **Insight Learning**
Read the panels above to learn how a crow named Betty was able to use a wire to obtain food.

✎ **Interpret Diagrams**
How was Betty's behavior an example of insight learning?

_____

_____

_____

 Lab zone® Do the Quick Lab *Become a Learning Detective.*

🗝 Assess Your Understanding

1a. Define An inborn response to a stimulus that is performed correctly the first time is called a(n) (instinct/learned behavior).

b. Compare and Contrast How are instincts and learned behaviors different?

_____

_____

_____

c. Apply Concepts Right after hatching, a duckling sees a child riding a tricycle. What will probably happen the next time the child rides on the tricycle by the duckling? Explain.

_____

_____

_____

_____

got it? ···

○ **I get it!** Now I know that the types of animal behavior are _____

_____

○ **I need extra help with**_____

    Go to **MY SCIENCE ⓢ COACH** *online for help with this subject.*

Patterns of Behavior

UNLOCK THE BIG ?

🔑 **What Are Three Ways That Animals Communicate?**

🔑 **What Are Examples of Competitive and Cooperative Behaviors?**

🔑 **What Is Cyclic Behavior?**

my planet Diary

FUN FACTS

Do You Speak Gorilla?

Animals communicate in many ways, but they don't usually say things like, "My tooth hurts." That's more or less what Koko the gorilla said in 2004, when she needed to go to the dentist. Koko uses hand signals, based on American Sign Language, to communicate with humans.

Koko was born in 1971 at the San Francisco Zoo. When she was just one year old, she began to learn how to sign words, working with Dr. Francine Patterson. Through signs, Koko has shown emotion, creativity, and intelligence. Koko can make around 1,000 signs. She can also understand around 2,000 spoken words—but she herself can't speak. Gorillas can make noises, but they don't have the mouth structures necessary to form spoken words.

Read the text and then answer the questions below.

1. Once, Koko was trying to describe an object but did not know the word. She signed "bracelet" and "finger" together. What do you think she was trying to say?

_____

_____

2. If you could talk to Koko, what would you ask her?

_____

_____

_____

Lab zone® Do the Inquiry Warm-Up *Communicating Without Words.*

▶ **PLANET DIARY** Go to **Planet Diary** to learn more about patterns of behavior.

Vocabulary

- pheromone • aggression • territory
- courtship behavior • society • circadian rhythm
- hibernation • migration

Skills

↻ Reading: Identify the Main Idea

△ Inquiry: Communicate

What Are Three Ways That Animals Communicate?

Animal communication comes in many forms. Perhaps you've seen a cat hissing and arching its back. It is using sound and body posture to send a message that says, "Back off!" 🔑 **Animals use sounds, scents, and body movements to communicate with one another.** An animal's ability to communicate helps it interact with other animals. Notice the gecko's body movements in **Figure 1.**

Animals communicate many kinds of messages using sound. Some animals use sound to attract mates. Female crickets, for example, are attracted to the sound of a male's chirping. Animals may also communicate warnings using sound. When a prairie dog sees a coyote or other predator approaching, it makes a yipping sound that warns other prairie dogs to hide in their burrows.

Animals also communicate with chemical scents. A chemical released by one animal that affects the behavior of another animal of the same species is called a **pheromone** (FEHR uh mohn). For example, perhaps you have seen a male house cat spraying a tree. The musky scent he leaves contains pheromones that advertise his presence to other cats in the neighborhood.

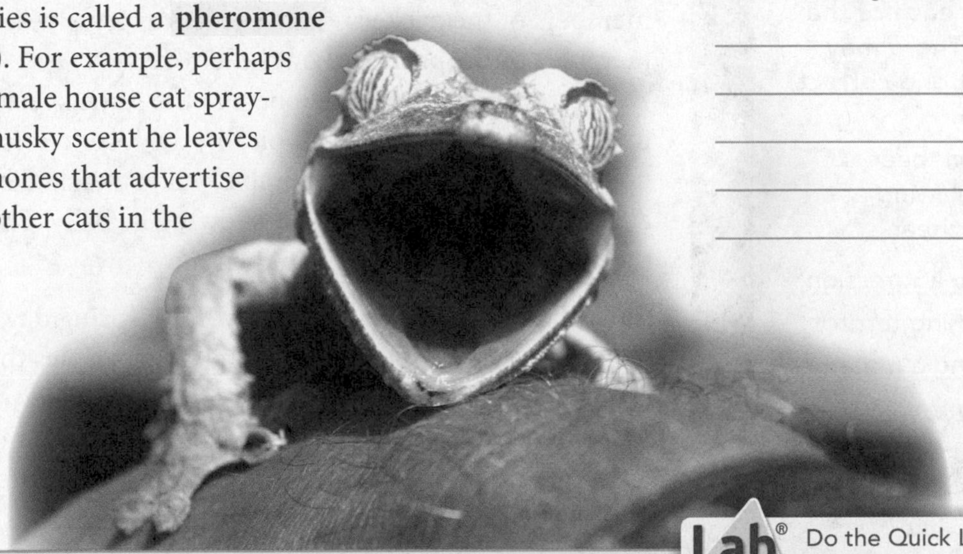

FIGURE 1 ·····························

Body Language
This giant leaf-tailed gecko opens its mouth when it senses danger.

✎ **Infer** What might the gecko be communicating with its body movement?

_____

_____

_____

_____

_____

 Do the Quick Lab *Modeling Animal Communication.*

🔑 **Assess Your Understanding**

got it? ·······························

◯ **I get it!** Now I know that animals communicate using _____

_____

◯ **I need extra help with** _____

Go to **my science** COACH *online for help with this subject.*

What Are Examples of Competitive and Cooperative Behaviors?

Do you ever fight with family members over the last slice of pizza? Is it easier to do chores by yourself or with other people? Sometimes you compete with people and sometimes you cooperate. Animals in the wild also compete and cooperate.

Competitive Behavior Have you ever fed pigeons in the park? They fight over every crumb because there usually isn't enough food to go around. 🔑 **Animals compete with one another for limited resources, such as food, water, shelter, and mates.** Competition can occur among different species of animals or within the same species. For example, a pride of lions might steal prey from a troop of hyenas. Or a female aphid might kick and shove another female aphid for the best leaf on which to lay eggs.

Showing Aggression When they compete, animals may display aggression. **Aggression** is a threatening behavior that one animal uses to gain control over another. Before a pack of wolves settles down to eat its prey, individual wolves demonstrate, or show, aggression by snapping, clawing, and snarling. The most aggressive members of the pack eat first. The less aggressive and younger members of the pack feed on the leftovers.

Aggression between members of the same species rarely results in serious injury or death. Typically, the loser communicates "I give up" with its behavior. For example, when attacked by an older dog, a puppy will roll onto its back, showing its belly. This signal calms the older dog. The puppy can then move away.

Establishing a Territory On an early spring day, you may hear a male oriole singing. He is alerting other orioles that he "owns" a particular territory. A **territory** is an area that is occupied and defended by an animal or group of animals. If another animal of the same species enters the territory, the owner will attack the newcomer to drive it away. Birds use songs and aggressive behaviors to maintain their territories. Other animals may use calls, scratches, droppings, or pheromones.

By establishing a territory, an animal protects important resources such as food and possible mates. A territory can also provide a safe area for animals to raise young without competition from other members of their species. Most male songbirds cannot attract a mate unless they have a territory.

FIGURE 2 ······························

Fighting in the Forest
This forest is full of competing animals.

✎ **Identify** Select which type of competition is happening in each of the four photos. There may be more than one correct answer.

This older black bear is pushing and clawing at a younger black bear.

○ Showing aggression
○ Establishing territory
○ Attracting a mate

A blue jay calls loudly from the top of a tree after he sees another blue jay.

○ Showing aggression
○ Establishing territory
○ Attracting a mate

In the space below, explain why you chose your answer.

_____

_____

_____

_____

_____

This male deer rubs his scent against several trees.

○ Showing aggression
○ Establishing territory
○ Attracting a mate

A male frog inflates his throat to make a loud call. He advertises his location to females.

○ Showing aggression
○ Establishing territory
○ Attracting a mate

Attracting a Mate A male and female salamander swim in the water, gracefully moving around one another. They are engaging in **courtship behavior,** activities that prepare males and females of the same species for mating. Courtship behavior ensures that the males and females of the same species recognize one another, so that mating and reproduction can take place. Courtship behavior is typically also competitive. For example, in some species, several males may perform courtship behaviors for a single female. She then chooses one of them to mate with.

273

FIGURE 3 ••••••••••••••••••••••••••

Safety in Numbers

When threatened by a grey reef shark, these fish form tight groups, called bait balls.

✎ **Interpret Photos** How does the bait ball help an individual fish escape from being eaten by a predator?

_____

_____

_____

_____

✎ **Identify the Main Idea**

Living in the wild is hard work! Some animals cooperate in order to survive. In your own words, write three important reasons why animals show cooperative behaviors.

_____

_____

_____

_____

_____

_____

_____

Cooperative Behavior Not all animal behaviors are competitive. 🔑 **Animals living in groups cooperate to survive.** Although many animals live alone and only rarely meet one of their own kind, other animals live in groups. Some fishes form schools, and some insects live in large groups. Hoofed mammals, such as bison and wild horses, often form herds. Living in a group helps some animals stay alive. For example, group members may protect one another or work together to find food.

How can group members help one another? If an elephant gets stuck in a mudhole, for example, other members of its herd will dig it out. When animals such as lions hunt in a group, they can often kill larger prey than a single hunter can.

Safety in Groups Living in groups often protects animals against predators. Fish that swim in schools, such as the ones in **Figure 3,** are often safer than fish that swim alone. It is harder for predators to see and select an individual fish in a large group.

Animals in a group sometimes cooperate to fight off a predator. For example, North American musk oxen form a defensive circle against a wolf or other predator. Their calves are sheltered in the middle of the circle. The adult musk oxen stand with their horns lowered, ready to charge. The predator often gives up rather than face a whole herd of angry musk oxen.

FIGURE 4 ·····················

The Hive Is Alive!
A hive may have tens of thousands of worker bees.

✏ **Explain** Why do you think a honeybee society has more worker bees than any other type?

_____
_____
_____
_____

Queen bee

Worker bees

Animal Societies Some animals, including termites, honeybees, ants, and naked mole rats, live in groups called societies. A **society** is a group of closely related animals of the same species that work together in a highly organized way. In a society, there is a division of labor—different individuals perform different tasks. A honeybee society, for example, has only one egg-laying queen. But there are thousands of worker bees that build, defend, and maintain the hive. Some workers feed larvae. Some bring back nectar and pollen from flowers as food for the hive. Other worker bees guard the entrance to the hive. **Figure 4** shows a honeybee society.

apply it!

⌃**Communicate** Discuss with your classmates one way that you have cooperated with your friends at school. Then describe how the cooperative behavior helped you.

_____
_____
_____
_____
_____
_____
_____

Lab Do the Lab Investigation
zone *One for All.*

🔑 Assess Your Understanding

1a. List What are two cooperative behaviors?

_____

b. Explain How are aggression and establishing a territory related?

_____
_____
_____

c. Apply Concepts Male red-winged blackbirds display red patches on their shoulders to defend their territory. What would happen if these red patches were dyed black?

_____
_____
_____
_____

got it? ··

○ **I get it!** Now I know that examples of competitive and cooperative behavior are _____

_____

○ **I need extra help with** _____

  Go to **MY SCIENCE COACH** *online for help with this subject.*

What Is Cyclic Behavior?

Some animal behaviors, called cyclic behaviors, occur in regular, predictable patterns. **Cyclic behaviors usually change over the course of a day or a season.**

Daily Cycles
Behavior cycles that occur over a period of approximately one day are called **circadian rhythms** (sur KAY dee un). For example, blowflies search for food during the day and rest at night. In contrast, field mice are active during the night and rest by day. Animals that are active during the day can take advantage of sunlight, which makes food easy to see. On the other hand, animals that are active at night do not encounter predators that are active during the day.

Hibernation
Other behavior cycles are related to seasons. For example, some animals, such as woodchucks and chipmunks, are active during warm seasons but hibernate during the cold winter. **Hibernation** is a state of greatly reduced body activity that occurs during the winter when food is scarce. During hibernation, all of an animal's body processes, such as breathing and heartbeat, slow down. This slowdown reduces the animal's need for food. In fact, hibernating animals do not eat. Their bodies use stored fat to meet their reduced nutrition needs.

Migration
While many animals live their lives in one area, others migrate. **Migration** is the regular, seasonal journey of an animal from one place to another and back again. Some animals migrate short distances. Dall's sheep, for example, spend summers near the tops of mountains and move lower down for the winters. Other animals migrate thousands of kilometers. Arctic terns fly more than 17,000 kilometers between the North and South poles.

Animals usually migrate to an area that provides a lot of food or a good environment for reproduction. Most migrations are related to the changing seasons and take place twice a year, in the spring and in the fall. American redstarts, for example, are insect-eating birds that spend the summer in North America. There, they mate and raise young. In the fall, insects become scarce, so the redstarts migrate south to areas where they can find plenty of food.

Scientists have discovered that migrating animals find their way using sight, taste, and other senses, including some that humans do not have. Some birds and sea turtles, for example, have a magnetic sense that acts something like a compass needle. Migrating birds also seem to navigate by using the positions of the sun, moon, and stars. Salmon use scent and taste to locate the streams where they were born, and return there to mate.

know?

Every November on Christmas Island, located in the Indian Ocean, about 120 million red crabs migrate from their forest home to breeding grounds on the coast. Sometimes, the crabs must pass through towns to get to the ocean. The people who live on this small island find crabs in the roads, schools, and even their homes!

FIGURE 5 ·····················

On the Move

The migration route of monarch butterflies is sometimes as long as 3,600 kilometers. In the fall, monarchs fly south from Canada and the United States and spend the winter in the mountains of Mexico.

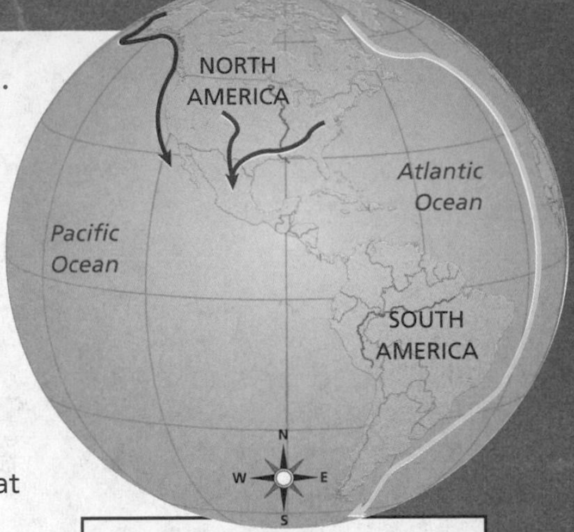

🖉 **Use the map to answer the following questions.**

1. **Interpret Maps** Circle the animal that has a migration route that passes more than one continent. Then, write the name of the animal on the line below.

A.  B. C.

_____

2. **CHALLENGE** Why do you think gray whales travel to warm, southern waters to give birth to their calves?

_____

_____

_____

_____

NORTH AMERICA

Atlantic Ocean

Pacific Ocean

SOUTH AMERICA

N
W · E
S

Key to Migration Routes
Arctic tern
Monarch butterfly
Gray whale

▲ This gray whale and her calf will travel for two to three months to return to their feeding grounds in the north.

Birds of a Feather...

How does an animal's behavior help it survive and reproduce?

FIGURE 6 ·······························

▶ REAL-WORLD INQUIRY Black-browed albatrosses live in colonies that can number close to 500,000 birds. Albatrosses behave in ways that enable them to reproduce and successfully raise their chicks.

✏️ Read the descriptions of black-browed albatross reproduction and behavior. Then, answer the questions on the lines provided.

2 Reproduction

This parent albatross is sitting on its egg. Which type of fertilization resulted in this egg?

_____

Why would external fertilization be difficult for albatrosses?

_____
_____
_____

1 Courtship Behavior

Albatross courtship behavior involves calling and dancing. Why is it so important that these two albatrosses perform courtship behavior?

_____
_____
_____
_____
_____
_____

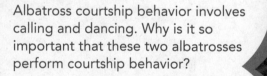

Colony Life

How is this chick able to recognize and take food from its parent?

_____

_____

_____

_____

In the photo below, you can see a colony of albatrosses. What type of cooperative behavior are they showing? How does this behavior help them survive?

_____

_____

_____

_____

_____

Assess Your Understanding

2a. Review The regular, seasonal journey of an animal from one place to another and back again is called (migration/hibernation).

b. Compare and Contrast How are circadian rhythms and hibernation alike and different?

_____

_____

_____

_____

_____

c. CHALLENGE Why may building a road through a forest interfere with migration?

_____

_____

_____

d. ANSWER THE BIG ? How does an animal's behavior help it survive and reproduce?

_____

_____

_____

_____

_____

_____

_____

_____

got it?...

○ **I get it!** Now I know that cyclic behaviors

_____

_____

○ **I need extra help with** _____

Go to MY SCIENCE COACH *online for help with this subject.*

279

In _____, animals live in groups to survive. Another type of behavior, called _____, leads to mating and reproduction.

LESSON 1 Animal Reproduction and Fertilization

🔑 Animals undergo either asexual or sexual reproduction to make more of their own kind or species.

🔑 External fertilization occurs outside of the female's body, and internal fertilization occurs inside the female's body.

Vocabulary
• larva • polyp • medusa
• external fertilization • internal fertilization
• gestation period

LESSON 2 Development and Growth

🔑 The growing offspring, or embryo, may develop outside or inside of the parent's body.

🔑 Young animals undergo changes in their bodies between birth and maturity.

🔑 Most amphibians and reptiles do not provide parental care. Most birds and mammals do.

Vocabulary
• amniotic egg • placenta • metamorphosis
• complete metamorphosis • pupa
• incomplete metamorphosis • nymph • tadpole

LESSON 3 What Is Behavior?

🔑 All animal behaviors are responses to stimuli.

🔑 The types of animal behavior are instincts and learned behaviors.

Vocabulary
• behavior • instinct • learning
• imprinting • conditioning
• trial-and-error learning
• insight learning

LESSON 4 Patterns of Behavior

🔑 Animals use sounds, scents, and body movements to communicate with one another.

🔑 Animals compete with one another for limited resources, such as food, water, space, shelter, and mates.

🔑 Animals living in groups cooperate to survive.

🔑 Cyclic behaviors usually change over the course of a day or a season.

Vocabulary
• pheromone • aggression • territory
• courtship behavior • society
• circadian rhythm • hibernation
• migration

Review and Assessment

LESSON 1 Animal Reproduction and Fertilization

1. External fertilization is common for organisms that live in

a. trees.　　　b. water.

c. deserts.　　d. open fields.

2. The _____ is an immature form of an organism that looks very different from the adult.

3. Classify Label each body form of the moon jelly. Then on the lines below identify whether each form represents an asexual or sexual stage.

_____
_____
_____

4. Infer All land animals undergo internal fertilization. Why do you think this method is an adaptation for life on land?

_____
_____
_____
_____

5. [Write About It] Consider the following statement: *Organisms that reproduce asexually are at a higher risk of extinction than organisms that reproduce sexually.* Do you agree or disagree? Explain your answer.

LESSON 2 Development and Growth

6. Which of the following organisms lays amniotic eggs?

a. fish　　　b. insect

c. turtle　　d. rabbit

7. Both _____ and _____ care for their young.

8. Sequence Label each stage of complete metamorphosis. Then number each stage to put it in the correct order.

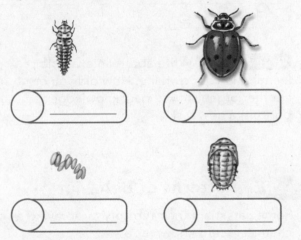

9. Compare and Contrast How is the development of an embryo in an amniotic egg and in a placental mammal different?

_____
_____
_____
_____
_____
_____

10. Make Generalizations Why is parental care so important for newborn birds and mammals?

_____
_____
_____

CHAPTER 7 Review and Assessment

LESSON 3 What Is Behavior?

11. All animal behaviors are responses to

   a. pheromones.   **b.** learning.

   c. aggression.   **d.** stimuli.

12. A bird builds a nest correctly the first time it

tries. This is an example of a(n)_____

13. Draw Conclusions How does learning increase an animal's chance for survival?

_____

_____

_____

14. Write About It Write about an example of learning in your own life. How did you or another organism use past knowledge to perform a new task?

LESSON 4 Patterns of Behavior

15. Some cats mark their territory by spraying a chemical scent known as a

   a. courtship behavior.

   b. circadian rhythm.

   c. cooperative behavior.

   d. pheromone.

16. Animals use _____

to find a mate.

17. Make Generalizations How do migration and hibernation help animals to survive?

_____

_____

_____

_____

APPLY THE BIG ? How does an animal's behavior help it survive and reproduce?

18. This male giraffe, a mammal, uses its neck to fight a male competitor. Using at least four terms from this chapter, describe how this male giraffe's behavior helps it mate and reproduce.

_____

_____

_____

_____

_____

_____

_____

_____

_____

_____

_____

_____

_____

_____

Standardized Test Prep

Multiple Choice

Circle the letter of the best answer.

1. The larval form of the frog shown in stage 3 is called a

   A nymph.   B pupa.

   C tadpole.   D adult.

2. Circadian rhythms are cyclic behavior patterns that occur

   A daily.   B weekly.

   C monthly.   D yearly.

3. An amniotic egg is the result of _____

   and _____.

   A asexual reproduction; external fertilization

   B asexual reproduction; internal fertilization

   C sexual reproduction; external fertilization

   D sexual reproduction; internal fertilization

4. A chimpanzee climbs on a box to reach a banana. When the banana is placed in a higher location, the chimpanzee stacks two boxes on top of each other to reach the banana. This is an example of

   A trial-and-error learning.

   B insight learning.

   C imprinting.

   D conditioning.

5. Which of the following is an example of a competitive behavior?

   A bees living together in a hive

   B a school of fish escaping a predator

   C a bear defending a territory

   D wolves hunting prey as a group

Constructed Response

Use the diagram below and your knowledge of science to help you answer Question 6. Write your answer on a separate piece of paper.

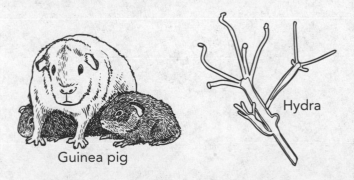

Guinea pig   Hydra

6. Identify what type of reproduction occurs in the guinea pig and the hydra. Then, compare and contrast the two types of reproduction.

SPECIAL DELIVERY!

Seahorse Reproduction

In warm, coastal waters all over the world, just after sunrise every day, a dance-like scene takes place. Tails intertwined, pairs of seahorses spin and twirl under water. Some use their long tails to hold onto strands of seaweed. These long tails that are adapted for grabbing and holding things aren't seahorses' only unusual feature. Seahorses also have some unusual reproductive habits!

Seahorses practice sexual reproduction, like other fish do. Unlike fish—or any other vertebrate for that matter—it's the male seahorse that carries fertilized eggs, provides the eggs with oxygen and nutrients, and gives birth. The males can do this because they have pouches, called brood pouches, in their abdomens.

When mating, the female seahorse deposits about 2,000 eggs inside the male's pouch each time, and he does the rest. He fertilizes the eggs, which become embedded in his pouch wall, and carries them for several weeks. During this time, the eggs receive oxygen and nutrients through a network of tiny blood vessels.

In about three weeks, the male seahorse's brood pouch expands until it is almost spherical. It stays this way for several hours, until the seahorse suddenly gives birth to between eight and 200 baby seahorses. These tiny seahorses can swim and feed by themselves, although they will not be ready to mate with their own partners for many months. About an hour after giving birth, the male is ready to mate again.

Design It Pipefish are another species with unusual reproductive habits. Find out about their reproductive cycles. Create a Venn diagram to compare and contrast the pipefish cycle and the seahorse cycle.

▲ The male seahorse's brood pouch expands as the baby seahorses grow.

Teen GUIDE DOG Trainer

Wherever Lena Cole goes, a puppy named Davey goes with her—even to school. Davey is just one of the puppies Lena trains so that one day they can serve as guide dogs for blind people.

Lena began training guide dog puppies when she was 15. She cares for the puppies for the first two years of their lives. Lena says, "What I do is socialization, basic obedience, and getting Davey used to all the possible situations that might occur when he is a guide dog." Socialization involves helping a puppy learn appropriate behaviors for different settings. This can include taking the puppy to movie theaters, train stations, and other public areas. After two years with Lena, a dog is ready for more advanced training as a guide dog.

Praising Good Behaviors

Lena uses conditioning to train and socialize the dogs. First, she carefully observes a dog's behavior. She praises the dog for positive behaviors, such as waiting quietly in a busy environment. Through repetition, the dog learns to associate certain behaviors with praise and to stop repeating behaviors that do not earn praise.

Rewarding Work

Lena says that raising guide dog puppies is rewarding because the dogs go on to receive training as guide dogs. Eventually they serve as companions and helpers for blind people. Lena also enjoys the close bonds she forms with the puppies, even if it makes for difficult farewells. "It's hard to say goodbye, but this is what you raise the dog for," she says. "You hope that he will be able to go on and help someone else."

Write About It How might you use conditioning to teach a dog to stop and sit at a red light? Predict what methods might work best. Based on your prediction, write a how-to manual describing your training methods.

APPENDIX

Using a Microscope

The microscope is an essential tool in the study of life science. It allows you to see things that are too small to be seen with the unaided eye.

You will probably use a compound microscope like the one you see here. The compound microscope has more than one lens that magnifies the object you view.

Typically, a compound microscope has one lens in the eyepiece, the part you look through. The eyepiece lens usually magnifies 10×. Any object you view through this lens would appear 10 times larger than it is.

A compound microscope may contain one or two other lenses called objective lenses. If there are two, they are called the low-power and high-power objective lenses. The low-power objective lens usually magnifies 10×. The high-power objective lens usually magnifies 40×.

To calculate the total magnification with which you are viewing an object, multiply the magnification of the eyepiece lens by the magnification of the objective lens you are using. For example, the eyepiece's magnification of 10× multiplied by the low-power objective's magnification of 10× equals a total magnification of 100×.

Use the photo of the compound microscope to become familiar with the parts of the microscope and their functions.

The Parts of a Microscope

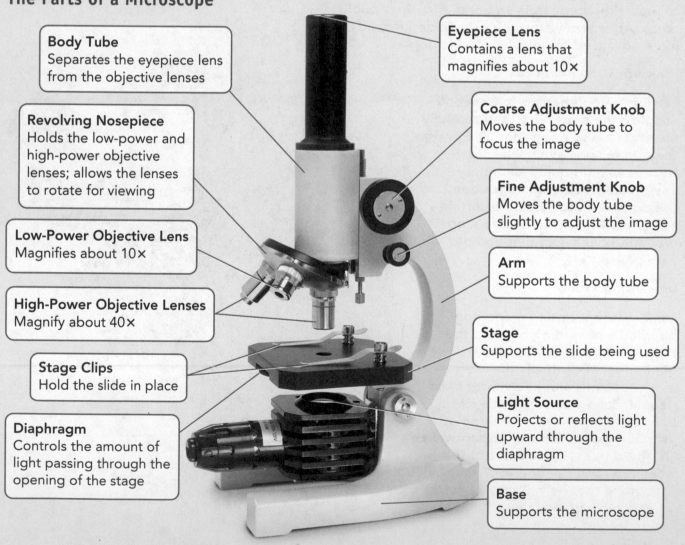

Body Tube
Separates the eyepiece lens from the objective lenses

Revolving Nosepiece
Holds the low-power and high-power objective lenses; allows the lenses to rotate for viewing

Low-Power Objective Lens
Magnifies about 10×

High-Power Objective Lenses
Magnify about 40×

Stage Clips
Hold the slide in place

Diaphragm
Controls the amount of light passing through the opening of the stage

Eyepiece Lens
Contains a lens that magnifies about 10×

Coarse Adjustment Knob
Moves the body tube to focus the image

Fine Adjustment Knob
Moves the body tube slightly to adjust the image

Arm
Supports the body tube

Stage
Supports the slide being used

Light Source
Projects or reflects light upward through the diaphragm

Base
Supports the microscope

Using the Microscope

Use the following procedures when you are working with a microscope.

1. To carry the microscope, grasp the microscope's arm with one hand. Place your other hand under the base.
2. Place the microscope on a table with the arm toward you.
3. Turn the coarse adjustment knob to raise the body tube.
4. Revolve the nosepiece until the low-power objective lens clicks into place.
5. Adjust the diaphragm. While looking through the eyepiece, also adjust the mirror until you see a bright white circle of light. **CAUTION:** *Never use direct sunlight as a light source.*
6. Place a slide on the stage. Center the specimen over the opening on the stage. Use the stage clips to hold the slide in place. **CAUTION:** *Glass slides are fragile.*
7. Look at the stage from the side. Carefully turn the coarse adjustment knob to lower the body tube until the low-power objective almost touches the slide.
8. Looking through the eyepiece, very slowly turn the coarse adjustment knob until the specimen comes into focus.
9. To switch to the high-power objective lens, look at the microscope from the side. Carefully revolve the nosepiece until the high-power objective lens clicks into place. Make sure the lens does not hit the slide.
10. Looking through the eyepiece, turn the fine adjustment knob until the specimen comes into focus.

Making a Wet-Mount Slide

Use the following procedures to make a wet-mount slide of a specimen.

1. Obtain a clean microscope slide and a coverslip. **CAUTION:** *Glass slides and coverslips are fragile.*
2. Place the specimen on the center of the slide. The specimen must be thin enough for light to pass through it.
3. Using a plastic dropper, place a drop of water on the specimen.
4. Gently place one edge of the coverslip against the slide so that it touches the edge of the water drop at a 45° angle. Slowly lower the coverslip over the specimen. If you see air bubbles trapped beneath the coverslip, tap the coverslip gently with the eraser end of a pencil.
5. Remove any excess water at the edge of the coverslip with a paper towel.

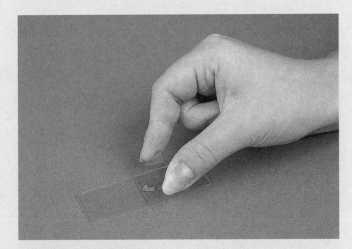

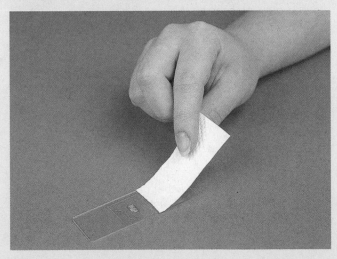

GLOSSARY

A

adaptation An inherited behavior or physical characteristic that helps an organism survive and reproduce in its environment. (139)
adaptación Comportamiento o característica física heredada que ayuda a que un organismo se reproduzca y sobreviva en su medio ambiente.

aggression A threatening behavior that one animal uses to gain control over another animal. (272)
agresión Comportamiento amenazador que un animal usa para controlar a otro.

algae Plantlike protists. (61)
algas Protistas con características vegetales.

amniotic egg An egg with a shell and internal membranes that keep the embryo moist; a major adaptation to life on land characteristic of reptiles, birds, and egg-laying mammals. (253)
huevo amniótico Huevo con cáscara y membranas internas que mantiene al embrión húmedo; adaptación principal a la vida en la tierra, característica de los reptiles, las aves y los mamíferos que ponen huevos.

amphibian A vertebrate whose body temperature is determined by the temperature of its environment, and that lives its early life in water and its adult life on land. (160)
anfibio Animal vertebrado cuya temperatura corporal depende de la temperatura de su entorno, y que vive la primera etapa de su vida en el agua y su vida adulta en la tierra.

angiosperm A flowering plant that produces seeds enclosed in a protective fruit. (98)
angiosperma Planta con flores que produce semillas encerradas en una fruta protectora.

annual A flowering plant that completes its life cycle in one growing season. (111)
anual Planta con flores que completa su ciclo de vida en una sola temporada de crecimiento.

anus The opening at the end of an organism's digestive system (in humans, the rectum) through which waste material is eliminated from the body. (214)
ano Apertura en la porción final del sistema digestivo de un organismo (el recto en los seres humanos) a través del cual se eliminan los desechos del cuerpo.

arthropod An invertebrate that has an external skeleton, a segmented body, and jointed appendages. (152)
artrópodo Invertebrado que tiene un esqueleto externo, un cuerpo segmentado y apéndices articulados.

asexual reproduction A reproductive process that involves only one parent and produces offspring that are genetically identical to the parent. (7)
reproducción asexual Proceso reproductivo que consiste de un solo reproductor y que produce individuos que son genéticamente idénticos al reproductor.

atrium An upper chamber of the heart that receives blood. (228)
aurícula Cavidad superior del corazón que recibe la sangre.

autotroph An organism that is able to capture energy from sunlight or chemicals and use it to produce its own food. (11)
autótrofo Organismo capaz de capturar y usar la energía del Sol o de las sustancias químicas para producir su propio alimento.

auxin A plant hormone that speeds up the rate at which a plant's cells grow and controls a plant's response to light. (120)
auxina Hormona vegetal que acelera la velocidad del crecimiento de las células de una planta y que controla la respuesta de la planta a la luz.

B

bacteria Single-celled organisms that lack a nucleus; prokaryotes. (47)
bacteria Organismos unicelulares que no tienen un núcleo; procariotas.

behavior The manner in which an organism reacts to changes in its internal conditions or external environment. (262)
comportamiento Manera en la que un organismo reacciona a un cambio en sus condiciones internas o en su medio ambiente externo.

biennial A flowering plant that completes its life cycle in two years. (111)
bienal Planta con flores que completa su ciclo de vida en dos años.

bilateral symmetry A body plan in which a single imaginary line divides the body into left and right sides that are mirror images of each other. (144)
simetría bilateral Esquema del cuerpo en el que una línea imaginaria divide el cuerpo en dos partes, izquierda y derecha, que son el reflejo la una de la otra.

binary fission A form of asexual reproduction in which one cell divides, forming two identical cells. (51)
fisión binaria Forma de reproducción asexual en la que una célula se divide y forma dos células idénticas.

binomial nomenclature The classification system in which each organism is given a unique, two-part scientific name indicating its genus and species. (16)
nomenclatura binaria Sistema de clasificación en el que cada organismo tiene un nombre científico específico de dos partes que indica el género y la especie.

bird A vertebrate whose body temperature is regulated by its internal heat, lays eggs, and has feathers and a four-chambered heart. (162)
ave Vertebrado cuya temperatura corporal es regulada por su calor interno, que produce huevos y que tiene plumas y un corazón de cuatro cavidades.

brain **1.** An organized grouping of neurons in the head of an animal with bilateral symmetry. (183) **2.** The part of the central nervous system that is located in the skull and controls most functions in the body.
encéfalo **1.** Conjunto organizado de neuronas ubicado en la cabeza de animales con simetría bilateral. **2.** Parte del sistema nervioso ubicada en el cráneo y que controla la mayoría de las funciones del cuerpo.

branching tree diagram A diagram that shows probable evolutionary relationships among organisms and the order in which specific characteristics may have evolved. (27)
árbol ramificado Diagrama que muestra las relaciones evolucionarias probables entre los organismos y el orden en que ciertas características específicas podrían haber evolucionado.

budding A form of asexual reproduction in which a new organism grows out of the body of a parent. (68)
gemación Forma de reproducción asexual en la que una porción del cuerpo de un reproductor se separa y forma un nuevo organismo.

C

cambium A layer of cells in a plant that produces new phloem and xylem cells. (102)
cámbium Una capa de células de una planta que produce nuevas células de floema y xilema.

capillary A tiny blood vessel where substances are exchanged between the blood and the body cells. (227)
capilar Vaso sanguíneo minúsculo donde se intercambian sustancias entre la sangre y las células del cuerpo.

carnivore A consumer that obtains energy by eating only animals. (207)
carnívoro Consumidor que come sólo animales para obtener energía.

cartilage A connective tissue that is more flexible than bone and that protects the ends of bones and keeps them from rubbing together. (159, 177)
cartílago Tejido conectivo que es más flexible que el hueso y que protege los extremos de los huesos y evita que se rocen.

cell The basic unit of structure and function in living things. (6)
célula Unidad básica de la estructura y función de los seres vivos.

cellular respiration The process that releases energy by breaking down glucose and other food molecules in the presence of oxygen. (50, 217)
respiración celular Proceso en el que se libera energía mediante la descomposición de glucosa y otras moléculas de los alimentos ante la presencia de oxígeno.

chlorophyll A green photosynthetic pigment found in the chloroplasts of plants, algae, and some bacteria. (85)
clorofila Pigmento fotosintético verde que se halla en los cloroplastos de plantas, algas y ciertas bacterias.

chloroplast An organelle in the cells of plants and some other organisms that captures energy from sunlight and changes it to an energy form that cells can use in making food. (86)
cloroplasto Orgánulo de las células vegetales y otros organismos que absorbe energía de la luz solar y la convierte en una forma de energía que las células pueden usar para producir alimentos.

chordate An animal that has a notochord, a nerve cord, and throat pouches at some point in its life. (155)
cordado Animal que tiene un notocordio, un cordón nervioso y bolsas en la garganta en determinada etapa de su vida.

cilia Tiny, hairlike projections on the outside of cells that move in a wavelike manner. (59)
cilios Pequeñas y finísimas proyecciones del exterior de una célula que se mueven formando ondas.

GLOSSARY

circadian rhythm A behavioral cycle that occurs over a period of about one day. (276)
ritmo circadiano Ciclo de comportamiento que ocurre durante el transcurso de aproximadamente un día.

circulatory system An organ system that transports needed materials to cells and removes wastes. (225)
sistema circulatorio Sistema de órganos que transporta los materiales que la célula necesita y elimina los desechos.

classification The process of grouping things based on their similarities. (15)
clasificación Proceso de agrupar cosas según sus semejanzas.

closed circulatory system A circulatory system in which blood moves only within a connected network of blood vessels and the heart. (227)
sistema circulatorio cerrado Sistema circulatorio en el que la sangre viaja sólo dentro de una red de vasos sanguíneos hacia el corazón.

cnidarian A radially symmetrical invertebrate that uses stinging cells to capture food and defend itself. (149)
cnidario Invertebrado de simetría radiada que usa células urticantes para obtener alimentos y defenderse.

complete metamorphosis A type of metamorphosis with four distinct stages: egg, larva, pupa, and adult. (256)
metamorfosis completa Tipo de metamorfosis de cuatro etapas: huevo, larva, pupa y adulto.

conditioning The process of learning to connect a stimulus or a response with a good or bad outcome. (267)
condicionamiento Proceso en el que se aprende a relacionar un estímulo o una respuesta con un resultado bueno o malo.

cone The reproductive structure of a gymnosperm. (114)
cono Estructura reproductora de una gimnosperma.

conjugation A form of sexual reproduction in which a unicellular organism transfers some of its genetic material to another unicellular organism. (51)
conjugación Forma de reproducción sexual en la que un organismo unicelular transfiere su material genético a otro organismo unicelular.

contractile vacuole The cell structure that collects extra water from the cytoplasm and then expels it from the cell. (58)
vacuola contráctil Estructura celular que recoge el agua sobrante del citoplasma y luego la expulsa de la célula.

controlled experiment An experiment in which only one variable is manipulated at a time. (9)
experimento controlado Experimento en el que se manipula sólo una variable a la vez.

convergent evolution The process by which unrelated organisms evolve similar characteristics. (29)
evolución convergente Proceso por el cual organismos no relacionados exhiben una evolución de características similares.

cotyledon A leaf produced by an embryo of a seed plant; sometimes stores food. (98)
cotiledón Hoja producida por el embrión de una planta fanerógama; a veces almacena alimentos.

courtship behavior The behavior in which males and females of the same species engage to prepare for mating. (273)
comportamiento de cortejo Comportamiento de los machos y las hembras de una especie en preparación del apareamiento.

critical night length The number of hours of darkness that determines whether or not a plant will flower. (121)
duración crítica de la noche El número de horas de oscuridad que determina si florecerá una planta o no.

crop An internal organ in some animals where food is softened and stored. (214)
buche Órgano interno de algunos animales en el que se ablandan y almacenan alimentos.

cuticle The waxy, waterproof layer that covers the leaves and stems of most plants. (88)
cutícula Capa cerosa e impermeable que cubre las hojas y los tallos de la mayoría de las plantas.

cytoplasm The thick fluid region of a cell located inside the cell membrane (in prokaryotes) or between the cell membrane and nucleus (in eukaryotes). (47)
citoplasma Región celular de líquido espeso ubicada dentro de la membrana celular (en las procariotas) o entre la membrana celular y el núcleo (en las eucariotas).

D

day-neutral plant A plant with a flowering cycle that is not sensitive to periods of light and dark. (121)
planta de día neutro Planta con un ciclo de floración que no es sensible a la luz o la oscuridad.

decomposer An organism that gets energy by breaking down wastes and dead organisms, and returns raw materials to the soil and water. (55)
descomponedor Organismo que obtiene energía mediante la descomposición de desechos y organismos muertos y que luego devuelve la materia resultante al suelo y al agua.

development The process of change that occurs during an organism's life to produce a more complex organism. (7)
desarrollo Proceso de cambio que ocurre durante la vida de un organismo, mediante el cual se crea un organismo más complejo.

dicot An angiosperm that has two seed leaves. (98)
dicotiledónea Angiosperma cuyas semillas tienen dos cotiledones.

diffusion The process by which molecules move from an area of higher concentration to an area of lower concentration. (218)
difusión Proceso por el cual las moléculas se mueven de un área de mayor concentración a otra de menor concentración.

digestion The process that breaks down complex molecules of food into smaller nutrient molecules. (212)
digestión Proceso que descompone las moléculas complejas de los alimentos en moléculas de nutrientes más pequeñas.

digestive system An organ system that has specialized structures for obtaining and digesting food. (213)
sistema digestivo Sistema de órganos que tiene estructuras especializadas para ingerir y digerir alimentos.

dormancy A period of time when an organism's growth or activity stops. (122)
latencia Período de tiempo durante el cual se detiene el crecimiento o la actividad de un organismo.

E

echinoderm A radially symmetrical marine invertebrate that has an internal skeleton and a system of fluid-filled tubes. (153)
equinodermo Invertebrado marino de simetría radiada que tiene un esqueleto interno y un sistema de apéndices en forma de tubos llenos de líquido.

ectotherm An animal whose body temperature is determined by the temperature of its environment. (157)
ectotermo Animal cuya temperatura corporal es determinada por la temperatura de su medio ambiente.

embryo **1.** The young organism that develops from a zygote. (106) **2.** A developing human during the first eight weeks after fertilization has occurred.
embrión **1.** Organismo joven que se desarrolla a partir del cigoto. **2.** Un ser humano en desarrollo durante las primeras ocho semanas después de llevarse a cabo la fertilización.

endoskeleton An internal skeleton; structural support system within the body of an animal. (153)
endoesqueleto Esqueleto interno; sistema estructural de soporte dentro del cuerpo de un animal.

endospore A structure produced by prokaryotes, such as bacteria, in unfavorable conditions; a thick wall encloses the DNA and some of the cytoplasm. (52)
endospora Estructura que las procariotas, como las bacterias, producen en condiciones desfavorables; capa gruesa que encierra al ADN y parte del citoplasma.

endotherm An animal whose body temperature is regulated by the internal heat the animal produces. (157)
endotermo Animal cuya temperatura corporal es regulada por el calor interno que produce.

esophagus A muscular tube that connects the mouth to the stomach. (214)
esófago Tubo muscular que conecta la boca con el estómago.

eukaryote An organism whose cells contain a nucleus. (24)
eucariota Organismo cuyas células contienen un núcleo.

evolution Change over time; the process by which modern organisms have descended from ancient organisms. (26)
evolución Cambios a través del tiempo; proceso por el cual los organismos modernos se originaron a partir de organismos antiguos.

excretory system An organ system that rids a body of nitrogen-containing wastes and excess salt and water. (231)
sistema excretor Sistema de órganos que elimina desechos que contienen nitrógeno, y excesos de sal y agua del cuerpo.

GLOSSARY

exoskeleton External skeleton; a tough, waterproof outer covering that protects, supports, and helps prevent evaporation of water from the body of many invertebrates. (152)
exoesqueleto Esqueleto exterior; una cobertura fuerte e impermeable que protege, soporta y ayuda a prevenir la evaporación del agua del cuerpo de muchos invertebrados.

external fertilization When eggs are fertilized outside of a female's body. (250)
fertilización externa Cuando los óvulos se fertilizan fuera del cuerpo de la hembra.

F

fertilization The process in sexual reproduction in which an egg cell and a sperm cell join to form a new cell. (112)
fertilización Proceso de la reproducción sexual en el que un óvulo y un espermatozoide se unen para formar una nueva célula.

filter feeder An animal that strains its food from water. (209)
comedores por suspensión Animal que filtra sus alimentos del agua.

fish A vertebrate whose body temperature is determined by the temperature of its environment, and that lives in the water and has fins. (159)
pez Vertebrado cuya temperatura corporal es determinada por la temperatura de su medio ambiente, que vive en el agua y que tiene aletas.

flagellum A long, whiplike structure that helps a cell to move. (47)
flagelo Estructura larga con forma de látigo, que ayuda a la célula a moverse.

flower The reproductive structure of an angiosperm. (108)
flor Estructura reproductora de una angiosperma.

frond The leaf of a fern plant. (94)
fronda Hoja de un helecho.

fruit The ripened ovary and other structures of an angiosperm that enclose one or more seeds. (117)
fruto Ovario maduro y otras estructuras de una angiosperma que encierran una o más semillas.

fruiting body The reproductive structure of a fungus that contains many hyphae and produces spores. (68)
órgano fructífero Estructura reproductora de un hongo, que contiene muchas hifas y produce esporas.

fungus A eukaryotic organism that has cell walls, uses spores to reproduce, and is a heterotroph that feeds by absorbing its food. (67)
hongo Organismo eucariótico que posee paredes celulares, usa esporas para reproducirse y es un heterótrofo que se alimenta absorbiendo sus alimentos.

G

gametophyte The stage in the life cycle of a plant in which the plant produces gametes, or sex cells. (110)
gametofito Etapa del ciclo vital de una planta en la que produce gametos, es decir, células sexuales.

genus A classification grouping that consists of a number of similar, closely related species. (16)
género Clase de agrupación que consiste de un número de especies similares y estrechamente relacionadas.

germination The sprouting of the embryo out of a seed; occurs when the embryo resumes its growth following dormancy. (107)
germinación Brotamiento del embrión a partir de la semilla; ocurre cuando el embrión reanuda su crecimiento tras el estado latente.

gestation period The length of time between fertilization and birth of a mammal. (251)
período de gestación Tiempo entre la fertilización y el nacimiento de un mamífero.

gill A feathery structure where gases are exchanged between water and blood. (219)
branquia Estructura filamentosa donde se realiza el intercambio de gases entre el agua y la sangre.

gizzard A muscular, thick-walled organ that squeezes and grinds partially digested food. (214)
molleja Órgano muscular y de paredes gruesas que exprime y tritura los alimentos parcialmente digeridos.

gymnosperm A plant that produces seeds directly on the scales of cones—not enclosed by a protective fruit. (96)
gimnosperma Planta que produce semillas directamente sobre las escamas de los conos—sin estar encerradas en un fruto protector.

H

heart A hollow, muscular organ that pumps blood throughout an organism's body. (225)
corazón Órgano muscular y hueco que bombea sangre a través del cuerpo de un organismo.

herbivore A consumer that obtains energy by eating only plants. (207)
herbívoro Consumidor que come sólo plantas para obtener energía.

heterotroph An organism that cannot make its own food and gets food by consuming other living things. (11)
heterótrofo Organismo que no puede producir sus propios alimentos y los consigue mediante el consumo de otros seres vivos.

hibernation An animal's state of greatly reduced activity that occurs during the winter. (276)
hibernación Estado de gran reducción de la actividad de un animal que ocurre en el invierno.

homeostasis The condition in which an organism's internal environment is kept stable in spite of changes in the external environment. (13, 139)
homeostasis Condición en la que el medio interno de un organismo se mantiene estable a pesar de cambios en el medio externo.

hormone 1. A chemical that affects growth and development. (120) **2.** The chemical product of an endocrine gland.
hormona 1. Sustancia química que afecta el crecimiento y el desarrollo. **2.** Producto químico de una glándula endocrina.

host An organism that a parasite lives with, in, or on, and provides a source of energy or a suitable environment for the parasite to live. (41)
huésped Organismo dentro del o sobre el cual vive un parásito y que provee una fuente de energía o un medio apropiado para la existencia del parásito.

hyphae The branching, threadlike tubes that make up the bodies of multicellular fungi. (67)
hifas Delgados tubos ramificados que forman el cuerpo de los hongos multicelulares.

I

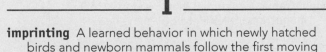

imprinting A learned behavior in which newly hatched birds and newborn mammals follow the first moving object they see. (266)
impronta Comportamiento adquirido de las aves y los mamíferos recién nacidos que consiste en seguir al primer cuerpo en movimiento que ven.

impulse An electrical message that carries information in the nervous system. (182)
impulso Mensaje eléctrico que transporta información por el sistema nervioso.

incomplete metamorphosis A type of metamorphosis with three stages: egg, nymph, and adult. (257)
metamorfosis incompleta Tipo de metamorfosis de tres etapas: huevo, ninfa y adulto.

insight learning The process of learning how to solve a problem or do something new by applying what is already known. (269)
aprendizaje por discernimiento Proceso de aprendizaje de cómo resolver un problema o hacer algo nuevo aplicando lo que ya se sabe.

instinct An inborn behavior that an animal performs correctly the first time. (264)
instinto Comportamiento innato que un animal ejecuta correctamente en su primer intento.

internal fertilization When eggs are fertilized inside a female's body. (251)
fertilización interna Cuando los óvulos se fertilizan dentro del cuerpo de la hembra.

interneuron A neuron that carries nerve impulses from one neuron to another. (182)
interneurona Neurona que transporta los impulsos nerviosos de una neurona a otra.

intestine An organ where digestion is completed and food is absorbed. (214)
intestino Órgano donde se completa la digestión y se absorben los alimentos.

invertebrate An animal without a backbone. (140)
invertebrado Animal sin columna vertebral.

J

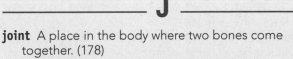

joint A place in the body where two bones come together. (178)
articulación Lugar en el cuerpo en donde se unen dos huesos.

K

kidney A major organ of the excretory system; removes urea and other wastes from the blood. (231)
riñón Órgano importante del sistema excretorio; elimina la urea y otros desechos de la sangre.

GLOSSARY

L

larva The immature form of an animal that looks very different from the adult. (248)
larva Forma inmadura de un animal que luce muy distinta al adulto.

learning The process that leads to changes in behavior based on practice or experience. (265)
aprendizaje Proceso que conduce a cambios de comportamiento basados en la práctica o la experiencia.

lichen The combination of a fungus and either an alga or an autotrophic bacterium that live together in a relationship that benefits both organisms. (73)
liquen Combinación de un hongo y una alga o bacteria autotrópica que viven juntos en una relación mutuamente beneficiosa.

long-day plant A plant that flowers when the nights are shorter than the plant's critical night length. (121)
planta de día largo Planta que florece cuando la duración de la noche es más corta que la duración crítica.

lung 1. An organ found in air-breathing vertebrates that exchanges oxygen and carbon dioxide with the blood. (219) **2.** In humans, one of two main organs of the respiratory system.
pulmón 1. Órgano de los vertebrados que respiran aire, responsable del intercambio de oxígeno y dióxido de carbono en la sangre. **2.** En los seres humanos, uno de los dos órganos principales del sistema respiratorio.

M

mammal A vertebrate whose body temperature is regulated by its internal heat, and that has skin covered with hair or fur and glands that produce milk to feed its young. (163)
mamífero Vertebrado cuya temperatura corporal es regulada por su calor interno, cuya piel está cubierta de pelo o pelaje y que tiene glándulas que producen leche para alimentar a sus crías.

mammary gland An organ in female mammals that produces milk for the mammal's young. (163)
glándula mamaria Órgano de los mamíferos hembra que produce leche para alimentar a sus crías.

marsupial A mammal whose young are born at an early stage of development, and which usually continue to develop in a pouch on their mother's body. (163)
marsupial Mamífero cuyas crías nacen en una etapa muy temprana del desarrollo, y que normalmente continúan el desarrollo en una bolsa del cuerpo de la madre.

medusa A cnidarian body form characterized by an open umbrella shape and adapted for a free-swimming life. (248)
medusa Cnidario con cuerpo que tiene la forma de una sombrilla abierta y que está adaptado para nadar libremente.

metabolism The combination of chemical reactions through which an organism builds up or breaks down materials. (6)
metabolismo Combinación de reacciones químicas mediante las cuales un organismo compone o descompone la materia.

metamorphosis A process in which an animal's body undergoes major changes in shape and form during its life cycle. (255)
metamorfosis Proceso por el cual el cuerpo de un animal cambia de forma radicalmente durante su ciclo vital.

migration The regular, seasonal journey of an animal from one environment to another and back again for the purpose of feeding or reproduction. (276)
migración Viaje estacional y regular, de ida y vuelta, que hace un animal de un medio ambiente a otro con el propósito de alimentarse y reproducirse.

mollusk An invertebrate with a soft, unsegmented body; most are protected by a hard outer shell. (151)
molusco Invertebrado con cuerpo blando y sin segmentos; la mayoría tienen una concha exterior dura que les sirve de protección.

molting The process of shedding an outgrown exoskeleton. (176)
muda de cubierta Proceso de cambiar un exoesqueleto viejo por uno nuevo.

monocot An angiosperm that has only one seed leaf. (98)
monocotiledónea Angiosperma cuyas semillas tienen un solo cotiledón.

monotreme A mammal that lays eggs. (163)
monotrema Mamífero que pone huevos.

motor neuron A neuron that sends an impulse to a muscle or gland, causing the muscle or gland to react. (182)
neurona motora Neurona que envía un impulso a un músculo o glándula, haciendo que el músculo o la glándula reaccione.

multicellular Consisting of many cells. (6)
multicelular Que se compone de muchas células.

muscle A tissue that contracts or relaxes to create movement. (179)
músculo Tejido que se contrae o relaja para crear movimiento.

N

nervous system An organ system that receives information from the environment and coordinates a response. (181)
sistema nervioso Sistema de órganos que recibe información del medio ambiente y coordina una respuesta.

neuron A cell that carries information through the nervous system. (182)
neurona Célula que transporta información a través del sistema nervioso.

nonvascular plant A low-growing plant that lacks true vascular tissue for transporting materials. (90)
planta no vascular Planta de crecimiento lento que carece de tejido vascular verdadero para el transporte de materiales.

notochord A flexible rod that supports a chordate's back just below the nerve cord. (155)
notocordio Cilindro flexible que sostiene la columna de un cordado, debajo del cordón nervioso.

nucleus 1. In cells, a large oval organelle that contains the cell's genetic material in the form of DNA and controls many of the cell's activities. (23) 2. The central core of an atom which contains protons and neutrons. 3. The solid core of a comet.
núcleo 1. En las células, orgánulo grande y ovalado que contiene el material genético de la célula en forma de ADN y que controla muchas de las funciones celulares. 2. Parte central del átomo que contiene los protones y los neutrones. 3. Centro sólido de un cometa.

nymph A stage of incomplete metamorphosis that usually resembles the adult insect. (257)
ninfa Estado de la metamorfosis incompleta que generalmente se asemeja al insecto adulto.

O

omnivore A consumer that obtains energy by eating both plants and animals. (207)
omnívoro Consumidor que come plantas y animales para obtener energía.

open circulatory system A circulatory system in which the heart pumps blood into open spaces in the body and blood is not confined to blood vessels. (226)
sistema circulatorio abierto Sistema circulatorio en el que el corazón bombea la sangre a espacios abiertos del cuerpo y ésta no se limita a los vasos sanguíneos.

organ A body structure that is composed of different kinds of tissues that work together. (143)
órgano Estructura del cuerpo formada por distintos tipos de tejidos que actúan conjuntamente.

organism A living thing. (5)
organismo Un ser vivo.

ovary 1. A flower structure that encloses and protects ovules and seeds as they develop. (109) 2. Organ of the female reproductive system in which eggs and estrogen are produced.
ovario 1. Estructura floral que encierra y protege a los óvulos y las semillas mientras se desarrollan. 2. Órgano del sistema reproductivo femenino en el que se producen los óvulos y el estrógeno.

ovule A plant structure in seed plants that produces the female gametophyte; contains an egg cell. (114)
óvulo Estructura vegetal de las plantas de semilla que produce el gametofito femenino; contiene una célula reproductora femenina.

P

parasite An organism that benefits by living with, on, or in a host in a parasitism interaction. (41)
parásito Organismo que vive dentro de o sobre otro organismo y que se alimenta de él.

pasteurization A process of heating food to a temperature that is high enough to kill most harmful bacteria without changing the taste of the food. (54)
pasteurización Proceso de calentamiento de los alimentos a una temperatura suficientemente alta como para matar la mayoría de las bacterias dañinas sin que cambie el sabor.

peat Compressed layers of dead sphagnum mosses that accumulate in bogs. (126)
turba Capas comprimidas de musgos esfagnáceos muertos que se acumulan en las marismas.

perennial A flowering plant that lives for more than two years. (111)
perenne Planta con flores que vive más de dos años.

petal A colorful, leaflike structure of some flowers. (108)
pétalo Estructura de color brillante, similar a una hoja, que algunas flores poseen.

pheromone A chemical released by one animal that affects the behavior of another animal of the same species. (271)
feromona Sustancia química que produce un animal y que afecta el comportamiento de otro animal de la misma especie.

phloem The vascular tissue through which food moves in some plants. (93)
floema Tejido vascular de algunas plantas por el que circulan los alimentos.

photoperiodism A plant's response to seasonal changes in the length of night and day. (121)
fotoperiodicidad Respuesta de una planta a los cambios estacionales del día y de la noche.

photosynthesis The process by which plants and other autotrophs capture and use light energy to make food from carbon dioxide and water. (85)
fotosíntesis Proceso por el cual las plantas y otros autótrofos absorben la energía de la luz para producir alimentos a partir del dióxido de carbono y el agua.

pigment **1.** A colored chemical compound that absorbs light. **2.** A colored substance used to color other materials. (61)
pigmento **1.** Compuesto químico que absorbe luz. **2.** Sustancia de color que se usa para teñir otros materiales.

pistil The female reproductive part of a flower. (109)
pistilo Parte reproductora femenina de una flor.

placenta An organ in most pregnant mammals, including humans, that links the mother and the developing embryo and allows for the passage of materials between them. (163)
placenta Órgano de la mayoría de los mamíferos preñados, incluyendo a los seres humanos, que conecta a la madre con el embrión en desarrollo y que permite el intercambio de materiales entre ellos.

placental mammal A mammal that develops inside its mother's body until its body systems can function independently. (163)
mamífero placentario Mamífero que se desarrolla dentro del cuerpo de la madre hasta que sus sistemas puedan funcionar por sí solos.

pollen Tiny structure (male gametophyte) produced by seed plants that contain the cell that later becomes a sperm cell. (96)
polen Diminuta estructura (gametofito masculino) producida por las plantas de semilla que contiene la célula que más adelante se convertirá en un espermatozoide.

pollination The transfer of pollen from male reproductive structures to female reproductive structures in plants. (108)
polinización Transferencia del polen de las estructuras reproductoras masculinas de una planta a las estructuras reproductoras femeninas.

polyp A cnidarian body form characterized by an upright vase shape and usually adapted for a life attached to an underwater surface. (248)
pólipo Cnidario con cuerpo de forma tubular y que está adaptado para vivir fijo en un fondo acuático.

prokaryote A unicellular organism that lacks a nucleus and some other cell structures. (23)
procariota Organismo unicelular que carece de un núcleo y otras estructuras celulares.

protist A eukaryotic organism that cannot be classified as an animal, plant, or fungus. (57)
protista Organismo eucariótico que no se puede clasificar como animal, planta ni hongo.

protozoan A unicellular, animal-like protist. (57)
protozoario Protista unicelular con características animales.

pseudopod A "false foot" or temporary bulge of cytoplasm used for feeding and movement in some protozoans. (58)
seudópodo "Pie falso" o abultamiento temporal del citoplasma que algunos protozoarios usan para alimentarse o desplazarse.

pupa The third stage of complete metamorphosis, in which a larva develops into an adult insect. (256)
pupa Tercera etapa de la metamorfosis completa, en la que la larva se convierte en insecto adulto.

R

radial symmetry A body plan in which any number of imaginary lines that all pass through a central point divide the animal into two mirror images. (144)
simetría radiada Esquema del cuerpo en el que cualquier número de líneas imaginarias que atraviesan un punto central dividen a un animal en dos partes que son el reflejo la una de la otra.

radula A flexible ribbon of tiny teeth in mollusks. (210)
rádula Hilera flexible de minúsculos dientes de los moluscos.

reptile A vertebrate whose temperature is determined by the temperature of its environment, that has lungs and scaly skin, and that lays eggs on land. (161)
reptil Vertebrado cuya temperatura corporal es determinada por la temperatura de su medio ambiente, que tiene pulmones y piel escamosa y que pone huevos en la tierra.

respiratory system An organ system that enables organisms to exchange gases with their surroundings. (219)
sistema respiratorio Sistema de órganos que permite al organismo intercambiar gases con su entorno.

response An action or change in behavior that occurs as a result of a stimulus. (7, 181)
respuesta Acción o cambio del comportamiento que ocurre como resultado de un estímulo.

rhizoid A thin, rootlike structure that anchors a moss and absorbs water and nutrients for the plant. (91)
rizoide Estructura fina parecida a una raíz que sujeta un musgo al suelo, y que absorbe el agua y los nutrientes para la planta.

ribosome A small grain-shaped organelle in the cytoplasm of a cell that produces proteins. (47)
ribosoma Orgánulo pequeño y en forma de grano del citoplasma celular que produce proteínas.

root cap A structure that covers the tip of a root, protecting the root from injury as the root grows through soil. (101)
cofia Estructura que cubre la punta de una raíz y la protege de cualquier daño mientras crece en la tierra.

S

seed The plant structure that contains a young plant and a food supply inside a protective covering. (96)
semilla Estructura vegetal que contiene una planta joven y una fuente alimenticia encerradas en una cubierta protectora.

sensory neuron A neuron that picks up stimuli from the internal or external environment and converts each stimulus into a nerve impulse. (182)
neurona sensorial Neurona que recibe estímulos de un medio interno o externo y que convierte a cada estímulo en un impulso nervioso.

sepal A leaflike structure that encloses and protects the bud of a flower. (108)
sépalo Estructura similar a una hoja que encierra y protege el capullo de una flor.

sexual reproduction A reproductive process that involves two parents that combine their genetic material to produce a new organism which differs from both parents. (7)
reproducción sexual Proceso de reproducción que involucra a dos reproductores que combinan su material genético para producir un nuevo organismo que es distinto a los dos reproductores.

shared derived characteristic A characteristic or trait, such as fur, that the common ancestor of a group had and passed on to its descendants. (27)
característica derivada compartida Característica o rasgo, como el pelaje, del ancestro común de un grupo que éste pasa a sus descendientes.

short-day plant A plant that flowers when the nights are longer than the plant's critical night length. (121)
planta de día corto Planta que florece cuando la duración de la noche es más larga que la duración crítica.

society A group of closely related animals of the same species that work together in a highly organized way for the benefit of the group. (275)
sociedad Grupo de animales de la misma especie y estrechamente vinculados que trabajan conjuntmente de manera organizada para el beneficio del grupo.

species A group of similar organisms that can mate with each other and produce offspring that can also mate and reproduce. (16)
especie Grupo de organismos similares que pueden aparearse entre sí y producir crías que también pueden aparearse y reproducirse.

spontaneous generation The mistaken idea that living things arise from nonliving sources. (8)
generación espontánea Idea equivocada de que los seres vivos surgen de fuentes inertes.

spore In bacteria, protists, and fungi, a thick-walled, tiny cell capable of surviving unfavorable conditions and then growing into a new organism. (64)
espora En las bacterias, los protistas y los hongos, una minúscula célula de paredes gruesas capaz de sobrevivir condiciones desfavorables y crecer hasta convertirse en un organismo.

sporophyte The stage in the life cycle of a plant in which the plant produces spores. (110)
esporofito Etapa del ciclo vital de una planta en la que produce esporas.

GLOSSARY

stamen The male reproductive part of a flower. (108)
estambre Parte reproductora masculina de una flor.

stimulus Any change or signal in the environment that can make an organism react in some way. (7, 181)
estímulo Cualquier cambio o señal en el medio ambiente que puede hacer que un organismo reaccione de alguna manera.

stoma Small opening on the underside of a leaf through which oxygen, water, and carbon dioxide can move (plural: stomata). (104)
estoma Pequeña abertura en la superficie inferior de la hoja a través de cual ocurre el intercambio de oxígeno, agua y dióxido de carbono.

stomach An organ in the form of a muscular pouch where food is broken down, located in the abdomen. (214)
estómago Órgano en forma de bolsa muscular donde se descomponen los alimentos; ubicado en el abdomen.

swim bladder An internal gas-filled organ that helps a bony fish stabilize its body at different water depths. (188)
vejiga natatoria Órgano interno lleno de gas que ayuda a un pez con esqueleto a estabilizar su cuerpo a distintas profundidades.

T

tadpole The larval form of a frog or toad. (258)
renacuajo Estado de larva de una rana o un sapo.

taxonomy The scientific study of how living things are classified. (15)
taxonomía Estudio científico de cómo se clasifican los seres vivos.

territory An area that is occupied and defended by an animal or group of animals. (272)
territorio Área ocupada y defendida por un animal o grupo de animales.

tissue A group of similar cells that perform a specific function. (86, 143)
tejido Grupo de células semejantes que realizan una función específica.

transpiration The process by which water is lost through a plant's leaves. (105)
transpiración Proceso por el cual las hojas de una planta pierden agua.

trial-and-error learning A type of learned behavior in which an animal learns to behave in a certain way through repeated practice, to receive a reward or avoid punishment. (268)
aprendizaje por ensayo y error Tipo de comportamiento aprendido en el que un animal aprende cierta conducta por repetición, para obtener recompensa o evitar castigo.

tropism The response of a plant toward or away from a stimulus. (119)
tropismo Respuesta de una planta acercándose o apartándose del estímulo.

U

unicellular Made of a single cell. (6)
unicelular Compuesto por una sola célula.

urine A watery fluid produced by the kidneys that contains urea and other wastes. (231)
orina Fluido acuoso producido por los riñones que contiene urea y otros materiales de desecho.

V

vaccine A substance used in a vaccination that consists of pathogens that have been weakened or killed but can still trigger the body to produce chemicals that destroy the pathogens. (44)
vacuna Sustancia usada en la vacunación y que consiste de patógenos que se han debilitado o matado, pero que aún pueden provocar que el cuerpo produzca sustancias químicas para destruir a los patógenos.

vacuole A sac-like organelle that stores water, food, and other materials. (86)
vacuola Orgánulo en forma de bolsa que almacena agua, alimentos y otros materiales.

vascular plant A plant that has true vascular tissue for transporting materials. (93)
planta vascular Planta que tiene tejido vascular verdadero para el transporte de materiales.

vascular tissue The internal transporting tissue in some plants that is made up of tubelike structures that carry water, food, and minerals. (88)
tejido vascular Tejido interno de algunas plantas compuesto de estructuras tubulares que transportan agua, alimentos y minerales.

ventricle A lower chamber of the heart that pumps blood out to the lungs or body. (228)
ventrículo Cavidad inferior del corazón que bombea sangre a los pulmones o el cuerpo.

vertebrae The bones that make up the backbone of an organism. In humans, one of the 26 bones that make up the backbone. (156)
vértebras Huesos que componen la columna de un organismo. En los seres humanos, cada uno de los 26 huesos que componen la columna vertebral.

vertebrate An animal with a backbone. (140)
vertebrado Animal con columna vertebral.

virus A tiny, nonliving particle that enters and then reproduces inside a living cell. (40)
virus Partícula diminuta inerte que entra en una célula viva y luego se reproduce dentro de ella.

W

water vascular system A system of fluid-filled tubes in an echinoderm's body. (188)
sistema vascular de agua Sistema de vasos llenos de líquido en el cuerpo de un equinodermo.

X

xylem The vascular tissue through which water and minerals move in some plants. (93)
xilema Tejido vascular de algunas plantas por el que circulan agua y nutrientes.

Z

zygote A fertilized egg, produced by the joining of a sperm cell and an egg cell. (112)
cigoto Óvulo fertilizado, producido por la unión de un espermatozoide y un óvulo.

INDEX

INDEX

Page numbers for key terms are printed in **boldface** type.

INDEX

Page numbers for key terms are printed in **boldface** type.

Index

ACKNOWLEDGMENTS

Staff Credits

The people who made up the *Interactive Science* team—representing composition services, core design digital and multimedia production services, digital product development, editorial, editorial services, manufacturing, and production—are listed below.

Jan Van Aarsen, Samah Abadir, Ernie Albanese, Zareh MacPherson Artinian, Bridget Binstock, Suzanne Biron, MJ Black, Nancy Bolsover, Stacy Boyd, Jim Brady, Katherine Bryant, Michael Burstein, Pradeep Byram, Jessica Chase, Jonathan Cheney, Arthur Ciccone, Allison Cook-Bellistri, Rebecca Cottingham, AnnMarie Coyne, Bob Craton, Chris Deliee, Paul Delsignore, Michael Di Maria, Diane Dougherty, Kristen Ellis, Theresa Eugenio, Amanda Ferguson, Jorgensen Fernandez, Kathryn Fobert, Julia Gecha, Mark Geyer, Steve Gobbell, Paula Gogan-Porter, Jeffrey Gong, Sandra Graff, Adam Groffman, Lynette Haggard, Christian Henry, Karen Holtzman, Susan Hutchinson, Sharon Inglis, Marian Jones, Sumy Joy, Sheila Kanitsch, Courtenay Kelley, Chris Kennedy, Toby Klang, Greg Lam, Russ Lappa, Margaret LaRaia, Ben Leveillee, Thea Limpus, Dotti Marshall, Kathy Martin, Robyn Matzke, John McClure, Mary Beth McDaniel, Krista McDonald, Tim McDonald, Rich McMahon, Cara McNally, Melinda Medina, Angelina Mendez, Maria Milczarek, Claudi Mimo, Mike Napieralski, Deborah Nicholls, Dave Nichols, William Oppenheimer, Jodi O'Rourke, Ameer Padshah, Lorie Park, Celio Pedrosa, Jonathan Penyack, Linda Zust Reddy, Jennifer Reichlin, Stephen Rider, Charlene Rimsa, Stephanie Rogers, Marcy Rose, Rashid Ross, Anne Rowsey, Logan Schmidt, Amanda Seldera, Laurel Smith, Nancy Smith, Ted Smykal, Emily Soltanoff, Cindy Strowman, Dee Sunday, Barry Tomack, Patricia Valencia, Ana Sofia Villaveces, Stephanie Wallace, Christine Whitney, Brad Wiatr, Heidi Wilson, Heather Wright, Rachel Youdelman

Photography

All uncredited photos copyright © 2011 Pearson Education.

Cover, Front and Back
David Doubilet/National Geographic Stock.

Front matter
Page vi, Kevin Schafer/Alamy; **vii,** Marevision Marevision/Photolibrary New York; **viii,** Michael Newton/Robert Harding/Newscom; **ix,** pogona22/Fotolia; **x,** Stephen Dalton/Science Source; **xi,** Kenneth M. Highfill/Science Source; **xii,** DLILLC/Corbis; **xiii t,** iStockphoto.com; **xiii m1,** iStockphoto.com; **xiii b,** iStockphoto.com; **xiii m2,** iStockphoto.com; **xxii bl,** Mark Turner/Garden Picture Library/Photolibrary New York; **xxii,** Imagebroker/Alamy; **xxiii,** Riccardo Savi/The Image Bank/Getty Images.

Chapter 1
Pages xxiv–1 spread, Kevin Schafer/Alamy; **1 br inset,** Jane Allan/Fotolia; **3 t,** Mau Horng/Shutterstock; **3mt,** Joshua Haviv/Fotolia; **3 mb,** Rod Williams/Nature Picture Library; **3 b,** Eye of Science/Photo Researchers, Inc.; **4,** Sam Ogden/Science Source; **5 tl,** Scott Camazine/Alamy; **5 tm,** Mau Horng/Shutterstock; **5 tr,** Matt Meadows/Peter Arnold; **5 b,** Kjell Sandved/Photolibrary New York; **6 tl,** Biophoto Associates/Photo Researchers, Inc.; **6 tr,** Kerstin Hinze/Nature Picture Library; **6 b,** Science Photo Library/Photolibrary New York; **7 t,** John Kaprielian/Photo Researchers, Inc.; **7 m both,** Ingo Arndt/Nature Picture Library; **7 b,** Gentoo Multimedia/Fotolia; **8 t,** Jürgen and Christine Sohns/Photolibrary New York; **8 b,** Lee Rentz/Alamy; **9,** Ian Thraves/Alamy; **11,** Arco Images GmbH/Alamy; **12 t,** Pichugin Dmitry/Shutterstock; **12 b,** Jose Fuste Raga/age Fotostock/Photolibrary New York; **13 l,** Tony Campbell/Fotolia; **13 r,** Steve Byland/Shutterstock; **14,** Smithsonian/Associated Press; **15,** Ilian Animal/Alamy; **16 t,** Joshua Haviv/Fotolia; **16 bl,** Eric Isselée/Shutterstock; **16 br,** Rod Williams/Nature Picture Library; **17,** Alan Gleichman/Shutterstock; **18,** FloridaStock/Shutterstock; **20,** Stuart Wilson/Science Source; **21 tl,** Armando Frazao/iStockphoto.com; **21 tm,** WizData, Inc./Shutterstock; **21 tr,** Eric Isselée/Shutterstock; **21 bl,** Hemera Technologies/JupiterUnlimited; **21 bm,** Kim Taylor/Nature Picture Library; **21 br,** Joseph Calev/Shutterstock; **22,** alle/Fotolia; **23 t bacteria,** SciMAT/Photo Researchers, Inc.; **23 b archaea,** Eye of Science/Science Source; **24 l inset,** Eric V. Grave/Science Source; **24 r inset,** Eye of Science/Photo Researchers, Inc.; **24–25 bkgrnd,** Ron Erwin/All Canada Photos/Corbis; **25 inset,** NICOLAS LARENTO/Fotolia; **26,** Dave Watts/Nature Picture Library; **28 t inset,** UTHAI TREESUCON/Associated Press; **28 b inset,** Tim Laman/Nature Picture Library; **28–29 bkgrnd,** Elenathewise/Fotolia; **29 lemur,** Nick Garbutt/Nature Picture Library; **29 camera,** Jasmina007/Shutterstock; **30 t,** Biophoto Associates/Photo Researchers, Inc.; **30 m,** Alan Gleichman/Shutterstock; **30 b,** Eric V. Grave/Science Source; **32,** JP5\ZOB/WENN/Newscom.

Interchapter Feature
Page 34 bkgrnd, Explorer/Photo Researchers, Inc.; **35 br,** Rebecca Ellis/iStockphoto.com.

Chapter 2
Pages 36–37 spread, Topic Photo Agency IN/age Fotostock; **39 t,** Marevision Marevision/Photolibrary New York; **39 b,** Visuals Unlimited/Getty Images; **40,** Evan Kafka/Stone/Getty Images; **44,** evok20/Fotolia; **46,** Odua Images/Fotolia; **47,** Brian J. Ford; **48 l,** VEM/Photo Researchers, Inc.; **48 m,** Chris Bjornberg/Photo Researchers, Inc.; **48 r,** CMSP/Getty Images; **49 tl,** James L. Amos/Corbis; **49 bl,** Ted Kinsman/Science Source; **49 m,** RGB Ventures LLC dba SuperStock/Alamy; **49 r,** Rob Whitrow/GPL/Photolibrary New York; **50 tl,** SciMAT/Science Source; **50 tr,** Science Photo Library/Photo Researchers, Inc.; **50 b,** Comstock Images/age Fotostock; **51,** Dr. Linda M. Stannard, University of Cape Town/Science Source; **53,** Stuart Westmorland/Getty Images; **54 t,** Scimat/Science Source; **54–55,** RGB Ventures LLC dba SuperStock/Alamy; **56 inset,** Gioiaphotography.com; **56 bkgrnd,** ALEXANDER JOE/AFP/GETTY IMAGES/Newscom; **57 l,** Eye of Science/Photo Researchers, Inc.; **57 m,** Steve Gschmeissner/Science Source; **57 r,** Andrew Syred/Science Source; **59,** Larry West/Photo Researchers, Inc.; **61 t,** Biophoto Associates/Science Source; **61 b,** Steve Gschmeissner/Photo Researchers, Inc.; **62 tl,** David McC Photo Researchers, Inc.; **62 tr,** Steve Gschmeissner/P Researchers, Inc.; **62 m,** Marevision Marevision/Ph New York; **62 b,** marinethemes.com/Kelvin Aitk 3-D; **63 tl,** Marevision Marevision/age Fotost

ACKNOWLEDGMENTS

New York; **63 tr,** David McCarthy/Photo Researchers, Inc.; **63 bl,** Steve Gschmeissner/Photo Researchers, Inc.; **63 bm,** Lawrence Naylor/Photo Researchers, Inc.; **63 br,** Biophoto Associates/Science Source; **64,** Biophoto Associates/Science Source; **65,** Elenathewise/Fotolia; **66,** Scott Camazine/Photo Researchers, Inc.; **68 l,** SPL/Science Source; **68 r,** Biophoto Associates/Science Source; **69 l,** Michael Lander/Getty Images; **69 inset,** Oxford Scientific/Photolibrary New York; **70–71,** Gary Meszaros/Photo Researchers, Inc.; **72 tl,** Emilio Ereza/age Fotostock; **72 tr,** Jeff Barnard/AP Photos; **72 bl,** Genevieve Vallee/Alamy; **73 t,** Jeffrey L. Rotman/Corbis; **73 b,** Photolibrary New York; **74,** evok20/Fotolia; **75 l,** Chris Bjornberg/Photo Researchers, Inc.; **75 r,** VEM/Photo Researchers, Inc.

Interchapter Feature
Page 78 cartoon faces, Dean Murray/iStockphoto.com; **79 b,** Michel Viard/Jacana/Photo Researchers, Inc.; **79 t,** Science Photo Library/Alamy.

Chapter 3
Pages 80–81 spread, Laurent Bouvet/age Fotostock; **83 t,** Howard Rice/Dorling Kindersley; **83 b,** Nigel Bean/Nature Picture Library; **85 l,** iStockphoto.com; **85 r,** Theodore Clutter/Science Source; **86 t,** ZTS/Shutterstock; **86 b,** Perennou Nuridsany/Photo Researchers, Inc.; **88,** Kjell B. Sandved/Photo Researchers, Inc.; **90,** Francesca Yorke/Garden Picture Library/Photolibrary New York; **91 bkgrnd,** czamfir/Fotolia; **91 inset,** John Serrao/Photo Researchers, Inc.; **92 t,** Adrian Davies/Nature Picture Library; **92 b,** Daniel Vega/Photolibrary New York; **93 bkgrnd,** Howard Rice/Photolibrary New York; **93 inset,** David T. Webb/University of Hawaii; **95 l,** Philippe Clement/Nature Picture Library; **95 r,** Albert Aanensen/Nature Picture Library; **97 t,** Christine M. Douglas/Dorling Kindersley; **97 m1,** Peter Anderson/Dorling Kindersley; **97 m2,** Joanna Pecha/iStockphoto.com; **97 b,** M. Philip Kahl/Photo Researchers, Inc.; **98 t,** K. Kaplin/Shutterstock; **98 m,** Howard Rice/Dorling Kindersley; **98 b,** Anna Subbotina/Shutterstock; **100,** Fletcher & Baylis/Photo Researchers, Inc.; **101 l,** Lynwood M. Chace/Photo Researchers, Inc.; **101 r,** Derek Croucher/Alamy; **102 l,** Peter Hestbaek/Shutterstock; **102–103,** Rob Cole Photography/Alamy; **104–105,** Pakhnyushcha/Shutterstock; **108 tl,** Kim Taylor/Nature Picture Library; **108 tm,** All Canada Photos/Alamy; **108 tr,** Barry Mansell/Nature Picture Library; **108 bl,** Barry Mansell/Nature Picture Library; **108 bm,** Niall Benvie/Nature Picture Library; **108 br,** Simon Williams/Nature Picture Library; **110,** Ocean/Corbis; **112,** Ed Reschke/Peter Arnold, Inc.; **113 t,** Michael Newton/Robert Harding/Newscom; **113 b,** Christine M. Douglas/Dorling Kindersley; **114–115,** Andrew Browne/Ecoscene/Corbis; **115 t,** blickwinkel/Alamy; **115 m,** Breck P. Kent; **115 b,** David R. Frazier Photolibrary, Inc./Alamy; **116 l,** Medio Images/Photodisc/Photolibrary New York; **116 seedling,** Nigel Cattlin/Alamy; **117 berry bush,** Nigel Bean/Nature Picture Library; **117 tm, tr, bm, and br,** Peter Chadwick/Dorling Kindersley; **118,** Dr. John Runions/Science Source; **120,** Maryann Frazier/Photo Researchers, Inc.; **121,** Mark Turner/Garden Picture Library/Photolibrary New York; **122,** Carole Drake/Garden Picture Library/Photolibrary New York; **124 bkgrnd,** Gary K. Smith/Nature Picture Library; **125,** Albinger/age Fotostock; **126, ** David Tipling/Nature Picture Library; **127,** Tom Mayes/

Cal Sport Media/Zuma Press; **128 t,** Kjell B. Sandved/Photo Researchers, Inc.; **128 b,** David Tipling/Nature Picture Library.

Interchapter Feature
Page 132 br, Susumu Nishinaga/Photo Researchers, Inc.; **133,** Ames/NASA; **132 ml,** sgame/iStockphoto.com; **132 tl and bl,** Tim Messick/iStockphoto.com.

Chapter 4
Pages 134–135 spread, age Fotostock/SuperStock; **137 t,** Bruce Davidson/Nature Picture Library; **137 m1,** Winelover/Fotolia; **137 m2,** Andrew J. Martinez/Photo Researchers, Inc.; **137 b,** Juniors Bildarchiv/F191/GmbH/Alamy; **138 inset,** Bruce Davidson/Nature Picture Library; **138–139 bkgrnd,** DLILLC/Corbis; **139 tl inset,** Pixtal/SuperStock; **139 tr inset,** PaulDidsayabutra/Fotolia; **139 bl inset,** Jason Edwards/National Geographic Stock; **139 br inset,** Anthony Mercieca/Science Source; **141 tl,** Don Hammond/Design Pics/Corbis; **141 tr,** Connie Coleman/Photographer's Choice/Getty Images; **141 br,** Volodymyr Krasyuk/Fotolia; **141 bl,** Keith Leighton/Alamy; **142,** Comstock Images/JupiterUnlimited; **143,** Neil Fletcher/Oxford University/Museum of Natural History/Dorling Kindersley; **144 t,** Winelover/Fotolia; **144 bl,** Andrew J. Martinez/Photo Researchers, Inc.; **144 bm,** Stephen Frink/Photographer's Choice/Getty Images; **144 br,** Zeng Wei Jun/Shutterstock; **144 br bkgrnd,** Bill Curtsinger/National Geographic Stock; **144–145 bkgrnd,** D. Hurst/Alamy; **145 t,** B.A.E., Inc./Alamy; **145 ml,** Image Source/SuperStock; **145 mr,** D. Hurst/Alamy; **145 bl,** Photodisc/Alamy; **145 br,** Tatiana Popova/iStockphoto.com; **146 l inset,** Kaz Chiba/Stockbyte/Getty Images; **146 r inset,** WaterFrame/Alamy; **146 bkgrnd,** Gray Hardel/Corbis; **147,** Purestock/Getty Images; **148,** Nature Production/NPL; **149 r inset,** Michael DeFreitas Underwater/Alamy; **149 l inset,** Malcolm Ross/Alamy; **149 bkgrnd,** WaterFrame/Alamy; **150 l inset,** PHOTO FUN/Shutterstock; **150 m inset,** M.I. (Spike) Walker/Alamy; **150 r inset,** Steve Gschmeissner/Science Source; **150–151 bkgrnd,** Tim Gainey/Alamy; **151 m,** Andrew J. Martinez/Photo Researchers, Inc.; **151 r,** David Fleetham/Mira.com; **151 l,** Sebastian Duda/Shutterstock; **152 arachnid,** pogona22/Fotolia; **152 insect,** Dave King/Dorling Kindersley; **152 flower,** JupiterImages/Creatas/Alamy; **152 crustacean,** Dave King/Dorling Kindersley; **152–153 bkgrnd,** Grant Faint/Getty Images; **153 sea cucumber,** Andrew J. Martinez/Science Source; **153 sea star,** Kaz Chiba/Stockbyte/Getty Images; **153 sea urchin,** WaterFrame/Alamy; **153 brittle stars,** NatureDiver/Shutterstock; **154 t inset,** Silver/Fotolia; **154 b,** Tsuneo Nakamura/Volvox Inc/Alamy; **155,** Heather Angel/Natural Visions/Alamy; **156 t inset,** Dave King/Dorling Kindersley; **156 bkgrnd,** David Peart/Dorling Kindersley; **157 tl,** Juniors Bildarchiv/F291/GmbH/Alamy; **157 tr,** Alan & Sandy Carey/Photo Researchers, Inc.; **157 bl,** Juniors Bildarchiv/F191/GmbH/Alamy; **157 br,** John Cancalosi/age Fotostock; **158,** Richard Cummins/Corbis; **159 lamprey,** Marevision/Getty Images; **159 lamprey mouth,** Heather Angel/Natural Visions/Alamy; **159 goldfish,** Pavlo Vakhrushev/Fotolia; **159 bkgrnd,** Stephen Frink/Getty Images; **160 l inset,** Arterra Picture Library/Alamy; **160 r inset,** Nick Garbutt/Nature Picture Library; **160–161 bkgrnd,** Alex L. Fradkin/Stockbyte/Getty; **161 t,** Karl Shone/Dorling Kindersley; **161 m inset,** blickwinkel/Alamy; **161 b inset,** Sarah Leen/

National Geographic Stock; **162 tl inset,** Hermann Brehm/ Nature Picture Library; **162 r inset,** rhfoto/Fotolia; **162 bl inset,** Marvin Dembinsky Photo Associates/Alamy; **162–163 bkgrnd,** Shunsuke Yamamoto Photography/Getty Images; **163 t,** Joe McDonald/Corbis; **163 bl,** Ingo Arndt/Nature Picture Library; **163 br,** Tom McHugh/Photo Researchers, Inc.; **164 t,** PaulDidsayabutra/Fotolia; **164 ml,** Andrew J. Martinez/ Photo Researchers, Inc.; **164 mr,** David Fleetham/Mira.com; **164 bl,** Juniors Bildarchiv/F291/GmbH/Alamy; **164 br,** Ingo Arndt/Nature Picture Library; **166,** JupiterImages; **167 l,** Geoff Brightling/Peter Minister, modelmaker/Dorling Kindersley; **167 m,** Jerry Young/Dorling Kindersley; **167 r,** Stephen Frink/ Photographer's Choice/Getty Images.

Interchapter Feature
Page 168, Bart Nedobre/Alamy; **169 t bkgrnd,** Doug Steley C/Alamy; **169 t inset,** Tom McHugh/Photo Researchers, Inc.; **169 b bkgrnd,** Cornel Stefan Achirei/Alamy; **169 b inset,** Ed Reschke/Peter Arnold, Inc.

Chapter 5
Pages 170–171 spread, Stephen Dalton/Science Source; **173 t,** Warren Photographic; **173 m1,** HorusVisual/Fotolia; **173 m2,** Stephen Dalton/Science Source; **173 b,** Will & Deni McIntyre/Corbis; **174 b,** Alan Carey/Corbis; **174 t,** David A. Northcott/Corbis; **175,** Gallo Images-Denny Allen/Getty Images; **176 t,** Warren Photographic; **176 earthworm,** Frank Greenaway/Dorling Kindersley; **176 shell,** Keith Leighton/ Alamy; **176 cicada,** Lynwood M. Chace/Photo Researchers, Inc.; **176–177 b bkgrnd,** Vibrant Image Studio/Shutterstock; **178 l,** HorusVisual/Fotolia; **178 r,** Steve Bloom Images/Alamy; **180,** Robert Marien/Corbis; **181,** Stephen Dalton/Science Source; **184 inset,** Geoff Brightling/Dorling Kindersley; **184–185 bkgrnd,** Dave Watts/Nature Picture Library; **185 tr inset,** Rod Planck/Science Source; **185 m inset,** Deco Images II/Alamy; **185 br inset,** Mark Conlin/Alamy; **186 kite,** D. Hurst/Alamy; **186 beach,** Platinum GPics/Alamy; **187 m,** Steve Goodwin/ iStockphoto.com; **187 r,** Peter Burian/Corbis; **187 l,** Delpho, M./ Arco Images GmbH/Alamy; **189 sea star,** Will & Deni McIntyre/ Corbis; **189 penguins,** Blickwinkel/Alamy; **189 frog,** Natural Visions/Alamy; **189 squid,** Mark Conlin/Alamy; **190 t,** Charles Stirling (Diving)/Alamy; **190 m,** Blaine Harrington III/Alamy; **190 b inset,** Smaointe/Alamy; **190–191 spread,** Remi Benali/ Corbis; **191 tl inset,** Juergen Hasenkopf/Alamy; **191 tr inset,** Perytskyy/Fotolia; **191 b inset,** Gallo Images/Alamy; **192 t,** Gijs Bekenkamp/Alamy; **192 b,** Imagebroker/Alamy; **192–193,** PhotoLink/Getty Images; **193 tl inset,** Bob Jensen/Alamy; **193 m,** Idamini/Alamy; **193 butterfly,** Ellen McKnight/Alamy; **193 grass,** D. Hurst/Alamy; **193 tr,** Rolf Richardson/Alamy; **196 t,** Steve Bloom Images/Alamy; **196 m,** Rod Planck/Science Source; **196 b,** Rolf Richardson/Alamy; **198,** Gallo Images/Alamy.

Interchapter Feature
Page 200, Stephen Frink/Digital Vision/Getty Images; **201 bkgrnd,** Niels Poulsen/Alamy.

Chapter 6
Pages 202–203 spread, Kenneth M. Highfill/Science Source; **205 alligator,** Warren Photographic; **205 elephant,** Photodisc; **206 t,** Eric Isselée/iStockphoto; **206 b,** Joel Sartore/National

Geographic Stock; **207 caterpillar,** Nancy Nehring/iStock Exclusive/Getty Images; **207 elephant,** Photodisc; **207 raccoon,** Photodisc; **207 lion,** Keith Levit/Shutterstock; **207 bear,** Tom Brakefield/Digital Vision/Getty Images; **207 jellyfish,** Darren Greenwood/Design Pics/JupiterImages; **208 t,** Gregory G. Dimijian/Photo Researchers, Inc.; **208 m,** SCPhotos/Alamy; **208 bl,** Duncan Noakes/Fotolia; **208 br,** Warren Photographic; **208–209 whale bkgrnd,** Blickwinkel/ Alamy; **209 t inset,** Marevision Marevision/age Fotostock; **209 l inset,** louise murray/Alamy; **210 tl,** Steve Kaufman/ Photolibrary New York; **210 tr,** Gary Lewis/Photolibrary New York/JupiterImages; **210 b,** Stuart Westmorland/Corbis; **210–211 snake,** Kim Taylor & Jane Burton/Dorling Kindersley; **211 tl,** Rich Reid/National Geographic Stock; **211 tr,** Nomad/ SuperStock; **211 m,** George Grall/National Geographic Stock; **216,** TOM MCHUGH/Science Source; **217,** Mike Kemp/ Rubberball Productions/Getty Images; **218,** Mark J. Barrett/ Alamy; **219 t,** Jurie Maree/Shutterstock; **219 bl,** Steve Noakes/Shutterstock; **219 br,** Igor Gorelchenkov/Shutterstock; **220 t,** Georgette Douwma/Nature Picture Library; **220 bl,** Rico/Shutterstock; **220 br,** Peter Leahy/Shutterstock; **221 t,** Dreamstime.com; **221 m,** George Grall/National Geographic Stock; **221 b,** Lukáš Hejtman/iStockphoto.com; **222 l,** Karen Givens/Shutterstock; **222 r,** DLILLC/Corbis; **222 m,** Karen H. Johnson/iStockphoto.com; **223,** Linn Currie/Shutterstock; **224,** David Fleetham/Alamy; **225,** Sapsiwai/Shutterstock; **226 t,** Jeff Lepore/Photographer's Choice/Getty Images; **226 b,** Dwight Nadig/iStockphoto.com; **228–229,** godunovatatiana/ Fotolia; **230,** Eric Isselée/iStockphoto.com; **231,** Stubblefield Photography/Shutterstock; **232–233,** Riccardo Savi/The Image Bank/Getty Images; **234 t,** Stuart Westmorland/Corbis; **234 m,** Igor Gorelchenkov/Shutterstock; **234 b,** Eric Isselée/ iStockphoto.com; **235,** Steve Noakes/Shutterstock; **236,** George Grall/National Geographic Stock.

Interchapter Feature
Page 239, Geoff Brightling/Dorling Kindersley; **238,** Natural Visions/Alamy; **238 crab illustration,** Jill Hartley/ iStockphoto.com.

Chapter 7
Pages 240–241 spread, Martin Harvey/Getty Images; **243 t,** Oxford Scientific/Getty Images; **243 tm,** Juniors Bildarchiv/ Photolibrary New York; **243 bm,** Thomas Kitchin & Victoria Hurst/Getty Images; **243 b,** EcoView/Fotolia; **244 both,** Kathy Keatley Garvey/University of California at Davis Department of Entomology; **245,** Colin Milkins/Photolibrary New York; **246 b,** Paul Bricknell/Dorling Kindersley; **246 t,** DLILLC/Corbis; **247 t,** K.L. Kohn/Shutterstock; **247 b,** David Chapman/Alamy; **250–251,** Oxford Scientific/Getty Images; **252,** David G. Knowles; **253,** Juniors Bildarchiv/Photolibrary New York; **255 inset r,** Alistair Dove/Alamy; **255 bkgrnd,** Andrew J. Martinez/Photo Researchers, Inc.; **255 inset l,** George D. Lepp/Corbis; **256 r,** Rick & Nora Bowers/Alamy; **256 l,** Rick & Nora Bowers/Alamy; **256 m,** SF Photo/Shutterstock; **257 r,** Design Pics Inc./Alamy; **257 l,** Design Pics Inc./Alamy; **259,** Patricia Fogden/Corbis; **260–261 t,** WizData, Inc./Shutterstock; **260–261 b,** Keren Su/ China Span/Alamy; **262 r,** Jesse Kunerth/Shutterstock; **262 l,** Brian Weed/Shutterstock; **263 t,** Cathy Keifer/Shutterstock; **263 b,** Joe Mercier/Shutterstock; **264–265,** Thomas Kitchin & Victoria Hurst/Getty Images; **265,** M & J Bloomfield/

ACKNOWLEDGMENTS

Alamy; **266–267,** Nina Leen/Getty Images; **268 t,** John Cancalosi/Peter Arnold, Inc.; **268 b,** Tony Wear/Shutterstock; **270,** Ron Cohn/Knight Ridder/Newscom; **271,** PhotoStock-Israel/Science Source; **272,** Linda Freshwaters Arndt/Photo Researchers, Inc.; **272–273,** Mark Turner/Photolibrary New York; **273 tl,** Robert Muth/Shutterstock; **273 b,** EcoView/Fotolia; **273 tr,** blickwinkel/Alamy; **274,** Doug Perrine/Alamy; **276,** FLPA/SuperStock; **276–277,** Mark Carwardine/Nature Picture Library; **278 b,** Kevin Maskell/Alamy; **278 t,** Doug Allan/Nature Picture Library; **278–279,** Kevin Schafer/Photolibrary New York; **279,** T.J. Rich/Nature Picture Library; **280 t,** Paul Bricknell/Dorling Kindersley; **280 tm,** Cathy Keifer/Shutterstock; **280 bm,** Joe Mercier/Shutterstock; **280 b,** PhotoStock-Israel/Science Source; **282,** Olma/Fotolia.

Interchapter Feature
Page 284, Mark Conlin/Alamy; **285,** Boris Djuranovic/iStockphoto.com.

this is your book

you can write in it